CW01370985

The World Needs Dialogue!
One: Gathering the Field

This edition first published in 2019

Dialogue Publications
The Firs, High Street
Chipping Campden
Glos GL55 6AL UK

All rights reserved

Book Copyright © Dialogue Publications, 2019
All individual authors featured in this publication retain copyright for their work
'Dialogue as a Whole-System Healthcare Intervention'
© Macy Holdings Management, LLC, 2018

Without limiting individual author's rights reserved, no part of this publication
may be reproduced, distributed or transmitted in any form or by any means, including
photocopying, recording, or other electronic or mechanical methods, without
the prior written permission of the publisher, except in the case of brief quotations
embodied in critical reviews and certain other non-commercial uses permitted
by copyright law. For permission requests, write to the publisher at the address above.

Typeset by Ellipsis, Glasgow

Ordering Information:
Quantity sales. Special discounts are available on quantity purchases by libraries, associations, and
others. For details, contact the Special Sales Department at the address above.

The World Needs Dialogue! / One: Gathering the Field – 1st ed.

Classifications:
UK: BIC – Society (JFC): Cultural Studies and JFF: Social Issues)
US: BISAC – SOC000000 Social Science

ISBN: 978-1-9161912-0-4

Printed in Great Britain

Contents

Chairman's Foreword   v
Editor's Introduction   vii

Section One
Organisations Need Dialogue!

Engaging Fragmentation, Subcultures and Organisational Power   3
Peter Garrett

Dialogue as the Heart of Strategic Change   21
Mechtild Beucke-Galm

An Entry-Level Practice for New Professional Dialogue Practitioners   41
Francis Briers

Conversations at the Mall: Dialogue, Debate or Negotiation?   53
Thomas Köttner

Section Two
Criminal Justice Needs Dialogue!

Dialogue through the Offender Resettlement Journey   73
Jane Ball

Dialogue and a Healing Environment in the Virginia Department of Corrections   93
Harold Clarke and Susan Williams

Fluxen Prison Dialogues in Norway   113
Trine-Line Biong and Christian Valentiner

The Legacy and Potential of Dialogue in the Criminal Justice System   133
Mark Seneschall

Section Three
Healthcare Needs Dialogue!

Dialogue as a Whole-System Healthcare Intervention   155
Beth Macy

Teaching and Using Dialogue in an American Academic Health Center 175
James M. Herman, Alan Adelman, and John Neely

Dialogue and Communities of Practice in American Graduate Medical Education 185
Beth K. Herman

Section Four
Society Needs Dialogue!

Dialogue, Politics and the Search for Global Solutions 197
Claudia Apel

Economics and Time Management as a Vehicle for Dialogue 217
Lars-Åke Almqvist

Indigenous Affairs, Border Services and the Path of Dialogue in Canada 239
Peter Hill

Dialogue as a Working Model in Degerfors Municipality 253
Per Hilding

Section Five
Acorn Dialogues

Dialogue Is a Spiritual Practice 273
Robert M. Sarly

Learning Dialogue in a Higher Education English Course 285
Mirja Hämäläinen and Eeva Kallio

Autism Dialogue 293
Jonathan Drury

Dialogue as Dynamic Energy in Living Communities 305
Ove Jakobsen and Vivi ML Storsletten

Participants 319

Chairman's Foreword

This volume acknowledges and celebrates 25 Professional Dialogue Practitioners and the wide variety of good work they have delivered. Some have been actively developing their Professional Dialogue careers for decades, whilst others add the innovative energy of being relative newcomers. Their work has provided a unique service, addressing and resolving fragmented situations in a wide variety of organisations and communities in different sectors and countries around the world.

The publication is the first collection of such accounts and thereby provides the first benchmark for the field by recording the state of Professional Dialogue in late 2018. It sets a standard that others will emulate and no doubt surpass in the future. The authors had their work considered at the first international conference of the Academy of Professional Dialogue, *The World Needs Dialogue!* Their papers were written and circulated to participants before the Academy's inaugural gathering. Extracts from the considerations with participants at the conference are included, along with their subsequently written postscripts.

The Academy of Professional Dialogue itself has taken a long time coming into form. Its origins lie in the gathering with David Bohm I convened in the English Cotswold Hills in 1984, that gave birth to a new kind of Dialogue. The essence of this endeavour was a deep concern for the well-being of society, humanity and the planet. It turned on the recognition of the damaging and pervasive fragmentation in human consciousness – and a developing awareness of the movement of thought and thinking that could move us beyond a state of fragmentation. During the early years, the primary endeavour was the practice of proprioceptive awareness, undertaken by privately convened groupings of keen individuals who shared this concern about fragmentation and wanted to experiment with what could be done about it.

Following David Bohm's death in 1992, the focus moved into the use of Dialogue within organisations. Here fragmentation was just as blatantly evident as elsewhere in society, but there were significant differences. The participants shared the local history and state of their organisation, they were not necessarily participating on a voluntary basis, and systemic feedback was immediately available. The result was a commercialisation of Dialogue and often a greater focus on communication skill-building than on proprioceptive awareness. The field deepened, however, with the recognition that thought is collectively held in the memory of subcultural groups. This enabled conscious work with the lines of fragmentation along the interfaces between different subcultural groupings, and bore fruit in terms of improved understanding, better working relations and collaborative innovation. A further significant step was my developing an understanding of the inherent power structures of organisations, locating Dialogue in relation to decision-making and accountability. That enabled better alignment of purposeful activity, and self-sustaining cultural regeneration.

The key elements were now in place for whole-system change through Dialogue, and it was only at this point that I realised we had given birth to a profession. So in 2016 I registered the Academy of Professional Dialogue as a legal entity. I waited patiently, and a year later I gathered a small group of ten colleagues from the UK, US, Sweden, Germany and Austria to consider what, if anything, we might be able to offer to society through the Academy of Professional Dialogue. We met a few miles from where I had met originally with David Bohm a generation earlier in 1984. There was resolute agreement that as a professional body we could do some things that were not being provided by others. We could inspire people to use Dialogue, acknowledge those already doing good work, provide a programme of training and development for people who want to become practitioners, and we could further develop the whole field of Professional Dialogue.

We raised the flag in 2018 with our first international conference, *The World Needs Dialogue!* The three days were attended by 80 participants from four different continents and the Academy of Professional Dialogue had finally taken form. The conference was led by the four Trustees, each of whom also hosted one the primary themes – namely Lars Åke-Almqvist (Society), Jane Ball (Criminal Justice), Jim Herman (Healthcare) and Peter Garrett (Organisations). I want to express my appreciation to my colleagues for their initiative, confidence and hard work. We issued a Founders Call and were remarkably fortunate to have a sufficiently generous response to clear the entire setting up costs of the Academy. The ten key sponsors were Lars Åke-Almqvist, Jane Ball, Flux Foundation, Gaiasoft, Peter Garrett, James Herman, William Isaacs, Robert Sarly, Henrik Tschudi and Renate van der Veen.

This book is the first publication of our new imprint *Dialogue Publications*, and I am proud of the fact that since the first conference we have established our own publishing company in order to make this conference material and other Professional Dialogue material widely available. This particular part of the overall initiative is the fruit of a long-standing friendship between me and Cliff Penwell, the editor, that goes back almost 40 years. We jointly resourced the formation of the company and between us we have spent hundreds of hours working on the papers and transcripts in our care. We are conscious of the contribution we are making by helping to create the language of Professional Dialogue, as well as disseminating the good work Dialogue Practitioners are doing.

My closing acknowledgement is for David Bohm, without whom we would not be walking this particular path with such a robust foundation and ontology. Were he alive today to witness what is happening, I know how interested, engaged and fulfilled he would be with the emergence of the Academy of Professional Dialogue.

Peter Garrett
Chairman, Board of Trustees,
Academy of Professional Dialogue

Editor's Introduction

If this collection of reflections does its job well, it will not be remembered as a book about dialogue. Rather, much like the conference that made this volume possible, it will be held as something akin to a circle of practice, a place to pause with others and reflect for a little while. As in the conference, the words shared in these pages are closer to invitation than to exposition.

All told, the voices of 25 people are represented here – a little under a third of the number that participated in this first *The World Needs Dialogue!* conference. All of the contributors are practitioners, but a smaller number would consider themselves authors. A little under half speak English as their native tongue. Yet here we all are – no matter our language – setting aside both hesitancy (*will others understand me?*) and certainty (*I'm sure they won't!*), in favor of showing up and letting others find their way alongside us.

The papers featured here were written in preparation for the conference but, as Peter mentioned, were not read at the event itself. They were distributed beforehand to allow us time to digest and then engage in dialogue rather than listen to presentations. While inevitably not everyone had read the papers, the authors offered their themes as points of departure for explorations in small groups. This served a couple of good purposes; besides expanding the topics, it allowed presenters to further refine the thinking that is now contained in this volume.

Like the conference, this book is organized into five categories: Organizations, Criminal Justice, Healthcare, Society and Acorn Papers. The first four areas we've called "Working Papers," and I believe they are self-evident. "Acorn Papers" may need a little context. Where the Working Papers offer a place for consideration of established Dialogue practices, The Acorn Papers are reserved for experimental, or less-established fields of work – for example, Robert Sarly's facilitation for troubled church congregations, or Jonathan Drury's circles with those who are a part of the autism spectrum. These may, with interest and support, become well established in the Dialogue community in the time ahead. All of them have global-change implications in one way or another.

At the end of each paper you'll find two additional sections: Conference Session Extracts, which are small excerpts of conversation from the smaller-group considerations on each of the themes. These are not intended as full transcripts or even as comprehensive accounts, but rather as a flavor of the conversations. Following this is a Postscript for each paper, the post-conference reflections of the authors after having time to digest their session and add whatever insights that may have emerged. Both of these sections are somewhat free-ranging, offering thinking-in-progress perspectives.

Some words of explanation about the use of shared language and terminology are probably needed, particularly for those of us who notice how words have impact. This applies here at three levels. First, you may notice a variety of editorial styles used over the course of the book. This is intentional; the idea (whether successful or not) was to honor

– *honour* – the form of English used by each of the authors, so as to preserve a sense of voice in their writing. While featuring each work in their native language wasn't a realistic option at this time (we are considering it for the future), we could at least offer some distinction within our shared currency. This means, for example, that papers originating in Europe have largely followed British conventions, including punctuation, turns of phrase and spelling; US works (and our Argentinian paper) are rendered American; and our Canadian offering follows the sort of UK-US blend common to the country. (And astute readers already will notice the difference in Peter's British voice in his foreword and my American one in this introduction.) All of this has been something of a challenge to keep straight, but hopefully it has brought some nuance to the reflections.

Second, our writers come not only from different countries, but also from different areas of professional concentration, ranging from healthcare providers to government officials to criminal justice professionals to educators, along with several others. Some are more academically oriented, and their work is full of citations, while others aren't, and they offered reference-free explorations. As in a dialogue circle, it's all part of the mix, and I made little attempt to homogenize these styles other than to follow academically accepted standards.

Finally, you will see some of the same people, terminology and practices mentioned across many of the papers: David Kantor, and his seminal Four-Player system; Peter Garrett and Jane Ball, with Peter's foundational work with David Bohm and, with Jane, decades of work in the Criminal Justice System; Bill Isaacs, with his almost-universal influence; Glenna Girard and Linda Ellinor, with their influential book and the steady work behind it; and of course David Bohm himself. I mention these people (and could highlight others) because they are part of the language and tradition that many of us have in common. At the same time, I am aware that not everyone who practices dialogue may be familiar with the legacy shared by our writers (each of whom has a remarkable story, as you will see). If you come across terms or examples that don't seem easy to grasp in one paper, chances are very good they will be described in another, from a different perspective and experience of practice.

This leads me to a final, short reflection on the path ahead for dialogue. In the context of a discipline that spends much of its time exploring new territory, a sense of shared tradition and language is useful and welcome. It gives shape to a field that has been, in modern times, largely ineffable, and it adds warmth to the circle. Like all living things, however, dialogue thrives in diversity, in its adaptability and eagerness to embrace the unfamiliar. It is not a "closed system," to borrow a term from both thermodynamics and systems theory. And dialogue will thrive now as it has over the centuries: through hospitality, vulnerability and inclusion.

It is a pleasure to join you in this work of a lifetime.

Cliff Penwell
Editor,
Dialogue Publications

Section One

Organisations Need Dialogue!

Engaging Fragmentation, Subcultures and Organisational Power

Peter Garrett

Did it ever occur to you that human thought may be the cause of most of the challenges we face in the world today? Some problems are the result of natural disasters like earthquakes, tsunamis, droughts and cyclones. Most, however, are caused by people, and the way they behave towards one another and the environment. The problems of crime, wars, substance abuse, deforestation, pollution, depletion of the ozone layer and so on, all arise from the way people think, feel and act. At the core of this is an identity which is fragmented, rather than being a natural part of the whole. If you stop to think about it, it is undeniable that we all live in one socially, economically and ecologically interdependent world, but so much of the time we act as if only our own interests matter. Curiously, this is just as much the case for 'good' people as it is for the 'bad' ones. We find ourselves putting our country (and our trading advantage), our community (and our local quality of life) and our personal career (along with our status and salary) ahead of others. This is an extractive way of relating to the world, where people want to know what they can get out of a situation rather than what they can contribute. Politicians stand for particular causes, but we find few statesmen who stand for the world.

The Pervasive Issue of Fragmentation

A significant shift in my own thinking occurred when I met David Bohm, a theoretical physicist, who introduced me to the notion of *pervasive fragmentation* in human consciousness. One of the things that impressed me deeply was David Bohm's distinction between parts and fragments. *Parts* work together, like the various organs in the human body or the symbiotic relationship between flora and fauna in nature. *Fragments* are not meaningfully related; for example, neither a bottle nor a wristwatch, smashed with a hammer, is thereafter able to hold liquids or show the time, and the fragments cannot be reassembled to their former state. David's observation was that human consciousness is suffering from widespread fragmentation.

With him I undertook an extensive private and experiential exploration into the nature and dynamics of human consciousness through agenda-free enquiries amongst large groups of voluntary participants. That resulted in what we called *Dialogue*. The key discovery lay in the relationships between the immediate experience, memory-bound thought and thinking. We discovered that the way to coherence is through understanding, and thereby a common content of consciousness.

Our early Dialogues were explorations into the roots of fragmentation in human consciousness. We were not trying to reassemble the fragments. We wanted to move upstream towards the source, which is the existing state of participatory wholeness. This phenomenon of fragmentation is very widespread. It has been fostered by the influences of fundamentalism: nationally (resulting in wars between countries); ethnically (leading to persecution); culturally (promoting sexism and racism); and religiously (fostering inquisitions, crusades and jihads). In current times these trends are exacerbated by economic dependencies. Oil-rich countries tend to ignore or question the connection between burning fossil fuels and global warming. Others who derive less income from sales of oil are convinced this is the cause of the destruction of the atmosphere. There are many such problems. When you have any problem, you think about it to find a solution. But what if *thought itself* is the problem? This is the assumption we made and tested.

Thought is held in the memory, and in muscular reactions in the body. It is thinking from the past that re-presents itself automatically and rapidly. That is the basis of learnt response that is essential for everyday tasks, like crossing the street or driving a car. The emotions are included. What has been *felt* in the past represents itself rapidly too, often in the form of intuitive impulses. This is a difficult field for enquiry because so much of what appears to be spontaneous actually happens automatically and is prompted unconsciously. We realised that an agenda-free approach to our Dialogues was the only way to succeed with this difficult enquiry. No dos, don'ts, or rules to follow – simply a common and singular intention to understand how consciousness works. It quickly became evident that limited awareness is one of the main problems. We are hardly able to discern what is immediate, and what are 'thoughts' (past thinking) and 'felts' (past feelings) being re-presented rapidly from our memory of prior experience. In the physical body, the awareness of movement is called proprioception. It is how you find the light switch in a dark room where you cannot use sight. You may remember where the light switch should be, and you are proprioceptively aware of raising your arm to the right height and feeling for the switch with your hand, despite the fact you cannot see anything.

We recognised the need for a similar proprioceptive awareness of movements in consciousness – not just a reflective capacity to understand later, but an awareness of what is happening in the moment *as it is happening*. We found that almost all the reactions, misunderstandings and challenges within the Dialogue Groups were based on limited awareness of what was being thought or felt by the speaker and by the listeners. So we took the unusual step of encouraging people to say what was in their minds and hearts in order to establish this proprioception of consciousness. We did it in the moment, which felt particularly dangerous at times, and we explored it together – what we thought we knew, the assumptions we were making, the responses and reactions, the implications, the sense of cynicism or reverence, and so on. We started to coin some jargon. *Suspending* all this (as a chandelier is suspended from a ceiling) openly and in words, enabled us to enquire collectively. It began to establish *proprioception*, meaning an awareness of what was happening as it happened, along with a common content of consciousness and coherence within the group. Where some people talk about wanting to 'go below the surface', we rather talked about going *upstream* into more subtle areas where impulses originate, and first begin to take form. As one colleague humorously observed, "an idea coming towards you is very different from an idea moving away from you!" Not insignificantly, this kind of sensitivity also created a feeling of impersonal fellowship or communion, a form of love that the Greeks referred to as *koinonia*.

I found these experimental Dialogues to be profoundly useful and I have applied the learning from them to address fragmentation in many sectors. During the three decades since that time I have worked with 30 or more individual commercial organisations, including small-to-medium-enterprises, and extensively with four different multinationals for four or five years each. I have supported environmental groups and Third-World development projects, trained consultants in top consulting groups, and introduced Dialogue as a consulting methodology to several MBA programmes. I am drawing on this broad range of experience to assert that *Organisations Need Dialogue!*

Subcultural Thought

In 1993, six months after David's death, I started a Dialogue Group in a maximum-security prison. It came about through meeting Patrick de Maré, a colleague of David's. Patrick believed Dialogue was the way to socio-therapy, and encouraged me to work with a student of his, a Probation Officer called Dave Parsons. This prison was a brutal and unfamiliar environment, and a challenging opportunity to engage raw social fragmentation. Things matter deeply to people living and working in a prison, and there could be immediate and long-lasting consequences as a result of what people said in the Dialogues I facilitated. I returned each week to meet with prisoners, staff and management in the prison, and there was feedback about the consequences of our previous week's Dialogue. It would have been very difficult to determine whether or not the private Dialogues with David Bohm and a range of loosely-related volunteers had any meaningful influence on society. But in the closed society of the prison it was easier to track the impact. Fragmentation was rampant, and any easing of it yielded immediate dividends. One Dialogue led to the resolution of a hostage situation elsewhere in the prison, and others over time led to deeply resistant prisoners asking to attend therapeutic classes. All led to greater awareness and respect between participants and a reduction of violation and violence.

This is where I learnt about the collective nature of thought, which is held in subcultural groupings. People's beliefs are formed from things they have experienced, heard or read.

These give them the basic 'facts' that, formed through their logic, result in beliefs. I began to see that prisoners, officers and management, who were in the same Dialogue, each selected their facts differently. Also each subcultural grouping automatically used a distinct logic. So they believed different things from the same situation. I saw that what they noted in any situation, and how they interpreted it, was reinforced by their colleagues, even when it was illogical or incoherent. This is the essence of social fragmentation. Our Dialogues worked so well because the prisoners challenged the officers' subcultural beliefs, and vice versa. They did this within the genuine and respectful containment of the Dialogue Group. These often blunt exchanges shifted the understanding and rapport between prisoners, security officers and other staff, and the participants gave weekly evidence of the consequences. It was here that I realised that a person's identity is partly an individual story and partly a collective matter. People identify themselves with particular groupings, and these subcultural groupings hold one's identity within collectively reinforced patterns of thought. Cultural change, I realised, is essentially about shifting the subcultural relationships and subcultural memory. That in turn affects the disposition of individuals and their behaviour.

This thinking was reinforced when, concurrently with the prison Dialogues, I was invited to help improve poor staff relations in one of the largest industrial complexes in Scotland where management and unions were in conflict. In this case there were four trade unions and three businesses operating on one site, and they were all at odds with each other. It was a complex fragmentation that led to endless, factious misunderstandings and misrepresentations. Members of each of the subgroups spoke with their colleagues and thereby reinforced their own beliefs and attributions whilst criticising the others. This could only be resolved by addressing different subcultural groupings separately, then bringing them all together. So I started to learn how to map subcultural groupings and how to use Dialogue to increase the awareness of interdependency so that they contributed as parts of a larger social system, rather than breaking it up.

Organisational Power

The third significant leap for me began with the pattern of repeated reorganisations I was encountering in my commercial consulting Dialogue work. It had set me thinking. Each new leader reorganises, and each reorganisation is rarely completed before the next one starts. Then it dawned on me that although every organisation is different, they have features in common globally. So I began with the question: *What do organisations organise?* There are many possible answers, including work, results, work forces, investment, time, etc. My realisation was that fundamental to their structure is *power*. Organisations are essentially power structures. One thing they all organise is power. People within organisations are subject to authority and constraints within the power structure that determine what they can and cannot do.

This power is delegated hierarchically in the form of *decision-making authority*, along with the accountability for those decisions. Typically, the owners (voting shareholders) delegate to the executive board. That board in turn delegates to managers, then perhaps through various levels to supervisors, and on to basic-grade staff members in a series of vertical lines of power. These 'power lines' are the primary means of delivery, and they determine how the organisation functions. There may be different dominant power lines for different products, services or geographies. They are often experienced as silos, where more attention is given to those above or below in the hierarchical line, than to what is required elsewhere or in the organisation overall. Those higher in the power line usually have more responsibility for the vision, strategy, policies, levels of resourcing and speed of change, whilst those lower down are often responsible for the planning, scheduling and the practical activities that determine timely delivery. Generally these vertical lines are competitive, because their heads meet at the executive board level where the critical decisions are determined. If there are limited resources, for example, the business lines will naturally compete for them.

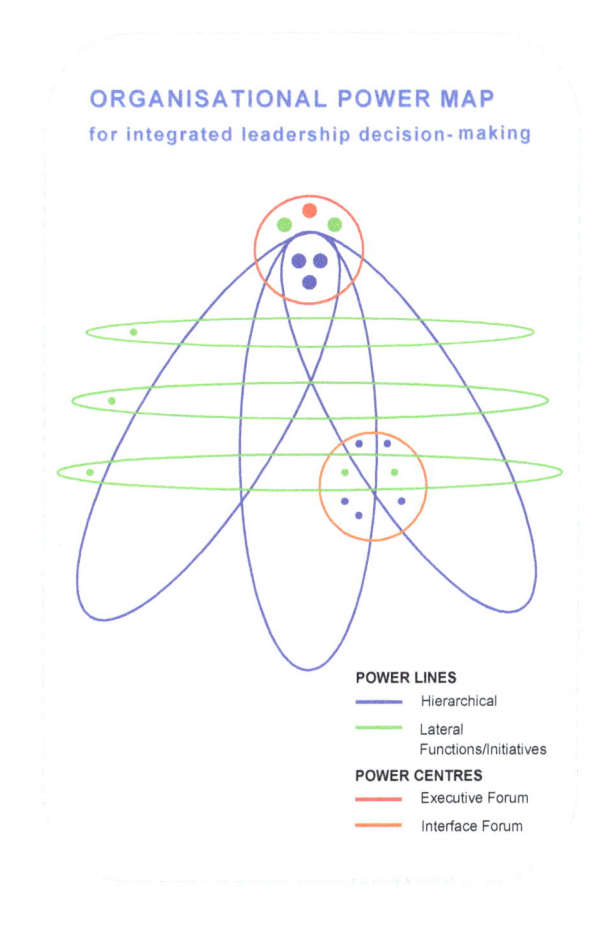

Adding to the complexity, there are a series of lateral power lines that are often called functions. Each of them has representation on the executive board as well. These horizontal power lines cut across all the vertical power lines. They provide financial, HR, legal, legislative compliance, marketing, public relations and other 'across-the-board' specialist services. They are intended to be of service to all the vertical business power lines, but sometimes they are regarded as being primarily interested in their own (partially self-determined) remits, whilst constraining the performance of the main business delivery. The functions often depend on those people working within the vertical business power lines to achieve their targets, both to introduce and to monitor changing standards.

Despite being employed in the same organisation, those working in the vertical and lateral power lines have different interests from one another. Those in the vertical power lines want the discretion to customise their services according to their clients' needs and interests, and to best suit their various products, services, geographies and so on. They want the space to run their business in what they see to be the most efficient, effective and profitable way. The lateral power lines, on the other hand, seek the economy of centralised specialist resources, rather than having them duplicated in every business unit and geography. They want records that prove compliance with industry legislation and they thrive on standardisation. Their power is often the power to say 'no'. So throughout the organisation there is a tension between the lateral and vertical power lines. It is worth noting that this tension plays out in some way for every employee. The demands of the competing interests are a daily experience to be met and negotiated. Sometimes it is a matter of saying 'yes' to the demands from the vertical and the lateral power lines, knowing it is not feasible to satisfy both. Switching roles from lateral to hierarchical, or vice versa, is generally a real eye-opener to employees.

In my observation this is the typical situation for every organisation where there is more than one location, or more than the number of employees who can sit together in one room to address conflicting interests.

One solution is to design a matrix organisation of some kind, where individuals are given roles in both vertical and lateral power lines, but the conflicts still have to be reconciled at an individual level because it is inherent in the structure of any organisation. This inevitable conflict between power lines is a basic gripe of employees who, from their fragmented local perspective, believe that others ('they') are being unhelpful or unrealistic. Some managers spend a lot of time and energy trying to make people happy by attempting to minimise the tensions, rather than understanding the underlying cause. So, is the conflict a good or a bad thing? Skilful senior leaders will not try to remove the tension. They will instead value and balance the various power lines at play. These tensions could be likened to the guy ropes of a traditional tent. Slack guy ropes leave the canvas flapping in the wind, whilst a similar taut tension across them all manages the wind and rain far better.

It is when the tension, and resulting conflict, gets out of hand that an intervention is required. This is evidently the case when there is more 'noise' and 'heat' in some part of the organisation than work being done. Such a situation could be escalated into a senior power play and a directive from on high about how to proceed. The better means of resolution, I propose, is to gather a representation of all the affected staff into a multi-stakeholder (i.e., multi-subcultural) Dialogue. With everyone present and able to speak for themselves, it is feasible with a little skill to understand one another, to establish a common view about what has been happening and to agree the best way to proceed. This is one reason why Dialogue skills are needed in organisations – to resolve inevitable conflicts of interest.

I call these kinds of representative forums *Power Centres*. There are two types of Power Centre. One is an Interface Forum that is placed in the appropriate part of the organisation to resolve the friction and misalignment between several of the vertical and/or lateral power lines. Who is in the room matters, and the clue to the absence of necessary people is when the conversation is about 'them' and 'they' are not in the room to answer for themselves. These Interface Forums can be convened wherever and whenever needed for a working Dialogue to establish or re-establish awareness, coherence and participatory respect.

The other Power Centre is the Executive Forum. There is always the need for the executive group to function as a Power Centre. That means that all the vertical and lateral power lines are represented in one forum, and everyone involved is required to wear two hats: one to represent the interests of their own particular power line, and the other to represent the interests and well-being of the whole organisation. Few organisations achieve this kind of versatility at the executive level because of the competing organisational and personal interests in the room, but those that do benefit enormously.

A further phenomenon to note is the shifting emphasis between centralised and decentralised decision-making and power. Each new leader, making his or her mark through a reorganisation, will move more in one or other direction. Moving more power into the centre will give him or her more immediate control, tends to favour the lateral power lines and results in greater standardisation, more reporting, less local discretion and a more directive culture. Making such a change can improve the performance of a loose organisation where everyone is accustomed to doing what they prefer. The other direction is to decentralise because the businesses are too constrained and spend too much of their time facing and answering to head office. They know their market, their clients and their products or services, so let them get on with their business! We set the targets and policies centrally, and they deliver the goods in whatever way they find works best. This clearly adds strength to the vertical power lines, and can feel liberating for the majority of staff, who sit in these power lines, and can improve the morale and performance.

One cannot do both, however, so there tends to be a pendulum swing – from decentralised vertical power line dominance to centralised, lateral power line dominance, and then back again every few years. This pendulum swing costs time and money. People are expected to reorganise themselves whilst still doing their normal day job. Changing roles and, often, reducing headcount, adds to the anxiety and tension. A more balanced state is preferable and more sustainable, so as well as using the Power Centre Dialogues as a remedial intervention, they can be proactively positioned at key nodes across the power structure of the organisation and at an appropriate frequency. As the Power Centres are used less reactively and more proactively, they can maintain this balance by designing early responses to changing external market conditions.

Why Professional Dialogue Is Necessary

The essential point to make is that *every* organisation of any size will inevitably suffer fragmentation. This is not necessarily because they are badly managed or poorly led, but because of the inherent power structure of organisations per se. The specialisation they depend on – and reward – encourages employees to become increasingly competent and experienced in one particular area of service and at the same time to have less awareness and hence less understanding of other parts of the organisation in which they work. Careers develop accordingly, resulting in silos. Typically, in any organisation I have come to know as a consultant, employees in nearby rooms at the head office have little to no understanding about what each other do, let alone how they may be impacting each other.

It is worth pausing to consider how widespread organisations have become. In the past century, as agriculture has become mechanised, populations across the world have moved from rural locations into the cities. Organisations have proliferated to manage the more concentrated mass of humanity to such an extent that this could be called 'the age of organisations'. We earn our living wages through organisations – or our investment interest, pension or governmental support. We depend on organisations to hold and transfer our money, to process our credit card payments and to issue us with banknotes. We buy our food through supermarkets, shops and delivery organisations. We fly in aircraft, or travel in trains and cars on rails and roads made by organisations. We are educated in organisations and buy our entertainment and holidays from organisations. We pray in organisations. Many of us are born, and will be cared for and die, in organisations – with even our funeral being arranged by an organisation. Organisations are now the pervasive universal phenomenon. Along with this is the widespread need to address aspects of inevitable fragmentation within those organisations. So clearly the need for Professional Dialogue is also pervasive!

As users, customers or clients we have come to expect that different parts of an organisation we are dealing with do not talk to one another, and we know that there is always a potential gap between the communication of our needs and the service provided. These failings are now so common that commercial organisations allocate substantial funds to pay noncompliance fines, people do not expect political parties and governments to act in each other's interests or for the well-being of the whole, and we watch debate and disagreement in the media as the norm rather than the exception.

The good news – and saving grace – is that this ubiquitous problem of fragmentation is the same problem being replicated everywhere. It appears in many guises, but the way through fragmentation to the existing state of participatory wholeness is not complicated. It does require understanding, skill, disposition and commitment. That is what we are in the process of building in the Academy of Professional Dialogue.

Addressing Organisational Fragmentation: Working Cases

The practical development of Professional Dialogue in an organisational setting depends on the context and history, as I hope these three working cases will bring to life. The first case describes the development of a Power Centre (an Interface Forum) to address subcultural fragmentation. The situation had a long history. At the outset, members of the various management and union groupings were pleased to recite this history of being wronged by each other. It took almost a year to get the relevant groupings into the room and into Dialogue together. The resulting forum ran monthly for years and became a generative, forward-looking Dialogue that delivered significant results across a large workforce.

The second case describes the steps we took towards creating a Dialogic Organisation, something that includes but goes well beyond a 'learning organisation'. The initial Power Centre was with the Executive Leadership Group, and then extended to include the whole organisation of several hundred people in an open and fully informed, ongoing consideration of the future of the organisation. The final case shows the power of creating an Executive Leadership Power Centre from the very inception of an organisation, before its official launch. This was a master class in executive leadership alignment and the business results were evident.

A Dog's Breakfast
A Partnership Forum within a Scottish Industrial Complex

In the late 1990s I had a call from the colleague of a manager on one of the largest industrial complexes in the UK to see if I would be willing to provide some help regarding industrial relations. Margaret Thatcher had decimated the power of the trade unions in the UK during her time as Prime Minister, but her first Labour Party successor, Tony Blair, had made promises to the unions in return for their support to get his party back into government. Those unions that had retained certain levels of membership and activity would have the automatic right to return to the collective bargaining of their pay increases. Historically, each round of bargaining had been long, drawn-out and fraught with problems for the site, causing extreme industrial relations tensions. The four unions on site all met the necessary criteria of support and anticipated, with relish, the approaching return to collective bargaining.

I worked with a former business partner, Bill Isaacs, on the initial meetings, whilst some months later he moved on to other work in the US (where he was based) but retained a direct interest. I returned to the site monthly over the following three years. During our first interviews of the three business unit leaders we found that they were concerned about the return of collective bargaining and had little respect for the union leadership. There was friction between the three of them, and they had different reporting lines back to their London head office. The HR manager, whose remit included industrial relations across all three businesses, was in a difficult position managing their conflicting interests. Next we discovered that there were four unions in the complex, each holding considerable animosity towards the management, as well as fighting openly with each other. (This is what, colloquially, the English call a *dog's breakfast*. The saying refers to the leftovers from the previous day's meal dropped into the dog's bowl for his breakfast. It implies a completely disorganised mess.)

It was clear that we would make no progress without first establishing agreement between the three leaders, so we went off-site with them to stay in a country hotel for a couple of days. The informal setting helped, along with the fine Scottish roast beef served with Bordeaux wine at a private table for five on the first evening. They did not trust the union leaders and wanted pre-emptive negotiations for a settlement before the collective bargaining rights were resumed. They had some ways to apply pressure to try to achieve that. It seemed naive to us ("Wouldn't the unions realise what you are trying to do?") and it avoided the primary problem that was one of poor relationships. Our alternative was a radically open partnership with the unions. As we talked together and learnt more about the history of the site, and their personal situations, we made headway. By the second evening we had a reasonable agreement to pursue a partnership approach. We sensed the possibility of regression, however, and asked each of them to put in writing their willingness to attempt an open partnership with the unions. Two did so the following day, whilst the third procrastinated and took nearly a week before finally agreeing in an email. But it worked, and the agreement held through the rest of the intervention.

The door was now open for us to engage the senior Leadership Team, including all the key managers on site, in order to develop their collective thinking and disposition to a partnership approach. We did this partly through the introduction of Dialogue skills – which inevitably led to the spirit of partnership – and partly through themed Dialogues. This in turn gave us the permission to engage the unions.

Asking the leaders for free access to their extended organisation was a key test of confidence and trust. They gave it, and we invited every union official on site to meet with us in one large gathering. There had never previously been such a meeting, and who knew what might happen? In retrospect, we did not do adequate preparatory work, and we were lucky to get through that meeting as well as we did. Separate interviews with more of them would have helped. As we entered the room there was an argument already under way between the different factions of the four unions represented by the 35 people in the room. They were more interested in arguing with each other than engaging us, and immediately proposed that we leave. They then proposed we meet them in several different groupings. It took skilful negotiation to stay in the room, and then to make our case for a different approach to their upcoming collective bargaining and relationship with management. Their broad Scottish accents were not always easy to understand, but we impressed them sufficiently to be taken seriously, and to remain in the room with them to explore the options going forward.

The next step was to get management and union in the same room, but in a spirit of Dialogue rather than one of debate or negotiation. It came right down to picky disagreements about seating, with the unions refusing to attend unless they sat at tables, rather than the circle of chairs we preferred. This was a strong indicator of both a lack of confidence in the process and a jockeying for a power position. I came up with an ingenious solution by finding eight long but narrow desks, which I put in an octagon with three people seated at each desk. We had the symbolic circular seating we wanted where no seat was more important than any other, whilst they had the tables they demanded.

We discovered that a significant portion of the workforce (over 30%) was not represented by the unions, although they were awarded the same pay increases that were negotiated by the unions. So we established their representation in the emerging Partnership Forum. Their elected officials called themselves 'The Independents'. So we now had three groupings, and this gave the chance of hearing a third perspective whenever things deteriorated into a debate between management and union. I created a structured feedback process to address the problematic subcultural beliefs. Management, Unions and the Independents each wrote two flip charts to present to the other two groups. Each sheet had two parts: a) what they liked and wanted the other group to keep doing or do more often, and b) what they did not like and wanted them to stop doing or to do in a different way. These requests were read aloud and the flipchart sheets were physically given to the relevant other grouping. Everyone heard all the feedback, then departed with their two flip charts of written feedback from the other two groups, to consider them in a private room. They had an hour to prepare their responses. It was eye-opening how often the feedback they had in writing was still misheard or misunderstood, and how often the new proposals to address the specific feedback points were ineffectual. We had round after round of feedback and response. The flip charts were handed to others with increasing respect, and new working practices emerged that everyone supported. So we began to shift the subcultural thought, and began a process of thinking together to establish a common understanding in a practical way.

Eventually we had a forum that met for a day each month. It had representation of the senior managers and leaders from all three businesses, all four unions and the non-unionised independents. It had taken over a year to convene the Dialogue! I described an image for the workings of this Dialogic forum, comparing its dynamics to playing cards. In a traditional card game each of us is trying to win, so we carefully hide our cards from each other then use our aces and trumps at critical moments to do so. In this Partnership Forum, I proposed that we all lay our cards face up on the table in front of us so that everyone can see everyone else's cards as well as their own. Then we work together to find the best way to play the cards to everyone's advantage, and to nobody's disadvantage. Surprisingly, there is always a way, I emphasised. Collective bargaining was reintroduced, and the negotiations took place according to the new rules. The spirit of engagement was completely different from in the past. People managed their responsibilities in a way that recognised the needs and interests of others, and little of the past tensions, criticisms and recriminations remained.

The Partnership Forum proved able to address serious issues. On one occasion the company had several safety incidents involving explosions, which are extremely dangerous in a petroleum environment. The matter was raised under Parliamentary privilege in the House of Commons and appeared across the media as a matter of public concern. In the past, leaked union revelations would have been designed to embarrass or hurt the leadership at a moment of vulnerability, and a little of that did happen, but not much. The opportunity was taken to invite the local Member of Parliament to attend the next Partnership Forum monthly meeting, which he did. He was last to speak in the opening check-in and was clearly impressed to see the entire site working together effectively. It was a completely different situation from what he had anticipated, and it had been surprisingly easy to provide him with a well-informed perspective.

There were other factors that enabled this intervention to work so well. A confident ex-union official (since promoted and now an independent) who was well-informed about management, union or independent ranks alike, accepted a full-time role supporting industrial relations. That gave me an internal facilitation partner. Secondly he, along with the HR manager, one of the business leaders, one of the union leaders and others joined our nine-month Leadership for Collective Intelligence programme. Bill Isaacs and I were both on the faculty. This meant the practical changes I was realising on the ground we reinforced by substantial Dialogic skill development.

By the time I moved on, the Partnership Forum was a self-sustaining *Power Centre* within the working of the industrial complex. It addressed day-to-day issues of practice, reviewed policies and fed into strategic planning. The impact of market and business developments were understood and accommodated proactively rather than reactively, and it was a fine example of key subcultural groupings functioning as parts of an organisation rather than working in fragmented silos.

How Boring Can You Get?
Trinidadian Integrated Planning and Scheduling

The first time I flew to work with a client in Port of Spain, Trinidad, there was an executive from the UK head office of the same multinational oil and gas company on the flight. I had been introduced to him in the airport lounge just before departure, and on arrival we travelled together to our hotel. I had been invited to introduce Dialogue for 'better communication' amongst the 250 staff in the business there, which I thought was a rather weak brief. I preferred to be more directly tied into the operations. When I heard that he was there to introduce a new planning process, I thought 'how boring can you get?' He enquired whether the Dialogue process could help the introduction of his work, and so a little reluctantly I explored the idea with him. I was surprised, because during the following couple of years we completely turned around the performance awareness of that business.

I began with a series of introductory sessions to get the Leadership Team familiar with a range of Dialogue skills. They were responsive individually but didn't function particularly well as a team. Because of transfers, a number of people had joined or left the team. They were not of a common mind, engaging each other at a rather superficial level. So an internal change person and I together designed an open feedback process. We met with the extended Leadership Team of around 75 for a day-long, off-site retreat in a large hotel meeting room. Each of the Leadership Team members was seated with his or her own direct reports around a table that displayed its team name (such as 'Finance', 'HR', 'Exploration' or one of several 'Operations' teams). We asked the teams to write feedback letters to other teams. They looked around the room to identify which of the other ten or so teams they wanted or needed to address, conferred about what should be said, and how best to say it, then collaboratively wrote their letters to those other teams. The letters were put into envelopes, addressed and delivered to the other teams around the room. They were either appreciative thank-you letters or requests for a change of some kind, and it was clearly stated which team was the author of the letter. Each table in turn read its correspondence from the other teams aloud, so everyone heard all the feedback given. Inevitably, HR had the largest mailbag. It was fun, engaging and serious. We had broken through the politeness. The communication lines were starting to flow between the silos and functions, reducing the earlier fragmentation that had kept them from talking together more seriously. The planning executive, who attended and enjoyed the session, was now convinced I could help the introduction of his new planning process, so we worked together on doing just that.

His idea was that every division, department or function would have its own plan, owned by a member of the Leadership Team. This plan would have four stages: an eight-year strategic display that showed proposed options for that part of the business; a two-year plan of committed delivery, since their capital expenditure was fixed two years out; a three-month schedule of defined activities; and a one-day operator's schedule for daily coordination. The eight-year and two-year stages would each be displayed on a single sheet of paper, whilst the three-month and one-day schedules would be held in a computer programme to enable detailed coordination of multiple activities. Schedule coordination was critical because much of the activity occurred offshore on platforms accessed by helicopter or boat, and was managed in a confined space with limited staff.

The starting point was the eight-year plan. The senior executive, the internal consultant or I spoke individually with each Leadership Team member about what was required. Some found it a simple matter to put their thoughts about the next eight years onto a single-page timeline. Others were seemingly clueless, and clearly worked on a purely reactive basis. Yet others realised how interdependent they were. The IT, HR and procurement requirements, for example, were contingent upon the business developments that lay in other people's plans. We coached them, explored options with each of them and helped them to form a clearer strategic view. The two-year plan would be easier, because their budgets had been allocated, but these would be tackled later, once the larger picture was clear. This preparatory exercise vividly showed how inherently fragmented organisations are because of the decision-making power lines. Previously, each made their own plans separately, and presented them to the CEO to be signed off. That meant the CEO was unwittingly the integrator of the many disparate activities.

The whole Leadership Team was together for a day in one room. We took a full day to see, understand, support and challenge the eight-year strategic plan of each Leadership Team member. They presented their plans one at a time and heard everyone's response. It was a tough experience for many of them, with their limited vision and their lack of significant proposals laid bare. The group was genuine in its support and challenge, and there was a kindness in the room, partly because each one knew they would have their turn. The CEO was unusually forthright at times, and some new options began to percolate. By the end of the day, an overall picture and common content of consciousness was emerging for the first time in the group. It revealed some large holes in the sustained profitability of the business unit, given the contracts they were chasing, and this significantly altered their investment proposals for the period four or five years out. Everyone was asked to revise their eight-year plans on the basis of what they had seen and heard. Coaching was now being requested by those who most needed it. A couple of weeks later, these new eight-year plans were circulated, and the teams began crafting their two-year plans.

Achieving the kinds of changes in awareness and coordination we were making had clearly required that I have a good rapport with the CEO and his full trust. I deliberately created an executive coaching relationship with him. I offered to do a Deep Cut interview with him, involving an audio-recorded, two-hour interview based on questions sent in advance, and with further ones added live. This proved particularly effective with this CEO ("I love your questions!"); as a result we worked together well. (In fact, our work together later led to developing a formal partnership between the company and the Ministry of Security to address violent crime in Trinidad.)

The CEO was socially adept and amiable, as well as being successful in significantly growing the business. He had strong support from his workforce, who looked forward to his performances at the town halls and other large venues where, in a theatrical way he combined vision, practice and humour (which in Trinidad can be quite risqué). He was what I call a 'circular thinker'. That is, he did not go straight to the point he wanted to make, but instead circled around before landing near it. This was very effective in large meetings because on the way round he picked up and included the many different interests and styles of people in the room. It had not, however, served him so well in coaching the senior staff members reporting directly to him. In looking at this with him, we saw that the strategic plans were an absolute godsend. So when he sat down with one of his direct reports he now did so with the eight-year and two-year plans on the table. Everything he needed to talk about was on those two sheets, and if the Leadership Team member wanted to talk about some other option, he would ask why it was not in the strategic plan. He had easy access to a detailed focus, which sat within an integrated plan before him.

What he did next was quite radical. He made the eight-year and two-year plans available to all employees on the company's intranet – and he didn't just make them available, he had days where they were posted on the wall and people were encouraged to walk around the room and get familiar with all of them. Members of the extended Leadership Team were on hand to explain the plans and to answer questions. When he put the plans on their intranet, he included a request for anyone to contribute their observations, proposals or concerns to the relevant team. There was no excuse for anyone to be uninformed or to lack feedback. The IT team, for example, could see what developments were coming and when, so they could support the data processing and communication needs. They could accumulate requirements across the business to acquire better systems, and so on. Individuals could explore changes in career paths. Most importantly, everyone could see the long-term viability and profitability of their business, all of which was dependent on them playing their part in the delivery. It cut across the norms of organisational power structures that generally inhibit what people are allowed to know or to talk openly about. It was fast becoming what I would call a Dialogic Organisation.

A Business Established on Professional Dialogue Principles
European Fuels Marketing

Shortly before Christmas in 2006, a global fuels marketing executive requested that I facilitate a critical team meeting about reorganising their operation. In the few days between Christmas and New Year I interviewed his direct reports in preparation for that meeting, some by telephone and others in their London offices, including a precise and pleasant Turkish executive. He had joined the company through his earlier employer being acquired, and he still felt himself to be a bit of an outsider. Within 15 minutes of our first meeting he asked me if I would coach him. I liked him, thought I could help and so accepted his proposal. In the reorganisation he would be in charge of the European operations.

We developed an understanding that I would coach him and his Leadership Team through the initial years of establishing his European organisation. We began monthly team meetings, preceded and followed by coaching sessions with him, and we had three of these monthly meetings before the inception of his business. They were for two days each, and during these meetings we formed the team and developed a vision, strategy and plans. We aimed to hit the ground running, and did so. Our formal launch took place in Barcelona, where we rented Gaudi's apartment for a black-and-red dinner jacket dance. The goal was to have a leaner organisation than the one it replaced, and to increase sales turnover and margins whilst reducing costs, which again is what we did. There was a decision not to have a head office building; instead, the European leader gathered his Leadership Team in a different country office each month. These offices ran from Portugal to Poland, from the UK to Turkey and everywhere in between, and it was good for each hosting office to meet the various country and central functional leaders personally. And it was a fun team – we celebrated Christmas and acknowledged people's successes.

The most significant success factor, however, went well beyond these welcome qualities. It lay in the decision-making process. We did what I have never seen done before by a team with such a broad geography: we met together in a different country for three full days every month. Given preparation work and travel, that took the best part of a week out of each month. People said you might do that for the business set-up, but it could not be done on a sustained basis. But we did, and it worked remarkably well, because every Leadership Team member was in the room for every significant executive decision made. As a result, it was very rare that a decision needed to be revisited or reworked. This was a simple solution to organisational fragmentation – a Power Centre at the executive level.

After finalising the vision, strategy and plans, we worked on contingencies. We took the view that it was quite predictable that something unpredictable would happen in the marketplace to affect the business. So we brainstormed half a dozen of the most extreme scenarios we could imagine. We then worked out contingency plans for what we could do to survive or even benefit from such an occurrence. The aim was to produce a set of levers that could be pulled if needed to change the trajectory of the business. These covered all parts of the business, were quite specific, and covered shorter and longer-term options. The availability of this collective thinking made available a remarkable sensitivity to changing market conditions and the ability to be proactive where competitors were often evidently reactive.

We then honed the efficiency of the monthly meetings themselves. For every item on our agenda I required the presenter or lead to explain why they wanted the consideration, and what he or she would like the rest of the team to do. The intention usually was either to inform people (in which case a quick walk-through a handout designed to be read later was significantly better than a 45-minute PowerPoint slide presentation), to ask others' views about a decision he or she was going to make, to delegate a decision for others to make, or to seek a consensus in the room for a way forward. This simplified roles and led to clear decision-making. It was intended to be a learning organisation and became one. Also, for each three-day gathering we secured a different and impressive dinner guest speaker with an unusual knowledge, talent or achievement that would broaden the imagination and skills of the team.

Privately I had been introducing Dialogic skills to the leader before introducing them to the group. We incorporated these skills into the design of each meeting, and a reflection afterwards on how the meeting had gone. In addition to the Deep Cut interview I had done with him, I undertook a facilitated 360-degree leadership review with his peers, seniors and direct reports. The leader's style changed, his confidence grew and the team and business thrived. He is now one of the most senior leaders in the multinational and no longer considers himself an outsider. Of course I thrived too. What an opportunity to devise ways to establish a Dialogic Organisation that did not suffer the usual limitations of fragmentation – at least within the Leadership Team. I had not by that time had the chance to work with a whole organisation in depth.

In Closing

There are other Working Cases that inform my thinking, and I will list a few to show the breadth and relevance of Professional Dialogue in organisations: A $5bn technology joint venture between two high-performing companies that was stalling on the basis that each knew their own proven (but different) methods were the right and necessary way to proceed; a failing English prison that was transformed into the highest performing local prison in the country; an Asian Scientific dispute that nearly cost several top executives their careers; a multinational China Business Forum and a six-year whole system change initiative in a US statewide government agency of over 13,000 employees.

These Working Cases may all appear to be different. The point to emphasise, however, is the saving grace. Fragmentation in the world may seem so extensive that it is beyond repair. But the pervasive fragmentation of consciousness is a *singular phenomenon* and each apparently unique manifestation can be addressed in the same essential way. We now have a reasonable understanding of what is involved, and that is what I am referring to as Professional Dialogue.

Conference Session Extracts

From conversation with 20 participants considering the paper with the author

One starting point: Did you notice in an organisation that you don't have the freedom to talk about anything anywhere? So how do organisations inhibit your talking and thinking? What's your experience of freedom of speech in an organization?

Well, we can talk about our dialogue project in the medical industry. We did a dialogue with the leaders on a team.

Exec top group?

It was the top – the top executives were there, yeah, in a group of three. Then they wanted the whole team to come together in the dialogue session. It was not long-term, Just one day. And it became very, very difficult. It became very clear from the beginning that there was not going to be said anything by the people sitting there with their leaders. You feel the power structure flowing through the thing so strong. Then there was a moment there that the dialogue was in a way being forced by the leaders, starting to tell the people how they should feel in a way. We had the feeling that we did not succeed in that situation to defragmentise the power structure in a positive way.

What do you think it is that led them not to be able to speak freely?

Well, my assumption is that the people from the team, they were just scared . . .

. . . of being punished for whatever they would say. They would have huge consequences for the way they would be treated afterwards.

So if they said the right thing, they might get some benefit. If they said the wrong thing, they might suffer?

I wouldn't worry about calling it fragmentation. Just people are inhibited. Outside the room, privately, they'll tell you all of it. In the room, they are shadier people. What is that?

I'd like to bring in something about – is it power or is it how we make decisions? Decisions, at some point, will be made, right? After a certain amount of dialogue in any group the leaders (or if we can truly come to a common ground within the group) some decision will be made, because we have to go out and do something ultimately. We need collective agreements around how decisions will be made because otherwise, they fall back into the existing power structure, which may or may not serve the community, the whole. I think there's something that in the dialogue community we overlook when we don't think about how decisions are formally made.

For me the gold dust in the room is that Peter exposed that there is a planning process in any organisation you work with. There are decision-making processes within organisations.

I am amused by the fact that – I think the first question Peter asked when he opened the dialogue was, "How free are we to speak?" And I think that was still hovering on several levels in the group. So that was a big learning.

The connection between process and content. For me, it was a very good learning, and I thank you how you went with that process also. The session encouraged me to focus more on the topic of power. And in terms of content, I'm very excited about your paper. I very much appreciate you wrote that. I think it's an important paper.

Postscript

The author's reflections written some months after the conference

When I sat down to write my paper several months before the inaugural *The World Needs Dialogue!* conference, I was surprised to find I had much more to say than I had realised. I have always been conscious that Dialogue is a verbal and participatory activity. Writing takes longer, and somehow needs more explanation because there is no immediate audience response or reaction to guide the communication. That is probably why I have written so little about Dialogue in the past.

On the other hand, I found the writing required more precision than speaking, and that has helped me to clarify my thinking. Also, the specificity required to put my experiences in writing, along with the learning I have derived from those experiences, revealed the degree to which I value first-hand self-learning above second-hand stories and third-hand book knowledge. I discovered the authority and depth in what I learnt from direct involvement, and that informs my professional work.

I had been aware that the recognition of collective thought and identity as sub-cultural groupings affected everything – from the convening of the Dialogues I have designed and run, to understanding the 'work to be done' (in terms of reconciling subcultural differences within a genuine collective understanding). Similarly, I knew that, without the analysis I had made of the power structure of organisations, I could not have succeeded with the organisational interventions I have made over the years.

What was less apparent to me was the relationship that I had identified and defined between Dialogue, decision-making and accountability. This is what has enabled my whole-system change work. Without this, I believe Dialogue would have to depend either on speaking from the heart or seeking spiritual insights, neither of which are reliable enough for sustainable change. Although my Dialogue work can and does accommodate both of them, it is not dependent on either. I have been focused on establishing a common understanding, sense and purpose amongst people who may have long-standing reasons to see the world differently. This shift of everyone's perspective, along with a shift of the ground out of which the relationships arise, is dependent on first-hand learning in the immediate situation.

During the conference itself, I was keen to explore how freedom of speech is curbed by the structural power of organisations. The phenomenon arose in the session, as I anticipated, but whilst many in the room felt some level of inhibition to speak up freely, few seemed to recognise it proprioceptively as an organisational phenomenon. Astuteness in this regard, in my view, is essential for intervention work, and I would like to develop the thinking further within the Academy.

So in conclusion, I learnt a lot from the whole process of offering the paper, choosing my subject more specifically, organising my thoughts as I wrote the paper, receiving editing feedback, hearing others' responses at the conference itself, and now reflecting on the progressive learning to write this postscript. I certainly do not have the end answer, but I am strongly encouraged by the progress I, and we, have been making. I hope to contribute again in future years.

Dialogue as the Heart of Strategic Change

Mechtild Beucke-Galm

People have always been concerned with what they could do to be well prepared for future events and uncertainties. One of the skills of a successful entrepreneur is foresight, the ability to make the right decisions for an uncertain time ahead. The technical and biotechnical developments of the last 25 years, and the resulting possibilities of their use, are immense. They have changed working and thinking. The time periods between introduction and widespread usage are getting shorter and shorter, whilst networks and interdependencies are getting larger and larger. Not only multinational corporations, but also small companies with 50 to 100 employees now have core markets all over the world.

How can we recognize the future when we encounter only its latent (and largely undefined) phenomena in the present? Which skills, processes and structures do we need for this?

In response to these questions, I present as a case study our consulting approach and experience of a strategy development and change process in a medium-sized European company. For this project, our team was comprised of three consultants from the Institute of Organizational Learning and Dialogue, Frankfurt: Richard Timel, Othmar Sutrich and me. Each of us had a special expertise in strategy development, organisational development, group dynamic and dialogue.

In this change process, large-group dialogues play an important role.

Aaxco – A Medium-Sized Company and Its Desire for Change

Aaxco (as we'll call it) was a group of companies with about 1,500 employees, covering various areas within the social market and the service industry. Aaxco had been founded 50 years ago as an institution for the care of the disabled, offering workshops and workplaces for the disabled. It had grown strongly in the last ten years. New business units had been added, such as e-commerce, IT training and a language school. These areas were not subsidised; they generated profits and operated in the markets under their own names.

The 'social market' in which Aaxco operated had changed dramatically in the previous ten years. As the state had withdrawn from many social tasks and would continue to do so, the funding – also for the care of the disabled – was significantly reduced. This forced institutions in this field, such as Aaxco, to consider other financing options and to develop new business models.

At the time we joined Aaxco, the situation was characterised by three distinguishing factors:

1. A decline in revenues in the core business (care for the disabled and workplaces for the disabled)
2. A variety of different business models within the company group (i.e., some business units operated and proved themselves in one market and made a profit, whilst others were financed by the state and were dependent on public funds)
3. Different working cultures in the business units, resulting in tensions and prejudices within the workforce

The management wanted and had to act in this situation. Its aim was to counter the decline in government funds through a changed company business model, which would reduce costs through rationalisation, use synergy effects to link the individual business units more closely together, make better use of existing resources, promote innovative forces and skills to prepare for further slumps in the traditional core markets.

The Change Process
Findings from the Initial Interviews

We started with a series of interviews to get a more precise picture of the situation. We spoke with the three directors (the management); with the heads of the various business units; with managers from different departments, teams and projects; with the heads of specific functions such as Human Resources and controlling; with the Workers Council; and with representatives of the owner.

In these interviews it became clear that the various business units held different perspectives on work, leadership, participation, performance, customer orientation, competition and cooperation. In some business units, there was a rather hierarchical culture; the culture in others was more participatory. While leadership was accepted and recognized as a meaningful function in some business units, employees in others approached managers with mistrust and distance. "We realize we need them, and at the same time we could work much better if they weren't there", one employee noted. In the core units of the company, employees had a broad say, which was evident from the fact they regarded the Workers Council as a sort of 'second' management team.

The interviews showed as well that the heads of the different business units managers had developed their strategy and their ways of operating relatively independent of each other, and that they had pushed their own expansion separately from one another. Decisions were made within the business units, based on the needs of daily working life, unrelated to a common strategic orientation. Know-how and competence, were built up by trainings, which the individual employees selected themselves following their individual interests, with no evident consideration of corporate strategy. These inconsistencies, largely incomprehensible to other employees and managers alike, consistently caused disappointment across the ranks.

Through the interviews we became aware of a latent anger as well about the poor information policies of the upper levels of management and about the competition that had developed between the different business units. Employees felt being isolated from important information, and they experienced colleagues from neighbouring business units competing in the same market segment as them, without being informed about those activities.

The differences between the large traditional core business units and the young, vital, small ones were of course the greatest: some wanted to preserve the 'tried and tested' whilst others wanted to develop and market new products. The management had already tried several times – with the help of different consultants – in recent years to reduce the tensions and conflicts within the organisation. In the interviews we were told that we were not the first ones and that Aaxco had already endured various change projects without changing significantly. Employees had participated in the change processes, yet at the same time had continued in the same way as always. "There's a pattern with us, which means we start out strong and then we lose a lot of ground," said one manager. We were determined to interrupt this collective pattern.

The Parallel Learning Architecture

To make the change possible, we (the consultants) invented a special structure, which would enable management and employees to tackle the described differences and tensions appropriately and to develop another business model could. The 'architecture' took into account the decline in government funds as well as an increase of profits from services. Therefore we set up three interrelated processes: strategy development, development of rationalisation measures and development of new competencies. We called this structure 'Parallel Learning Architecture'. This 'Parallel Learning Architecture' was based on three key criteria: 1) to ensure the dynamic balance between hierarchy and employee participation; 2) to generate a strong pull of change; and 3) to correlate the intermediate states of the three development processes. Our process of change was therefore a top-down *and* a bottom-up approach, containing elements of self-organisation.

We started the three processes at the same time. Normally one first develops a new strategy, then introduces new structures or processes and then builds up new competencies, according to the strategy. We did it differently! We wanted to create a pull that would be stronger than the existing collective pattern of participating in the change process while continuing as before.

The simultaneous start and concurrent course of the three development processes enabled those groups, who were driving the change (the three directors = management, the project group rationalisation, and project group strategic personnel development) to exchange information about their progress during the ongoing change process. It was intended that they

24 | Organisations Need Dialogue!

© Mechtild Beucke-Galm

Strategy Development
- Analyse the current strategic position, the current structure and the current culture
- Analyse the core competencies and create scenarios of a worthwhile/desirable future
- Analyse potential markets, clients and competitors
- Develop a process to implement the strategy

Strategic

Potential for rationalisation
- Identify areas of rationalisation
- Build up knowledge management and quality management
- Foster innovation and product development
- Establish KVP – 'Kontinuierliche Verbesserungs-sprozesse'

Dialogue

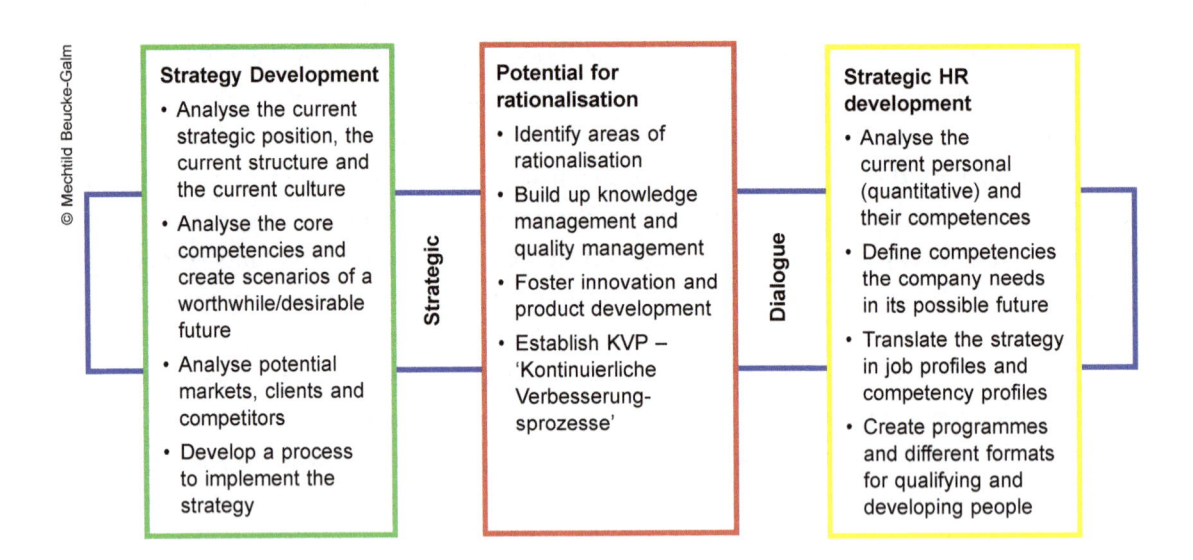

Strategic HR development
- Analyse the current personal (quantitative) and their competences
- Define competencies the company needs in its possible future
- Translate the strategy in job profiles and competency profiles
- Create programmes and different formats for qualifying and developing people

should influence each other's considerations and decisions, instead of only informing each other about the results after decisions have been taken. This was in line with our systemic consulting approach, to understand an organisation as an ongoing series of interactions between the various corporate functions and processes.

In our 'parallel learning architecture', we wanted to anchor employee participation. We chose the format of a large group, where employees and managers from different business units and levels would talk and think with each other and would consider together the intermediate status of the discussions in three change project groups. These large groups – which we called 'Strategic Dialogues' – would be like a microcosm of the company.

This 'parallel learning structure' was based on eight structural elements:

> **The Executive group,** consisting of three directors and two consultants. This group managed the overall process and was responsible for strategy development.
>
> **The Rationalisation project group,** consisting of six to eight key people in the company. This group examined the processes and structures in the various business areas and developed recommendations of measures for rationalisation and new organisational structures. This group received advice from time to time from a member of the consulting team.
>
> **The Strategic Personnel Development project group,** consisting of the HR manager, three junior managers and a consultant. This group developed a concept to build the competencies that the company would need in future. An important focus was on leadership and management, on communication and on decision-making.
>
> **The Self-Organised Pilot groups,** consisting of interested employees and created on their own initiative. They took up long-standing employee concerns and worked

out suggestions for improvement. As groups formed, the members, group appointments and work results were reported to the project office and published on the company intranet.

The Strategic Dialogues, in which 70 employees and managers from the various management levels and business divisions participated and considered the intermediate results from the groups one, two and three.

The group of Dialogue Facilitators, consisting of 20 junior managers who supported as co-facilitators the flow of the strategic dialogues. They also promoted this new and 'different' way of communicating in the company and would moderate pilot group meetings if required.

The Project Office, consisting of the project office manager and a small support team, who organised and coordinated all processes, collected and published all documentation and minutes. All organisational data and documents were gathered here and could be accessed from the Project Office.

The Consulting Team, responsible for the architecture for change and which accompanied and coordinated the overall process. They advised the three directors in developing a new strategy, supported the Rationalisation project group in analysing the data collected and in coming forward with recommendations for new structures and processes. They also helped the Strategic Personnel Development project group to create a new concept for skill development, which would be based in the new strategy. The team of three consultants was committed to the company as a whole, not to individual groups.

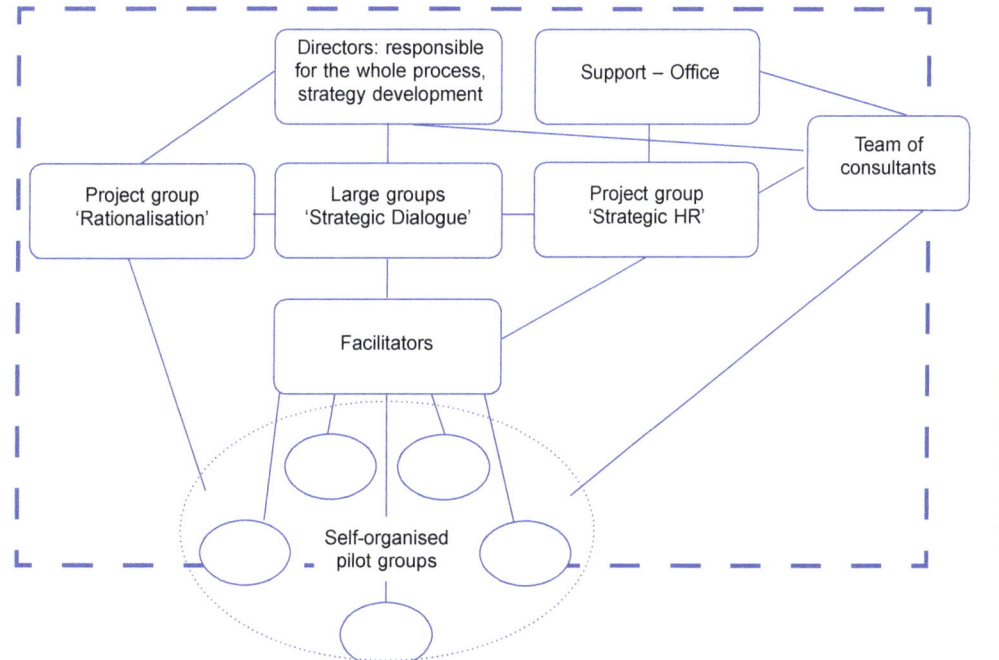

Dialogues As the Heart of Strategy Development and Change

When we proposed to the management to integrate dialogue forums into the strategy development, we encountered mixed reactions and feelings from the directors, interest and openness as well as scepticism and anxiety. We were asked why we thought it could be important. We referred to the results from the first interviews and argued for another way of strategy development, which could fit much better to a participatory company culture:

- The strategy should not be developed by only the management. Experiences and ideas of members from different company levels and business units should flow into the creation of the strategy as well. This would not only be an asset in terms of content, but it would also correspond to a corporate culture, in which employees already had a broad say.
- The interpretation framework for strategic decisions should be widely discussed by management and employees. This would lead to a better understanding of strategic statements and decisions and broader acceptance among employees.
- The existing 'political' communication style should be abandoned as much as possible in favour of an open, exploratory exchange.
- Relevant and provocative topics should no longer be discussed in reproachful and sometimes angry ways in small circles (often in breaks instead of meetings), but should be introduced, worked on and changed in an open exchange between management and employees.

Following these guidelines, we created the Strategic Dialogues as a series of large-group events. Seventy people from four hierarchical levels and from five or six different business units, met with members of the different project groups (the Strategy development group, the Rationalisation project group, the Strategic H/R Development project group) and the Workers Council. The one-day events took place every six to eight weeks. Here, the employees were able to publicly express their ideas for the future, which could then be incorporated into the thinking of the management. The current status of the three development processes (strategy, rationalisation, strategic H/R) were presented and discussed together. It was an opportunity for participation. Contradictions and commonalities became apparent and could be reflected in a new and different way, in a dialogic way.

The composition of the large group was based on heterogeneity and was a good mixture of personnel. While individual managers took part in several Strategic Dialogues, employees only participated once, and each time different employees were invited to the events. Over time around 35% of the employees would participate in a Strategic Dialogue. One the one hand, it was clear to us (consultants) that a one-off event could only provide an impulse and did not constitute a development. On the other hand, we could observe some "movement" in some areas of the company. Participants had talked to colleagues about their experiences – the atmosphere and what was said. Therefore a further proportion of the workforce was indirectly involved and attention was drawn to the change process and the new culture of communication.

This new communication differed significantly from the usual corporate one. Critical to its success were the following:

- Communication should no longer be one-way as in previous management conferences, in which the 'superiors speak and the lower ones listen', but an exchange of views between all.
- Communication should no longer be political and tactical, where 'one and two join against three and four', but should become a flowing sequence of arguing and listening, of assertions and questions.
- Communication should be an open expression of experiences and their meaning, of expectations and disappointments, of reservations and uncertainties.

Setting and Process

One condition for this other kind of communication, is the creation of a another 'space', another physically space and another 'cultural space'. Concerning the physical space, we changed the usual seating order in the company's conference room. Instead of a 'theatre seating order' (row after row with a stage in front, where the directors sat), we had a big (more like an egg) circle with 70 chairs. Everybody could see everybody. The stage was pushed into the background and covered by curtains. Everybody would be on the same level and nobody would speak from above.

In terms of the 'cultural or mental space', we did several things:

- We used a different language than the one which management used in their information
- We introduced a different invitation process, where participants were informed about the new meeting style, the intentions and its meaning in the change process
- We trained interested young team leaders in dialogue and had them talk with colleagues before the large group Strategic dialogues started about their experience with dialogue

David Bohm spoke and wrote about the different space which is needed for and created by a dialogic communication. He called it 'container', which could be compared to the 'holding environment' in Winnicott's theory about the environment children need in order to learn and develop. We think of a 'container' as a space for exploration and understanding, where shared points of view and contradictory ideas can stand side by side without having to be ironed out smoothly by consensus, a space that can absorb what motivates, touches, shakes or unsettles the participants. When feelings are not held, people defend themselves and fight, therefore remain stuck in repetitive routines.

We built the container for the Aaxco change process in several steps: through the wording of the invitation and the attached information; through conversations between the trained young team leaders and their colleagues; through the seating in a circle and through the introduction by consultants and directors the beginning of each Strategic Dialogue.

The invitation to participate in a strategic dialogue was signed by the three directors and was accompanied by various kinds of information:

- A description of the Strategic Dialogue as a new format
- A description of the process architecture
- An analysis by the directors of the company's situation in the expected social and economic developments
- Information about the first steps in different project groups
- A list of the existing pilot groups

All of this could also be found on the company's intranet.

The Strategic Dialogues took place in the largest room of the company. This was the room in which the management usually held their information events. At the front of the room was a stage where the directors normally sat to be better seen in their speeches, while the members of the lower and middle management levels and of the workers council sat in rows of chairs in front of them. The Strategic Dialogues were different. There were no pedestal, no rows of chairs and no tables. Seventy chairs were set up in a circle, just fitting into the room. When the participants in the morning met in front of the room, they found drinks, fruit and the obligatory name tags waiting. Most of the participants did not know each other as they were from different business units.

Imagine such a day . . . 70 participants sitting next to each other in a circle – more-or-less expectant and more-or-less sceptical, more-or-less waiting to see how the management would present itself. How could we turn these people from an audience into participants? Whoever would open the scene had to bring a spirit into this room in which exchanging ideas and speaking to each other could take place. Entry is everything!

The opening was made by one of the directors. He spoke of the intention of this day, about the company as a family and about current events. Then my colleague and I took the floor. We introduced ourselves, spoke about our relationship to the company, about the spirit of the day and also about the opportunities and the risk. Together with the in-house facilitators, we talked about a different form of communication and about our images of strategy development. We introduced the philosophy and practice of dialogue and created the 'field' for a new exchange and encounter: taking each other seriously, getting involved with each other, listening to each other and responding to each other. Here people from different business units came together with different stories and experiences. In this microcosm, for one day, the members behaved differently than they usually did.

After the introduction, the participants talked to each other in groups of three. We invited them to talk about a possible future for the company and to incorporate their more recent experiences. People seemed attentive and interested in what each other had to say. The whole room was filled with the murmuring of engagement. Then back into the big circle: an important moment! Who would start, and how? What would be the first contributions, what would come to the fore and what would remain in the background? A middle-aged man took the initiative, introducing himself, telling the group how long he has been with the company. He talked about his experiences in his department, what had changed in recent months and what it meant for him to work there. He was followed by the two partners of his trio. Both had been working in one of the new business units for just six months. They described the structure of this unit, the market movements and the business opportunities. Then a neighbouring participant spoke, and then another; in the first hour everyone spoke at least once. There was little connection between people – the conversation consisted of individual statements. There were also still few images of the future; more often, people talked of the recent past. Their interests, their personal hopes, their daily experienced contradictions were brought up for discussion. The style of conversation was hesitant and cautious, as there was still no sense of what could be said in this context. The flow of conversations was uneven and halting, the contributions followed each other according to the seating arrangement. There was something formal about it, as if there was still no 'ground' for the emotional content.

This phase was followed by a public interview with one of the directors, sitting in the centre of the circle. He spoke about the current business situation, about developments in society and about the direction, Aaxco should develop. During this time, the participants only listened – and nevertheless something happened inside them. The director's comments definitely generated a resonance in everyone, which made him or her aware of the own thoughts, beliefs and judgements.

Following the director's interview, members of the two other project groups presented their ideas as well as the members of the self-organised groups.

After this phase of listening, it was time for the participants to exchange their impressions, thoughts and feelings. In small groups they talked about what they had heard, where they disagreed and what questions arose for them. In the following large group session, people presented what they had discussed and what their thoughts or judgements were. Questions were put forward and answered by the director together with the project group members.

In the second half of the day, employees and managers – based on the morning's questions – contributed their ideas in thematic working groups. These results were then briefly presented to the large group and discussed in a publicly witnessed 'fishbowl' inner-circle conversation, which, after half an hour, became a large group dialogue. The Strategic Dialogue ended with a check-out with everybody.

Strategic dialogues as large-group events are a real challenge for all participants. Most people are not used to speaking in a large group or to openly addressing topics, and they are even less accustomed to speaking openly as employees when their own managers and also their managers' bosses and one of the directors are in the room. To make it easier for the people, we designed the Strategic Dialogues to alternate between large- and small-group conversations, between unstructured and structured formats. In the first three Strategic Dialogues the unstructured phases in the large group were 'only' about 1.5 hours in the morning and 1.5 hours in the afternoon. It was important to us not overwhelm the participants who were unfamiliar with this format.

Reactions Within the Company

What were the overall responses to the Strategic Dialogues over the course of one-and-a-half years? I would like to answer this question with quotations from discussions I had after each of the Strategic Dialogues. They showed the range of impressions, expectations and hopes.

One employee from the area of care for the disabled said:

I didn't expect anything from this day. Why should I? The management will make their case and they have invited us as an audience. You know what that's like! Yes, some things were interesting, but the managers will continue as before. I don't think I need to come here again.

A second person saw it quite differently:

I had expected nothing, like my colleague, but then I was surprised by the openness with which the director talked about their current strategic considerations, about the contradictions and about their own uncertainties. I didn't expect it at all and I was impressed.

A third person said:

I was very sceptical about these so-called Strategic Dialogues. Above all, because different superiors are sitting here and you have to be careful what you say in this big circle in their presence. This can cause problems later on. Nevertheless, it was good to exchange ideas with others. But I still doubt whether we will be able to talk openly to each other in our daily lives.

For many, the focus was not on management, but on the exchange with colleagues:

We have never had the opportunity to get to know colleagues from other business areas – therefore these strategic dialogues offered an interesting chance for exchange.

The directors shared different perspectives about the Strategic Dialogues as the series progressed. One of them put it this way:

I am confused and angry by the biased image our employees have and about the vehemence with which they sell their ideas as truth. I am also annoyed by the assessments they have of us as management. The company has grown rapidly in recent years, but I still thought we knew our employees and had a working atmosphere of trust. What strikes you here is an explosive mixture of admiration and mistrust towards the management.

And another:

For me it is completely surprising that people's loyalty is limited to their own business unit and that they don't have other business units and the company as a whole completely in their mind. The second surprise is that we are expected to do everything better and at the same time leave everything essentially as it is. How do you do that?

We consultants had a different view of what was happening. As one of my colleagues said:

I am deeply impressed by the reflectiveness that the employees showed and by the potential a lot of these people show. This becomes very visible through the Strategic Dialogues. It is a phenomenon how little the management does see this and promotes or uses the potential.

The Strategic Dialogues were experienced by all much like alternating baths, from hot to cold and back to hot: moving between high inner participation and ambivalent distancing, between intensive involvement and bored listening, between high esteem and derogatory commentary. There were boring information phases and cycles of high attention, lengthy hinting and violent clashes. Those who wanted to know what was going on in Aaxco during this time could experience this personally in the Strategic Dialogues. The participants came with a wide range of differing expectations. Some wished that the top management would be shown to be incompetent and found it boring if this did not take place. For others these forums were too threatening, because they might meet their own leaders there and did not want to speak openly in their presence. For some employees, the large groups were exhausting and they were happy to be there only once. For others, the Strategic Dialogues were examples of successful, lively communication in the company.

A Pivotal Moment in the Process

We consultants experienced again and again how difficult it was for participants to break away from their own assumptions and patterns, to step out of their own system of coordinates. And on the other side, people brought forward their reservations and disappointments, their anger and helplessness, their interest and commitment into this dialogue space. Bohm proposes that the space should be 'empty' so that one can move freely in one's mind. "We must have an empty space, where we are not obliged to do anything, nor to come to a conclusion nor to say anything or not say anything . . . Otherwise we are not free . . . It's open and free. It's an empty space." (Bohm in Nicholson 1996) Building such a space for dialogues therefore means creating a space in which the participants can become aware of their ideas and thus free themselves from the compulsion to perpetuate old behaviours and interpretations.

This became particularly clear in the fifth Strategic Dialogue. After the working groups, the discussion took place in the inner circle (fishbowl) with one of the directors and representatives from the various small groups. The public discussion was lengthy but seemed pointless, as the members switched between monologues and correcting each other. The outer circle became restless: some went out to get a drink or to smoke and talk to others rather than listen to the chatter in the inner circle. We consultants dissolved the inner circle and moved on to the planned exchange within the larger group. But the communication structure from the inner circle repeated itself. This led to a sense of time pressure, as if there would not be enough time to say the essential things. One of the participating directors took the floor. He had waited a long time, then he just burst. He wanted to express his view, to clarify, to reject, to say what from his perspective was wrong, to show some of the topics in another light. He was unstoppable . . . My attempts to limit his contribution failed. Suddenly, one of the young managers, who was one of the in-house facilitators that day, stood up abruptly and interrupted him: "Stop! It is as always – we are invited to participate and you take up most of the time for yourself and your view . . . " She was very upset. Fear, numbness, speechlessness, silence . . . What had just happened here? What did this mean? Was he destructive or helpful? Was it a breakdown or a breakthrough?

In the large group pressure had gradually built up, because no grouping could listen to what another wanted to say: all wanted to give their own views rather than to listen. The unspoken message of the employees, the managers and the members of the management was, "We have something essential to say. You don't hear it, that puts us under pressure! Listen to us . . . finally!"

This message, because it wasn't expressed verbally, stage-managed itself in the course of the exchange in the large group. What had the management and the employees wanted to say? What should the others hear?

The management saw Aaxco as a company that had come under pressure from increasing competition, despite successes to date. The employees (and on this day many from the field of traditional work with the disabled were present) spoke of their social commitment in working with the disadvantaged. They saw progress in improving methods and procedures in working with clients and thought of the future as a further development of the present.

The management tried to convey a new business model; its starting points were the development of completely new market segments, which meant this strategy should be the starting point for future action. The employees described the importance of security for their community.

The management spoke of insecurity and threat to the company. This description was perceived by many employees as an attempt to irritate, and experienced it as a loss; they themselves found no evidence of becoming effective in this situation.

The groups remained alone in their perceptions, assessments and concerns; there really was no listening. Each group was too preoccupied by their needs and views. This had been the 'reality' in this company for a number of years and it could be felt and experienced in the situation described above.

We consultants were at that moment also caught up in the dynamics described. We could see the pattern of not listening and referring to each other, but in this situation we were not really able to pivot and use it productively. I approached the young manager who had spoken so passionately. She answered and talked first to me and then explained to the director what was putting her under pressure, as well in the company as here in this dialogue session . . . and he answered her. This led to another colleague talking and bringing himself into the conversation. For a short time an honest exchange developed. Then the agreed-upon completion time was reached and we had to end the meeting. At the end, part of the numbness and speechlessness in the group had dissolved . . . but another part still remained.

The Evolution Throughout the Strategic Dialogues

Over a period of one-and-a-half years, six Strategic Dialogues had taken place, and they had improved in quality over the course of that time. An essential aspect was that the ideas concerning the new strategy of the directors and their drafts became more and more concrete, as did the considerations and initial results from the two project groups. Their statements became more understandable and comprehensible for the employees, who were therefore able to make a better contribution.

The dialogic communication we had introduced had an effect. The later Strategic Dialogues were more open and more direct, more conflictual and more appreciative. The workforce was on the move and there was a broader acceptance among many of those involved in the upcoming realignment. The opportunity to participate in the Strategic Dialogues or in the self-organised pilot groups (and thereby participate in shaping the organization) was positively received.

Thanks to the Strategic Dialogues, trust between the directors and between the employees and the directors had largely returned. One employee once addressed it to one of the directors: "I have not understood everything, that is at stake at the moment, and that is not my job. But I think you're doing a good job". Employees were able to observe the directors in the Strategic Dialogues and get to know their thinking. From this observation they learned about their leadership qualities and could make themselves a picture, whether these gentlemen would lead the company into a successful future or not and whether they would also be responsive to the employees.

A New Culture in the Company
The Culture of Dialogue

In order to consolidate the new culture of open exchange and to anchor it in the company, we felt it was necessary to develop dialogic competence and an appreciative attitude.

Superficially, it seems quite easy to enter into Dialogue with each other. You sit down and talk. Experience shows, however, that it is not that easy. Special skills and practices are needed – and can be learned. This includes:

- Listening to what the other person says and creating space for it within oneself. This means not only paying attention to the contents, but also to their 'emotional tinting' and to make the different dimensions of things accessible through enquiry.
- Meeting people and functions in an appreciative and trusting manner, being attentive and considerate, not rashly judging them according to inner images and ideas, but first perceiving what happens 'here and now'.
- Saying what you think. "This is what I mean, and . . . how do I express what I mean?" This includes asking questions not only of others, but also of oneself.
- Understanding and accepting contradictions and paradoxes as 'normal' and not trying to resolve them unilaterally.
- Distinguishing between observation and evaluation. Delay the evaluation and thus slow thinking down. Leave different and contradictory statements next to each other and resist the impulse to quickly put them into an ordered context.

We decided to start the 'anchoring' in training young managers, introducing the dialogue approach to them in several workshops. Out of a pool of junior staff which the HR manager had put together, 20 members were selected to be learn about dialogue. Afterwards they were asked to support us as facilitators in the Strategic Dialogues, using the newly gained dialogic skills, and to apply the dialogic practices in their own team meetings. Five of the 20 were involved as facilitators in each of the Strategic Dialogues. They presented the practices of dialogue to their colleagues at the beginning of each large-group session. In their presentation they talked about what would be different for them today as against their usual meetings. They spoke about their previous experiences with department meetings and about their hopes for the today's Strategic Dialogue.

We (consultants) passed on our experience as a kind of 'training on the job' to our junior staff. We tuned in to the Strategic Dialogue with them the day before and evaluated the day together with them the day after. We discussed with each other in advance what we wanted to pay particular attention to that day and, after the event, what had been successful, what had not and why. With the preparation and follow-up, attention was generated among the junior staff for the corporate reality that was shown in the Strategic Dialogue and for the difference between the dialogical attitude versus the pronounced political-tactical attitude that had been dominant in the company.

Through this joint communication, the young managers gained a different perspective of the company and of leadership, of the work and entrepreneurial action. They perceived the different positions between which the company moved back and forth during this time and saw the effects of the different leadership and communication styles. They learned to be able to work in the field of tensions, created by the simultaneity of different kinds of logic in the company, without relieving themselves of their own tensions by making judgemental and/or derogatory comments on the process or of the behaviour of others. Together with us consultants, the junior managers as facilitators formed an essential fund for the dialogue container described above.

The second area of 'anchoring' was at the middle management. For its members, the Strategic Dialogues were a (sometimes) difficult developmental process, a 'learning on the job'. They heard how the employees saw the company (or the various divisions) and they internally compared these views with their own images. They learned what the employees were critical about and what they were expecting. And they were (during the open discussions), repeatedly asked to express their views on individual topics and to take a public stand, which had never happened before. Managers had to accept and respect the different logic of the various sub-systems, seize opportunities and consciously grasp risks when the moment comes, and had to learn to make a fluent and flexible change of perspective in group processes.

From Social Work Orientation to Professional Business Understanding

The cultural change I described developed in co-evolution with a second change. Slowly but surely the company developed a new 'orientation': from a predominantly social work orientation to a professional business understanding. There were great differences between the employees of the disability sector and those of the profit-oriented young companies with regard to their respective notions of work, performance and effectiveness. The first group of employees was shaped in their attitudes by their background as social workers and directed their attention in their work to the people they cared for and worked with. The relationship with these people – the care, support and acceptance – was in the foreground for them. Business topics such as performance, efficiency or costs were not part of their everyday thinking and, from their point of view, was management's responsibility.

This was completely different for the employees of the young companies. Even though many of them also had a socio-pedagogical background and had worked in the disability sector, they were keenly interested in market and profit opportunities. They were innovative in the creation of new services and were keen to win new customers for the group. The relationship between investment (time, know-how, money) and profit played a relevant role in their thinking. For them it was a matter of course to deliver promised services at a defined point in time.

The differences in ideas and motivations became visible in the Strategic Dialogues and in the pilot groups. They caused irritation and defence, also astonishment, curiosity and interest. At the same time, a broader exchange on these topics was initiated, which over the next few years led to a professional understanding of their business.

Findings

We accompanied the company in the development of the strategy and the gradual restructuring over one-and-a-half years. During this time, a new strategy for the Group was developed in monthly workshops with the directors and in the quarterly Strategic Dialogues. This new strategy focused on growth in the young business units and on specialisation in traditional disability work. The growth strategy focused on identifying and winning new customers and developing new service products. In the disability work, the strategy was to focus on a reduced number of offers that would cover 80% of the needs in this region.

During this period, the Rationalisation project group developed various measures aimed at reducing costs. These measures included the standardisation of administrative processes, a more differentiated listing of subsidies and costs for the various disabilities and the development and introduction of a new controlling system in the traditional business area. A cross-divisional product development process was proposed for the young business units.

At the level of self-organisation, six to eight working groups were set up, which took up the concerns of employees and worked out suggestions for improvement. A working group suggested that rooms should be used for workshops by employees from different business units and not only by employees of the unit in which the rooms were located. The use of the rooms should be organised 'unbureaucratically' via a new intranet platform that could be created by the company's own IT business unit. Another idea was to organise an exchange of experience and knowledge across different business areas to specific products and customers.

The HR concept was fundamentally changed; the department, which had so far seen its job in organising trainings in technical and professional skills, now made the development of managers and employees its task. The H/R work would in future be oriented to the strategy and no longer only to individual (professional) interests. Quantitative and qualitative data were collected on the current situation and the number and skills of employees the company would need in the future were defined. The new Strategic Personnel Development led to other recruitment processes and to other learning offers for the management and the employees. H/R focused now on the topic of leadership and promoted a personal development through various formats such as in-house workshops, coaching, job rotation and mentoring.

In the following years, the company underwent a development that resulted in the separation of the profit and non-profit areas. The young companies joined forces, retained part of the company name and are now successful in the market. The area of care for the disabled and the workshops for the disabled have been reduced and concentrated on services that continue to be financed by the state.

Reflections in Retrospect

Looking back on the project and our work, it becomes clear that we had received a very special request from Aaxco. The request to advise and support the company as a whole – in strategy development, in the implementation and change process and in the development of a new HR – was extraordinary. Normally, we receive requests for one area or another and we are confronted with the fact that several consulting firms with different approaches and theories are working in the company at the same time we are. In Aaxco the management took a different path; maybe we got a leap of faith because my colleague had a good reputation in the 'consulting scene' for more than 30 years.

Looking back at our working hypotheses and the change architecture we introduced, from my perspective several things have proven to be useful and effective:

- The combination of a bottom-up and top-down process
- The (almost) simultaneous start of the three development processes (strategy development, the identification of rationalisation potential and the new personnel development)
- The combination of self-organisation and defined project groups
- Involving employees in the process of strategy development

We learned how the various architectural elements can mutually reinforce each other and thus have a powerful effect on the organisation. We also learned – again – more about dialogue, e.g., that dialogue in different social contexts must develop its own style and follow the circumstances of the situation. Strategic dialogues focus attention on the present and the future; they work in a strategy process by widening and simultaneously sharpening the view of a larger group. The large groups are like microcosms of the company, in that one could say that the company is 'talking to itself' here – it talks to itself and, if the dialogue succeeds, listens to itself at the same time. Those moments are special and fruitful. In such moments, the participants experience the dynamics they create together, the inner images from which they emanate and why they argue as they do. In the dialogues, the attention of the participants is concentrated, just as burning glasses do in optics. And therefore, participants can make observations and experiences which are otherwise inaccessible. At Aaxco the participants experienced in the Strategic Dialogues:

- That the 'centre' of the company had been lost due to the rapid development
- That many employees measure themselves by the quantity of their knowledge and not by business success
- That every form of control is experienced as a restriction, which creates a collective defence: 'Control is inhumane'
- That most employees are involved in a communication game: one member teams up with a second and both then act together against a third and fourth . . . and how this reduces learning and development
- That the drive to continue in this pattern is strong, and that there is no interest in really wanting to see what is 'going on'

We (consultants) have once again become aware of how challenging it is to work with unstructured large groups and how much uncertainty these groups are mobilising. They open up the possibility of articulating existing fears. An unstructured space that offers the possibility of making insecurity tangible contains the chance to make collective fears visible. Consultants and participants experience which fears are most important. Mostly, they are individual fears that then condense into collective fears. One can observe where and in which direction the transmissions take place: from the individual to the collective and/or from the collective to the individual. In Aaxco we have perceived the fear of demarcation due to globalisation and the associated acceleration. We have observed this fear among many employees in the traditional field of work with the disabled and it has shown its effect throughout the company as a collective fear. Without the large-group dialogues, neither we consultants nor the management would have been able to perceive and access this fear.

We have also learned – again – that phases of incomprehension and anger are an immediate part of the dialogue process and that it is not an 'accident' when conventional forms of conversation collapse. In dialogue the incompatible comes together, and contradictions and opposites become more clearly visible. The challenge in such phases is to stay in contact, not to retreat, and to see and understand one's own contribution in the unsuccessful interaction process. If one admits one's own part to oneself and others, then it becomes possible to change the quality of the conversation and one's own conversational behaviour; previous perceptions, ideas and interactions are put into perspective.

This requires a variety of skills. Besides the ability to listen with an open mind and to speak about what is in oneself or what is in the space, it also requires the ability to perceive and 'hold' anger and fear (one's own and that of the collective). And it requires various meta-competencies (cf. Beucke-Galm 2016) such as confidence that the discussion process will makes sense, even if there is a breakdown.

In hindsight, I can see that we have paid less attention to the phase of exiting than to the phase of entering. We have carefully considered how to start the entire process and the sub-processes and how to set up the container for the dialogues. We have not, however, planned and designed the exit and conclusion with the same mindfulness. Figuring out how to do this at the end of a dialogue session is not enough.

I would like to conclude with the following: Dialogue is not creating a feeling of well-being in a group or creating the myth that through dialogue the problems can be solved. I share Lee Nicholsen's statement that dialogue in a time of increasingly rapid abstraction and seamless digital images is a persistent "confrontation with the uncomfortable chaos of everyday tangible experiences". Today I would say "Through dialogue the 'invisible chaos' is made visible!"

References

Bohm, David (1998). *Der Dialog. Das offene Gespräch am Ende der Diskussionen* (Nichols, Lee, Hrsg.) Stuttgart: Klett-Cotta Cotta (4. Aufl. 2005).

Beucke-Galm, M. (2008). Coaching – ein Dialog mit sich selbst der Gruppe und der Organisation, in: *Supervision und Coaching*, VS-Verlag 2008.

Beucke-Galm, M. (2010). Coaching als Entwicklungsprozess, in: Zeitschrift OSC, 2/2010.

Conference Session Extracts

From conversation with 20 participants considering the paper with the author

How would you feel about running that process? It's an ambitious program, right? If next week you were heading in to run one of these 70-person groups and you had all these moving parts simultaneously, what would you be thinking or feeling?

I would feel a really strong sense of responsibility to be taking them on that journey. They might think, "You're one of the three people who should know what's going on". I'd feel a sense of responsibility in the face of that. I'm not sure I'd be up for that. That might be too much responsibility with too much at stake [laughter]. Some of those 70-people dialogues – if that goes really flat, they walk away going, "That was a freaking waste of time".

For me, is the most exciting but also worrying thing: "Oh, would I dare to engage in a dialogue with 70 people at the same time?" And I think I wouldn't. Up till now [laughter], we have dialogues in groups of seven people in ten tables or like 500 people but then in groups of ten and then bring that together. So a lot of respect to Mechtild and others that you dare to facilitate a process with that many people.

How was it then implemented? That's difficult in my opinion.

This was an exhaustive, extremely well-done diagnostic that clearly shows that our model was not sustainable. Our business was dependent on people to deal with volumes. And we couldn't afford to bring in the number of people to deal with the increasing volumes.

It's had consultants previously, either two or three rounds of consultants and nothing happened. If you were one of the three and the proposal was, "Let's do this", would you do this, or would you change it?

How do you raise the voices of the 1,500? I think, in the text, it said that there were a lot of interviews done before. I would be very interested in the project-group rationalization, the strategic HR group. Who are these people, the four or the six or eight, that are in there?

So I'm trying to come up with my bottom-line statement [laughter] . . . I think dialogue is critical, but it's not sufficient to actually deliver the change that's needed. And so what else is needed? There needs to be consequences for stepping out of alignment with a new change. I'm interested to know how you combine repercussion with dialogue.

How would it change what I'm going to do? I think be braver, maybe. I might think about the structure and how I draw it out visually for people, the effect I'm expecting to have. I'm quite a visual person, so think a bit about how I draw it out.

I think there's something about the simultaneous approach that also fits with dialogue, with the wholeness that is happening altogether, at once.

Here, it ended up with the separation of the for-profit from the non-profit. Is that a success? Is that in the name of wholeness, or is that a fragmentation?

Mechtild bringing her work for us to think about is a good way for us to learn. We are not telling each other what to do, or making one model, we are learning how to be more effective.

Postscript

The author's reflections written some months after the conference

This postscript results from a special situation. Since I could not participate in the conference and the exchange on my paper, I listened to the group discussing my text and the project five months later.

The audiotape transported me into the room of the conference centre on the afternoon of 16 October 2018, and it opened the space for me with its different voices and different perspectives. Listening for over 90 minutes and getting involved with the views and comments of the participants had an interesting effect on me. It brought the project, with its many levels, people and interests back to life – more than had been the case with writing. Writing is about focusing, structuring and working things out, bringing complexity into form and making it accessible. The discussion process of this group brought the diversity of the project back to mind; the strategic dialogues, with their different opinions, views and perspectives especially became very present again.

Through listening to the individual contributions and the flow of the discussion process the important aspects and the dynamic of a large group dialogue became clearer to me:

- Large-group dialogues – especially in the context of change processes – are a special challenge for participants and facilitators. They require ongoing attention, long breaths and trust in the process. As a facilitator, one must know and endure the fact that it is only over the course of time that a different quality of listening and speaking develops.
- In a large group dialogue a room is filled with different interests, backgrounds, experiences and emotions. Curiosity and openness to inquire are present as well as, uncertainty and ambivalence. Participants are stimulated, impressed and sceptical at the same time.
- The strategic dialogues developed over the course of the project into a central forum in which the intermediate results from the various subprocesses flowed together, and where they were presented and discussed.
- The strategic dialogues were not a decision-making instrument, but rather were a place of joint thinking, of debate, of joint consultation to better understand the complex issues and different interests, and their respective meanings for the company.

An Entry-Level Practice for New Professional Dialogue Practitioners

Francis Briers

It is my perception, which seems to be fairly commonly shared by others as reality, that the pace of change in the world is getting faster. There are various terms relating to this, whether they be the originally military 'VUCA' acronym (Volatility, Uncertainty, Complexity and Ambiguity) or 'Age of Accelerations', coined by Thomas L. Friedman. However this experience is labelled, leaders and teams in organisations need to find increasing levels of responsiveness and agility to stay competitive and require empathy and creativity to constructively shape the experience of customers or users – and resilience, quite frankly, to stay sane!

I have found in my work some simple practices for relating to each other which evoke the spirit of dialogue, as I understand it. They help groups build collective resilience, find creative solutions to tricky problems, and establish a habit of listening more deeply to themselves, to each other, and to their wider ecosystem so that they can be more responsive and less reactive. This has been true across diverse contexts, from talent and leadership development to culture change and Agile business transformation.

While this work may not engage people in Dialogue in the traditional sense, it is proving to be of genuine value, enabling them to enter into a different kind of conversation with each other, and to elicit deeper listening, awareness, and connection. This is especially true when combined with embodied approaches to state management – practices which enable people to swiftly manage their physiological state when they are emotionally 'triggered' by an event – so that participants have the capacity to regulate their own levels of stress and psychological arousal and we can all relate to one another as constructively as possible.

The practices I have been using with groups and teaching to teams, so that they can create different kinds of conversations for themselves, are fairly simple. I typically use these practices with groups of no more than 12 to 15. (I also use a 'pairs' practice which works well as part of a set of methods, but that is definitely closer to Nancy Kline's work with the 'Thinking Environment.') The group practices use the concepts of debate, discussion and dialogue as a way of framing the kind of conversation we want to elicit. I typically refer to the Latin root of these words to define them: *Debate* (its Latin root being the same as *bat*), meaning 'I take my ideas and seek to beat you over the head with them until you agree with me!' and *Discussion* (its Latin root being the same as *concussion* and *percussion*), meaning 'we smack our thoughts and ideas together and see what falls out the other side'. Both of these are essentially combative; they can be useful but create a particular relational tone. Finally, we speak about *Dialogue* (its Latin root being *dia* and *logos*, translating as 'flow of meaning').

Whilst discussion is typically shaped by a desired outcome – e.g., to make a decision – the way I have been working with dialogue is to shape the conversation using a focusing question. This helps establish a 'flow of meaning' and exploration rather than a more combative hunt for a predetermined conclusion. These conversations are then underpinned by a commitment to really listen to others as they speak, rather than planning what next to say. Also I ask people to pause, take a breath and speak what they are thinking and feeling when it is their turn. Through various versions of turn-taking and an intention to be concise, we seek to enable 'equal air-time' which various bodies of research have found is an enabler and outcome of high-performance teams.

There are more nuances to the practice, and ways I combine it with things like state management, as mentioned, but that describes the heart of it. I see the contribution it could make to the professionalisation of Dialogue as a well-tested 'entry level' practice: something that is time-efficient and accessible, but which lays the foundation for a genuinely different quality of relationship and a culture founded on a different set of underlying assumptions. The tangible shift in atmosphere and connectedness within a group from this practice can then be a springboard for exploring deeper Dialogue work and more systemic interventions.

The Purpose of the Work

I've described in broad terms some of the principles I have been working with as a very simple 'Dialogue' practice (i.e., providing a focusing question, committing to listening and holding an intention for equal airtime, etc.). I have also mentioned using state management methods – such as 'centring' – in connection with this work. Although there is a danger that this sounds like I am aiming to limit the conversation or in some way drive it into a particular emotional tone, I want to be clear that is not the case.

So what is the aim or intention? It is a little more numinous than this in my thinking, but here are some bullets to summarize. Our aim is to help people have the most useful conversation possible while relating to each other as constructively as possible. We do this through (as best we can):

- Creating equality of voice in the group
- Setting aside predetermined or habitual thinking
- Listening to each other openly and attentively
- Supporting everyone to continually anchor themselves in an expanded and responsive state rather than becoming entrenched in a contracted and reactive state

We do this so that we can, both in the moment and as a habit in our lives more generally, create and maintain connection with self and others rather than practising disconnection or dissociation. (Even this last is not an attempt to avoid emotionality or conflict, but to seek always to be aware and responsible with our emotions rather than allowing them to hijack our awareness and undermine our capacity for clear thinking and care.)

Some Examples of Application

I have applied this work in different ways in different environments. Mostly these are organisational settings, and most often in commercial enterprises though I have also worked in Health and Social Care, with the Police, and in some NGO organisations. Sometimes I have explicitly taught different ways to meet and speak together so that teams, groups or leaders can take the work away and use it themselves. At other times I have more implicitly used methods and practices as a facilitator to shape the work of a group I have been supporting. I will give examples of both.

Executive Team Facilitation

I have worked for several years with the Executive Team of a large creative agency. In my work with them I have seen the group grow, change and evolve, both in terms of the individual team member's capacity and with managing people who are leaving and joining the team. On most of the occasions when I have facilitated their sessions exploring strategy and organisational culture, I have used simple rounds of dialogue to help them listen more deeply to themselves and each other. It is a lively group, generally unafraid of conflict. They have fierce debates, but all too often what I have seen coming out of this is simply a re-treading of old ground. What I have observed – and what they have fed back – is that by slowing down, practising deeper listening, pausing and reflecting to really sit with a question before speaking, and hearing equally from all voices, they have elicited greater self-honesty about what really matters to them as leaders of the organisation. With this, they discover more creative solutions to long-standing problems and greater alignment around their approach to future challenges.

Just before my first offsite session with the team, a new CEO had been put in place. I chose to work with the group outdoors, to use the activation of peripheral vision to initiate higher levels of theta brainwave activity. This led to some focused conversation in pairs to reflect on their team's purpose, before coming back together to work in rounds to hear back from others. At another time we met after they had experienced an extended period of high stress when three key members of the team had left quite suddenly. I worked with some simple centring (embodied state management) exercises, then used some rounds of dialogue to express and hear from each other how they were feeling, and how they saw the morale and social climate of the organisation. In both cases, the group identified these interventions as turning-point moments in both our work together and the evolving capacity of the Executive Team to lead the business effectively.

Priming Agile Teams

As part of a large Agile transformation programme in a Financial Services business, we ran three-day 'priming' workshops to help the teams launch a new way of working, usually in newly formed teams. These were made up of three strands of learning: Agile theory and techniques, personal mindset, and team 'spirit' work. (The latter two were experiences to build strength of the team's relationship, along with learning tools and skills to take away and apply later). At the heart of the team 'spirit' work the simple dialogue practices offered a shared foundation of relationship and a way to have group conversations which gave equal airtime to all. This was important in three ways:

1. The teams needed to be self-managing groups of equals, albeit with different roles – a significant shift away from a fairly conventional hierarchy with very clear manager and decision-maker positions.
2. They were cross-functional teams made up of disciplines that had not previously worked alongside each other. For these teams the typical personality and communication styles were much more diverse than if they were working in more traditional teams organized by function.
3. The teams also consisted of people from different cultural backgrounds, both in terms of nationality and as a mix of employees and contractors.

In both the original three-day training and subsequent facilitated support sessions we used dialogue to create more open conversation where, in the moment, the dominant voices (either due to historical seniority or communication style) were more contained and other voices were heard. This enabled concerns and frustrations to surface which previously were being avoided, which in turn enabled a diversity of thinking. In this way, the group was able to find new solutions to challenges the groups had been facing. In some of the teams, regular rounds of dialogue became part of their team practice, helping to embed a culture of equal airtime and a different quality of listening in what were very diverse teams.

High-Potential Development

As one module of a high-potential talent development programme, we have been working with collaborative leadership and resilience. The link I have made between these two themes is that, as human beings, we are socially resilient. As such, working dialogically is the connecting medium between diverse topics. It is a wonderful ground on which to practice core skills for collaboration (social awareness, deep listening, creating a frame where diverse people can be heard), a great environment to explore some of the factors involved in collaboration (purpose, motivation, feedback and honesty), and an excellent way of building greater connection and trust swiftly, in support of social resilience.

Alongside this work with dialogue, we have explored embodied awareness (noticing our physical, emotional, mental and spiritual states and being more sensitive to when we become 'triggered'.) This, along with state management and mindfulness, cultivates greater awareness and choice in the moment. I have linked these to the work with dialogue as well by using listening as a kind of relational mindfulness practice (repeatedly bringing our attention back to the quality of our listening) and by attending more closely to our own state within the relationship with others.

We have worked with this design over two years, and in both the groups it has enabled previously more disengaged members of the cohorts to enter into a deeper relationship with my co-facilitator, me, and with the rest of the cohort. It has built capacity in the individuals to face immediate challenges more gracefully (as reported by them). These include high workloads, along with project work for the development programme. Significantly, we have also seen several instances (more than previously when the programme had a different session in the design at this point) of people making significant life changes as a result of the work – for the better, as far as we can tell!

Simple Practices to Start a Different Kind of Conversation

While there is nuance, detail and skill in how you can work with even quite simple practices, what I have found over the last seven or eight years is that, with some very simple guidelines and a little role-modelling from a skilled facilitator, people can shift the quality of their conversations. The most basic steps I follow are:

- If you are in the same physical location, sit in a circle – this helps to structurally reinforce equality so everyone is more likely to speak and feel heard, and it helps everyone to see each other
- Introduce the intention for everyone to have equal air time – if we all aim to speak concisely, that will help the conversation
- No one speaks twice until everyone has spoken once – we will take turns and go around the whole group
- Work in rounds, e.g., one, two or three rounds – if we want to speak longer we can repeat the core process and cycle back around
- Everyone responds to the same question – this is how we focus the conversation
- Ask everyone to pay full attention to the person speaking – listen, don't think or plan about what you are going to say
- Then, when it comes to your turn, pause, take a breath and speak what is on the surface for you – it doesn't have to cover every thought in your mind; trust that it is what is needed, and others may say some of the things you are thinking too
- Finally, just before beginning I invite everyone to take a moment to bring themselves

present, often saying 'Feel your feet on the ground and bum in the chair!' I then restate the question and invite anyone to begin
- After each person has spoken I say 'thank you' then turn my attention to the next person

I have found that, more than anything more complex or structural that might be added to this simple practice, it is the quality of presence the facilitator brings to the conversation that makes the greatest difference to the depth and quality of dialogue and relationship. There are foundational considerations such as the maturity of the group, the environment you are in, and how well the participants know each other, which will affect any activity you engage in. Beyond these, however, quality of presence can be a gateway to a different way of relating in a way that goes beyond methods or techniques.

How our Physiology Can Be Friend and Foe

Embodiment, sometimes referred to as 'somatics', is a field of study dedicated to exploring and understanding the subjective experience of the body. When I refer to 'state management' methods in this text, they are always in the context of embodiment as an approach or philosophy. The prevailing tendency in modern culture is to treat the body objectively – as an object: a vehicle to get your brain to meetings, a machine to be made more efficient or a thing to be made more beautiful. In this way embodiment is deeply counter-cultural in that it asks us to embrace our body as an integrated part of ourselves. This can feel uncomfortable, just as doing anything unfamiliar can be, but the benefits far outweigh the costs, and I think there is an interesting parallel between this counter-cultural aspect of embodiment and the countercultural move towards dialogue as rather than the more typical default towards discussion and debate.

My experience is that, as a facilitator, being aware of and able to attend to and manage my embodied state (anchored in the physiological but absolutely connected to emotional, mental and spiritual capacity) is a critical means by which I shape and influence the way a group engages with me, the work and each other. I can do this regardless of whether or not the subject of state management is appropriate or welcome as an explicit part of the work. However, when I have been able to work explicitly with state management as part of the work I have found that the dialogue practices I have described here have been even more powerful in helping people to deepen their relationships and have more generative conversations.

You may well have heard the phrase 'fight or flight'. This is the terminology in psychology for the state we enter when we perceive threat in our environment and has become increasingly common language as interest in psychology has grown in the public domain. However, the deeper process of what goes on in the body is less well understood.

Essentially, when certain finely-tuned elements of our nervous system detect a threat, we switch into a different gear. Some systems in our bodies are super-charged while others are suppressed as determined by what is essential and non-essential in a threatening situation; however, when this system was evolved our definition of *threat* was very specific: 'something is trying to kill me!' Our social evolution has moved faster than our physical evolution, though, so now if we perceive a social, emotional or intellectual threat the same hardwired threat response is triggered – albeit sometimes to a lesser degree. Some of the key things which happen when we are in 'threat-mode' are:

- Immune system is suppressed
- Digestion is suppressed
- Certain muscle groups tense, ready for action
- We end up shallow-breathing, using about 40% of our full lung capacity
- Blood thickens
- Heart rate increases and blood vessels can constrict
- Lymph system (which is involved in removing toxins from our bodies) has reduced function
- Cognitive function of the neocortex (human forebrain involved in rational, creative thought and risk-taking) is suppressed
- Capacity and inclination towards soothing and affiliation are suppressed

All of this makes sense in the context of life on the savannah, where a primary threat might have been getting savaged by a sabre-toothed tiger, but in our modern context, it makes less sense.

In the context of working together in organisations and creating inspiring and generative learning environments, most of these physiological shifts will be deeply unhelpful. With the pace of modern life the reality is that the emotional charge present in many work environments between team members, and the power differential which might exist in a group when working with teams (i.e., if you are my boss then I may see you as a threat) mean that, in all likelihood, most of us are going to be operating in low-level threat mode much of the time. And that is without considering the potential for people to be in the group who have a history of trauma, or even just the way that they can arrive to a meeting still upset after having had an argument at home.

I am not advocating suppressing what is real and relevant for participants in the moment – quite the opposite – but if we are going to have a conscious, useful, responsive conversation rather than a triggered and reactive one, then being able to reduce background levels of primal physiological triggering can be really valuable. It is no good internally 'telling' my brain that the person challenging my ideas is not a threat. As one Calvin and Hobbes cartoon said, 'Never in the history of calming down has anyone ever calmed down as a result of being told to calm down!' Embodied state management methods give us the means to intervene in a way which, with awareness, we can reduce the agitation in our physiological system and bring our whole brain and attendant capacity for clear thinking and positive relationship back online. Dialogue practices then build on this foundation to create connection and enable richer and empathic and reflective ways of relating.

Resilience and the 'Age of Accelerations'

As I referenced in my introductory paragraph, the world only seems to be moving faster and I would also say that society is generally becoming more atomised in communities and more divided along entrenched political lines. In this context, the declaration *'The World Needs Dialogue!'* as the title of this conference could not be more true. More broadly I think we are all going to need deep reserves of resilience if we are to navigate what seems to me to be a kind of transitionary time. We are coming into stark contact with the consequences of many of the technological, environmental and social changes which have been shaped and emerging from the past 20 years or more, and as they become clear we are still working out how to deal with these consequences constructively rather than reacting to them.

In these turbulent and uncertain times, both personal resilience and social resilience in families, groups, communities and organisations are critical and only seem likely to become more necessary as time goes on. Having simple, accessible practices for building these necessary capacities seems vital to me, and if we can interweave the personal and the social so that they are mutually reinforcing, then so much the better. My hope is that these can be entry-level methods (as suggested by the title) which then enable deeper practice, but even if these small practices are engaged with sincerely and with commitment over time, my experience is that there can be a deepening of presence and relationship that is rich and nourishing on its own.

Future Exploration

What I have presented here could be further explored in my own future work or by others in the field. I'm sure there are many more, but here are a few suggestions:

- In the intersection between state management and dialogue
    I am aware that working with some form of 'centring' is not unfamiliar as a part of work with dialogue and, to some practitioners, maybe a well-ploughed furrow, but as technology to measure and understand things like brain-wave state, hormones, heart rate variance and other physiological shifts, I think it would be fascinating to better understand the interplay between dialogue work and measurable shifts in state.
- In simple practices as gateways to deeper work with dialogue
    I am sure there will be other simple and very accessible practices which help

people to swiftly access different qualities of relationship and conversation. They may be seen currently as 'warm-ups' or learning exercises, but as someone who historically habitually always went to depth as fast as possible, I have been pleasantly surprised by the amount of value people have received from what seemed to me, on first working with them, as potentially shallow or over simplified practices. In the corporate world where I mostly operate, speed of learning and application is often vital if work is going to stick and see use outside the workshop. I wonder about having a catalogue of these more accessible practices that could be valuable in their own right, but that also serve as gateways to deeper work.

- In how a facilitator's quality of presence enables groups to relate differently
  In all of my work as a facilitator, coach, spiritual counsellor, Interfaith Minister, and performer, it is my experience that the quality of presence a facilitator brings to the work is the biggest single factor determining the value of work done with groups in a variety of contexts. I think this would be very rich territory to explore and build a rigorous understanding of, especially in the context of dialogue.

However you choose to take this work forwards, I hope it is of value to you and the communities you are part of.

Conference Session Extracts

From conversation with 20 participants considering the paper with the author

I was really interested in the amount of skill needed to take very complex ideas and practices and make them accessible for people. There's a tremendous amount of mastery required.

I think about Pablo Picasso, he was very good to paint in a classic way. But when he got older he began to paint like a child.

If you can create a qualitatively different experience with people in five minutes then you've got a good chance again to try it for ten minutes tomorrow and 20 minutes the day after that. And you start to build a bit of momentum. And actually quite magical things happen even with very inexperienced facilitators.

I just want to underline your thing around equal time. How many dinner parties has one been to where one person just hogs the space and goes for it? And it was just a simple thing that could change everything.

I'm wondering about this equal airtime. There's a function also for observers, for those who don't voice so much. It's good for everybody to be somehow voicing something but, equal airtime all the time? I don't know.

I found after maybe eight or ten years, eventually, four practises that I thought were critical, and what I hear in yours is emphasis on several of them. One is listening, without which you can't get a quality conversation, and another is being genuine. Then there is respect, and I think you're proposing that the bearing of the facilitator brings an atmosphere of respect. The fourth one we have called suspension, which is explain and explore your thinking. It took me a long time to reduce this to the key factors, and I hear you echoing a lot of them in your practise.

How do you let the dialogue go wild, and reveal things because you're giving attention to problems you need to deal with? Then how do you get to look at that constructively to get beyond it? It would probably be the next step on with this – to have wild periods and contained periods, if you like.

A myth about dialogue is that everybody's nice to each other all the time. There is a great deal of respect, but that's different than being nice.

I guess I go for more dangerous dialogue and so there is something for me about how we create a strong enough container that can hold the really difficult conversations.

When things started to get very tough with the Catalonian independence and all of the polarisation in our region, I recall I was so frustrated about how to bring all my skills. I just said, well, let's just have a picnic with a group of parents, because things were getting a bit heated. And it was so simple, we just sat there naturally in a circle, on the grass, and sharing something to eat, and just expressing how we felt. And that, for me, was a perfect example of bringing dialogue. And I'm trying to think, "Okay. So what is it that works? So what is it that we did at that moment?"

Authenticity is something so simple, but you can't teach it. Right? It's very difficult to teach. And it's something that seems to be at the core of dialogue.

Postscript

The author's reflections written some months after the conference

The methods I described at the conference had their genesis in my interest in exploring Dialogue, and through working with my friend Andy Bradley. How I work now owes a lot to Andy's thinking and practise. Through the process of submitting my suggestion, writing the paper, and being in dialogue around my piece, some things have bubbled to the surface for me. They are not all new things, but they are significant, and I think they will continue to shape my exploration for some time to come.

I have experienced a sense of the value of this simple work over time, but that has been reaffirmed by articulating it here – partly through reflecting on my practise and seeing how it is woven through so much of what I do, and partly in sharing it and receiving feedback from a wide and diverse group of practitioners.

This has also encouraged me to return to and elevate other simple practises which, as my work has become more complex over the years, can be easy to pass over. Listening, for example, really spending time exploring this and having people practise in different ways can be incredibly powerful in both work and general life.

My conviction in investing in these small and simple things is because investing in these fundamentals – given time and practise – enables a deeper exploration to take place. Without the fundamentals, that deeper exploration rests on a foundation of sand.

During the dialogue at the conference focused on my paper, someone shared a metaphor of a tiger in a cage – a kind of paradox. If you let the tiger out then it will likely kill you, or at the very least may go and harm others. But if you keep it caged that is incredibly cruel to the tiger, so you cause harm in another way.

That tiger is like the wilder territories of emotions, relationship and the complexity of organisational systems. At its depths, the tiger is the uncharted territory of consciousness with all its potential for both wholeness and fragmentation, elegance and destruction.

If we are to venture into these wilder territories and learn how to 'free the tiger' then we are best served by having established, through deep practise, discipline and structure, useful habits and a way of being that can find peace even in chaos.

In this 'Age of Accelerations' there can be a tendency to want everything to be instant, bite-size and on-demand. This is valid and understandable; and powerful, simple practises make it possible to respond to need with pace. However, we must remember to go beyond the quick-fix and continue to build the deeper capacity.

It is another kind of paradox: the structure and simplicity of the fundamentals can enable us to leap into the complexity of the wilds. This is true for us as facilitators and for the client groups we serve.

Conversations at the Mall: Dialogue, Debate or Negotiation?

Thomas Köttner

This exploratory journey was jump-started by an invitation to write about an economic crisis within a large commercial enterprise, and how dialogue played a role in overcoming not only that temporary situation, but also many other emerging challenges. The experience I will describe took place many years ago, but it makes an ongoing case for the dialogical challenges and opportunities in complex private businesses, where everybody is a client from a particular perspective.

It is also the story of how dialogue was instrumental in dealing with the effects of one of the worst inflationary phenomena the world had seen during the last two decades of the 20th century.

At the time of the events I'll describe I was a Tenant Relations Manager and acting General Center Manager in what was the largest shopping mall in Argentina. A shopping mall is an environment in which every human, technical and environmental variable impacts all the others, through an almost infinite multitude of interactions. It brings to mind that the life and evolution of a regional shopping mall is very close to the birth and growth of a planned city. It is similar in its initial concept phase, through its construction and operational stages, all the way to its evolution into a living environment. That living environment grows partly by itself, but also through the impulse of what is happening with the environment, the surrounding spaces, and the impact it is having on society at large.

At the risk of being obvious, it is also worth mentioning that every organization is, from a socio-linguistic perspective, a stable network of conversations. Things happen as a result of our conversations. The purpose of this paper is to share with you a story from my professional life that may lead you to explore and reflect on the different kinds of conversations that become necessary in different circumstances. I want to identify which conversations are deeply dialogical, which ones are partly so, and the other kinds of interactions – and what distinguishes them and why. My hope is that you may feel inspired or even challenged to think about the kind of approach you would have taken in the different situations I describe – which may bear some similarity to daily situations you are involved in from time to time.

Several questions that appeared for me and may arise for you, may be dependent on the meaning given to Dialogue. In my understanding and perspective, Dialogue is the conversational interaction where a deep connection can be established between the participants, so that an energy and vibrance of shared meaning can start and keep flowing. That connection goes deeper and beyond the exchange of rational views, opinions and arguments that may nurture a debate or a discussion.

Ideas and expressions come from an alignment of mind and heart and soul, and not only out of mental processing. In most cases throughout this written journey, it is from this perspective that I posed my own questions.

A Shopping Center as a Relational Place – Context

Imagine a small town where everyone makes a living from selling goods to visitors. The town has a Mayor and a Council whose members take care of promoting the town and keeping it in good shape with clean streets, pleasant public spaces and an always-friendly atmosphere. Attracting visitors is a duty for the council, but its success depends on the citizens maintaining their individual promises of offering quality products, tasty foods and beneficial services to every newcomer and regular visitor. The council also takes care that the goods and services are competitive enough to promote everyone's creativity and innovation for customer benefit – but not over-competitive, to ensure that everyone can have a good income and a prosperous life.

That is basically what a large shopping center is and how it aims to function. From an economic perspective, it is a commercial city for selling goods, organized in a synergistic way. It has offerings structured in "neighborhoods" in such a way that, whoever wants, needs or is inclined to buy a particular product, may be well-disposed to buy something in neighboring stores as well. The owner develops the infrastructure at his own risk, and rents the most suitable stores for the best development of each tenant. The tenant commits to running his business in the best way he can. He expects the owner to service, administer, promote and market the center to be most attractive to visiting shoppers. In exchange for that, the owner charges a monthly percentage of net sales, according to the typical economic margins for the different business categories.

From a social perspective, it is a meeting place, a safe environment for families and their children. Teenagers can start exploring independently by strolling around and entertaining themselves by getting together with friends for a meal or a drink. Security is organized to take care of visitors and their belongings. Car parking is built, and the peaks and lows of visiting traffic is managed.

From a cultural perspective, it is a place to have the latest and the most anticipated movies, live theater and musical performances. Bookstores launch new editions in their stores with events organized by the publishers and the center's management. Food fairs and cooking events are held by diverse chefs, sponsored by companies whose products will be sold in the center's food markets. In the same way, fashion shows will attract visitors to check the latest trends and see others who relate to their lifestyle.

From a labor perspective, it is a substantial employer and a strong job creator. Hundreds of people are involved daily in maintenance and basic services duties, while hundreds or even thousands are involved in the daily sales, promotions and ongoing development activities. Beyond that, externally, thousands of jobs are directly related to the shopping center's daily life.

When the mall closes its doors, night life begins in the form of cleaning, maintenance, facilities replacement and repair, painting, security and all the other behind-the-scenes services. Given the multiple systemic interactions that happen simultaneously, we can imagine how many dialogic situations present themselves every day, and how many could happen in a way that enhances people's lives, ideally in an "everybody wins" environment. So, this is a wonderful environment to experience Dialogue in so many ways . . .

About this Mall

This shopping mall was developed, having navigated the various usual (and unusual) bureaucratic stages, as the largest shopping mall in Argentina. It was partly a conversion of the premises of an old printing company, and partly new construction. It became a "regional" shopping center as distinct from a neighborhood one. The scale of the mall's footprint for the center and parking space to attract and accommodate visitors from far away made it necessary to buy two streets from the city. It was designed to accommodate 300 stores on three levels, including two large "anchor" stores. But there were not 300 established brands in the country. In fact, there were not even 50 well-known brands, in terms of the current brand recognition criteria! This meant scanning the market in search of single, small businesses that could supply the assortment of product categories needed, along with finding the strongest tenant mix possible.

The project needed to be attractive to attract the commitment of merchants into what was a completely new adventure in the Argentinian commercial real estate landscape. Those fortunate enough to have traveled abroad, and to have visited this kind of enterprise overseas, were clearly more eager to dream of being part of the first regional mall in the country, realizing it could add prestige to their own brand. Smaller family stores were very slow to respond to invitations to meetings, and only cautiously become involved and willing to take the risk.

So many ongoing and simultaneous institutional, group and individual interactions happen that the venture becomes a big multi-conversational network. Just consider the following as a short glimpse of the connections and interaction during planning in a culture that, for historical reasons, tends to be highly mistrusting and skeptical. A certain plot of land is envisioned, which could be a good geostrategic location for such an enterprise, and then identified. The vision forms in the mind of the developer, who needs to be bold enough to put his own money on the table, since the banks are extremely conservative. The vision becomes a plan, and the creative plan becomes a concrete possibility. Research is undertaken to validate assumptions about how people would like to live, socialize and spend their money, and to be sure the location will be a popular place to visit. If research confirms the potential and the economic sums seem favorable, then the land is acquired, architectural plans are plotted and construction tenders are requested. Meanwhile, permits and legal agreements need to be worked out with public authorities. Architects are selected, and the vision shared with them. Construction companies are selected – over 50 different companies worked on the construction.

Next we needed a marketing plan and had to select marketing agencies to work with us in communicating the new concept and getting merchants. We needed to hire commercial staff to work out the logistics of identifying and bringing in the right tenants. Our tenant mix needed the right balance of products and services to generate visitor and customer attraction. We needed a marketing department to keep promotions and communications messaging active; an operations department to manage security and keep maintenance, cleaning, gardening and air conditioning current; an architectural department to deal with the tenants' own architects while shopfitting their stores; and last but not least, we needed a legal department. That was my first assignment, dealing with the tenants' lawyers in the negotiation of the contracts. It was not an easy job because our contracts were unknown in the country at that time, and had extensive clauses to deal with the complexity of living in such a concentrated environment. Essentially, we had to educate tenants and their employees into a new way of cooperating while still competing with one another.

Each one of these stages needed a mix of effective communication, including negotiation, debating and discussion – and each of them was certainly an opportunity for dialogue.

Dialogue was a constant opportunity, but to what extent were we aware of it? Did we allow it to occur? Did we approach matters from a dialogic perspective? Is it always possible to do so? At which moment is it necessary? Let's walk through some of the developmental steps already outlined to get some perspective.

The Prospecting Process

When a mall requires a certain commercial return on investment (ROI), things need to happen in the shortest time possible. Our leasing process started with designing the tenant mix, where the planner takes into account the architectural design of different store units to arrange various product categories and brands to create variety and synergic attractiveness for visitors. The idea is to generate a positive psychological disposition for the buyer through neighboring stores that carry products complementary to their previous purchase. This is a lengthy process and it takes either experience or the interaction of different views and logic to discover what merchandise and services might work best together. How do shoe sales interact with those of children's clothing, or with kitchenware, and why? What are the categories in the mind of the buyer, if it is possible to know? What is the validity of your own view or insight from a scientific or psycho/sociologic perspective? It is most interesting to discover how very diverse and apparently completely unrelated products may live in the mind of a consumer at the same time, thus becoming completely connected in their buying priorities. This leads to very interesting enquiries and explorations, although definitive answers do not emerge quickly. We found it to be an opportunity for dialogue since, even when not finding shared meaning, new insights and visions were generated in the participants, empowering a dialogical participation in the group.

Once the tenant mix was designed, potential companies, brands or stores were identified that could occupy a particular space to create their own unique attractions, as well as contributing to the good of the whole center. As this step was completed and invitations extended, then the process had to be far more dialogic than the earlier, more general economic and leasing discussions. Why would we like or need to have them at the center? Why would the merchant be interested in joining us – what kind of mutual opportunity would exist? What kind of opportunity would we like it to be, and how could that strengthen our offer? At that point prospective tenants had to understand the concept, along with its particular demands and requisites. They also needed to envision how this shared environment might impact their growth if the adequate synergies were put to work together.

Naturally there may be questions about the extent to which the process is dialogic and from what perspective. Is it real dialogue, or is it a commercial debate? How much is the approach a "free" one, and how much is it negotiation inspired by the aim to achieve an intended result? It can be dialogic if a consideration of potential emerges in the interaction. Or it could be an induction process for the prospect to finally accept and close a deal, thereby complying with the landlord team's specific needs. The business interactions, in a culture where social trust levels are low, tend to create a transactional and speculative relationship between people in a deal-making situation. Is there place for a "win-win" approach when trust is low? Can Dialogue emerge and, if so, what kind of dialogue would it be? What part does intentionality, as it is referred to in philosophy, play in a conversational interaction that is called a Dialogue – or something else? It is the nature of commerce to try to have the fewest expenses and pursue the highest incomes and profits. In the complexities of the mall we quickly learned that several merchants would look for every opportunity to get some slick advantage or unexpected benefit at the expense of the landlord or the whole center's interests.

At certain fashion shows or live promotional events which would attract a lot of visitors, the required logistics would impact the entrances or shop windows of some stores. Store managers would then pursue a claim for some reduction of cost or increase in benefit because of a reduced influx of clients into their stores that day. Other merchants, running into difficulties within their industry or category, would legitimately request some additional financing or a modification of their economic contract conditions. For example, modifications of taxation for different industries could have an impact in the percentage of rent certain categories could pay without losing money.

So the challenge is to distinguish "speculators" from businessmen and try to keep balance for everyone's general good. What role do our intentions play within the dialogical dance in such situations? It is always possible to fall into fallacies in our Dialogical thinking. The distance between what we say and actually do reveals our rationalizations, those stories we tell ourselves in order to keep peace of mind when incurring some wrongdoing.

Fallacious thinking takes us into measuring ourselves by our intentions and others by their actions. Intentions are abstract and silent. Actions are observable and, by definition, will involve a potential for a margin of error. Fallacious thinking allows us to evade responsibility, because unavoidably in that kind of thinking responsibility will fall on somebody else.

When entering Dialogue, based on our good intentions to arrive at deeply felt agreements, do we really follow through and act in accordance?

In retrospect, during conversations for superior mutual commercial benefit, we might have told ourselves that we wanted to arrive at win-win situations. We might even come to witty and articulate arguments about the benefits of reaching certain agreements. However, were we really open to what could emerge from a fluent Dialogue even if it might eventually have different results from what we would have regarded as a positive outcome at the beginning?

How possible is it in business to give up control and "flow with the waters" of shared meaning and allow unexpected agreements? Are we ready to honestly look for another's interests even if they might have unexpected outcomes or – universe forbid – even appear against us, but are better for a longer-term relation? If we are not ready to be aware, to modify our intentions or get to rid of them, are we really free enough for Dialogue?

The Contracting Process

At a mall, tenants have to comply with contractual terms of use, mandatory opening times and different staffing requirements, and they must accept regular point-of-sale cashier and systems audits and several other responsibilities which are not usual in free-standing stores. This variety of new conditions generated longer processes of offers and counteroffers. In a culture which Darwin, in his 1835 visit defined as "a society that celebrates the transgression of the law," tenants' interest in being part of this new project had to be larger than their worries about what this submission to a landlord would mean. So this process with prospective tenants became a process of long conversations, partly to explain, partly to understand and take a first dialogic step together.

Once the intention for the merchant to join the mall was clear, a second dialogic stage appeared, this time with the lawyers of the respective interested companies. It was the first time that such a long and complete contract was put in the Argentinian market, with its several thick and bound annexes that previewed every single working obligation the tenant assumed. Lawyers would oppose many of the contract clauses and would let their clients know that such a contract was unacceptable. They recommended that the tenant not sign it.

Today such contracts have become common, and are signed almost with closed eyes, but at the time they were unheard-of. This meant that a lease-signing process which should have taken six weeks extended for months of back-and-forth negotiations. They often took hours of interaction, especially for the big leases. At times they were dialogic, and at times they were simply give-and-take negotiations. We needed to explain the sense and purpose of many clauses, just to create understanding that they were included for the benefit and common good of the whole commercial community.

The center finally had its grand opening in October 1988 with 12,000 guests invited to the party. It was featured in every business, architecture and social magazine. And it was the new wonder place to visit, with its initial 3,500 parking places full most of the time.

The Tenant Construction Coordination Process

Despite the mandatory construction guidelines in the contract, due to building layout the rules cannot always be fully respected. Some brands may have certain brand design icons or figures which they want to install in a certain position, or customer behavior issues that have been researched by the tenants' marketing staff, who then recommend a certain walking path, etc. Conflicts arise that have to be resolved. Signs, canopies and storefronts are all often discussed and generate explanatory requirements. Many things that appear one way when considered from a design perspective may seem different when considered from a business-generating perspective, or as an insurance-related risk. To what should we pay the most attention? Sometimes debates arise. Should the landlord's general requirements for the individual premises prevail, or should the tenants' commercial interest be put in front? This often resulted in heated discussions, because so many different perspectives need to be taken into consideration (technical, aesthetic, functional, economic, commercial, promotion potential), yet each professional tends to look at the issue from his or her own perspective. Finally a conversation that allows each to understand the others' priorities becomes necessary, in order to balance the functional and economic needs of each party as well as the benefit of the whole community. How can dialogue contribute to this? Is the technical conversation, or business-based conversation in this field or domain actually a dialogue? And what would tell us if it is not a dialogue?

Dealing with Contractors to Maintain Opening Dates

Developing a mall is very different from developing a regular building complex where the contractors are more or less directly under the developers' control. In a mall development they are working at the same time as the contractors for each of the 300 other tenants. One of the main challenges that had not been foreseen was that there was not a sufficient supply of some building materials. The country had never seen or heard of such a demand of some materials for floors or walls as were required for the defined designs in our mall. We had to coordinate and troubleshoot all the material shortages, while keeping record of the timing in order to open before Mother's Day in October, and continuing to Christmas. There were many well-worded requests and pleasant conversations necessary in order to get suppliers to want to help us, even when they were desperate for the business. We did finally reach our target – and the night of grand opening, with all 12,000 guests at the party. But while the opening speech was being given by the company president, most of us workers and managers were still cleaning the premises on the other side of the ceremony ropes, which were about to be untied.

We certainly used every kind of conversational exchange in this stretched situation, and most probably dialogue was simply not possible. Our interactions had to be demanding or directive, while knowing at the same time that we were in the hands of suppliers. Nevertheless, it may be interesting to explore if there could be a place for dialogue in such demanding situations. We certainly needed to explain the situation more than once in order to create a willingness for the suppliers' side to respond to our urgency, but were those interactions ever a dialogue?

Managing the Tenant's Employees

Any action in such a multi-coordinated place as a shopping mall impacts and reflects the whole. This was a new trading environment for such an individualistic culture, and it created challenges for us when trying to harmonize commercial behaviors and customer-service approaches. Up to that point, retail had been mainly demand-driven, so people arrived to a store because they needed to purchase some particular merchandise. But now, in the kind of synergistic enterprise where added attractiveness would cause more sales for everyone (at least in theory), offer-driven commercial exchanges were crucial. We needed to experience the different service approaches first, and then educate the tenants' employees whenever we detected less-than-desirable attitudes and practices with customers. Sometimes we made a straight demand that employees behave in a defined way. But to make that a real learning, or an experience that would sustain itself over time, the conversation needed to be respectful and considerate. Yet what was the best way for a particular person to learn? How exploratory should the conversational approach be? How much time would it take? Was dialogue actually possible? Quite often, at the beginning, the flow of visitors was slower, which allowed time for the tenants' salespeople to have dedicated conversations. Would we, under our severe management pressures, actually have or make time for real dialogue? I would say we did not devote enough time to it and, in retrospect, it would have been a good investment. Yet the reflection is interesting – how would we, or you, dear reader, have promoted real dialogue in those situations?

Dealing with Consumers

From time to time customers experience a situation which to them is offensive, disrespectful or frustrating because they were disappointed with some product, quality or price. At that time in Argentinian retail, there was not even a basic understanding of returning purchased products for a refund. Among the tens of thousands of monthly transactions, there were always a number of claims from customers who did not feel well served with their purchases and did not receive a satisfactory response from the tenant – so their claims landed at central management office. This required a letter to the customer, or eventually a call to them to arrange a meeting to explore how to resolve the issue. This was generally a kind of mediation process, the complexity of which depended on the economic importance of the purchase to the buyer. We certainly did not want bad word-of-mouth circulating about the mall. No enterprise wants or can afford that. The best possible "arts of influence" were used, most frequently getting to an agreement, but a few negotiations would go on for quite some time. At a certain point we'd ask ourselves – and perhaps the other parties involved did as well – what is the ultimate purpose of this seemingly unending process? That exploration might be a dialogic approach to something that is usually a discussion or debate with fixed positions by each of the participants.

Again I could ask: Is that dialogue? Is there a common interest in getting things solved in the fairest and most balanced way? Or is it just the manager's intention to complete an emotionally consuming succession of meetings? In some situations we really had to have a dialogue – say, when a vehicle was stolen. It did not happen often, but it did in one severe situation when the individual involved made a serious claim and even called the press before a solution was found. We could not replace lost vehicles without establishing a dangerous precedent. It was before the days of street surveillance cameras, and someone could lose a vehicle anywhere and then claim that it happened at the center. Yet even then we would take the aggrieved person seriously and generate a dialogue for mutual understanding, calming them down. We would commit to helping in every possible way with security paperwork, insurance and so on, so that the person ultimately would be thankful for our involvement in attempting to reduce the damage.

Dealing with Neighborhood Residents

The shopping mall was situated in what had been a peaceful, big-garden residential area on the outskirts of Buenos Aires, and its opening obviously had a big impact on the daily travel of the local residents. Traffic through the once-quiet streets was intense; concerns were understandable, given that during the first weekends of our opening even the nearby highway would have a mile-long traffic jam of cars wanting to access the mall. The neighbors were worried about their lifestyle, for the impact of the center in their families' lives, for the potentially damaging impact on the value of their property, among many other issues. Some of the neighbors would close the access to their streets with large stones and sand-filled oil drums, something which would make the traffic congestion in the surrounding road system even worse. Then a committee of neighbors was set up, led by an influential journalist who lost no opportunity to complain about our mall. We held meetings with these neighbors, paid attention to their concerns and evaluated what we could do to make things easier for them. We knew that good relations were important and we really wanted to act with goodwill, knowing as well that some things would need to be delayed until things settled and that certain new habits would become accepted.

The exchanges eventually became more focused, and even dialogic. I think that was because the facts and information we were sharing gave a renewed perspective of the impact of the mall. It inspired the neighbors to develop a more appreciative perspective and to think of ways to adapt their lives to benefit from this new situation in their neighborhood, instead of only suffering from the lost opportunities. We wanted to promote understanding of the different reasons the mall could eventually benefit their property values and even their lives as a whole, as actually did happen after some time. Real estate rose in value, neighbors became regular visitors, their children of all ages had a safe environment to meet and stroll around with friends, and families had a place for movie-going and dining.

As you may have already realized by reading these few examples, a shopping mall can be an interesting, even amusing, place to manage. The perspectives from which interactions emerge are almost unending and never boring. At this point we could still ask ourselves: Is this, then, a dialogic environment? Is this where interacting people build meaning together, for a benefit that exceeds the interests of the individual parts involved? It could be – it almost should be – but two factors get in the way: social culture and economic culture. These two aspects are the ones which ultimately sourced and led to a serious crisis in the whole country and consequently in this young enterprise, and only a few months after its successful grand opening. In order to understand how that crisis evolved, it is necessary to understand a few more cultural facts and factors.

Some Notes on Argentina's Social Culture

By some time frames, Argentina is a young country. It declared its independence from the Spanish throne in 1816. In 1854 it gave itself a Constitution which was considered by many world-renowned constitutionalists to be as close to perfect as any society could give itself. It became the sixth-largest economy in the world during the 1920s. Argentina had many services, infrastructure, public institutions and educational institutions which were known as superior to those in many of the European countries. This brought a lot of European immigration and, as happens in most migratory situations, it created defensiveness in the locals regarding the diverse attitudes natural to immigrants.

We were a new country with a drive for development and improvement, but without a clear national identity. That accentuated an individualistic society. And the lack of a national identity is disguised by a culture of "looking like," rather than being alike. A reflection of this is the use of foreign languages in advertising and in store promotional signage, even when sales persons might not even understand what is being said. It is usual to make this advertising in English, assuming that the foreign language will give a certain feeling of upscale flair or sophistication.

In closed economies, which commonly tend to decrease the quality of products by non-competitiveness in business, the idea that everything foreign is better gets into the collective unconscious.

Naming stores and local brands with English, German or Italian names, and then advertising in those languages, makes no difference in the quality of the locally produced goods. Another example of pretending, or "looking like," is copying store designs or layout concepts which are impactful in one culture but not in another. A large minimalist store layout with just a few clothes displayed here and there is something that suggests wealth and luxury in some exclusive Tokyo districts, where the rent per square feet can be the highest in the world. But copying minimalism in Argentina in those years meant no more than an empty store, even suggesting that the merchant did not have enough money to afford displaying more merchandize.

"Looking like" implies copying without understanding, which creates paradoxical results all over. For example, season's-end sales are copied from the US, though it is another empty message. In the US and many other countries and cultures, a seasonal sale is intended to get rid of as much remaining inventory as possible, so as to get another turnaround squeezed out of the yearly calendar; price reductions tend to be significant and impactful. However, in an inflationary-minded society that tends to keep inventory, or even one that doesn't produce enough to have remainders, advertising a sale creates in customers frustration and a sense of being deceived, since seasonal sales in Argentina usually do not offer the price opportunity their advertising suggests. They are just small reductions in prices for merchandize already price-inflated in random ways. There is no real benefit to the consumer.

The Argentinean collective unconscious is unable to define itself clearly. Jorge Luis Borges, one of the country's most renowned writers, said: "Argentinians are Italians who speak Spanish, think as the French and would like to be English." This confused identity may create a sense of insecurity, which generates defensiveness, and a general attitude of being polite but reserved and defensive – as if by exposing oneself to a deeper conversation one would be discovered to be inexcusably ignorant. Even when relationships develop, my own experience is that most of the time conversations are held with a strong need to be right. Losing face would be devastating, which in turn is why discussion prevails over debate, and of course over dialogue. Dialogue may make us vulnerable when we are exposed to insights that may shake the structure that sustains our image.

Defensiveness often presents itself as the proactive request of objectivity, and this works in subtle ways. Who can claim to be carrying the flag of objectivity? Isn't requesting objectivity a way of asking others to comply and "surrender" to the acceptance of my own views? It brings me to the question of how the pursuit of objectivity plays in our minds when wanting to promote dialogue. Is it possible – or is the risk of maintaining a fallacy once again very high?

Hyperinflation Impacts Our Mall

Next comes the story of how we realized the need for a deeper conversational interaction. People say it takes two Christmas seasons for a new shopping mall to settle down. Opening just before Christmas generates an initial positive energy that keeps spirit high with new and expectant tenants. Our mall's most intense construction stage was during 1987 and 1988. Inflation was already high, registering an accumulated inflation of 175% in 1987 and 388% in 1988 when the mall was opened to public on October 12th. It was already concerning and unsettling, but not unheard-of, in a country where an average of 100 to 150% yearly inflation had been normal for decades. But it galloped into 1989 with 3,079% that year and 2,314% in 1990. The monthly rate went from 9.6% in February 1989 to 200% in July of that same year, and the acceleration let loose the social debacle that every hyperinflation generates.

It brought a crisis of trust and a feeling of despair amongst many of our merchants. With hyperinflation you really do not know what it is best or right to do. You tend to act by instinct, caring most about reducing risk. In this climate, we needed to keep spirits positive and put up our best show for our first-tier clients (the merchants) and our joint second-tier clients (the end-consumer). A mall is supposed to be a supplier of enjoyable experiences and, as the old entertainment business adage says, "The show must go on!" Yet frustrations and merchant fears meant increased visits to management offices. We had several meetings a day with people who wanted and expected us to have some magic forecast, or some clear strategy to reverse the inflationary spiral. When it became evident that nobody had a formula for resolution, a certain confrontational climate appeared. The first reaction to frustration, a very human one, was blaming. People blamed the developers, management – everybody who could be considered as "other" to the sufferer.

As I paid attention to many of the arguments, it was evident that conflicts arose from frustration and a sense of impotence, spreading blame for things that could not have been handled in any other way. Big crises usually develop slowly, step-by-step, but then suddenly they happen "overnight." This creates many diverse reactions, the first usually being self-deception. Of course we felt it was our duty to keep spirits calm. We were looking to navigate the mall through the crisis in the best possible way and, hopefully, to do this in joint good spirits with all tenants.

The first block to a rational interaction is self-deception by one, some or all. I ask myself: Can real dialogue occur within self-deception? Of course everyone has a degree of self-deception, but how far can it go? Even when we could momentarily calm down the emotions, we could not really find sustainable ways of keeping emotions at bay. So antagonism and conflict became a daily climate.

As time passed, the problems in the general environment were seen to be much larger than what was happening inside the mall. Then people started to accept what was going on in the center, and instead of reparations they started looking for some kind, any kind, of solutions or preventions. This was a time when conversations for understanding started to take place. Many tenants started weighing up whether to clench their teeth and try to survive the situation, or to jump ship as soon as possible and cut losses to rescue whatever could be saved. Individual tenants and representatives of the larger franchises that inhabited the mall started approaching the mall's management in search of guidance, information, resources and, ultimately, whatever words could bring hope.

We wanted to avoid any kind of surprise in addition to the already-hard situation. We knew that once stores start to close, the risk of a domino effect is high. So the best way to keep things running for the good of everybody was doing whatever was necessary to keep tenants betting on the positive every new day. At the same time, from the developers' perspective, when one's huge investment in hard currency starts melting down six months after the grand opening, and the general monthly income is scarcely enough to pay the light bill, the situation becomes very unsettling.

Social unrest was at high levels. At a national level, street demonstrations and turmoil were common and supermarket looting and food scarcity were part of daily life. Some of the unrest was played up by political parties, and part of it was real desperation. And the contagion of frustration and impotence spread to every corner of the country. The microclimate an upscale mall offers, one of those posh, clean and "everything taken care of" places, was not immune to this at all, and negative emotions were all around. Conflict of every kind had to be observed in detail, because any spark could create a scalable negative environment.

We started holding general meetings. A big-store shell, still unoccupied, served as a kind of theater and tenants and/or their managers were invited to the meetings. They were usually led by the company's major shareholder and president, a very smart and strong business man. He was notoriously charismatic, tough and very human at the same time, with an intense and rich experience in "big-box" format retail environments. His personal and physical presence was key to people trusting, at least, that the vessel had a competent captain. He would open the meeting with words of understanding for the general disturbance, conveying the idea that these difficult times would one day pass as they had always done before. Then, appealing to a certain pride in those who would one day feel that overcoming this situation was a significant learning experience in their lives, he got to the core of the matter.

He made one simple assertion: "Nobody can take the country away!"

Even if we reached economic ruins, nobody could take the country away, and this would always provide ways of rebuilding for those who were ready to face the challenge. "Nobody can take the country away" became a kind of internal motto. It promoted the idea that even at its worst, there would still be possibility of rebuilding, even from scratch if necessary. Curiously this blunt, frighteningly realistic approach had a positive effect and somehow kept the internal society knitted together. It impressed me. I learned how a certain motto, a certain driving idea, could become instrumental in building constructive conversations. If Dialogue becomes a conversation with a center, the presence of such a motto could provide the initial building block.

The business needed to be kept alive and there was a dilemma. On one side, as the landlord's management, one of our responsibilities was to keep rent collection as high as possible, but on the other hand there was an implicit need and obligation to keep the whole system viable from a landlord, tenant *and* end-consumer perspective. General meetings were held regularly, explaining the situation, explaining the company's vision and plans, sharing and describing previous difficult times along its history, and how they had been managed for a positive outcome. All of this was in the expectation of keeping spirits up. Nevertheless, inflation makes the whole system so vulnerable that every small economic adjustment creates unforeseen waves on a daily basis. The eroding force is too big.

Store managers and franchise owners started requesting meetings with management, with no clear purpose than just to share their worries, confusions and anguishes. These emerging conversations probably had the most naturally dialogic character. They were usually conversations that leveled everyone's doubts, vulnerabilities and humility. In economically healthy times, the landlord is often seen as the Goliath that rules a world of many small Davids, who in turn have to comply with strict contracts and demanding operational rules. On the landlord's side that is often necessary to keep order, particularly in societies that are not naturally accustomed to standards of excellence. But in crisis times such as the one described, the asymmetry of power vanishes. We were all faced with our vulnerabilities, limits and broken-heartedness.

Meetings with small groups and individuals began taking place as a natural way of feeling the togetherness required for the general task at hand. Exploring visions of possible futures, some people would have preferred to cut their losses and leave, but when faced with their potential next step, they realized that there was not much alternative for the future if they quit at that moment. Deeper existential aspects emerged. Many tenants were third-generation Mom and Pop store owners. Exploring the "whats," "whys" and "what-fors" of their activities kept the meaning of their business life in perspective and made the daily challenges more acceptable. Reconnecting with their activity and its purpose of progress, family support or just learning how to become a stronger brand became a challenging but enlightening and inspiring exercise. I could see that it was in those moments, when their activities and worries connected with their heart's intuitions, that they became positive in the midst of the reigning external confusion.

The daily work on the side of management was of course in permanent troubleshooting mode. But that mode, which involved financial care and reducing operational costs to a minimum, became progressively more about taking care of the concerns of those who were ever closer to jumping ship. Some of them eventually did so, and empty stores were disguised as best possible, with decorated plaster walls and fancy messages, as is done in present times. This lasted for some months after the peak monthly inflation of 196% in July 1989. Then severe restrictions in the following months reduced the inflation rate.

The possibility of recovery, from a landlord's perspective, was – given the skyrocketing value of foreign currency and the locally established habit of saving in US dollars – that it would become affordable in local money to invest in fitting out a store, and some saw the opportunity to do so. The interesting thing was how, as this transition happened, the tone of negotiation had changed. The internal message and approach was much more cautious, and it was not the usual hard-nosed negotiation approach that had reigned in the commercial real estate business.

The economic impact in society and the increasing social turmoil led to the country's president resigning before the end of his term. The newly installed president and his cabinet tried to tame inflation in an orthodox way, and it rebounded yet again to a peak of 119% in March of 1990. In this second wave, the new constellation for the center was already established. People knew who had already survived as a tenant, who could not and who did not. It was now a "known" situation and therefore easier to deal with. Learning had been enormous for everyone and in every sense in particular for the then-young executive who, almost 30 years later is writing this story.

What Did this Experience Enable Me to Learn About Dialogue?

No experience would reveal its richness if not for what we learn from it. This learning is a unending journey, and of course I now have the advantage of hindsight, of looking back on recollections, many of them quite precise, but many years after the described events took place. I have been looking at things from a different personal and professional perspective because at the time I had no theoretical frames about dialogue at all. This suggests that Dialogue, despite our more-or-less developed skills, may be a very basic or innate human trait whether or not we are aware of it.

I am still, and will always be, a learner on the subject, but I can already place reasonable questions about the subject which may, in turn, inspire some insights and learning for us all. I invite you to reflect on some of the learnings I am sharing and on the questions that emerge from them. Some of the points may come as affirmations and others as questions, knowing as well that every question has a background assumption in order to be made in the first place. Here are some areas upon which I am reflecting:

- I can see that I participated in and witnessed conversations that could have been called dialogues, in that they were creating renewed meanings or understandings for the participants. Yet I could also perceive that they had different dialogical intensities. (What do I mean by *dialogical intensities?* The amount of authentic dialogue that emerges in a conversation.) What would reduce this kind of intensity? Being unable to let go of a particular intention or position, and holding it as necessary that it prevail. Interacting with architects, for example, could be dialogical. Sense and meaning would form and transform yet, ultimately, the creative pride of the designing "artist," or the business and economic sense of the development side, would at certain moments push the conversation in directions that would turn them into argumentative exchanges. Could it be different? Probably yes, but under what conditions and with what effect on the participants?
- I could participate in dialogues of mutual understanding, where each participant would make sense of the motivations of the other as, for example, when dealing with lawyers around particular clauses of the contracts. But is every clarifying and respectful conversation a dialogue? I can see that understanding emerged, confrontation did not arise, but . . . did something new arise? Had the situation evolved to a scenario that previously had not existed? And if this is not real dialogue, what would have made it so?
- I participated in mediation conversations in conflicts between tenants competing

with the same products, where unfair competition or contract breaches had occurred. Is mediation a Dialogue? The situation certainly changed for the participants in their conflict, but how dialogic is it when the intention or scrutiny of a third party, even when trying to keep intellectual honesty at its best, intervenes, with the unavoidable biases that the third party may bring with them?

There were heated exchanges that I participated in, which, curiously, were very dialogic, and I believed they were positive because behind the strong words the participants could sense, at a basic level, that we were honestly looking for a solution. Does intention play a role in Dialogue? Which one? To what degree?

Then there were deep dialogues that I participated in. Looking at what they had in common, I found that this depth took place only when the situation was so bad that all masks and speculation would fall away for all the parties involved. It was only in the later stages of the conflicts that dialogue appeared more real, open and honest, while the earlier stages had a feel of negotiation or transaction. What made the difference with the more real dialogue? I believe it was at the point of really looking to rescue ourselves from very difficult situations that we would really care for the other in deep understanding. I learned that people were more open when they came to the very core of the reason why they were in that business, and in that particular environment. The connections were much stronger when the dialogue related to the personal implications of the changing situation. This made me ask: how context-based is the possibility of real dialogue? When can it be promoted? Does dialogue only emerge naturally between us as a last resource? How deep and long can our masks, egos and drive to win hold us from interacting at a deeper level?

From a strictly business perspective, I asked myself: Why does openness and trust only appear as a last resort, rather right from the beginning? Is this socially and culturally related? Is it somehow inherent in business to have a win-lose mode?

A Final Word

This was a stage of my early executive life which I remember fondly, and with gratitude. I was fortunate to learn so much from the experience, and to understand many of my own professional and personal drivers. These have brought me, over the years, into situations which are externally different but underneath are actually very similar. I have more understanding of why we human beings behave as we do, and how to get ourselves out of confusion or trouble when we need to – and to do what we are called to do in the most helpful ways. It does leave with me a driving question, which will guide my future research and professional development:

Why do we invest so much time reacting to unfortunate situations, when we could have avoided them by investing a fraction of that time and effort in clarifying, reflecting, and reaching a simple level of agreement through the practice of dialogue?

Conference Session Extracts

From conversation with 20 participants considering the paper with the author

I've done work in commercial organizations, which is what I call a closed system, where the power lines quite clearly go to those in authority. I've done work in open systems, which are more social, a community where people answer to anybody or nobody. What interests me here is this is halfway in between. The mall is contained, it's a set number of people, it's commercial and has commercial capability, but it's cultural, and you go into the culture in Argentina. I'm thinking if we want to get good at cultural work, it's very interesting to look for situations which are halfway in between. So there's enough containment to understand if we're making progress.

I agree with all this. When you describe it as a small city, that's somewhere in between the local and the global, and we all know that we're immersed in business in this world, and on a more or less greedy level, and how are we going to manage? I think it's very, very interesting and important.

I read the paper, and just now, ten days later, a penny dropped that my work in churches is similar in one respect to your work with the law, in that I'm called in to do dialogue at moments of desperate crisis.

Dialogue takes us to our edge. This has taken us to our edge. Every single dialogue that I've personally been in over the last couple of days has in some way or shape or form, taken us to our edge in one way or another. And what I'm noticing is that we're talking about the experience of being at the edge and also noticing that the world is at an edge. And the crisis points are all around us, in all the very many ways in which we all care about. If we are to beholders, conveners, enablers of dialogue, we need to become very comfortable with always being at our edge. And we need to figure out, for ourselves, how we will self-care when we're at our edge.

I'm having a chicken or egg moment, is it the edge that brings you to dialogue or dialogue that brings you to the edge [laughter]?

What we want to do is have content, but also have process. How can we combine the content with the process? Which is what's required if we're going to make a difference in the world.

As dialogue practitioners there are a number of places one could intervene. One would be with the initial set up of the mall, that it has a deliberate culture of competition and collaboration in its contracting. The second would be to intervene by providing training and development on how to pull people together when there is a dispute or a challenge [inaudible]. The third would be how to make the best use of situations which are breaking down, how do you provide the necessary skills to do that? The fourth one is that this is an example of what's happening cyclically in Argentina, and is happening repeatedly. The real intervention is understanding how a country which pays too many people repeatedly borrows US dollars. So the ultimate intervention is at that level. Ideally, we'd have the scope to do all of those.

Postscript

The author's reflections written some months after the conference

While writing the paper for the conference, I realized that the shopping mall as a scenario was a complex system with several subsystems, while being itself a subsystem of larger ones. What unfolded in that scenario in terms of Dialogue experiences could be applied to many other complex socio-cultural-economic-political systems as well.

In writing this story from my past and later sharing it during the conference, I learned that Dialogue emerges through the genuine awareness in participants, that a shared energy and subject will happen if we give ourselves into it with a contributor's mindset. This energy appears if we engage with the moment from a perspective of contribution and relegate the defensive barriers of our self-interest.

When guided by our self-interest, what comes to mind are arguments; while looking at our larger common interest, in which we are self-rescuing us all, we embrace our vulnerability and let go of our barriers. That dialogue emerges more naturally when hearts are open, be it out of joy or of anguish. We need to create a context that helps us to give up the harmful fiction of non-vulnerability.

I could connect past and present in the observation that, every time we want to guide, limit or condition the environment, the venue, or the meeting, what could have become a convergent dialogical exploration may turn into a defensive debate or a divergent discussion.

With the conference being a good observation environment I became more aware of the kaleidoscope of perspectives that multiculturality generates, and how we improve dialogue when cherishing the acceptance of what is understood above the relevance of what is said.

I have learned that we need to allow for enough time. Time, in dialogue, just turns against us if we rush it, turning the emotional energy and involvement into rational discussion. An adequate timeframe allows the biological phenomenon of hearing to become the beautiful cultural phenomenon of listening as construction of meaning.

I have learned that Dialogue connects with our loving selves rather than the fearful defensiveness present in transactional or confrontational discussion. This emerged beautifully for me in some of the comments I received from readers. This made me realize that an open story may allow for learning about dialogue in many more ways than if it had been written to teach what dialogue is, or should be.

I became aware of the dialogic nature of private conversations – namely my own thinking process – when reflecting about the meaning of past events.

As an evolving step of the conference, I am exploring and learning through the Dialogue Circles that keep developing within the Academy, and paying attention to avoid fragmentation due to our human need to categorize and define professional domains, while Dialogue seems to be a meta-communication approach that involves them all.

Section Two

Criminal Justice Needs Dialogue!

Dialogue Through the Offender Resettlement Journey

Jane Ball

What is the purpose of the Criminal Justice System? Is it punishment? Or retribution? Perhaps rehabilitation? Deterrence? Public safety? While there is undoubtedly a little of all of these in practice, rehabilitation is at the heart of modern penal policy in the UK and US systems where I have worked. In my experience the reality of the aspiration to provide rehabilitation (defined as 'the reintegration of a convicted person into society') is hampered by the fragmentation of the Criminal Justice System that leads different organisations, divisions and people to act in isolation rather than together. The Offender Resettlement Journey (ORJ), created by Peter Garrett and me, is a Dialogic response to integrate the activity of the whole system – including the offender – to achieve the common goal of successful resettlement. The theory and practice of the ORJ is based on knowledge generated over many years of Dialogue with offenders and people who work in the Criminal Justice System at all levels, alongside our experience of organisational consulting. In this paper I'd like to explore some of the key features of the ORJ, how they developed, and the relevance of the ORJ for effective Professional Dialogue within the Criminal Justice.

My Journey with Dialogue in the Criminal Justice System

Over the last 19 years my work has been based entirely on Dialogue in many fields, both commercial and social, and continuously within the Criminal Justice System. Over this time I have worked in 15 different prisons in the UK, and in six different State and city corrections departments in the US, under the auspices of the charity Prison Dialogue and the consulting business Dialogue Associates. I am director and co-owner of Dialogue Associates with Peter Garrett, who has been my teacher, mentor and colleague continuously throughout this period. We have partnered on many initiatives, co-designed, facilitated and supported each other in the intervening years.

When I started the work was focussed on improving the prison, without any additional resourcing or policy changes, through Dialogue and the way that people talked with each other. As we developed partnerships with prison Governors and senior managers, they asked us to use the Dialogues to address specific issues. For example, conflict between a healthcare provider and the prison operation and security staff; the transition from one prison Governor to another; an Equality and Diversity review across prison policy and practice; and union management strategy. Our thinking, practice, and vision also moved from unit-level Dialogues for staff and prisoners to whole-prison transformation, to groups of prisons working together with local communities, to state-wide systems. The core of the work has been bringing together people from the different, and relevant, subcultural groups to address individual and collective thinking within the Criminal Justice System. Things change as a result. The practice, theory and skills have developed through repeated application and practice here, as well as drawing on work in the commercial sector.

Most of the work has involved the engagement of offenders. Time after time, I have seen individuals flourish through the experience, and start to take hold of their own lives, and I've witnessed the awakening of an intelligence in the system that is not often included in decision-making. Why wouldn't the whole Criminal Justice System provide the conditions for this change to be nurtured in everyone? Why wouldn't it provide a place for a generative, rather than destructive, relationship between the offender and the system? We have developed the Offender Resettlement Journey through practice over many years, driven by the desire to create such a system – or to provide the conditions for its creation. It is a now a fundamental framework for our Professional Dialogue work in the Criminal Justice System.

The Offender Resettlement Journey in Theory and Practice

The Offender Resettlement Journey tracks the 'archetypal' path of an offender. It is the journey an offender takes from committing an offence and arrest, through sentencing, incarceration (although not in all cases), supervision by probation agencies in the community, release (from prison or probation commitments) and re-entry into the community, then resettlement - to be independent and law-abiding, and ultimately to make a positive contribution to their community. I have heard many, many stories from offenders over the years, and of course everyone has a unique experience. Despite the variations, we have found core features of the ORJ: common routes, transitions and crises, things that help people to succeed and others that trip them up. Understanding this helps to make those journeys a success in life; and informs the design and facilitation of ORJ Dialogue interventions. Here are some of the characteristics we have found.

The offender journey is *material*. That is, the physical experience progresses from court to a prison cell, to a probation hostel, a bedsit, and possibly to home with your family. Your clothing, accommodation, meals . . . everything changes. It is *relational*. As you are incarcerated you say goodbye to your family and friends, and in prison you share a cell with someone you have never met. You live closely with a large group of strangers and have a range of personal and professional relationships. When you return home upon discharge, you try to sever ties with offending 'associates'. The offender journey is *emotional*. It consists of anger, sadness and loss, despair, desperation, hope and expectation. It is *mental*, in that your thinking changes as you learn to navigate a new environment with different rules, norms, processes and ways of working and living. The journey travels from *dependence* – be it on drugs or alcohol, someone to unlock doors, social security or health benefits – to *independence* and, with it, increasing choice about where you live and work and spend your time.

Finally, at its core, this is a journey of *identity*: from offender and prisoner to worker, student, entrepreneur, father, mother, neighbour. (This is why the naming of those who have offended society and its laws is so significant. Are you a *con, inmate, offender, prisoner, man* or *woman*?) The journey may be a one-time passage from arrest to resettlement, or it may repeat and repeat, each time activating the whole cycle, with identity at its centre.

There are some key points in the journey when circumstances change, and care and attention is required to navigate these successfully. As on a road trip, things are different when you depart – you realise the petrol gauge is low, you forgot your bag, can't remember if you locked the back door! – to when you are cruising down the motorway and the only choice is whether to turn the radio on or what speed to drive. They are different again as you arrive – traffic builds up as you reach a major city – and then you are suddenly at a stand-still and you don't know why.

As an offender enters the Criminal Justice System they may be waiting for the police to pick them up, preparing to go to court or be incarcerated, saying goodbye to family, drinking their last can of strong lager, or trying to get hold of drugs that they might try to take in with them. They may know it is coming, or the police break through their front door in the middle of the night. Whatever the specifics, something strong and particular happens at this point. We have called it the *Crisis of Entry*. As the offender's release from prison approaches another crisis arises: the *Crisis of Release*. A new range of questions await: Where will they go? Will old associates be waiting for them? Will they be able to stay clean? What they will do for money? All this, combined with the excitement and anticipation of freedom: choosing what to wear, eating good food, seeing their partner, being with their children . . .

Once across the threshold of the prison gate the reality of coping with those freedoms hits home: Why did the police just stop me? What do I do about the noisy neighbour? What do I tell that employer about where I have been? How do I get to see my probation officer at noon and my drug agency at one in a different town? These are all real challenges that I have heard offenders talk about during Dialogue work, reflecting on what went wrong and sometimes looking ahead to how to manage. These transitions are intentionally named as crises because it is very easy for things to go wrong, and people feel – and are – vulnerable. During research work for the UK Ministry of Justice, offenders described a crisis at the end of their probation supervision in the community, when no one is watching what they are doing any more, there are no routine visits, and no advice or interest. We found that each crisis could be managed best with a 'clear line of sight', a view of the whole journey to resettlement. With a clear line of sight offenders can see the route ahead, anticipate problems, discover what is required and make better decisions as a result.

Fragmentation in the Criminal Justice System

In my experience most people who work in the Criminal Justice System are remarkable, dedicated and resourceful individuals. They work hard and achieve what is required of them in demanding conditions. According to where they work they have a different focus: it may be running an orderly regime (lock and unlock prisoners, serve meals, supervise movement around the prison); testing urine for drugs; checking where probationers are living and working; managing the budget; delivering a treatment programme according to set guidelines; tracking of the number of assessments completed within a set timeframe – any one of the hundreds of tasks required to run the system. Staff meet their targets, yet are not routinely expected to consider their impact on the offenders' journey to resettlement, nor to take an interest in what other parts of the system are doing. The education department in one prison where I worked complained repeatedly that offenders couldn't complete their classwork because they were always late for their sessions. This was because they were held up by residential prison staff who made sure that the prisoners had what they were entitled to (breakfast, medication, a chance to raise queries) before they left.

Beyond the prison, fragmentation in the Criminal Justice System is even more pronounced and difficult to address because it is part of an open system. In an open system, even though the offender may still be under the jurisdiction of the Criminal Justice System, there is no one person to whom everyone ultimately reports, as there is in even the largest multinational corporation, who can lay out the common purpose and expectations.

Dialogue can support a successful journey to resettlement and provide something of an antidote to fragmentation by providing the opportunity for offenders to talk and think about their situation with the right people who are part of that journey. For example, Dialogue between offenders, family members and probation staff will help people prepare for family life, with the demands that a probation licence dictates. However, the Criminal Justice System is complex – multiple agencies and many people affect the offender journey. The ORJ reveals the interconnectedness of the agencies, and the departments within agencies, through the perspective of the offender, and their common goal of creating successful journeys. Criminal justice staff start to think from an offender's perspective about the current conditions, their role in creating them (whether they are a prison officer, drug counsellor or senior leader), and what they can do to improve those conditions. With that awareness and use of Dialogue skills to talk and think together, everyone can act more intelligently and make better decisions. The awakening in staff in Dialogue groups when they are given a chance to talk and think with offenders and colleagues is inspiring. Some staff respond in action, such as the semi-retired prison officer who galvanised local agencies to come into the prison to offer their services, rather than waiting until prisoners were released. Others notice the quality of the engagement, such as the police officer who told me he talked about things in the Dialogue that he had never spoken about with his wife.

ORJ Intervention Skills

The ORJ as an intervention requires vision to create an integrating image that reveals the interrelatedness of the system, convening skills to include the right people from the right parts of the system and Dialogue facilitation skills for working with offenders and different agency subcultural groupings. In the pages below I will describe four examples of ORJ work in the Criminal Justice System that demonstrate these skills and vision in action to begin to address the problem of fragmentation within the Criminal Justice System. Along with other interventions and experiences not included here, they have been foundational in building the understanding that has underpinned the theory of the ORJ, and in developing the skills and experience required for a Resettlement Journey intervention. Each one is a also valuable Dialogue intervention that could be replicated, with the right support.

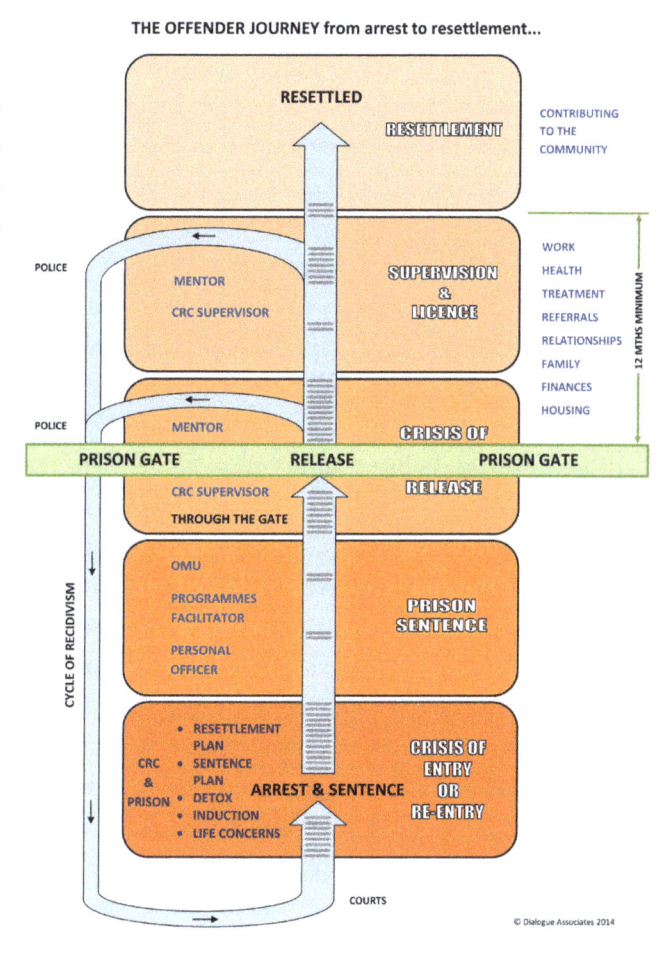

THE OFFENDER JOURNEY from arrest to resettlement...

This graphic is an example of how to break the ORJ down into sections to engage participants in research. The research was commissioned by the Ministry of Justice of England and Wales

Facilitation Skills to Change the Discourse
Staff–Prisoner Dialogue At HMP Blakenhurst

Context
This was one of my first experiences of Dialogue work in a prison. In 1998 Prison Dialogue had been awarded the contract to run monthly two-day Dialogue groups at HMP Blakenhurst, a private prison in the Midlands region of England. I joined in 1999 and facilitated Dialogues between prisoners, staff and managers there for up to four days a month until 2003. Though the Governor in charge of the prison at the time was interested in the potential of Dialogue to improve the prison environment, it was only the requirement for the prison to run non-accredited programmes that enabled us to be there.

The Work

The aim of the work was to improve relationships between the sub-groups of prisoners, staff and managers, and hence their experience living and working in the prison. Therefore, the Dialogue groups were roughly structured to represent a microcosm of the prison. Up to 20 prisoners from each of the four housing units, two uniformed staff and one prison senior manager (different each time) participated. It was socio-therapeutic in that people could work out issues in the social dynamic of the group. At times they gave and received direct feedback from other people, and they learnt about themselves by listening to others. As one prisoner noted after the sessions, "Hearing ourselves speak has helped us understand ourselves and others".

We met for two full days each time and talked together without a set agenda, allowing the theme to emerge from the group. The first challenge was that some people – offenders, staff and managers alike – didn't want to be there at all. A check-in, in which each person was invited to speak in turn, got everyone engaged immediately, listening, talking, thinking about what they would say, interested in other people, and usually having some fun. A check-out at the end of each day allowed the content of the Dialogue to settle and prepared participants to transition to relationships back out on the prison landings.

Once engaged and with the permission of an open agenda, the sessions typically began with prisoners complaining about prison conditions, poor food, lack of rehabilitation, behaviour of some staff, etc., and petitioning staff and managers for improvements. At times facilitation needed to be strong, enabling people both to vociferously put forward their point of view and stop to listen and understand the perspective of others. As all sides offered this to each other they learnt more about why things were the way they were, how things might be improved and (probably less often) what was good about this prison.

We began to deliberately introduce the Dialogic Practices in sessions: Voice, Listening, Respect, Suspension. We explained that *Voice* meant to be genuine, not saying one thing in the room and something different outside of the room. *Listening* was to give your attention and try to understand what others were saying and meant. *Respect* was to take the stance that other people thought and did what they did for a reason that made sense to them; even if it was not what you would do there was a reason for them doing it. *Suspension* was to hold your views openly, and consider why you thought what you did, like a chandelier suspended from the ceiling so that you could see it all of the way round. I learnt about the Practices from Peter. His input to the development of these Practices was based on his experiences in high-security prisons HMP Whitemoor and HMP Long Lartin, so they were powerful in this context. They made perfect sense to the prisoners and staff, and they easily picked up the practice and the language.

The Outcomes and Limitations

Month after month we created a good rapport between staff and prisoners in the Dialogues, even when unpopular staff attended, or housing units sent along their 'baddest' prisoners. Staff and prisoners found they had common interests; that is, prisoners wanted safe prisons just as much as the head of security did, but they lacked the understanding of the others' perspective without Dialogue. The more focussed use of the Practices deepened the quality of the container. (The *container* is the term Peter introduced to me at that time, that names the quality of atmosphere among people.) I found that the Practices created a strong container that was safe enough for people to be more open about themselves. There was energy of genuine engagement and a quality of relationship that was unusual, and a feeling that change was possible. One prison officer named the changing dynamic: "At first I thought it was about inmate-to-officer but was pleased that we were able to speak as person-to-person."

In this container we saw individual offenders transform as they realised themselves in the Dialogue group. Take 'Eddie' – in the first two or three sessions he attended he sat in the corner, arms folded, head down, refusing the opportunity to speak. I was surprised that he came back. By perhaps his second or third session when he was asked a question he responded with explosive street talk that was hard to even understand. Gradually his words became sentences, and he began to engage more critically in complaints about the prison. Then one day he started to tell his story and described in detail his offence, robbing people at a cashpoint (ATM). He described clearly his sense of hopelessness and inability to see any other way to make a success of himself, and the pleasure of being able to buy the designer clothes he wanted. In time he was able to talk more thoughtfully with others about his upbringing and community, and then to wrestle with questions about his future. There were other individuals like Eddie who came month after month to explore their life, their storyline, in depth. It is surprising how clearly I can recall those people, even after all these years. Eddie and others contributed to the container, and as a result other people could engage with the same questions about themselves, in depth, even if they were only there once. The focus of the Dialogue changed from 'what others should do to make things better for me' to 'what I need to address to improve things for myself'.

As a group I found prisoners more interested in thinking about their journey and resettlement as they found themselves in the safety of the container. As one prisoner put it to his group, "What is more important, that you can't buy tuna on the canteen (prison shop) or that you need to deal with your drug problem so that you don't end up back here again? What would your family want you to be talking about?" Officers who came to the Dialogues saw how they could have an impact on offenders' lives. One officer, after attending a series of Dialogues, chose a new role managing the work groups who tended the grounds of the prison. As he told me, "We have Dialogue every day, and I can see what a difference it makes to [the prisoners], and I love my job again."

The development of individuals and relationships between staff and prisoners was encouraging, but still there was no structure to take what was being learnt in the Dialogue into the wider prison or Criminal Justice System in a sustainable way. I remember thinking as Eddie was released that he needed to continue this quality of Dialogue in the community, but there was no way for him to so.

Learnings for the ORJ

Through repeated practice I learnt the critical facilitation skills required for this work, the foundation for any ORJ intervention. Most important is the use of – and encouragement for others to use – the Dialogic Practices, creating a container that enables a rich authentic enquiry with an offender about their life and circumstances. It leads even the most cynical staff to listen and understand the offenders' experiences, and others to think about how they are leading their own lives. It is an engagement between people, not an interview or assessment, and that requires the facilitator to be equally authentic and willing to talk about their own experiences, thoughts and feelings, appropriately and professionally. "They left their key in the car and went into the shop, that was why I stole it", said a prisoner innocently on one occasion, as if it was the most obvious thing in the world! I expressed my disbelief in no uncertain terms, and my straightforward, authentic response deepened the quality of Dialogue. The Dialogue facilitation skills also enable an effective conversation between subcultures. Over time, this moves beyond an us-and-them debate to a common enquiry. This is a necessary skill to integrate a fragmented system. A typical example of such a debate occurred between the prisoners and the Head of Security about security measures in the prison, particularly how family members were searched when they arrived for a visit. Facilitation encouraged them to listen to each other, enquire about each other's views, explain their own and why they held them. As a result, they discovered their common interest in keeping the prison safe and secure, and beyond that, something of their common humanity.

The developing enquiries in the Blakenhurst Dialogue groups revealed how much more opportunity there was in prison to enable offenders to change their story, and therefore be less likely to reoffend. Many of the offenders had been in prison many times before, and their stories of how they came to be back in prison. ("It is like snakes and ladders: it's hard to climb up a ladder, but when you slide down like a snake it is fast", said one prisoner.) These repeating, predictable patterns revealed where the system was and was not working.

Mind the Gap
Resettlement KPI Conference with HMP Blakenhurst, HMP Brockhill and HMP Hewell Grange

Context

While our Dialogue groups in HMP Blakenhurst focussed increasingly on the offenders' story of resettlement, HMPS ('Her Majesty's Prison Service' in England and Wales) announced the introduction of key performance indicators (KPIs) relating to resettlement. The measures were the first time in the UK that prisons would be monitored on what was provided to help offenders re-establish themselves in the community after they left the prison. I had worked in two prisons adjacent to HMP Blakenhurst: a women's prison HMP Brockhill, and an open prison (the lowest security level in England and Wales) HMP Hewell Grange, so we took advantage of our relationships there to centre a conference on these three prisons. The aim was to learn more about how Criminal Justice System could better support the resettlement of offenders – what was working, what was not and how things could be improved.

The Work

For the first time we created a map of the system that highlighted the factors affecting whether an offender was reconvicted or resettled. We played on the iconic wording from the London Underground notice that says 'Mind the Gap' as you get on or off the train, but here The Gap referred to the gap between incarceration as an *offender* and independent life in the community as an *ex-offender*.

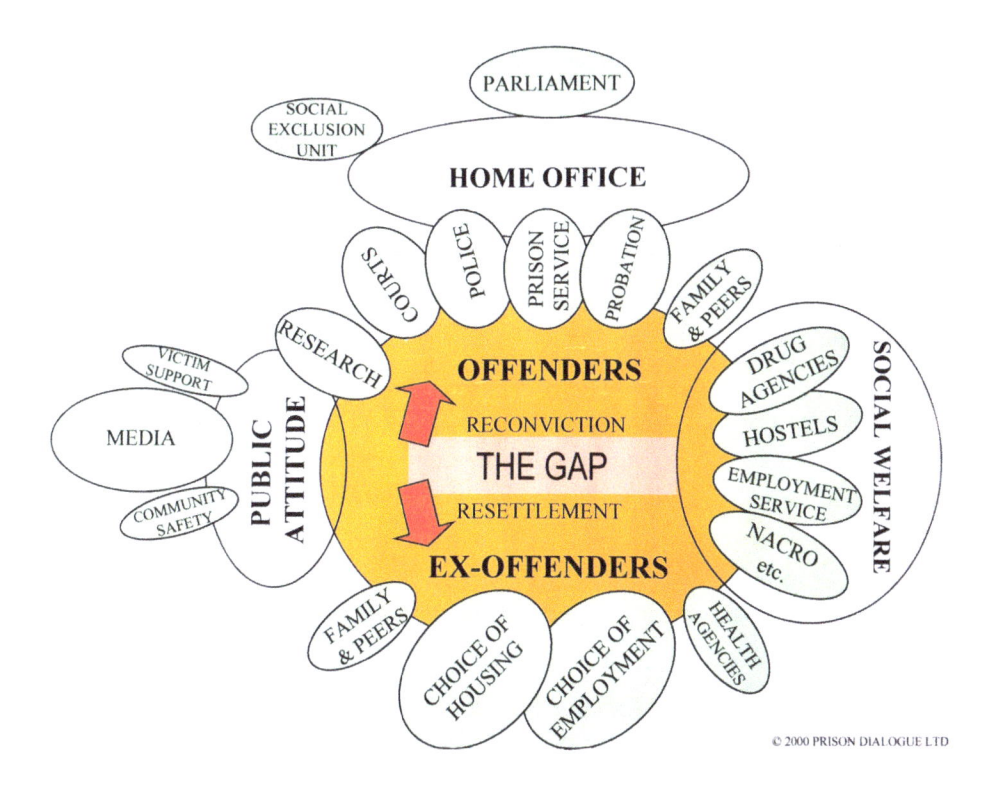

As we began our conference, we required every subgroup to be represented at the gathering. We invited people by name from each agency and, if they didn't reply, we called them until they did. If they were not available we asked them to send an appropriate representative, and we persisted until we had a guarantee that the right person would be there. I still remember Peter calling the Home Office (in the US, something of a combination of the Justice Department and the Department of Homeland Security) to ask them who they would send – and they did send someone! There were 45 participants, including police officers, magistrates, victim representatives, drug treatment counsellors, prison officers, prison managers, voluntary sector support staff, employment service managers, public health and social policy advisors, , an academic criminologist, family members, prisoners and ex-prisoners.

The conference was structured around four themed Dialogues: 'Arrest and Conviction', 'Imprisonment', 'Release and Resettlement', and a final reflection on the whole journey. Participants sat in two concentric circles. Participants with direct experience of the theme – the aspect of the journey under consideration – sat in the inner circle and spoke in an open Dialogue. Those in the outer circle listened and added awareness, which they shared in observations at the end. As such, the Imprisonment Dialogue included the prison staff, prisoners, family members, while the police, magistrates, victim support, and the employment service listened from the outer circle.

Outcomes and Limitations
The primary outcome of the conference was learning about the fragmentation and inter-connectedness in the Criminal Justice System (documented in a full report and published at *www.prisondialogue.org*). Agencies had little awareness of the impact they had on the ability of others to do their work. Drug treatment counsellors described how they could not work effectively in prisons because of lack of cooperation from prison staff who saw them as a burden rather than an asset to the prison, and policy advisors were disconnected from the experience on the ground, and were making uninformed policy decisions. Security staff could undermine prison visits through their attitude to family members, yet resettlement staff were trying to encourage strong family ties in the knowledge they improved chances of successful resettlement. There was little to no understanding between different phases of the journey, apart from the knowledge held by the offenders and their families. The Magistrate, who sentenced people to custody, was not interested in what it was like in prison. Police were told that how they made an arrest (always based on a professional risk assessment) affected how the offender thought about Criminal justice agencies, and therefore their attitude to prison staff once they were incarcerated.

As a one-off event, the session generated a high level of awareness and new understanding about the inter-relatedness of the criminal justice agencies, the offender and their family. Previously I had not thought of a Dialogue needing to lead to a plan of action, rather that each participant would make their own decisions about what they would do as a result of what they had heard and learnt. However, the Criminal Justice System is large and complex and the individual motivation at the end of the session was unlikely to lead to the policy or practice changes I could see were needed.

Learnings for the ORJ
The map, graphic and naming (The Gap) provided a strong and clear external display of the system that everyone could see and refer to. We could show *Offender–Ex-offender* at the heart of the image and depict the relative positioning of the agencies. The concentric circle design of the session reinforced the image. The offenders and ex-offenders were the only people seated in the centre circle for each Dialogue, and it was obvious that they were the only group to have continuous first-hand experience of every phase of the journey.

Participation by all relevant stakeholders is essential. With each perspective brought out by people talking openly about their first-hand experience, the inter-relatedness of the system and its impact is clear. As the Criminal Justice System is an open system – meaning that there is no one person with authority over everyone – it requires skilful convening to achieve this. This includes understanding and mapping the system to identify the relevant agencies or sub-groups, sending invitations purposefully to the right people, taking care to explain why it is relevant for them to be there, and following up to secure their participation. In a closed system, with sponsorship at the right level, you can require people to attend. In an open system, where people do not have a common leader, you have to make the case for them to be there.

Threshold Dialogue
An Open System Working Together to Improve Resettlement

Context
From 2003 to 2006 Prison Dialogue worked consistently with the Governor (in charge of the prison overall), all of the senior managers and staff at HMP Dorchester in the south of England in support of a prison turnaround. Dialogue was at the heart of the transformation that took the prison from a ranking of 135th of 136 prisons in England and Wales in 2004, to 35th by 2006 – the highest ranking it could achieve for a prison of its type. It also ranked 1st or 2nd in the country across 12 different Measures of Quality of Prison Life (MQPL). The work at the prison was noticed by the Governor, who let us know that "The Director General called me to pass on his personal congratulations for what was seen as an extraordinary shift in the prisoners' custodial experience".

This was only the beginning. The vision went beyond the custodial experience to the creation of a whole-prison approach to resettlement. The Governor wanted the prison to be what was known as a "beacon establishment", one that shone out among other prisons and had influence beyond the prison walls. Partnering with the prison Governor, we introduced our thinking about the offender journey and developed Threshold Dialogue to operationalise a wider partnership within the Criminal Justice System to reduce recidivism in the local community.

The Work
Bournemouth Threshold Dialogue was launched in January 2006 and for the next five years I worked to develop a structured Dialogue intervention, designed to address fragmentation in the multiple ways it occurred in this system: between different phases of the journey, particularly prison and the community; between different agencies and between offenders and the agencies; also between line staff (practice), senior managers (procedure) and chief officers (policy). In reality this meant that we created a network of interrelated Dialogue groups at three prisons and three community sites that tracked the offenders' journey in and out of prison.

We did not set it up as a grand design. The network was built over a period of time as we engaged regularly with groups of offenders and discovered what they needed. We knew that offenders experienced a crisis of release that builds up towards the end of their sentence and hits them as they step through the prison gate. The experience of freedom can be unsettling, and there is a lot of pressure to secure accommodation, income and medication, re-engage with family, and avoid past associates. We began in HMP Dorchester with Dialogues focussed on preparing for release, and then in the large seaside town of Bournemouth, where many of the offenders lived. The sessions were run on the same day every week within prison and the community – one week a young man would attend a Dialogue in the prison, and on the same day the following week he would be in a Dialogue in the community. This was particularly helpful for the significant group of offenders whose journey took them in and out of prison repeatedly, with sentences too short to receive any interventions in prison. They could continue to engage in the socio-therapeutic intervention of Dialogue regardless.

This was another open-system intervention; therefore, we understood that we would have to establish how Threshold Dialogue met the organisational interests of each and every one of the agencies to secure their participation. It needed to help them be successful in their day job. Every agency accepted that they needed to engage with offenders, but it was difficult to achieve. Few recently released offenders want to be seen talking to the police. It can take hours for a housing worker to see one offender on a prison visit. Threshold Dialogue provided engagement in quantity and quality. In a session with 15 offenders for 90 minutes they achieved 22.5 hours of engagement with offenders from their local community. The impact was significant. For example, police usually got to know offenders when they were arresting them, a time when there was little opportunity to build a relationship. They rearrested people time and time again, and as a result frequently held negative assumptions about offenders. In Threshold Dialogue they could support the offender's thinking about their journey and build mutual understanding and rapport. I knew of a previously violent offender who willingly went to the police station with one of the police officers he had met in the Dialogue when he breached his probation licence. In the past that would have required force, a team of officers and probably some injury. Housing workers who got to know offenders in depth while they were in prison were more able to support them once they were released and dealing with the challenges of communal living.

Prisons, police, local government, housing providers, employment service, and a drug treatment service became primary long-term partners in this intervention. Their staff participated regularly in Dialogues at a number of sites, and some of them trained as facilitators so that the process could be self-sustaining. Facilitators worked in pairs and we created a reporting mechanism to support the development of their facilitation skills. This required them to listen and become more aware of what was happening. After his first session, one officer learnt that if he tried to remember good quotes he wasn't listening, and he couldn't remember what people said. If he just listened, he could recall significant comments easily.

In time there were Threshold Dialogues tracking the offender journey – a local prison which incarcerated offenders serving short sentences, a medium security prison for those with longer sentences (many of whom started out at the local prison), and a young offenders institution, a night shelter and day centre for those whose lives were more chaotic, a supported housing unit for ex-offenders who were recently released, and at a community hall for people who were living more independently.

We developed the concept of the Line of Sight for the view that offenders have of their resettlement journey. We found that many offenders do not have a clear Line of Sight. They cannot see what they must do, either fully or in good enough time to succeed; or they get stuck no view of where they are trying to get to, or what they have to do to get there. Threshold Dialogue helped to create a clear Line of Sight for prisoners over their entire journey, with a destination worth aiming and for and manageable steps for each major transition. The participation of agency staff was critical – for example, staff from community agencies came into the prison for a Dialogue about preparing to be in the community.

The Threshold Dialogue system was supported by an Operations group of senior managers and a Governance Board of chief officers from every agency involved. This structure took learning from Threshold Dialogues into management and resourcing of operational services and the development of policy and strategy. After five years we held a Line of Sight event sponsored by the Local Criminal Justice Board to mark our withdrawal and hand over to local ownership. This included use of graphic maps and a spatialised offender walk (described in the following example) to display the system to itself.

Outcomes and Limitations

I witnessed and tracked changes in many individual offenders, including prolific offenders who were stuck in the revolving door of short-term sentences and short-term release who did not re-offend for the duration of our connection with them. Relationships between offenders and staff from every agency developed constructively. Interagency cooperation was more effective, leading to tangible service changes. As a direct result of Threshold Dialogue, a project was set up to provide a package of social security benefit, rent assistance, private sector accommodation and employment advice for offenders on release. One of the participants, the Manager of Bournemouth Safer and Stronger Communities Team, emphasised the value of Dialogue against this backdrop: "We talk about partnership working a lot, but I think actually what dialogue does is really strengthens some of those partnerships at various different levels – right from the people who are working on the ground, maybe managing offenders or ex-offenders on a day-to-day basis, in hostels, Police Community Support Officers and community workers, but also at a more strategic level: prison governors; superintendents from the police and community safety managers; probation managers; actually working together and understanding what the system looks like in their local area."

The limitation was the lack of sustainability. Despite the achievements of Threshold Dialogue, including the creation of the local Governance structure and facilitation team, it folded once we withdrew. It was disappointing but not surprising. Local leaders (primarily in prisons and police) who had partnered with us to set up the programme had moved on, without establishing the commitment from those who replaced them. Without leadership, participation fell away. HMP Dorchester closed in 2013.

Learning for the ORJ

Through Threshold Dialogue we learnt about the larger offender journey, between prisons and into the community, and the experience and impact of repeated cycles of re-offending. This included the development of our understanding of and language for the Crisis of Release, Crisis of Entry and Re-entry, and the Line of Sight.

I believe that Threshold Dialogue helps offenders prepare for and successfully make their journey to resettlement and develops the skills of staff to support that journey more effectively. It requires widespread participation from criminal justice agencies – and we found participation can be achieved in an open system where agencies find the value to their individual organisational interests or targets. Even so, you need senior partnership and sponsorship. In an open system you need it across key agencies, from key influencers, and you must work hard to secure the commitment of new leaders.

ORJ for Organisational Development
A State-Wide System

Context

The ORJ can be used at scale for organisational development, as we have shown in a state-wide system in the US. This was the first time we named the intervention the Offender Resettlement Journey, and it was a consistent image as Peter and I partnered with the Director and his team to cascade Dialogue skills and practice throughout the agency. The foundation was completely different to anywhere else and, as a result, the potential was more significant. Working steadily with the agency over six years, all of their 12,000 or so employees were introduced to Dialogue skills for engagement and communication, every supervisor exposed to the use of Dialogue skills for management and coaching, and every leader to the use of a Working Dialogue pattern as a business practice for participatory change. The introduction to these skills included an organisational infrastructure to embed the training and practice of Dialogue in a practical way. This whole-system skill-building was cascaded from the Director and Deputies to the Executive team, every Unit Head, every Deputy unit head, on down through the ranks.

Intervention Design

The ORJ was introduced at stages alongside the other skills. At the first ORJ we included an ORJ 'Walk' event, held over an afternoon, within a Dialogue Skills Training session with executives and unit heads. In those early days the focus of the cultural change was the communication between ranks, up and down the chain of command in this hierarchical system. The aim of the ORJ was to introduce the idea that you could also think from the point of view of the offender, to understand the system and inform decisions. This was a challenging proposition for some people. It was a 'walk' because we physically walked an offender up and down the room to show their journey through the system from the point they were sentenced, to the current time – I'll outline more about the spatialisation and facilitation below. It was an event because there was no structured follow-up. People were definitely moved and affected. The memories were at times very emotional and, for many of the leadership, a great reminder of the human impact of their work, in that they spent more time with emails and in meetings as a result of the walk. I remember one of the older warden's touching reaction to being thanked by an ex-offender for the words of advice he gave him as his counsellor, perhaps 30 years before. The ORJ 'walk' had a personal impact on people, but there was no designed change as a result.

Later, as the Dialogue skills were in broad use across the agency and accepted because of their value, we ran three large-scale, in-depth ORJs to show the potential for organisational development. These ORJs focussed on a maximum-security prison, a medium-security prison and a low-security prison in partnership with nearby Community Corrections districts. We worked closely with a steering group for each site so that locally they owned the process (from the research to identify the ORJ through their unit, to giving practical support to the design to the convening and logistics), the organisational learning and the resulting change proposals and implementation.

There were three phases. In the first phase we talked regularly with the local team to understand the flow of offenders into and out of their care and draw the graphic image of the journey centred on their prison. This required data to identify the common journeys and significant points of transition. The enquiry revealed five different archetypal journeys which we named on the graphics and provided useful language to refer five quite distinct experiences.

Local data informed the choice of which journeys it would be helpful to understand, and therefore which offenders, other prisons, probation units or other criminal justice agencies should be invited to the session. Where there were significant drug problems they selected and invited male and female offenders who had been incarcerated for drug-related offences

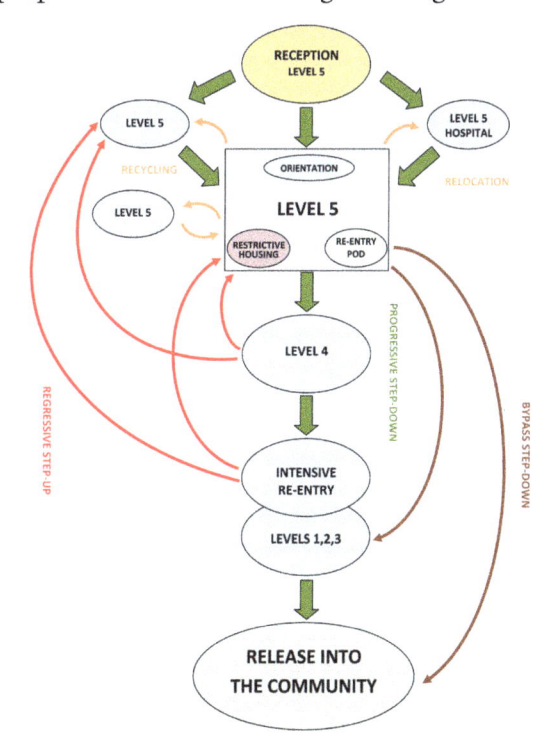

OFFENDER RESETTLEMENT JOURNEY

and had been in treatment. Where prisoners we re-released on parole after decades of incarceration, they selected a man who had served nearly 40 years, and where they wanted to learn about the most challenging offenders they selected a man who had been in the highest security conditions and was working his way down the system. Other invitations were also made to specific individuals – not just any probation officer or Sheriff was invited, but rather a probation officer from the office who received most offenders on release from that prison, and the Sheriff who ran the jail that sent more offenders to that prison than any other jail.

Spatialised Facilitation
The second phase was a facilitated event, bringing the system together in one room. These days began with a process of engagement to build the container: first a check-in, then exercises and small-group skilful conversations to introduce and activate the Dialogic Practices. One check-in led people to think about their own journey through corrections (when they joined the agency, their first job, next job, when they expect to retire). Questions were posed to give permission to think about how the agency could be improved from a financial, operational and community perspective. The final question was a moral one – if your son, daughter, or some other relative was incarcerated here, would you be happy with the treatment they received?

Next we spatialised where participants were seated in the room. At one end were those who worked in the community, at the other end those who worked in maximum-security prisons. In between were staff from prisons at reducing levels of security until you reached the prison gate – represented by thick silver tape across the floor, or tables or chairs – something that marks a significant change between prison and community. Stepping across that threshold is a distinct and significant change for anyone, and the spatialisation has to represent that. Everyone was seated in a relevant place where there were no observers. Family members sat centrally in the community so they had clear sight of their partner or child as they walked through the system. Then Peter and I took turns facilitating a process for the ex-offender or offender to tell their story from the moment when they were sentenced, beginning with how long they were sentenced for, to set the length of the story. Sometimes they went back before then, and though we assured them they didn't need to name their crime, many of them did. We spoke with them some days beforehand to help them to feel confident in us and comfortable about what would happen, but not to hear any details of their story. As we walk and talk we want to achieve genuine, spontaneous human engagement, not hear their rehearsed speeches nor our prepared questions. We included other participants as we went, turning to family members, a Sheriff, prison or probation officer or others, to ask what their experience was of the same journey. For example, turning to a mother to ask what they were thinking as their daughter was incarcerated for the first time, to a 'zero-tolerance' judge why he sent someone back to prison, or to prison staff who received the offender as they arrived in a maximum-security prison.

These offender walks were followed by a whole-group Dialogue to digest together what people noticed or learnt about the system by considering it from the point of view of the offender. Next, we facilitated a process of support and challenge to identify and name specific needs and opportunities that could be addressed to improve outcomes, stimulated by the earlier experience. This required focus and persistence, given the emotional as well as intellectual response to what people had seen and heard.

The final phase took each need or opportunity into a proposal and action, using a participative change methodology including engagement of offenders and other stakeholders. The proposals were integrated into the organisations' reporting systems as business improvement projects.

Outcomes and Limitations
The ORJ led to greater awareness and understanding of interdependencies across the system and the benefits of thinking from the offenders' perspective to see how the system works. As a result the agency is looking to embed the ORJ as a regular organisational development process, led by their own staff. On the whole, the proposals that came out of the ORJs were seriously considered and implemented, or rejected with clear feedback. Some simple, practical solutions were introduced (e.g., transferring money to offenders as they arrive in prison, or use of prisoner mentors in prison reception), and others addressed bigger cultural issues that were more difficult to shift, but at least they were being talked about (for example, the practice of moving prisoners with mental health problems to higher-security prisons). They identified opportunities where people recognised common interests and the potential they could achieve together, particularly with willing community partners.

We have not yet developed other practitioners to be able to facilitate an ORJ, with the skills that we have developed over many years of practice. The ORJ pattern is still complex and will need more work to be simplified as a pattern that can be replicated. These steps are important to make the ORJ more widely available.

Learning for the ORJ
We know the phases required for an ORJ intervention for organisational development, including: research to map the system and understand which journeys will be fruitful to focus on; selection of offenders and other participants; convening; design and spatialisation; facilitation for an authentic, often emotional, experience; and how to take that response into proposals and then to action. Each phase requires certain understanding and skills.

Dialogic facilitation skills for an ORJ are notables, and an extension of those we used in prison Dialogues. To manage the event you need to discern how to use the time available to tell the story, and how to pick out the important aspects of this story. Crucially, you need to engage authentically in depth with someone you have just met, enabling them to willingly describe profound, painful and exhilarating personal experiences in front of an audience of 40 to 80 people that includes police, prison staff, judges, priests, and their own mother . . . You must develop the confidence to ask questions that you don't know the answers to, and to respond genuinely when you hear things that affect you. Simultaneously, you have to be aware of and engage the rest of the participants. They will be a diverse group of people, from many agencies and ranks, with different experiences and attitude. You need to use your presence and your own authenticity and invite them into the conversation.

Relevance of and Possibilities for the ORJ

The Offender Resettlement Journey provides theory and practice for the integration of the Criminal Justice System through the perspective of the continuous journey of the offender. Without this, the Criminal Justice System is fragmented and different parts act without reference to each other, and without reference to the offenders they mean to help. The integration enables everyone, including offenders, to make better decisions knowing the impact they will have on others. The ORJ could be used widely in the Criminal Justice System to integrate practice, procedure and policy. It could also be extended to include the journey before arrest to identify preventative opportunities, or journeys that end in prison because there is a growing group of aging prisoners who may die before they are released. The same approach would be relevant in other fields where there is a clear purpose and integrating focus. For example, I designed and facilitated a session for a multinational oil company that was based on the journey of crude oil from extraction to sale, and Peter and I have recently used the Migrant Journey. It may have relevance in education – the child's learning journey, in healthcare – the patient's journey, in social care – the journey of aging. I would welcome others stepping forward to explore these applications.

Conference Session Extracts

From conversation with 20 participants considering the paper with the author

It raises the question that you alluded to at the beginning, Jane, around convening as a critical component of how this works well. And I really appreciate your words because convening can look different, I'm imagining, based on this context and the circumstances that you're in. Are there any general tips, I'm wondering, that you might offer around the convening?

So the simplest one is, if you talk about them, they should be in the room.

The other thing I think is important is about the organisational knowledge. There are some things that are practise-based, there are some things that are kind of about resources and allocation of resources, and some that are policy-based. What we had on the Threshold Dialogue that I showed you was the practise. But we also then had an operations group where all of the agencies involved, the operational managers, were in a regular meeting together. It used dialogue skills, but it was a meeting. And there was the chief executives of all the agencies, a governing body.

For me, I saw how important all those skills are when it's a really complex system and somehow really, really important things are going on in people's lives.

I'm yearning to continue to develop these skills that we've been learning and training on to effectively change the culture within our agency, to ultimately then be more effective to our clients and our community.

So I am yearning for an ability and a desire to continue to use dialogue in creative ways in how I deal, not only with my offenders, but with my colleagues, victims. I'm in domestic violence unit, so I interact a lot with victims and also with collateral contacts for the offenders, to keep it a circle approach, a wraparound approach.

To create a space where people like me, who hold competing thoughts and feelings and ideas about the subject of criminal justice, and to have a space to work through that through dialogue. I remember before I left, there was a defence attorney who wanted to know what the prosecutor said about her clients so that she could prepare what she would say in support of her client. And I thought to myself while we were here, it would be interesting if this happened in dialogue.

Yes. And for me, it's very much about changing paradigms and changing systems. How do we go from seeing that criminal, that drug dealer, and instead see Bernhardt, the person, and what your needs are, to put away that punishment and see the needs, how to adapt to society again? That's what I'm taking from this, so.

There are so many thoughts. But what I can do, is take Dialogue into Sweden, to get this into the criminal system in Sweden.

I'm with you. I'm tremendously inspired by the way you do it, by the systemic approach, well-thought, and the combination, the beautiful combination of the sincerity I feel in when I'm a role, I feel in your questions. They're well-thought-through, they're spot on, and they're brought from the heart. And it touched me. That touches us, and I think that is a tremendous compliment for you. You really did something here. You brought magic. Thank you.

Postscript

The author's reflections written some months after the conference

During the Working Paper session, I learnt more about the power and value of spatialisation, which I introduce in my paper and is fundamental to the Dialogic facilitation of the Spatialised ORJ. Rather than talking about the paper, or the work, I used spatialization in the session and as a result all the participants were engaged and had a live, common experience to consider together. Through two spatializations we achieved balanced participation from all the perspectives in the room, despite the differences. I knew this was necessary.

The introductions and check-in revealed that while some people were experienced practitioners, others were beginners, or had no practice experience. A few worked in the Criminal Justice System. Less than half had read the paper, and the others had not only read it but were excited and stimulated by what they had read and wanted to hear more. This reflected my experience during earlier sessions in the conference where some wanted to understand the content of papers, while others explored live their own thoughts and feelings about what was happening in the room. This was quite a mix to engage in a consideration!

First, I replicated the Spatialised Offender Resettlement Journey Walk. Every person was given a role – the Warden of a maximum-security prison, a probation officer, a policeman, judge, etc. Just as in the work I had written about, I marked the prison gate. Those that worked in prisons in their imagined roles sat to one side, those that worked in the community to the other. One person stood up alongside me as the ex-offender, and another was his mother, and a neighbour. I walked with the "ex-offender" and I raised the sort of questions I would use. What happened in court? Can you remember the judge giving your sentence? Tell me about your first night in prison. What happened on your day of release? I turned to the "police officer" and asked if he remembered this young man, and to his mother who said she was not happy to have him home when he was first released! The emotion in the room was palpable, and one or two people had tears in their eyes.

In the paper I have written about this process facilitated in correctional systems, and the honest, frequently emotional reaction from people who work in the system. However, this was a role-play, and in my experience, these are usually awkward affairs. Yet the theatre of the spatialization and process was powerful; it engaged the whole person, not just their abstract intellect, and their reaction was equally integrated. Someone mentioned a family experience of the Criminal Justice System, and others were inspired to develop this approach in their own work in different fields. The process revealed the theory and practice of the ORJ, and provided a common immediate experience related to the content of the paper that participants were able to explore. This combined the work and the in-the-room experience that had not been connected in other sessions.

I briefly spatialised a representation of the Threshold Dialogue structure and process, which I had not done before, and the value was different. We set up a circle of chairs each side of the prison gate and the "offender" moved between them as he entered prison and was released, again, and again. It allowed a sometimes-complex concept on paper to be externalised, understood and considered by everyone. We could talk about the work as we saw it in the room and add thinking to it.

There is more to learn about the use and value of spatialization and this was a great opportunity to try some things out.

Dialogue and a Healing Environment in the Virginia Department of Corrections

Harold Clarke and Susan Williams

Personal Background for Susan

I am the Organizational Development Manager for the Virginia Department of Corrections (VADOC). In this role, I am responsible for the implementation, coordination, and management of the initiatives that enable the Department to achieve its strategic goals. I lead the business practice of Dialogue for the Department but have not always been in this position. I started with the VADOC in January 2008 as the Mental Health Supervisor for Probation and Parole. I supervised the transition of individuals with mental health needs from incarceration onto probation, ensured their linkage to services in the community, and assisted probation officers with managing their cases. Along with my direct reports, I served as the liaison between institutions, including prisons and jails, probation, psychiatric hospitals, and community mental health providers. I also provided training across the Department on various topics including mental health and mental illness, stress management, leadership, and evidence-based practices. Although the VADOC Dialogue story began in 2010, I didn't enter the Dialogue scene until later.

So begins our story . . .

Creating the Conditions

In 2010, the Virginia Department of Corrections (VADOC) was in transition. The goal of the newly elected Governor was to enhance public safety with a focus on reducing victimization, improving the outcomes for offenders returning to their communities, and reducing recidivism by strengthening re-entry programs. Thus the Virginia Adult Re-Entry Initiative was established. The Governor searched for a new Director for the Department to further that mission. The question for the appointed Director, Harold Clarke, then became "How could the Department best enhance the programs and services that are working and eliminate those that aren't, while motivating employees and engaging external stakeholders towards a common purpose of effective reintegration of offenders into the community?" Having previously been the Director in Massachusetts, Washington State and Nebraska, Harold Clarke had an idea of what would help move the Department forward.

When Director Clarke was newly appointed in Nebraska, he reflected upon what the Department needed. At the time he thought, "The best way to create lasting systemic change is through the culture." With the assistance of the National Institute of Corrections (NIC), the Department conducted a Future Search Conference. Over the course of 2½ days, over 80 stakeholders representing the Department and the community engaged in Dialogue to find meaning and common ground to envision a better reality for everyone. Out of that conference, Director Clarke thought about having a "clean, clear, sanitary, healing environment, just like a hospital."

By the time he was Director in Massachusetts, while still working with NIC, the idea of a Healing Environment was formed. As described in the book *Healing Corrections: The Future of Imprisonment*, the NIC Norval Morris Project was established to create a more "just, effective and humane Criminal Justice System." (Chris Innes, 2015, pp 14-15) The project participants, including Director Clarke, wondered how they could "transform correctional leadership and the workforce in ways that would empower staff to reduce recidivism and promote prevention." There, the concept of the Healing Environment expanded from just the physical aspects to include the cultural aspects: a place and an atmosphere where staff could engage with one another to address issues and impediments in order to become better performers. That, in turn, would impact the inmates, thus benefitting the whole organization.

Around the same time as he was pondering on the creation of a Healing Environment in Nebraska, Director Clarke was introduced to the concept of Dialogue through one of the pioneers of Dialogue work, Peter Garrett. As the agency was exploring the idea of the Healing Environment, he realized it could do so dialogically. This would mean that all employees could use their voice, which would bring about a better understanding and more staff support. As he experimented with Dialogue and the Healing Environment, Director Clarke saw that results included a stronger culture and employee engagement focusing on offender re-entry and reduced recidivism. After the Director left Nebraska, he shared the Healing Environment concept in Washington State with similar tangible results and then again in Massachusetts before heading to Virginia. With Peter Garrett, he introduced in each state the concept of Dialogue as the foundation to build the Healing Environment. He believed that all initiatives were better when Dialogue was used to pull them together. Dialogue creates a foundation and a format for better understanding and communication. Director Clarke did not force leaders to conform to the concept. One of his aims was to change the "command-and-control" culture and mindset. Therefore, he didn't command people to follow the principles. He nurtured those leaders who were interested as well as next-level supervisors who desired the changes and tapped them to model the way and inspire others.

By the time Harold Clarke arrived in Virginia, its Department of Corrections had already begun work in moving toward a re-entry-focused agency through the Virginia Adult Re-Entry Initiative Strategic Plan. Many programs and projects were being piloted and introduced. Additionally, the VADOC aimed to be a learning organization and more effective agency through the use of evidence-based practices and programs, and the introduction of Learning Teams. (Learning Teams are small groups of employees that meet regularly to communicate, learn together, practice skills, grow professionally, and continually develop the organizational culture to better achieve its mission.)

The Director realized the VADOC needed a vision and mission to pull the various initiatives and strategies together in a manner that could be understood by every employee, offender and stakeholder. Creating a Healing Environment was the perfect solution. The VADOC began to purposefully establish a culture where everyone – employees, offenders, and stakeholders – would be treated with dignity and respect; they would create together an organizational culture that would prioritize helping people be better through support and accountability. He realized that, more than ever before, the vehicle for the expression of the Healing Environment had to be Dialogue.

Dialogue was the foundation that supported the cultural change. Dialogue has been key in aligning goals, breaking down silos, integrating separate pieces, and creating common expectations. Dialogue became the means of bringing people together to talk, think, and learn. Dialogue introduced a common language and specific skills which allowed people to engage with one another with less misunderstanding and increased participation amongst all levels of employees. Dialogue created the atmosphere where voices could be heard and new ideas could emerge.

Laying the Foundation

The introduction of Dialogue at the VADOC occurred in a top-down fashion. After discussing it with his Deputies, the Director introduced the topic through his reading list. All of the Executive Team members and Unit Heads (wardens, superintendents of facilities, and probation chiefs) received the book *Dialogue and the Art of Thinking Together* by William Isaacs. In it, Isaacs emphasizes the power of a Dialogue to open possibilities and see new options by speaking in a way that contributes one to the other.

Following the assignment of the reading, Dialogue Associates Founders Peter Garrett and Jane Ball were brought in to train the Executive Team members in some basic Dialogue skills. They began by looking at the history of the organization and having the leaders think about the culture of the Department at the time they began. David Robinson, the Chief of Corrections Operations, serving directly under the Director, viewed the session as an opportunity for growth. He observed that by reflecting on the history, and learning to think together, the agency would be propelled forward like an arrow from a bow. Following a period of transition and uncertainty, there would be growth, movement forward, and the rise of new leaders.

The first dialogic skills introduced were "check-ins" to learn how to get everyone in the meeting attentive, participating and focused. Executive Team members and Unit Heads were tasked with going back to their staff meetings and using check-ins and then come back together to reflect on the results. For those familiar with Dialogic skills, this will seem like a basic task. However, at the time, it was the first hint of a cultural shift. The VADOC culture did not value hearing everyone's voice, and many meetings were held in a monologue fashion. In fact, many participants were so unaccustomed to speaking in meetings that they resisted participating in the check-ins initially. Deputy Director Cookie Scott recalled appreciating this change the most. She reflected that this was a different way of interacting; it provided the opportunity to sit within the Executive Team in a better way. The meetings were less directive and there was more conversation. The team members were able to learn about one another, hear one another's authentic voices, and get a sense about not only what other people were thinking, but about who each individual was as a person and as a leader.

Meanwhile, Chris Innes was continuing with the Norval Morris Project and working on his book, *Healing Corrections* and Dialogue Associates was developing a plan to bring the Dialogue skills across the entire Department.

In 2012, Dialogue Associates began meeting with the Executive Team and Unit Heads on a quarterly basis. They taught them Dialogue skills for talking and thinking together and engaged them in thinking about and developing visions and initiatives for the Healing Environment in each of their Units. What would each institution, facility, probation office, and administrative department do to create a Healing Environment for their offenders and staff members? Greensville Correctional Center, for example, is the largest prison in Virginia and houses over 3,000 offenders. Greensville is the site of separate residential treatment programs, including mental health, medical, sex offender, and a veterans' unit. Additionally, Greensville includes a work center and a death chamber. With there being so many different functions and employees at Greensville, they needed a Healing Environment Initiative to bring them together. Greensville felt like several different institutions, with different goals, each with distinct staffs, who happened to be working on the same 1000-acre compound. They were working in "silos" with limited communication or cooperation. They chose the motto "One Team, One Mission" as their Healing Environment Initiative. This made it clear to everyone that although Greensville was made up of a lot of components, they were all one team working towards the same goals.

Some Unit Heads struggled with the idea of working with their employees to develop Healing Environment Initiatives. They were still confused about the concept and not used to hearing the voices of their staff members when making decisions. However, over the course of the year, all of the Units managed to develop something that contributed to the Healing Environment. The impact was immediate in many areas. Employees had been allowed to contribute their thoughts and ideas to a major Department Initiative. Many were hopeful and enthusiastic about having been allowed to share their voice, and even more excited about the possibility of the Unit making the changes necessary to attain the Healing Environment goals. Many people expressed cautious optimism for the development of a respectful and supportive environment.

In 2012, Dialogue Associates also recognized the need to introduce Dialogue skills to all of the nearly 12,000 employees in the VADOC system. They began a Dialogue Practitioner Development Program (DPDP). The DPDP would start with the training of 24 individuals from across the Department to learn Dialogue Skills and then train and introduce these skills to others in the agency. I received an email saying I had been selected to be part of this group of trainers. I was excited to learn the new skills. I had heard the word *Dialogue*, but other than that had very little understanding what it was about. I also had been conducting many trainings around the Department and didn't mind adding another one. Little did I know that Dialogue was going to be something completely different than what I had been doing and would ultimately change my world!

As our training as Dialogue Practitioners progressed over three days, our understanding of the concepts increased. We could see the value in the skills, especially the practices. We practiced with one another and learned how to deliver the Dialogue skills in the seven-hour standardized format of the Dialogue Skills Training. Despite understanding the importance of the subject, our ability to use the skills and our image of ourselves and our roles was limited. We believed ourselves to be "trainers" and focused on the definitions and explanations of the skills and, in some regards, more than their use. Along with my fellow 23 colleagues, we began systematically and enthusiastically training each and every person in the VADOC on the basic Dialogue Skills – with a focus on getting the trainings completed. Within a couple of months, many of the Dialogue Practitioners began to run into difficulties. Their supervisors did not want them being away from their positions for days or even weeks at a time, and they were finding it difficult to juggle their regular work with their Dialogue duties. Some Dialogue Practitioners were running into strong resistance at the Assistant Unit Head and Middle Manager levels. Nevertheless, the Director and his Deputies were not swayed from the goal. They continued to engage with the Unit Heads on the importance of the Dialogue skills. The Dialogue Skills Trainings were conducted at every institution, facility and probation office; on average about 24 participants were taught at a time until all employees had taken the training. Additionally, the Dialogue Skills Training was incorporated into the Basic Skills Training for new officers and employees.

The Dialogue Skills Training focuses on interaction through check-in/check-out and the modes of engagement. Awareness of the modes of engagement helps determine how the conversation will proceed; the right mode should be selected according to the goals of the conversation. If, for example, the purpose is to only convey brief information and not engage the participants in any exchange, then a monologue may be the correct mode. If the aim is to hear people's thoughts and have input from different perspectives, then Dialogue would be the preferred mode. The training also emphasizes how to have functional conversations using the actions as well as quality conversations having the practices in place. The Dialogic practices of "Voice," "Listen," "Respect" and "Suspension" set the tone for quality conversations. Through these practices, an environment where people feel comfortable sharing and learning is developed. People feel safe to share their thoughts, and genuine exchange of ideas can happen.

The reaction to the Dialogue Skills Training was overwhelmingly positive, especially amongst the frontline employees. It was really the first time a concept was introduced that emphasized the value of their opinions or even the ability to provide their thoughts on a subject. As one Correctional Officer stated, "The Dialogue Skills Training explained that I am allowed to have a voice and my opinion should at least be respected even if it's not the final decision." The more often employees were exposed to the concepts, the more deeply established the skills became. Understanding was deepened in several ways. The initial introduction was accompanied by Dialogue posters that were placed in every Unit. There were separate posters for each skill set to help keep things simple. At a glance, a person could see the types of skills and a word that helped define each.

While the initial Dialogue Skills Trainings were being conducted, Peter Garrett began writing articles about Dialogue for the monthly newsletter that is electronically distributed to every employee. The articles explained the dialogic skills and principles in more depth than when introduced in the Dialogue Skills Training. They offered staff members the opportunity to read at their leisure and understand the larger purpose of the initiative. The first article was "What is Dialogue?" Here is an excerpt:

> *There are times when clear instructions need to be given in a command-and-control mode, particularly in times of crisis and with issues concerning security. There are other situations in which it is more helpful to think things through with others before reaching a decision, particularly when making changes that affect other people. The simple principle here is to include people who are affected by the change in the decision-making process, and this is where Dialogue is needed. In Dialogue people are encouraged to contribute their thoughts, experience and understanding in order to improve the quality of decisions.*
> —Peter Garrett, Around Corrections: Vol 1. Issue 3 – Feb. 2013

Another way in which the Dialogue skills were reinforced was through the Learning Teams. Learning Teams are small groups of 10-15 employees that meet regularly to communicate, learn together, grow professionally, and continually develop the organizational culture to better achieve its mission. At that time, Learning Teams were established within the Probation and Parole Districts, where they mainly focused on teaching the officers skills in motivational interviewing and effective communication with their probationers. A few of the institutions also had Learning Teams which focused on effective communication and case studies/scenario reviews. That is, within the Learning Team, the members would discuss a real-life situation that had occurred to examine what went well and what could or should have been done differently. Learning Teams were scheduled to meet for an hour, twice a month. Those Learning Teams were efficient in teaching and practicing certain skills, including reflective listening, asking open-ended questions, using affirmation, and conducting "change talk." However, those skills alone could not address a deeper level of effective communication, especially amongst colleagues. Dialogue holds the practices that set the climate, and changes the way people treat one another, respect one another. It opens their minds to new perspectives. Those are the added elements of more effective communication. It was imperative that all employees received these skills.

Dialogue Associates continued to work in separate sessions with the Executive Team, the

Unit Heads, and Dialogue Practitioners on their development. Then they also began to work with selected staff members from those various groups to strengthen and expand the Learning Teams. The group developed a series of seven Dialogue Learning Plans. The purpose of the Learning Plans was to reinforce and practice the Dialogue skills within the Learning Team to support the use of Dialogue throughout the Department. More impressively, the group developed a comprehensive plan to systematically introduce Learning Teams across the Department in the Units that did not have them, develop and train facilitators known as Subject Matter Specialists (SMS), and conduct the Dialogue Learning Plans and assess the knowledge gained at the end of the seven Learning Plans.

The plan started with six pilot sites. Those sites were allowed to develop their own system for assigning employees to Learning Teams, scheduling Learning Teams, training their facilitators (SMSs), and conducting the Learning Plans. Some lessons could be completed in one session and other lessons needed two sessions to be completed, but it was at the discretion of the Units and the Specialists. After the pilot sites began, the workgroup continued to convene and examine which aspects were most effective and which were least effective, and to make recommendations and develop guidelines accordingly. The rest of the Department, with over 40 institutions and facilities and over 40 probation and parole offices, were incorporated into a 15-month Dialogue and Learning Team rollout with Units being brought in each quarter. Everyone in the Department was assigned – and new employees continue to be assigned – to Learning Teams. Revised Learning Team vision, mission, and policy were created. The Learning Team Model, a visual representation of the agency's values, practices, initiatives, and purpose of the Learning Teams was created so that every employee would know that the VADOC is a learning organization and the Learning Teams are the mechanism to create and sustain a safe environment for staff to learn together in a way that fosters positive change and growth.

After the first year of training, it was clear that more Dialogue Practitioners would be needed to assist in getting the entire Department trained. An additional 60+ Dialogue Practitioners were brought into the Dialogue Practitioner Development Program (DPDP) while the first group of Dialogue Practitioners earned certificates as Dialogue Practitioner

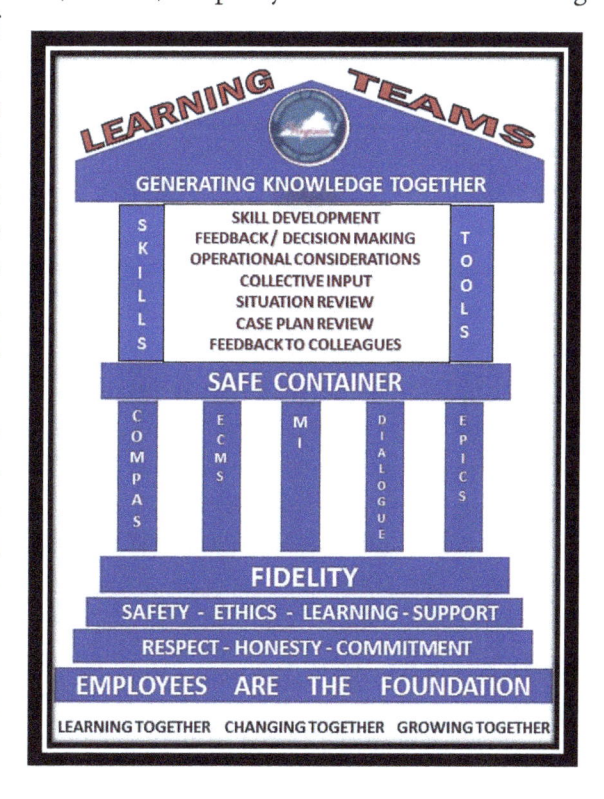

Trainers. Over the years, the DPDP has continued to grow as Dialogue Practitioner cohorts have been systematically brought in across the State and trained in the basic Dialogue skills at the same time as the more experienced Dialogue Practitioners, who have continued to grow in using their skills, gaining more knowledge about Dialogue and learning new skills. It was clear to the first cohort after the first year that they were more than trainers. They realized the impact of Dialogue and how they were change agents for the Department. Presently there are approximately 275 active Dialogue Practitioners in the Department. The Practitioners span across levels from Correctional and Probation Officers to Wardens, Probation Chiefs, and Regional Administrators. They come from diverse fields such as Education, Food Service, Medical, Agribusiness (agricultural operations), Environmental Services (chemical, industrial, and waste management), Research, Technology, Treatment, Security, and more. Every Unit has at least one Dialogue Practitioner and some larger Units have six or seven. We will continue to examine the activities of the Dialogue Practitioners and, later, the impact of their work.

Following the large wave of introducing and reinforcing the basic Dialogue skills through the Dialogue Skills Training, the introduction of Dialogue Learning Plans in the Learning Teams, and the articles written in the newsletter, the Department was ready for the next level of skills. Dialogue was not only a way to communicate and engage, but also a way of developing accountability. As Peter Garrett noted, Dialogue provides a forum to think through together the consequences of our collective actions and to shift our expectations of one another. It was time to move the Department from learning and talking about the skills into using the skills. This meant using the skills for better communication and quality interactions, and even more so to further the mission of the agency. It was especially incumbent upon the leaders in the Department to establish initiatives that serve a purpose and for employees to understand that purpose.

Thus, the idea of *"Serving the Commonwealth of Virginia"* was created. Dialogue Associates designed a poster which captured the essence of all of the activities of the Department and placed each of them into one of four categories. Every activity or decision of the Department should support at least one of these categories: Fiscal accountability, Operational accountability (incarceration), Community accountability (re-entry and probation), and Moral accountability (doing the right thing as well as the things that help individuals become better citizens). Over time and with new research and knowledge, the actual activities or initiatives may and should change, but the overall goal of reducing recidivism remains the same under the umbrella of serving the Commonwealth (Virginia is called a Commonwealth instead of a State as a largely symbolic term).

Just as it was important for employees to understand not only what they were expected to do but also why, it was also important for leaders to be accountable in how they lead. A good manager manages things and processes and meets the set requirements. A good leader leads people by the way he or she talks to and guides them to determine the way forward while accomplishing the tasks required. The VADOC had excellent managers. They had worked hard to develop safe and secure facilities. There was a very clear command-and-control

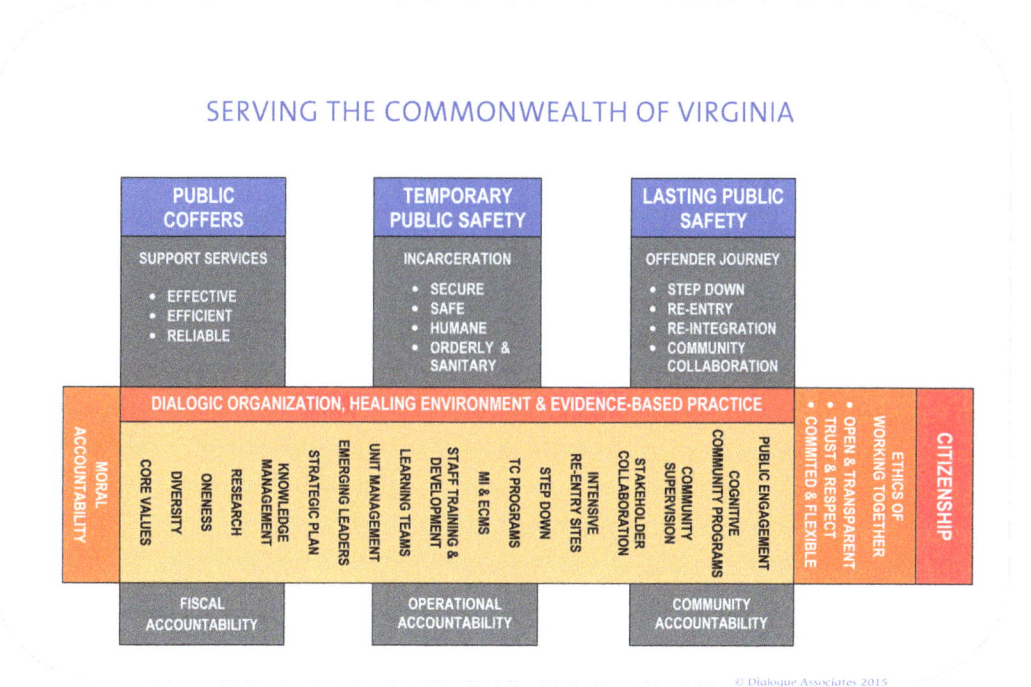

SERVING THE COMMONWEALTH OF VIRGINIA

PUBLIC COFFERS	TEMPORARY PUBLIC SAFETY	LASTING PUBLIC SAFETY
SUPPORT SERVICES	INCARCERATION	OFFENDER JOURNEY
• EFFECTIVE • EFFICIENT • RELIABLE	• SECURE • SAFE • HUMANE • ORDERLY & SANITARY	• STEP DOWN • RE-ENTRY • RE-INTEGRATION • COMMUNITY COLLABORATION

DIALOGIC ORGANIZATION, HEALING ENVIRONMENT & EVIDENCE-BASED PRACTICE

Left vertical band: **MORAL ACCOUNTABILITY** — CORE VALUES, DIVERSITY, ONENESS, RESEARCH, KNOWLEDGE MANAGEMENT, EMERGING LEADERS, STRATEGIC PLAN, UNIT MANAGEMENT, LEARNING TEAMS, STAFF TRAINING & DEVELOPMENT, MI & ECMS, TC PROGRAMS, STEP DOWN, INTENSIVE RE-ENTRY SITES, STAKEHOLDER COLLABORATION, COMMUNITY SUPERVISION, COGNITIVE COMMUNITY PROGRAMS, PUBLIC ENGAGEMENT

Right vertical band: **CITIZENSHIP** — ETHICS OF WORKING TOGETHER, OPEN & TRANSPARENT, TRUST & RESPECT, COMMITTED & FLEXIBLE

FISCAL ACCOUNTABILITY	OPERATIONAL ACCOUNTABILITY	COMMUNITY ACCOUNTABILITY

© Dialogue Associates 2015

structure in place. Yet even before Harold Clarke came to the Department, there was movement in developing the culture to be even better. It was certain that the leaders of the future would need to evolve. The next phase of Dialogue helped shape those nebulous ideas into structured, easy-to-understand principles. The Dialogue Coaching Training brought the concepts of Dialogue, accountability, coaching and leadership needs together in a seven-hour training. The idea of Dialogue and accountability was based on the premise that proactive support and challenge was more effective in shaping behavior than reactive disciplinary action.

The structure incorporates four levels of accountability actions: Dialogue, Coach, Hold to Account, and Discipline. The aim was for Unit Heads and supervisors to start building the foundation of the communication with Dialogue in their Units. Dialogue would be the mode for co-creating and taking ownership for ideas together, and for engaging with, supporting and challenging the day-to-day with each other. However, the coaching does not stop there. Supervisors needed to take the time to individually coach employees to improve their performance and support their individual development. Coaching is a matter of both support and challenge for actions, behaviors, and impacts. Even with coaching, sometimes people make mistakes, take shortcuts, or disobey directions and the supervisor has to respond. Even so, when the supervisor approaches the situation and engages the employee in a skillful conversation while using the Dialogue skills (e.g., listening with the intent to understand and respecting the person's perspective, keeping an open mind, authentically voicing their expectations), the result is more likely to be favorable. And finally, discipline may be necessary when certain policies or laws are violated.

The Dialogue Practitioners were trained in the principles of coaching and then sent to facilitate the Dialogue Coaching Training with the management teams of each Unit as well as the Executive Team and the supervisors at headquarters. During the Dialogue Coaching Training, the supervisors had the opportunity to practice the skills of coaching an employee and holding an employee to account by doing role plays in groups of four. The groups consisted of one person playing the role of being the supervisor, one playing the role of the employee, one person supporting the supervisor and coaching him or her if her or she became stuck or veered off track, and the fourth as the bystander, providing observations of the entire role play at the end. Each training included several Dialogue Practitioners so that each small group could also have a Dialogue Practitioner sitting in. The Dialogue Practitioner for each group served as a facilitator keeping everyone in role, coaching and bystanding.

During every training session, inevitably there would be supervisors, oftentimes many, who would express dismay at the thought of doing role plays. Many were reluctant participants. However, afterwards participants offered overwhelmingly positive feedback and support for that aspect of the training. The supervisors were excited to learn and practice strategies to effectively support, encourage, and hold their employees accountable. Many participants even had "light bulb" moments when they realized their role in the problematic behavior, either through lack of coaching, unclear expectations, or other reasons. One sergeant expressed his epiphany as "I realize that I am contributing to the problem of our turnover. I do not get involved individually with the new hires. I tell them what they need to know and then I wait to see what they're going to do. I do not make any investment in them until I know they're going to stay. Now I see that I need to make an investment in them and that is what may help them transition better and remain employed with us. I am going to work on coaching someone every day."

Another aspect of the Dialogue Coaching Training that helped the supervisors to think differently about coaching was the introduction of the Leading Energies. The Leading Energies give purposeful and productive direction to the coaching conversations. All of the Leading Energies are necessary for a successful outcome. Dialogue Associates defined the four Leading Energies as Visionary Energy, Performance Energy, Citizen Energy, and Wisdom Energy, and each has a distinct purpose. The Visionary Energy is thinking about the future. It is dreaming about what the future could hold and being able to see the big picture. Coaching with Visionary Energy asks questions such as "Where do you see yourself a year from now?" or "How do you envision your department?" Performance Energy is about getting the work done as expected. Performance Energy wants the numbers, data, and results. The positive use of the Performance Energy in coaching is setting targets and deadlines, checking in with the employee on the status of their progress or showing them how to track the data.

It only takes Visionary and Performance Energy to accomplish a task; set the direction (Visionary) and get it done (Performance). However, the other two Energies bring quality to the work. Citizen Energy involves being interested in the people, getting them participating, and making sure the right people are in the right positions, Citizen Energy coaching acknowledges the contributions of others, and provides them with the training or support needed for their success. Wisdom Energy brings perspective and reflection, as well as awareness, organization, and balance. The Wisdom Energy coach lives by the motto "Work smarter, not harder."

The VADOC, as many organizations, had a tendency to overuse Performance Energy and underutilize the other Energies. There were many things to get accomplished and many priorities. Therefore, the majority of the supervisors tended to fall into Performance-based coaching. It was all about the numbers and meeting target expectations. With that being the case, when an individual wasn't performing up to expectation, the supervisor naturally fell into reinforcing the targets and deadlines and using disciplinary actions if they were not met. The progression of the disciplinary process often consisted of a warning, a write-up, and then a disciplinary action. Supervisors who didn't want to be overly punitive sometimes went too far in the other direction and made several verbal warnings but did not offer any other consequence or coaching. The structured nature of the coaching practice using the Leading Energies within the Dialogue Coaching Training offered supervisors new ways of thinking about interacting with their employees and approaching issues. Using the Dialogue skills also helped them think about what was behind the behavior. Was it a training issue? Did the person need more support and guidance? Did the person not understand the importance of the task in the big picture? Did the supervisor need to set the expectations more clearly and follow up? It was clear after the trainings that the majority of the supervisors began to think about their roles and approaches to coaching in a different manner.

The goal of teaching the Dialogue Practitioners about coaching was to help them as trainers and leaders become proactive and to help the leadership in the Department learn to be more proactive as well. The Dialogue Coaching Training was specifically designed to reinforce how supervisors talk to, engage with, support, and train employees to attract and retain quality people to accomplish the mission. Additionally, through coaching, employees are better able to make good decisions on their own and bring creativity and innovation to the workplace by sharing their ideas. These important qualities are not prominent in a command-and-control culture. The VADOC is seeing gains from becoming a coaching culture. Employees are being recognized for establishing innovative programs and practices. The Dialogue Coaching Training became a standard day of the Basic Skills for New Supervisors Training and remains so to this day.

Dialogue in Action

Most of the employees of the VADOC either embraced or accepted the use of the Dialogue skills as part of the way business is done in the Department. However, even though they were participating in Dialogues, there was a disconnect about how to obtain results from the Dialogues. People were not putting the ideas and information into practice. Some were becoming frustrated with the Dialogues, claiming that they were "all talk"; some made statements such as "They are good for hearing all of the voices, but they don't get any real work done." It was clear that people would need more guidance in conducting Dialogues that were meant to solve problems and make decisions. Thus, Peter Garrett and Jane Ball designed the Working Dialogue with input from a small but diverse working group. The Working Dialogue is a structured method that uses the skills within a Dialogue to explore opportunities, enhance processes, solve problems, or make decisions by including those affected by the change.

The Unit Head conducts the set-up with the Dialogue Practitioner who will be facilitating the Working Dialogue. They review the purpose and focus, who should be invited and the event details. Then they send out invitations to the participants. The actual Working Dialogue consists of three phases including a) current situation, b) desired outcome, and c) changes required to get from the current situation to the desired outcome. The current situation highlights what is presently happening regarding the situation. All of the participants share their thoughts and the DP facilitator notes them on a flip chart. By the end of the session, the DP will summarize the points reflecting the common understanding of the group. At the end of the session, there is a "gate" before moving to the desired outcome. The gate consists of questions to make sure all considerations have been made before progressing. The questions include 1) Has anyone been left out? 2) Have we heard everyone's perspective? and 3) Do we have an agreed understanding? Each participant answers the questions on a scale from one to ten, giving the facilitator an opportunity to examine the issues further and possibly reconvene if key voices are missing or if there are scores below an eight. Alternately, they know they are clear to move forward if there is no issue.

The second phase of the Working Dialogue, the desired outcome, has the goal of thinking about new ways of working together to benefit the Department. The participants generate ideas of what they'd like to see happen or how things could ideally become. They tangibly describe what it would be like. The end of the session is then also closed by another set of gate questions. The third phase consists of looking at the changes required. The participants brainstorm as many different options as they can think of to achieve the desired outcome. Then they examine the risks and benefits of the options and make their selection. Once they have made their selections, they create an action plan detailing who in the room is responsible for doing what and by when. The session ends with another set of gate questions. The final aspect of the Working Dialogue is for the Unit Head and the DP to meet again to complete the follow-through by reviewing the process and the action plan to determine its effectiveness.

The response to the Working Dialogue was predominantly positive. As previously mentioned, a sizeable number of the employees of the VADOC are structured, performance-oriented individuals. Therefore, the structure of the Working Dialogue and the action plan, generated to monitor performance, fit with their personalities. They were able to see the tangible results of the Dialogue and felt a sense of accomplishment versus when they felt they were "wasting time" sitting in a regular Dialogue. All of the Units were charged with having at least two Working Dialogues going every quarter. This mandate was met with displeasure. Unit Heads who supported the process felt resentment at being forced to use it. It required the use of Visionary Energy to get them on board. They had to understand the big picture that new habits require practice to become ingrained. Any new process that isn't reinforced will be lost.

It was also pointed out that the Dialogue Coaching Training was provided to the Management teams. Then the Management Teams were expected to take it back to their middle managers and first-line supervisors. Because it wasn't required, only a few of the Units actually exposed all of their supervisors to the concepts. Then it had to be incorporated in the middle managers' and supervisors' annual training for a year to make sure that every supervisor had been introduced to the concepts. Furthermore, Management Teams did not use or reinforce the coaching and Leading Energy concepts amongst themselves and thus forgot some of the skills. Most Unit Heads accepted the rationale and attempted to use the Working Dialogue as a standard practice as much, if not more than, what was required.

At this time, Wisdom Energy has guided the Units in that they understand the Working Dialogue and it has become a business practice within the Department. They use it as needed and as appropriate. Several Units, especially Probation and Parole, are even using the Working Dialogue to address issues with external stakeholders and partners. However, this is not limited to Probation. Even institutions have used Working Dialogues with external agencies to accomplish joint ventures and goals. For example, one facility used a Working Dialogue with the Department of Transportation to plan how to use the offender roadcrew workforce in conjunction with the work to be done by the Department of Transportation. The results of the Working Dialogues have demonstrated a commitment by the staff for continuous improvement. People want to fulfill the mission of the Department and want their work to be meaningful. The future direction includes gathering the results of the Working Dialogues to share in a forum so that others can benefit by hearing ideas and information shared in other Unit Working Dialogues.

One of the most powerful interventions to affect systemic change is the Offender Resettlement Journey (ORJ). The experience an offender has from the time of arrest, through incarceration, then probation and until they are no longer supervised and out living as a productive citizen is their journey. To be resettled means to be successfully living in the community, free of involvement in the Criminal Justice System. A key event of the ORJ is to have one or more offenders recount their own personal journey in front of an audience of staff members, external stakeholders and partners and family members. They symbolically walk through their journey while answering questions from a facilitator. The DP facilitator asks questions about their experience, their emotions, and what helped or hindered them along the way. In this way, the audience connects to the person as a human being with feelings and an inside perspective. The audience gains insight into the pivotal moments, experiences, and conversations that impacted these peoples' lives and how they can work better for the people who are still under their care or supervision.

Dialogue Associates partnered with the National Institute of Corrections to pilot three ORJs in 2014. Those events focused on a) specific aspects of re-entry issues from a high-security prison as well as re-entry issues for offenders who were difficult to program, as they were moved around institutions because of their misbehavior; b) offender re-entry into probation to eventual successful community living; and c) intake issues for offenders when they first enter into the VADOC. All of them were considered to be successful even though success was measured in different ways for each. What made them successful was that staff members and community stakeholders heard the stories and thought differently about their systems and what was working and what was not. They created lasting changes as a result of the events. For example, in one community, they restarted a Council comprised of various community stakeholders including VADOC, local law enforcement, Department of Social Services, Community Mental Health Treatment, and more to collectively address offender re-entry issues and work together on the most difficult cases requiring multiple points of intervention. In one of the institutions they realized that a lot of time was spent sending the personal property of the new intakes back to their homes. However, if they could communicate that to the jails before they brought the offenders, then the offenders could give the property directly to their families before leaving the jail and heading to prison.

In January 2018, Dialogue Associates returned to conduct four more ORJs with a focus on intensive re-entry and examining the slice of the offender journey between the last year of incarceration, which focuses almost exclusively on re-entry programming, and the first year of probation, which focuses on getting the offender settled into the community. Since the regions of Virginia are quite different from each other, sites were selected to represent those geographical areas as well as a women's prison which serves offenders from across the Commonwealth. At the conclusion of each of those ORJs, the participants were placed into small groups to reflect upon the stories and generate topics or issues to be explored in more depth. Out of those groups, nearly 20 topics were brought up that needed to be examined. An ORJ Steering Committee determined that seven of those topics were universally applicable and should be examined from a statewide perspective. Working Dialogues were convened on the local level to address the site-specific topics. Working Dialogues also were convened with participants from across the Department for the seven universal topics. And as momentum works, those Working Dialogues prompted more issues to be addressed and more Working Dialogues, which are currently ongoing. For example, after a group discussed the need for enhanced peer support, increasing the use of external mental health peer supporters became a topic for a Working Dialogue. As a result of that Working Dialogue it was noted that peer support for substance abuse treatment is not substantially different from mental health peer support. Peer support is now recognized as a certified profession in Virginia. Therefore, a new group is working on developing the peer support requirements for certification of our offenders so they can have marketable skills upon discharge. This is just one example of the material benefits of the ORJ. There are many more tangible outcomes that improve the lives of the people under our custody and supervision.

Reaping the Benefits

There has been no other initiative that has penetrated through this organization at all levels as Dialogue has. Dialogue has taken root within the VADOC and has influenced every employee from every department as a true business practice that supports every other initiative. Dialogue has purpose and meaning for each employee, and has truly created an environment that encourages and enables each and every worker to know their role in working towards the mission.

Life in the Department has changed for all levels of employees. Everyone is encouraged to share their voice. Ideas and programs have been implemented because an employee – who may have previously kept quiet – was able to share their thoughts openly. Skillful conversations and Dialogues are happening at all levels, with people trying to gain common understanding and goals. By communicating more regularly and using Dialogue skills, people are more connected and willing to work together to resolve issues. There is a greater feeling of "oneness" that we are all in this together and have a shared vision towards which we are working.

Working Dialogues are happening every day across the VADOC to continually improve processes and procedures. The Department continues to be recognized as an outstanding leader and innovator in many different areas, including the response to the Prison Rape Elimination Act, reduced use of restrictive housing, Step-down (an incentive-based program for high-security inmates to progress within the system) and re-entry programming at maximum security prisons, Effective Practices in Community Supervision, Opioid addiction treatment, developing recycling centers (which have financially benefited the Department as well as produced marketable skills for offenders), focused mental health treatment while incarcerated and while on probation, and more.

All of the initiatives of the VADOC, beginning with the Healing Environment as the milieu and Dialogue as the mechanism, come together in service of the mission. The lead-in to the Strategic Plan quotes Director Harold Clarke: "We are in the business of helping people to be better." That is the mission condensed into one easy-to-understand sentence. And the Department must be doing something right. For the second year in a row, the VADOC has led the United States with the lowest recidivism level in the Nation at 22.4%, and it continues to decline. Other state agencies, Departments of Corrections from other states, and even other nations are looking to Virginia for guidance. The Secretary of Public Safety and Homeland Security for Virginia, Brian Moran, stated:

In 2011, under the leadership of Director Harold W. Clarke, the Virginia Department of Corrections initiated a multiyear transformation and has since undergone a wholesale culture change. The department consistently seeks opportunities to enhance existing practices. Now, other states and countries visit regularly to observe our practices and to understand how we have achieved success. The State Department has even partnered with the Virginia Department of Corrections to train other countries' correctional leaders . . . Clarke has created a healing environment within the Virginia Department of Corrections by instilling a culture in staff and offenders alike that motivates them to create and foster positive and progressive changes. He operates from the principle that how we treat and engage offenders on the inside affects our communities on the outside; it affects the victims and their families, families of offenders and the men and women in our care, 92 percent of whom will one day be our neighbors.

– Brian J. Moran, *Bristol Herald Courier*
via AP, June 15, 2018

However, as compelling as the story is from the Director, his supervisor and his employees, the most powerful testimony comes from the offenders under our care and supervision. A former offender who participated in the ORJs has formed his own business to help other formerly incarcerated individuals. He wrote an editorial to the paper about how the VADOC changed his life, excerpted below.

> *When I first arrived at DOC [Department of Corrections], I had no idea if I would make it out alive. With "life" hanging over my head, my incarceration started filled with darkness, despair, and hopelessness. This was during a time when the governor and director of DOC seemed to care nothing about our rehabilitation or our well-being, and there was no real access to programs.*
>
> *Then in 2012, Gov. Bob McDonnell appointed Harold Clarke as the director of the DOC, and Director Clarke changed everything about my experience in the DOC. From that point, he emphasized that re-entry begins on day one and began implementing programs to help inmates to think differently and acquire employable skills.*
>
> *I could immediately feel Mr. Clarke's presence throughout the system, especially in the re-entry department. Even if an offender had not accomplished anything during his or her entire incarceration, there was now a director who said, "I'm still going to give them an opportunity to succeed in their last six to 12 months, and have a chance to make it in society."*
>
> *The re-entry program also helped inmates get D.M.V. identification cards, which can be difficult to obtain. This made renting an apartment or applying for jobs possible upon release. These seemingly simple tasks can be huge barriers for incarcerated people.*
>
> *While incarcerated, I co-facilitated multiple treatment programs in re-entry, such as Thinking for a Change, Victim's Impact, and numerous other programs. I can relay countless stories of success by the men who participated, including me. When I was released from prison, I felt over-qualified to re-join society. I was armed with pro-social concepts and definitions, and the tools necessary to succeed.*
>
> – Paul Taylor, "Preparing for Life after Prison in Virginia,"
> *Richmond Times Dispatch*, June 2, 2018

Vision of the Future

The VADOC journey with Dialogue continues. To review up to this point, Dialogue Skills Trainings are conducted for new employees and Dialogue Coaching Trainings are conducted in every new supervisor's class. Dialogues are conducted on the different shifts to hear the voices of the correctional officers, during annual in-service trainings to have input from front-line officers, first-line supervisors, and middle managers, at monthly Unit Heads' meetings for leadership to think and grow together, and across the Units. Dialogues have been conducted with visitors to better understand their concerns. Working Dialogues have become a business practice and are conducted internally as well as with external stakeholders.

The skills have become part of the culture. There is still room for improvement in the culture change from command and control to direction and support as well as moving decision-making to the lowest possible level and making sure that all of the voices of the people who will be impacted by decisions are represented in the process.

Two developments currently in process include bringing offenders preparing for release (known as Returning Citizens) into the Dialogue fold and equipping them with the skills and knowledge of Dialogue in the final two years before their release. They will learn how to have more productive communication and better engagement. Over time, the skills could be introduced to the other offenders and even at intake so that they can have positive, quality conversations from the start. There are already instances of offender engagement in Dialogues with staff members, and teaching them the skills will only enhance those Dialogues. There is even potential for the "Elders" (higher functioning offenders charged with responsibility of encouraging, engaging, and guiding other offenders in the therapeutic program) to become Dialogue Practitioner trainers and coaches.

The other development is the evolution of the ORJ. The ORJ has been revised to reflect the goals of the VADOC. Now known as the Reentry, Reintegration and Reflection Experience (R3E), the enhanced purpose is discovering from the experiences, thoughts, and feelings of participants to reflect upon and learn current practices with the intent of gaining insight and understanding that will drive action for change, new areas of development, and overall improvement. The Department will continue to learn from the intensely personal experiences of the individuals under our care and supervision, and will delve deeper into areas in need of improvement.

References

Garrett, P. (2013). "What is Dialogue?" *Around Corrections*, publication of Virginia Department of Corrections. Vol. 1, Issue 3, retrieved from http://www.prisondialogue.org/files/files/What%20is%20Dialogue%20by%20Peter%20Garrett.pdf.

Innes, C. (2015). *Healing Corrections: The Future of Imprisonment*. Boston: Northeastern University Press.

Isaacs, W. (1999). *Dialogue and the Art of Thinking Together: A Pioneering Approach to Communicating in Business and in Life*. New York: Currency/Doubleday.

Conference Session Extracts

From conversation with 20 participants considering the paper with the author

I like that sentence: dialogue not just as a skill but as an attitude, which is what we're really trying to convey. When we say *dialogue*, we're not always thinking about the circle. For us, dialogue means the way you talk, interact, and engage with people on a daily basis.

We talked about what a dialogic prison looks like. Every prison is somewhat dialogic, but some, of course, are more than others. For example, the warden of one of our prisons asked to become a dialogue practitioner, and she says, "Command and control has its place, but we don't need it as often as we might have had it." So she has meetings with her management team and they have a voice in most of their decisions. And different line officers get to take turns coming to the management meetings. In their facility, it feels different when you go there. The morale trickles down, how they treat the offenders, how they think about them as returning citizens.

I think it is very different in Virginia where it's a clear decision-making business practice. So it's integrated.

So why do you think it has worked in Virginia? What do you think are the ingredients or the magic ingredient – because there can't be any other example in the world of an organization with 13,000 employees that has embraced dialogue, anything like the same extent.

Okay. So the magic is having a leader who has that vision and who has that insight to stick with it, bringing in the level of expertise that he brought in and that he was willing to spend to do that, to have those experts come in and then having just the first level, like the first 24 of us just having – just a small committed group to start with. We couldn't have done it without Harold Clarke.

I'd also like to mention Dave Robinson who is Harold's Deputy Chief of Operations. He was born in the department, literally born in the department, because his dad was a regional director or so at the time he was born.

So the Director has that strong visionary energy. But his Deputy, Mr. Robinson, has a strong performance energy of getting it done, the person who's going to make sure things happen. And so you put those together, and there's going to be momentum.

For me, the most important thing is that dialogue is an attitude. Really, it is. It is how I am, every day, in whatever I do. Yes.

First, you show up, then you're realizing yourself, then you're occupying the ground and you're doing it. And then at the next level, you're sort of affecting the field. This year I was occupying the ground. I sort of said, "Okay. I'm ready to take the reins and take the lead. Director Clarke, really, has pushed me to say – Peter and Jane have other things they have to do. The world needs dialogue [laughter], right? The world beyond Virginia needs dialogue, and he's thinking about what his next phase of life is in terms of dialogue, maybe national corrections, whatever he's going to do next. So thank you for supporting me. My step up to the leadership. [laughter] [applause]

Postscript

Susan Williams' reflections written some months after the conference

The response to our paper, "Dialogue and a Healing Environment in the Virginia Department of Corrections," was tremendous. The energy and enthusiasm that surrounded me at the Conference provided fertile ground to think through new ideas and ways to continue to shape our dialogic journey in the VADOC.

The most important theme that has emerged in my mind is about Dialogue not just as a set of skills, but as an attitude, a way of being. Once our Dialogue Practitioners and Unit Heads grasp this concept, the culture will permanently shift. It will no longer be part of our overused terminology of "another tool in the tool bag." A tool in the tool bag suggests that it can be put away until it is needed. The Dialogic skills are always needed. We need to talk about them differently.

Another principle that emerged is Dialogue is not always about talking. Sometimes it is being still and thinking together and, in this case, thinking, "What is the well-being of the whole?" Many of us think about the skills as they relate to ourselves or others: Am I using the skills? Is he using the skills? We don't think about the Dialogic skills as they relate to the whole. What are we contributing? How are we contributing?

In Dialogue with other Conference attendees, I developed some thinking around measurement. My question was, How do we measure our progress? A response recommended that instead of strict numbers measurement, sit in small groups and discuss strengths and opportunities – what and how you've done and where you need to grow. I was reminded that in measurement, sometimes you hit the target, but miss the point.

The Dialogic intervention that has had the most impact on the heart has been the Offender Resettlement Journey (ORJ) as described by Jane Ball in her paper. The ORJ is certainly an opportunity to realize gaps and strengthen care and programming but, more profoundly, it is the opportunity to connect with individuals who have been incarcerated, and genuinely understand their experiences and feelings. Then supervision and support can come from a more authentic understanding. Like the quote . . . we are spiritual beings having a human experience.

These themes and principles will lay the foundation for the VADOC to strengthen and deepen our Dialogic culture. Additionally, there are some tasks going forward that will help spread our story and learning for others. They include, but are not limited to, Dialogues and Dialogue Skills with offenders; Dialogues with offenders and staff; connecting offenders to the community with dialogues; connecting state agencies with dialogues; and connecting external stakeholders and private companies with dialogues.

Fluxen Prison Dialogues in Norway

Trine-Line Biong and Christian Valentiner

Flux

Flux has been working with dialogue in Norwegian prisons since the autumn of 2015 and, prior to that, with the practical application of dialogue since 2009. The story, however, begins before that.

Henrik Tschudi met David Bohm at a private dialogue Weekend in Copenhagen in 1989 and, although attending the conference because of Bohm's reputation as a scientist, Henrik walked away deeply inspired about dialogue. A similar private dialogue weekend was arranged in Oslo by friends of his during the following year, at which time he and Peter Garrett would video-record several conversations with Bohm in Henrik's living room.

In 1993 Henrik founded the Flux Foundation, which had as its primary purpose supporting work towards a harmonic and meaningful world. Its key focus has always been on *consciousness, society, dialogue* and *science*. The foundation has supported many projects to promote scientific approaches to understanding the world, including cosmology conferences and various types of dialogue work.

In 1993 the Flux Foundation established a life-philosophy magazine which ended its cycle as a print publication with its 50th issue in 2008. *Flux Magazine* is carried forward in an electronic format. In 2003 a book publishing business was added, and since 2009 this has been an independent business, still carrying the Flux name.

Experiential Programmes

Trine-Line Biong, a trained actor, director and coach, joined as chief editor in the Flux Foundation in 1997. Initially, her main role was the publication of *Flux Magazine*, and subsequently the books that would come out under the Flux imprint.

In 2009 Trine-Line and Christian Valentiner, an experienced facilitator and organisational development consultant, decided to turn some of the subject matter on dialogue into experiential programmes. Over the course of the following years dozens of people have been trained as dialogue practitioners and facilitators under the Flux brand.

Flux Dialog

In 2017 a non-profit organisation, Flux Dialog, was established. Its primary purpose is to support society's development through dialogue. The organisation was created separate from the Flux Foundation and from Flux Publishing to enable applying for donations, government funds and grants from other foundations. From January 2018, the Prison Dialogue work in Norway has been carried out under Flux Dialog. The organisation is also developing other dialogue-based projects in Norway.

The Norwegian Prison System

Prison systems provide their own context for dialogue work, and correctional systems have great differences from country to country. Therefore we are choosing to describe some highlights of the Norwegian context, as it guides how we work and what we can achieve. With dialogue we are not attempting to change the correctional system, rather we wish to influence how one may work inside the given framework. We find that to be an approach that creates immediate impact.

The directive of the Norwegian prisons is "to ensure a proper execution of remand and prison sentences, with due regard to the security of all citizens and attempts to prevent recidivism by enabling the offenders, through their own initiatives, to change their criminal behaviour".

The correctional system also operates with what is called 'the principle of normality', meaning that the punishment is solely a restriction of the prisoner's freedom. Otherwise, they retain all other rights as citizens. Also, they will not serve under stricter conditions than necessary for security.

Progression through a sentence is aimed at re-entering society. Given that, rehabilitation is thought to be a significant part of a stay in prison. Our experience is that in recent years there has been a political trend of focusing more on security than rehabilitation. Prisoners with long sentences will often move through the system from high security to low security and occasionally via halfway houses towards their release.

Norway has a capacity of almost 3,900 cells in 43 prisons spread over 61 locations. Approximately two-thirds of these are high-security facilities. In 2016 the average number of prisoners was 3,850 (up 2.7% from 2015). The total number of prisoners throughout the year was 13,528 (up 6.1%). Less than one in five prisoners are female. An independent study published in 2010 showed that 20% of people who were released from prison reoffended within two years, one of the lowest recidivism rates in the world.

The longest prison sentence in Norway is 21 years, although the new Penal Code provides for a 30-year maximum sentence for crimes related to genocide, crimes against humanity or some other war crimes. The average sentence is around eight months. More than 60% of unconditional prison sentences are up to three months, and about 90% are less than a year.

There are almost no escapes from prison in Norway and over 99% of all prisoners on temporary leaves return on time.

Some 3,600 full-time equivalent staff are employed in the prison service. Prison staff in Norway is unarmed and about 40% are female officers. Prison officers in Norway go through a two-year education at the Staff Academy, where they receive full pay and are taught in various subjects like psychology, criminology, law, human rights and ethics.

Flux Dialog does not currently work with offenders with severe psychiatric diagnoses and young offenders, and only on rare occasions with prisoners in preventive detention.

This context allows us to operate in a system that is still highly focused on the individual's journey to freedom. Many programmes are offered by both central and local government organisations as well as NGOs, but none actually combine the *prisoners with staff* and none are focused on understanding where our patterns come from. So, in the context of a prison system allowing human growth, dialogue currently occupies a relatively unique position in the Norwegian setting.

Prison Dialogues in Norway

Flux was approached in early 2015 by Oslo Prison with an invitation to participate in a cultural offering to the prisoners. Although we thought that dialogue sessions would be an interesting approach, after several rounds of conversation with leadership, this idea did not manifest. Our initial contact person returned to her permanent position in Bergen and, a few months later, contacted us about the possibility of working in Bergen.

This led to a series of monthly, one-day dialogue sessions in the Bergen Prison from autumn 2015 to spring 2016, a total of seven full days. The sessions were offered to a group of prisoners in a drug rehabilitation programme as well as to staff and selected civilian visitors.

Trine-Line contacted Peter Garrett and Jane Ball after finding 'Prison Dialogue' on the Internet. This led to a highly appreciated collaboration in which Peter and Jane, through regular calls, would mentor Trine-Line and Christian, using their 20-plus years of experience in the UK and US prison systems.

Through his personal network Christian approached Bredtveit Women's Prison in Oslo in the spring of 2016, and the facility's leadership quickly became interested in the work that had been done in Bergen. That initiated a collaboration between Flux and the prison that is currently the main focus of our prison work.

Aims and objectives

The purpose of our programme is to contribute to the rehabilitation and integration of prisoners and reduce conflict between prisoners as well as between prisoners and staff.

The long-term desired effect of the programme would be a changed culture of collaboration in the prison, though still subject to the strictly regulated environment that it is. The

Prison Dialogue work seems to have a positive effect on how individual participants see each other, and others, as human beings, and this supports long-term rehabilitation.

Initially the project was intended to improve the language skills of prisoners, many of whom do not have large vocabularies. This was to take place through conversation, increased listening to the thoughts of others and, eventually, to oneself. By mirroring each other we see much more than our own reflection; we begin to notice how much alike we are as human beings. Through dialogue prisoners and staff also gain insight into essential life topics.

From 2018, The Norwegian Prison Dialogue project contributes to documenting the positive effects of training as well as the frequent practice of dialogue as a means of rehabilitation and improving communication skills. It also provides further development and verification of the methods and models we use for initiating and conducting dialogues. These current models are described further below.

The project also requires the onboarding and potential training and mentoring of new facilitators, bringing more dialogue ambassadors into the world.

Method

The method employed in the Prison Dialogue sessions since 2015 is built on the foundation from the Flux Dialog training programmes. During the sessions in Bergen Prison the method further developed from experience in the unique context the correctional system provides. Our approach is inspired by the works of David Bohm, William Isaacs, Linda Ellinor and Glenna Gerard, Marjorie Parker and David Kantor, and the experiences of Prison Dialogues in the UK.

The approach in a 'Fluxen session' (the prisoners' name for our dialogues), outlined in more detail below, is currently as follows:

- Introduction of facilitators and/or visitors
- Interactively building the dialogic framework
- Check-in with all participants
- Dialogue on one or more themes
- Meta-dialogue
- Check-out with all participants

Introductions

After the participants have gathered, the facilitators introduce themselves if there are new participants in the group. On several occasions an external participant has also been invited into the session to add perspective. This person is also asked to introduce themselves. The significance of the introduction is to create trust and familiarity with the people who are guiding the conversations and who are not part of the daily life of those who are prisoners or workers there.

We move on to defining *dialogue* and emphasise that the intention is better understanding and deeper meaning, not to reach conclusions or agreement. We also explore the common interpretation of dialogue as "a conversation between two people" – the opposite of *monologue*.

The Dialogic Framework

The foundation of the Fluxen sessions are what we call the 'dialogic framework'. These are described on two posters that sit permanently on the wall of the common rooms we use, and are therefore available to the participants at all times, and not just during sessions:

The first part of the framework is the *Dialogic Guidelines*. These are a set of ground-rule statements that we get participants to agree upon at the beginning of each session. They are:

1. **Everyone is equal** – To the extent practical in this setting, we allow our roles and status to be less prominent and meet in the dialogue as human beings.
2. **Dialogue is a conversation with a centre, not sides** – We contribute to the inquiry, not to any particular person in the circle. Repeated exchanges of opinions between two individuals in the circle cuts the effectiveness of the circle.
3. **We all have a part of the truth** – When we share these truths in dialogue we see a bigger picture.
4. **It is equally important to listen as it is to speak** – We include those who wish to sit and primarily listen.
5. **Nothing is wrong** – Do not judge what you want to say; say it and see how it moves the dialogue.
6. **Only one person speaks at a time** – Self-explanatory!
7. **Everything that happens in the dialogue stays in the dialogue** – We create trust by agreeing that we do not take 'quotes' out of the context from the dialogue to people who did not participate. We may talk about the themes in general and new understanding.

The Dialogic Framework

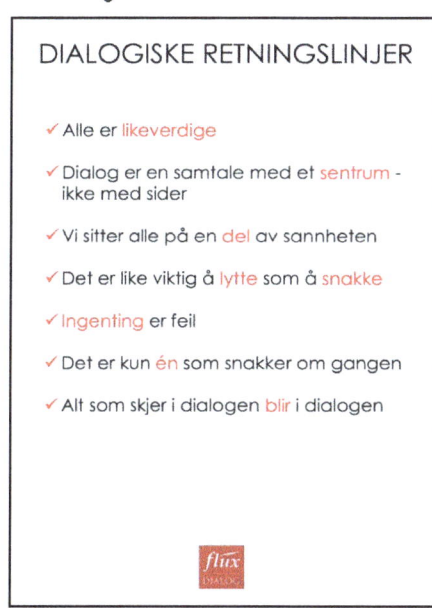

Dialogic guidelines (English in main text) 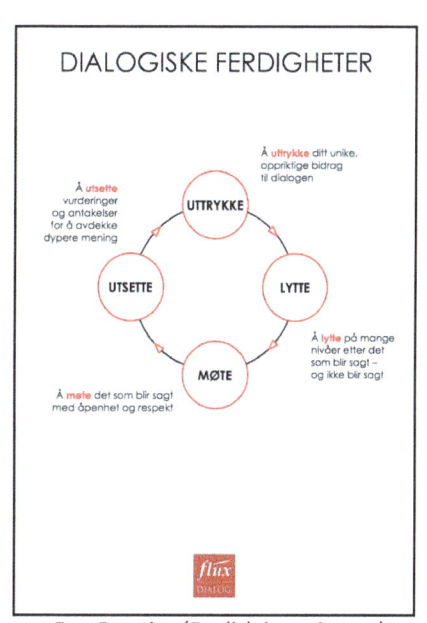 FourPractice (English in main text)

These seven guidelines are introduced by the facilitators on the first session and, given repeat participants, we start building it interactively and collectively going forward. That is, participants are invited to offer their interpretation of each of the guidelines, and the facilitators steer the conversation towards the shared understanding of the original intention of each of these.

Occasionally, mini-dialogues start out of this run-through of the guidelines. Usually, we do not allow them to be extensive, but sometimes some real learning is harvested at this early point.

The original purpose of the guidelines was to offer tools for facilitating a good conversation. They help the facilitators adjust the process during the dialogue sessions. In addition, we have noticed the bonus effect of repeating the guidelines at the outset of each session: the participants begin to see that these are applicable to many types of human interaction and conversations, and not only for the structured and facilitated dialogue sessions.

The second part of the framework is what we have called 'dialogic skills'. These are inspired by four Dialogic Practises:

- Listening
- Respecting
- Suspending
- Voicing

These are similarly introduced by facilitators and built interactively with the participants at the beginning of each session. They are primarily used to highlight learning moments of well-used skills (or Practices), and also manifest toward the end of each session in the meta-dialogue, described below. Occasionally, participants are invited to work on a skill of choice between sessions and we weave the learning into the introduction of the practices in the following session.

We often use the metaphor of a football game to describe the difference between 'guidelines' and 'skills': The former are the lines around the pitch; if they are crossed, the referee might blow the whistle (or throw down a flag, depending on your definition of football). These guidelines are non-negotiable unless we agree collectively to change them. Skills, however, are abilities for you can train and become increasingly better at, like kicking the ball far or running through defence. These skills can be practised and developed individually.

By upholding the discipline and investing time during each session to build the container, we create an ongoing embodiment of this framework in the participants, slowly enabling them to operate more intuitively in the sessions and possibly also outside.

Check-in

After establishing the dialogic framework, all participants are invited to check in. The purpose of the check-in is to activate all participants and get all voices present. It also marks the opening of the dialogic container.

The process consists of stating one's name and responding briefly to a question or theme introduced by the facilitators. We strive to keep the check-in theme appreciative as these dialogues often tend to circle into the darker side of life in prison and shut down those with a more positive mindset or get them to corroborate the negative. We therefore want to start the dialogues on a positive energetic note.

Some check-in questions and themes that have worked well are:

- "Talk about something good that has happened since last time" (this allows ample space to find something good even if one is feeling down in the moment)
- "How do you feel right now?" (can sometimes backfire if someone is very negative)
- "What is moving in you right now?" (is more open than the previous one, but can be too fluffy for some)

One benefit of the participants stating their name is that it establishes their individual identity in the circle. It also allows the facilitators to learn the names of participants, which builds intimacy and trust.

The check-in is usually started by one participant volunteering to speak first, and then going clockwise in the circle.

Dialogue

The theme for the main dialogue is invited from the participants. In many cases the facilitators bring a number of themes or questions that may be used, should the participants not find a useful topic. As facilitators we log topics that may arise in dialogues but are not followed through, and that may be useful later.

The facilitators will monitor the flow and energy of the dialogue and adjust accordingly, using either the guidelines or other facilitation techniques such as paraphrasing or asking questions. They may also add their own perspectives or inputs to the topics as a way of modelling the skills, or to facilitate the dialogue.

A dialogue session usually last about 90 minutes to two hours, with a short break.

Meta-Dialogue

After the dialogue the participants are invited to reflect upon the dialogue process itself – not the theme or where it took us content-wise, but rather how we used the guidelines and skills to improve the quality of the conversation.

We spend most of the time focusing on the skills, and how they can be further developed. We may even go through them one at a time and check with participants for reflections and observations. This is a low-threshold process debrief in which participants often gain new learning in their dialogic conversations skills or have deeper insights into their habits and patterns.

The information in the meta-dialogue is instant feedback to the facilitators, allowing adjustment of future sessions based on the experience of the participants.

Homework
Occasionally we will invite the participants to take on a piece of voluntary 'homework'. We then plan to debrief this in the following session. Oftentimes this is related to working with the dialogic skills. For example:

- In the next week, notice which of the skills you use most
- Before the next session, pick one skill you would like to work more on or improve

Our experiences with this have been varied. Often the participants may have forgotten by the time we leave the premises. Other times we have been surprised at what they have come back with in terms of new insight. One prisoner reported that she had suddenly noticed how she wasn't listening at all in the family context.

We plan on continuing this practice as we believe a lot of the transformation is created through a change of our behaviour. Even if you do not do the homework you commit to, just stating in a circle that you would like to work on the way you meet people (Respecting) has an impact on the individual as well as the circle. It also helps to anchor the dialogic framework.

Another interesting conversation may come out of debriefing homework: *Why is it that we 'forget' to do it or shy away from it?*

Check-out
Every session closes with an invitation for participants to check out. This is done in similar fashion to the check-in: participants state their names and respond to the question, "What do you take from this dialogue today?"

The information in the check-out is important for the facilitators to calibrate what themes and questions work to break the dialogue open, what parts of the framework that work and what needs to be emphasised in future sessions.

The check-out closes the dialogic container.

Examples of Dialogue at Work in the Prison Setting

Bergen Prison
The first dialogues at Bergen Prison were one- or two-day sessions with a group of men, largely from an addiction background and with long sentences. They were conducted in the autumn of 2015 and spring of 2016 for a total of seven full-day sessions. The work and learning from Bergen laid the foundational structures for effective dialogue in the work we are currently carrying out at Bredtveit Women's Prison.

The sessions in Bergen Prison provided an incredibly steep learning curve for being inside the correctional system and interacting face-to-face with prisoners, some of whom had very long sentences and severe addiction problems. We learnt that this requires good debrief techniques between facilitators in order to remain outside of the drama, quite similar to the guidance or counselling a professional therapist would seek out.

We also learnt how crucial the relationship is with the ambassadors of the prison staff. When you have sponsors, the navigation inside the walls become so much easier. In Bergen we were well anchored in our unit, but not with management. That provided some challenges when the unit decided to stop the sessions and try something else themselves. The prisoners wanted to continue with the dialogue. We know that Bergen Prison created a different dialogue forum at a later stage and are happy to have inspired that.

Process-wise, many things landed from our experience in Bergen. When we first started, we would introduce the dialogic framework at the beginning of a session, but only verbally. After we saw participants struggling to remember the core concepts, we started creating flip charts to illustrate the guidelines and skills. These later evolved into the posters mentioned above. As a pedagogical tool these work excellently, as any participant can step in and facilitate according to them, without having to memorise the materials.

Based on a comment from Peter Garrett's experience in UK prisons, we also found that bringing treats they would not normally get, such as fruits and biscuits – and particularly sweets – would attract people to the dialogue. As prisoner once told us, "I came for the sweets, but the dialogue was actually really good".

Participation in the Bergen dialogue circles was quite high and stable. This was related to the unit's drug rehab purpose, as about 70% of the participants were also part of an ongoing rehabilitation programme, and also because the ambassadors were active in recruiting prisoners and inviting staff.

One of the beautiful moments created in the Bergen Prison sessions shows how establishing these kinds of cross-group forums matters. It took place in a session to which a senior officer responsible for training officers, including summer temp replacements, was invited. In the dialogue he learned from the prisoners that the temps often work less effectively with the prisoners as they don't understand how the particular units work in their daily routines. This had for several summers created a lot of frustration and aggressive situations. One of the prisoners suggested that *they* train the temps, because they know how things work, as many of the prisoners had longer experience with the routines than even the permanent staff. Although this initially created some mirth, the senior officer took this seriously and later initiated a closer dialogue with the prisoners in advance of temp staff training.

Bredtveit Women's Prison

Since autumn of 2016 we have conducted biweekly, 2½ hour-sessions at the Bredtveit facility. Initially we worked on Ward Four, which is defined as a 'living unit' with less restriction of movement on the ward and more privileges for the prisoners. From the autumn of 2017 we expanded to covering two wards: Ward Four, as before, and also Ward Two, which has higher security. In total we have conducted almost 50 sessions on Wards Two and Four.

Earlier this year, the prison asked us to expand our work to their Open Ward B2 after several prisoners who had moved there talked about 'Fluxen'. This spring semester we have conducted ten sessions at B2, now biweekly after a weekly frequency initially. From autumn 2018, it looks like this will move to a weekly session on request by the prison.

Also, in 2018, we are conducting a pilot project funded by grants from the Scheibler Foundation and the Flux Foundation, both private funders. The pilot has the following activities as its work description:

- Conduct sessions in the three Wards and collect data to document the positive benefits of dialogue
- Train staff in the practice of dialogue as an introductory course to increase insight, lower scepticism and inspire use in other work processes in the prison
- Train and recruit facilitators to set the prison up for expansion to other prisons
- Follow-up on volunteer civilians who participate in the dialogues
- Develop a method for the dissemination of Prison Dialogues in Norway

Prisoner and Staff Participation

A significant feature of the Fluxen Dialog is that we invite both prisoners and staff to the sessions. This is key to our aim of creating a better understanding of each other as human beings and, in the long term, potentially improving the collaborative culture in Bredtveit Prison.

It is our experience that sessions in which staff participate – rather than those only with prisoners – are richer, more expansive and more rewarding to all participants. Of course, the more diversity in a dialogue the better, and staff and prisoners represent distinct polarities within the spectrum of the prison experience.

Sessions with prisoners alone tend to circle around in the group's thinking to the gloomy and negative side of prison life. Many prisoners feel victimised by the reality that they are convicted and imprisoned, rather than by the environmental factors that may have put them in crime's way. It is our observation from many sessions that the 'prison is shit' theme is a popular one between prisoners.

Sessions where at least one staff member participates offer more perspective. Occasionally, prisoners want answers or explanations from staff about (for example) conditions or decisions on the ward. We are careful to facilitate the dialogue with all participants having an equal voice, and the emphasis on participating as human beings and individuals. Although status or role are therefore less prominent, we still respect the authority and accountability of staff working within the prison.

That, of course, is challenging in a prison environment where the lines are so obvious, but we are succeeding with this direction of facilitation. Staff who are confronted with complicated prison issues in our sessions are invited to respond as an equal human being, as well as explaining their role where that is relevant.

The prisoners are very positive about the combined sessions, and often ask for more staff to participate. We see this as a sign of success that a forum has been created which allows a different type of communication between staff and prisoners.

Staff participation, unfortunately, is quite low. We hear many explanations, and are trying to address these with measures such as training. (See the *Staff and Management Training* section below.)

We have seen participation from senior management, vocational training staff, the prison vicar and several of her students, as well as prison officers and trainees. From the prisoners' perspective the real need is for the officers to participate, and they are also the staff group with the lowest participation rate. Increasing participation with this group would greatly increase the benefits from the programme, we believe.

The prisoners also appreciate management participation. We have seen positive effects, such as when one leader shared personal travel stories and was seen as more a human being than a uniform; they became a person and not a role. Another senior leader, through dialogue, was surprised by the impact that uniforms have on the prisoners – and arrived for the next session in civilian clothing!

Clergy participation always seems to flow well with the philosophy of dialogue, and the prison vicar and theology students have participated on several occasions, contributing beautifully to the sessions. The approach of the clergy is one of holding and seeing the human being without judgement and easing the journey through prison in their faith – and sometimes not, but just as a conversation partner. The formative education of clergy in Norway today appears to integrate well with our way of dialogue and with the nature of one-to-one conversations between prisoners and church representatives. The clergy participants intuitively understand the flow of Listening > Respecting (seeing the human being) > Suspending (not judging) > Voicing.

External Participants

By recommendation from Peter Garrett and Jane Ball from their positive experiences with Prison Dialogues in the UK, we began inviting external participants to the dialogue sessions in Bergen, and we have expanded and continued the practice in Bredtveit.

The purpose of inviting external 'civilians' is to add more diversity to the dialogue sessions as well as elements of normalcy not otherwise present in the circle of prisoners, staff and facilitators. It also builds a bridge between the prison system and society and helps break down the stigma that criminals typically carry.

These guests are people from our wider network who are interested in dialogue or societal development, those from other prisons or law enforcement, NGOs, potential facilitators – always good human beings!

The prisoners have generally responded positively to external participants as they bring the 'outside in'. Staff have occasionally wondered why these people were invited and how they have been selected. The prison holds a number of prisoners with significant sentences of public interest, and concerns have been raised by management of the real value to the sessions versus the risk of unnecessary exposure of the inmates (although confidentiality agreements have been signed).

The feedback from prisoners is that this external contact helps them stay 'normal' and counters the sense of isolation. They provide other impulses and variety and diversity to the dialogue, including new perspectives to prison issues. As one prisoner said, "It's good to be seen by a new face".

The external participants have, without exception, fed back that the sessions have been incredibly impactful on them. For most externals this would have been their first (and maybe only) visit to a prison or exposure to convicted criminals. The assumptions, judgements and stigma that society holds around convicted people are put into question when people actually meet other human beings in the dialogue. Apart from having been convicted for a felony, they are mothers, fathers, daughters, sons, lovers, lonely, skilled, etc., and from all walks of life.

Connecting the Inside and the Outside

Flux has for many years conducted dialogue circles where people can come and be in dialogue for two or three hours on various themes. During our work in Bergen we began a conversation between the Prison Dialogue group and one of our circles in Oslo, where they could send each other questions for inquiry through dialogue. This was continued with one ward at Bredtveit.

Some questions that were exchanged:

- What 'invisible' prison may you be in?
- What would you think about meeting a convicted person after he/she is released?
- Could you admit to yourself that you have done something wrong?

As a prisoner you have very limited contact with the world outside. Some questions you may want to ask are also difficult to share in a group of people that you serve time with and have not chosen to be in relationship with. It lowers the threshold to 'send it to others', yet it still lingers in the group subconsciously.

We found that this approach offered participants the opportunity to ask questions they may not have found the time, place or courage to do otherwise. Nor would most people have access to a group of prisoners – or ever visited a prison – and heard their unique perspectives.

We also found that most questions are universal. Although asked from a specific place, they enabled the inquiry to take many routes. Our experience is that prisoners require somewhat more facilitation to stay with the inquiry as they are attempting to 'answer' the question rather than explore it and discover why it may have been asked.

With every new session, the connected dialogue groups really looked forward to this exchange.

Staff and Management Training

In the autumn of 2018 we have been given the opportunity to conduct dialogue training sessions just for staff. This will allow us to provide some foundational learning for the method described above.

Our experience in Bredtveit has been that staff are much less likely to come to the sessions than prisoners. When staff do come, it is often management or educational personnel rather than the guards who have the daily interaction with the prisoners, even though the benefits of thinking together are thought to be highest with the guards.

There are several assumptions as to why the staff do not participate, or do not return to sessions after participating once. One is the myth that they will be criticised by prisoners for conditions in prison. Another is that they do not want to 'wring their souls' in front of the prisoners or share personal or vulnerable experiences. A third is that they do not have time.

By conducting staff training we intend to address the first two myths and build a strong understanding of and trust in the dialogue method, so that if the time challenge is real – which it sometimes is – they are more skilled in stepping in and out of session, rather than having to participate from beginning to end in order to learn the framework. We may also address their concerns in the learning groups before participating in sessions with prisoners.

In the dialogue training sessions only with staff we will be picking themes related to a recent organisational culture survey, which will give us a basis for talking about real-life issues for them. We are also making a pitch to train the two management teams at Bredtveit, so they can be role models, open to incorporating dialogue in their daily work. This is a longer-term process but the Chief Warden, the Deputy Warden and the Prison Inspector – First, Second and Third in their hierarchy – are all very positive towards this. Again, finding the time is an issue.

Both of these initiatives are supporting the aim of slowly changing the culture in Bredtveit Prison.

Challenges

Although the Bredtveit Prison wards where we work seem to respond well to dialogue, conducting such a programme is not without its challenges.

Language
Many prisoners are not of Norwegian origin, and quite a few have not lived in Norway long enough to get by, language-wise. This provides some challenges to the dialogue sessions, where

an eager participant may not be able to listen well or voice their perspectives. We always invite anyone to participate, but it seems that lack of language skill pushes many away. We have also translated into English, German and Spanish on occasion, but our experience is that this fragments the verbal aspect of the dialogue, and the translation conversely pushes away some Norwegians as it may appear tedious to them.

Time
Although a prison sentence according to the objectives of the Norwegian Correctional Services is the 'restriction of liberty' and one might assume that prisoners have a lot of time on their hands, we have found it surprisingly difficult to land 2½-hour time slots that do not collide with other activities in the prison.

With the aim of creating a communication forum including both prisoners and staff, the complexity further increases. When prisoners have time, it is often because staff members are otherwise engaged. We have gone several rounds on this with prison leadership, and although they encourage staff to participate in the sessions they, too, struggle to create the space for it. There is also the attitude/will part to this conundrum which we addressed above, and we are attempting to change this through training.

Impact
We have often wondered how we might measure the impact of Fluxen. After working for several years in the same system, we are sensing a change of attitude in a positive direction towards dialogue. It would be interesting going forward to learn from other practitioners how they measure both the short-term and long-term effects of ongoing dialogue practice and training.

Specific to the correctional system, we would like to understand if dialogue practice in prison has had an effect on prisoners once released: Do they communicate differently? Listen more? Suspend judgements? Is there a longer lead time before they end up in situations created by misunderstanding? Are they becoming more aware of thought patterns that no longer serve them?

Despite all these questions, we have logged a lot of feedback on the individual impact of dialogue on prisoners. They see that dialogue works, and can be used outside of prison too, e.g., in their romantic relationships. They see how many vantage points come out through dialogue. Also, they see that it may contribute to lowering conflict levels due to better understanding and more patience. As one prisoner put it, "We gain an insight into each other's daily lives. What if we used it every day? Talked about common problems?" They also notice after a while that taking up issues outside of the dialogue sessions is easier.

Learning
The funding that came into place at the beginning of 2018 led to more effort being put into a structured approach to project learning. We have chosen to follow an Action Research-inspired model.

Since the beginning of our work in Bredtveit Prison in 2016, we have kept detailed logs of each session, including themes, number of participants, challenges etc. From the beginning of 2018 we have also kept a learning log to help us evaluate and adjust the different approaches we are trying. Basically, we ask:

- What was needed?
- What did we do?
- What did we learn?
- What was wise?

This ongoing collection of learnings continuously develops our practice.

Themes

The topics, or themes and questions we explore in the dialogues, are essential to having fruitful sessions. Within prison we have found that these themes (in no particular order) are both recurring and impactful:

- Freedom
- Loss and grief
- Being misunderstood
- Respect
- Stress
- Prejudice and assumptions
- Being 'labelled'
- Resistance
- Hate
- Intimacy and love
- Relationships
- Attitudes
- Humanity
- Drug problems and rehab
- Isolation and loneliness
- Preparing for return to society
- Power and control

Facilitators

We always co-facilitate, working in pairs. Although it may seem resource-intensive, the benefits for the group and well as the facilitators are great. Particularly if we work with groups of over eight people, it works well having one facilitator hold the space (notice what is going on) while the other hosts the process.

In particular, if facilitation experience is limited then working with a co-facilitator will give you space to breathe and recover should you need to.

Facilitators are human beings, too! We are consciously making a point about this by showing our own humanity. This may happen when we mess up the walk-through of the framework, for example. We will point to it, laugh, and correct course. We will never try to be cool or all-knowing.

We will also participate in the dialogue with our own input to model the principle of equality in our guidelines. With larger groups that is rarely necessary, and the intervention will more likely be in the form of a question or summary than an opinion. Occasionally, and particularly in smaller groups, we as facilitators may be important contributors to the flow of the dialogue. Self-management is important in those cases, as we do want to be honest and authentic in our contributions, but do not want to manipulate.

Having worked in both men's and women's prisons, there are also different dynamics we have observed:

- In men's prison it seems prisoners are comfortable with both female and male facilitators, and although we have not tried an all-female facilitation pair in a men's facility we believe it would work fine here in Norway. The team we worked with in Bergen had two female officers leading a rehab programme and commanded great respect.
- In men's prison there seems to be more straight talk. Men tend to use fewer words but are powerful when they show up. When there are conflicts, they appear to be sorted with forceful communication, bordering on aggression. Conflicts that arise are short-lived. Facilitation requires an awareness of this and staying open if aggression seems to lurk.
- In women's prison it has been a benefit being a female-male pair of facilitators to balance out gender, and at least have one female representative. There seems to be a higher potential for maintaining distance with male facilitators, as many women's crimes are related to men. An all-female pair has also worked, but we have noticed that women prisoners also appreciate the presence of men, as they operate in a largely female setting around the clock. So, our recommendation would be to go with a female-male pair, or test it with the prison.
- In women's prison we notice tendencies to more drama and slander. There are more cliques and factions. Many things are not said in plenary sessions such as a dialogue but come out in little groups in private, creating a bad atmospheres and low level of trust. Interpersonal conflicts may go on for a long time. Facilitation requires an understanding of how the dialogues only address a snapshot of the current system.

Debriefing learning is another area where having two facilitators is very beneficial. Facilitating on your own, you are often very engaged in the process and may be missing what is going on in the bigger space. When there are two, the richness of observations from a session grows exponentially.

It is also useful to debrief what emotional impact the dialogue has had, as we occasionally hear some horrific stories. One intention of dialogue is to create impact, but carrying other people's emotions or trauma is not healthy. Co-facilitators have a role with each other normalising this. This could also be done as a faculty of facilitators, or through a Practitioner Circle in the Academy of Professional Dialogue. A debrief circle could cover more areas than criminal justice, e.g., people working with war or conflict dialogue, refugees, serious health issues – anywhere trauma is present.

Recommendations

Should you decide to offer dialogue to your own local prison or correctional system, we hope we have offered some insight into how we work through our methods and experiences above.

A few other pointers that may help you as it did us:

Get ambassadors – Find some people in the prison who are engaged in making things work. These could be staff doing training programmes, clergy or officers with rehabilitation responsibilities. That they have a positive attitude and work with prisoners is more important than their hierarchical status (at least in Norway).

Invite leadership – Mobilising senior staff to participate in the dialogues helps create an acceptance amongst staff. Also, prisoners are more positive towards participating than you may think. It is important that they are briefed so they understand that they do not necessarily represent their organisational role in the dialogue but are there as equal human beings.

Use the same method every time – We have seen the benefit of transparently using the dialogic framework every single time, also up to the point where we as facilitators find it nauseating! However, the discipline pays off when the participants start referring to elements from the framework themselves and that way help facilitate. Whatever method you use, make it visible.

Have good themes – We encourage the circle to select what they want to talk about, but often it is too superficial or irrelevant to the whole group. We log good themes that emerge in previous dialogues and keep them for future use. They are often relevant at a later stage. Good themes or questions are critical to a good dialogue. The participants will often conclude that 'dialogue does not work' when the real issue was 'The theme was not good'.

Train staff – Conducting introductory training sessions for staff only in the dialogic framework may lower the high threshold of them choosing to participate the first time. They get an understanding of the purpose, process and their role, so they feel confident going in.

Log your progress – We were encouraged early on by Peter Garrett and Jane Ball to log our experiences. We did some logging work in Bergen and created new structures with the commencement of the Bredtveit project. Currently we log both sessions and general learning as described above. This paper would not have been possible to write without our logs.

References

Bohm, D. (1996). *On Dialogue* (L. Nichol, Ed.). London: Routledge.

Ellinor, L. & Gerard, G. (1998). *Dialogue: Rediscover the Transforming Power of Conversation*. New York: John Wiley & Sons, Inc.

Hannevig, L. and Parker, M. (2012). *Dialog – en praktisk veiviser*. Oslo: Flux Forlag.

Isaacs, W. (1999). *Dialogue and the Art of Thinking Together: A Pioneering Approach to Communicating in Business and in Life*. New York: Currency/Doubleday.

Kantor, D. (2012). *Reading the Room*. Hoboken, New Jersey: John Wiley & Sons.

Flux website: www.flux.no

Prison Dialogue website: www.prisondialogue.org

Conference Session Extracts

From conversation with 20 participants considering the paper with the author

The thing I think that happens in a dialogue as opposed to other kinds of therapeutic approaches is that you actually become that person in the dialogue. I'm thinking of guys that I've known where listening is a real challenge. The first few times you meet them in the dialogue, they're completely incapable of listening. They talk over people. You realize that that inability to listen, and therefore understand people, and therefore empathise with other people, is part of the pattern of their offending.

So you transform that in the dialogue itself. You're not yet talking about their future story, but they are just transforming.

It kind of touches me what Jane said about the deep process of not being able to listen. And that process you were talking about. That's so empowering, the dialogue.

In the dialogue you don't just talk about things. You are in a living dynamic of how people behave. How they behave in the dialogue will reflect how they behave outside. So in the dialogue you look to transform the way people engage with each other so that continues when they leave the dialogue.

I just wanted to ask, is it possible to imagine a dialogical prison without addressing the question of power? Because there is so much power. There's the power – there's the structural power with the director and so on, or between inmates, so is it addressed right up front? Is it a topic of dialogue, the power, or how is it dealt with?

I'm curious about their relationship between shame and forgiveness. And is forgiveness a conditional thing? I depend on you to forgive me versus I forgive myself and in doing so I release some of the shame that I carry.

I'm thinking of my experience in the prison dialogue. It's exactly the place you want to explore those kind of issues about shame, and punishment, and what I think's going to help me personally. But you look to do it from first-hand experience. So what we're doing now is more theoretically, 'What's the relationship between shame and punishment?' But in the dialogue, you're looking for people to talk about their own shame, and their own experience of punishment and if it's made any difference to them. And in my practice one of the ways of achieving the equality is, as a facilitator, you can also do that.

So can I talk about times that I felt ashamed and when I've been punished for things. And what's the effect when I've tried to get away with things so I'm not punished and all of that behaviour. It's as much about allowing yourself to be a participant, a full participant, and that leads the equality and the common inquiry and understanding.

I am fully attentive to this engagement. I have a little bit of a different story. So sitting in dialogic circles such as this actually helps me heal as well. While I do work with offenders – I'm a probation and parole officer as well – my family has been directly impacted by a violent crime that – my uncle was murdered. And murdered by someone who was actually being supervised by my agency. So, for me, it's healing. And it's helpful. And this has been a good engagement.

Postscript

The author's reflections written some months after the conference

In the years of working in this field we have been quite disciplined in the way we have worked with establishing a good framework for dialogue in each session. The walk-through of the guidelines and practices could often take up to 30 minutes, something that was found tedious by 'seasoned' participants. Although we always intend to build this interactively, we don't always get the expected response from the group, and this section becomes a teaching rather than a conversation.

In recent sessions where a majority of participants have previous experience of Fluxen, we have allowed starting the dialogue without the walkthrough of the guidelines, but still make the group responsible for the joint facilitation of the session. This has created an easier flow into the subjects that matter more to the participants, and we are acutely aware of tying process-learning in the dialogue to the framework when learning moments arise. We also still debrief the process in the 'meta-dialogue' before checking out.

In addition, we have begun to assign roles to selected participants for a part of the dialogue, e.g., "you may only ask questions" or "you are only listening for assumptions or judgements – and call it when you hear them". The learning is debriefed, and this sharpens the focus on specific practices, giving the participants an experience rather than an abstract, conceptual teaching.

In our Dialogic Guidelines we have changed the sentence 'Nothing is wrong' to 'Nothing is wrong to say'. This is based on feedback from dialogues where both prisoners and staff have challenged this. The original intention of the guideline was to encourage people to speak without judging themselves, and that is captured in the new version.

The dialogue around the paper at the 2018 conference pointed to the importance of having both prisoners and staff participate. We are challenged having staff come and have only had some moderate success with getting access to train staff, even if the prison was offered this training for free and the pilot runs were very successful. The argument we hear over and over again is how difficult it is to free up time for the staff to participate both in the sessions and in training.

Flux Dialog has taken on new facilitators for prison dialogue work for 2019 as the sessions have increased to twice per week. Rather than training from scratch we have picked experienced people who have also done significant work with themselves.

The CEO of Hanover Insurance, Bill O'Brien, who after conducting and leading many processes of transformation and change summed up his own experience with the following words: *"The success of an intervention depends on the interior condition of the intervenor"*.

In prison we find that we need facilitators who have taken personal responsibility for their own 'interior condition'. Dialogue work is a healing journey for all participants, including the facilitators. However, the facilitators have a responsibility for creating and holding the right container for that work.

The Legacy and Potential of Dialogue in the Criminal Justice System

Mark Seneschall

I am writing this article as a Trustee of Prison Dialogue, a UK-based not-for-profit charity which seeks to promote the use of Dialogue in the Criminal Justice System, and especially in prisons. My route to arriving in this position was somewhat roundabout, as I am neither a Criminal Justice professional nor a Dialogue Practitioner. I encountered the concept of Dialogue in the course of my career in the oil business with British Petroleum as part of some work we were doing to strengthen team working across different departments and break down organisational silos. During this period I met Peter Garrett and Jane Ball and heard about some of the exciting Dialogue work they were doing in prisons. From a distance – and as a UK taxpayer – it seemed (and seems) to me that, at a purely pragmatic level, if a key part of the role of prison is to reduce the likelihood of those released re-offending again, then British prisons had plenty of scope for improvement.

Peter and Jane's work appeared to provide a means of intervening in some of the unhelpful dynamics in and around prisons, so that prisoners become better equipped to deal with the complexities and realities of their situations. This is particularly true of the challenges that surround relationships with other people, both whilst incarcerated and following their release. Equally, prison staff become better acquainted with and gain more understanding of the prisoners in their charge, seeing them as people as well as being prisoners. When this happens, prison staff treat prisoners in a way more conducive to helping them become law-abiding and contributing members of society after release. Nothing I have learned subsequently about the work and its impact has caused me to revise these views.

Despite this, the practical application of Dialogue in prisons and other parts of the Criminal Justice System remains confined to a small number of pockets where enlightened leaders have realised its potential and taken steps to apply it in situations where they are in a position to exert their authority. The challenge remains to convince prison authorities – and their political masters – of the critical role that Dialogue can play. This is to some extent our own fault since, whilst I am absolutely certain there is an important story to be told about Prison Dialogue work, those of us who have been involved with it have failed to tell it as powerfully as necessary. My aspiration in writing this article, and sharing some of the groundbreaking work and outcomes achieved over more than 30 years, is that it will prompt some interest from those responsible, and provide a fillip to the wider adoption of Dialogue in prison systems. I see this as a key mechanism in helping make prisons more successful institutions, and thereby contributing to a more effective Criminal Justice System, both in the UK and elsewhere.

With this in mind, I've written this article in two parts. The first is a brief history of Prison Dialogue, describing its evolution and providing a sense of how one piece of work led to another. The second consists of four case studies which describe in greater detail what seem to me to be the most important pieces of work with which the charity has been associated – a sort of 'Prison Dialogue Greatest Hits', providing a more in-depth analysis of what was done in each case, the challenges that had to be overcome, and the results achieved.

Prison Dialogue – A Short History

Prison Dialogue was established as a charity in 1995, with a view to extending the work commenced by Peter Garrett and various co-workers during the early 1990s at HMP (Her Majesty's Prison) Whitemoor, a maximum-security facility in Cambridgeshire. The prison was attracted to the idea of using Dialogue as a means of improving relationships and, in turn, the operation of the prison which was by definition highly fragmented. Peter's work had developed from a collaboration with David Bohm, the renowned physicist, who is generally acknowledged as the source of much of the early thinking about the critical role that Dialogue can play in overcoming the fragmentation of thought – thereby improving the way human beings make sense of what is happening around them. Peter sought to extend this into the application of Dialogue as a means of reducing fragmentation and conflict in practical situations. Following an introduction to a probation officer, it was agreed prisons provided an obvious context in which to pursue this. This resulted in the Whitemoor Dialogues, which ultimately ran for seven years. There was a consideration of the Dialogues being accredited by the Prison Service, but it was apparent that the independent facilitation was necessary for its success and Prison Dialogue was established to ensure the ethics and know-how of the process were not lost within the normal power structure in any prison.

The success of these Dialogues pointed to a wider application of the approach, and Prison Dialogue was the vehicle to promote this. The programme was extended to other prisons, starting with HMP Long Lartin in Worcestershire, and to what were called 'Community Dialogues' in the city of Cambridge. This was a partnership venture with Cambridgeshire Probation Service, involving ex-offenders still serving sentences but living outside the prison, meeting weekly with members of their local community with the objective of supporting their re-incorporation into normal society after leaving prison. This interim period is clearly one of considerable challenge and vulnerability for prisoners. The work was later furthered with the launch of the 'Threshold Dialogues', which commenced in Dorset in 2004, seeking to establish a collective Dialogue among a wide range of parties involved in the end-to-end process of offender resettlement. This included serving prisoners and those who had been released, prison staff, police, probation and housing personnel, and drug and alcohol rehabilitation groups, among others. The purpose of these Dialogues was to reduce the fragmentation among participants and organisations, thereby aiding the passage of released offenders across the prison 'threshold' and back into society.

Another theme that became apparent from these earlier Prison Dialogues was that Dialogue could address situations involving change and transition. The first example of this was again at Long Lartin, where – following the success of the ongoing Dialogue Programme at that prison – Dialogue was employed to support the opening of a new wing at the facility. The objective was to engage prisoners, staff and managers to ensure a trouble-free relocation, and to put in place a culture for the new unit which would be respectful, participatory and therapeutic. The intervention proved successful, with the relocation taking place without incident, and a constructive pattern of relationships between prisoners and staff being established. A subsequent activity involved the use of Dialogue to address performance problems in the Healthcare Unit at HMP Blakenhurst near Birmingham. This work in turn led to the application of Dialogue to help turn round a failing prison at HMP Dorchester, in Dorset, between 2003 and 2006.

These interventions had two distinctive features which were different from conventional change-management approaches. First was the active involvement in the change of all the different parties who would be impacted by it. This contrasts with the more typical approach, where the change is designed by managers who then attempt to impose it on the wider organisation – which then frequently attempts to resist it. In the Dialogue-based model of change, the change is designed by all parties (or at least representatives of all parties) who are affected by it, which often gives rise to superior and better-informed design, as well as readier acceptance. The second distinctive feature was the comprehensive nature of addressing fragmentation issues, which extended beyond the obvious one between prisoners and staff to other relationships. These included those between managers and staff, and between different managers and departments within the prison, which were often a major source of difficulty and ineffectiveness. Dialogue proved extremely valuable in both laying bare these internal relationship problems and in helping the participants address them.

This led to a series of interventions in a number of different prisons, many in the private sector, which at the time appeared more ready to engage with innovative operational improvement approaches than those in the public sector. These Dialogic interventions aimed at addressing particular problem areas or internal relationship challenges. Possibly the best example of this was the work undertaken by Dialogue Associates, an organisational Member of Prison Dialogue at HMP Birmingham for G4S (a private security firm) in support of the transition of the prison from public sector to private sector operation. This was a highly charged situation, with entrenched union opposition to the decision which the Government had taken to privatise the running of the prison, against the backdrop of a struggling prison characterised by poor relations between staff and the existing management. Aided by the extensive use of Dialogue and active engagement with all parties, the transition ultimately passed without incident – even though the union had initially stated their intention to call a national strike to resist the change, and the Government had developed plans to employ troops to staff prisons should such a strike take place.

Disappointingly, with resources becoming increasingly constrained in the UK prisons arena (including in the private sector), the work with G4S came to an end in 2014, although there remain pockets of high-quality local activity where those who were introduced to the concepts of Dialogue continue to make excellent use of it in their ongoing activities. Additionally, Prison Dialogue has also recently been offering bursaries to representatives from UK prisons to help them to participate in Dialogue training as a means of advancing the wider adoption of the approach.

At the same time, the focus of the Dialogue work being undertaken in prisons has shifted from the UK to the US. Work in the US had initially commenced in 1999, when Harold Clarke, then the Director of Corrections in Nebraska, met Peter Garrett at a conference convened by the Shell oil company, at which Peter had been speaking. Interested in Peter's experiences in UK prisons, he introduced his leadership team to Dialogue to help them manage some problematic relationships and move towards a less hierarchical way of operating. Subsequently, Director Clarke moved on to head up corrections departments in a number of other states (Washington, Massachusetts and, most recently, Virginia), and in each case sought to employ Dialogue as a key means of creating a more effective and humane way of operating.

This has taken its richest and most complete form in Virginia, where Dialogue sits at the core of Clarke's efforts to achieve 'Lasting Public Safety' within Virginia through the creation of a 'Healing Environment' across the entire Corrections Department, both for offenders who came into the Department's care and for the staff who looked after them in prisons and during probation.

The Lasting Public Safety programme focused on the need not only to protect society from those who offend against it by securely incarcerating them, but also to seek to ensure that once offenders were released – as 90 per cent of those imprisoned in Virginia are – they did not offend again. A Healing Environment envisaged prisons and corrections as institutions which supported constructive change for offenders and – critically – for the staff responsible for them. This environment would help staff manage issues and improve the quality of their workplace lives, in turn freeing them to provide more effective assistance to offenders. Implicit in the creation of the Healing Environment was the need to change the culture and behaviour of staff, so that they align with and support the successful rehabilitation of offenders.

Effecting these changes in a system comprised of 45 prisons housing about 30,000 inmates, and 43 probation districts responsible for about 60,000 people – and employs approximately 11,500 people – is a multi-year undertaking. Dialogue has been central to changing the way people individually interact and the relationships between the different subgroups within the system, breaking down the established 'command-and-control' culture and increasing individual autonomy and accountability, thereby providing a new model of effecting change. The transformation of the system continues, and its success to date is clearly demonstrated by the fact that Virginia has the lowest level of recidivism in the United States. As a result, other states are also beginning to explore the potential of Dialogue to help improve the quality of their own departments of corrections.

In 2013 Prison Dialogue celebrated its 20th Anniversary, with a day event in the Hotel du Vin in Oxford, that had been tastefully converted from its historic use as a local jail. All the records covering Peter and Jane's work over 20 years had been gathered in one place, for Peter and Jane, along with Liz Leigh and me, to write 41 Case Studies which we gave as a gift set to each of the participants. This paper, exploring the application of Dialogue in Criminal Justice, is based on Peter and Jane's records.

Case Studies
HMP Whitemoor Dialogues

This is an obvious case study to select, given that it was the first application of Dialogue in a prison setting, and paved the way for all subsequent work. It demonstrated the range of different benefits that Dialogue could provide, including:

- As therapy, it was a vehicle for enabling prisoners living in a confined and constrained environment to express themselves openly
- As a means of improving interrelationships, it created a space where people from different groups – even where there has been tension and conflict – can come together and start to build mutual understanding and respect
- As a vehicle for learning and education, it helped participants build new skills, notably in 'articulacy' (that is, the ability to express oneself and be understood) and social interaction, which better equipped them to succeed, both inside and outside prison

Context
The first-ever Dialogue Group started in a prison began in September of 1993 on the main wings of the Whitemoor high- and maximum-security facility in Cambridgeshire. Dave Parsons, a Probation Officer working in the prison, conceived of the group and based his proposal to prison management on the paper "Dialogue – A Proposal", co-authored by David Bohm, Peter Garrett and Don Factor. The idea was to bring together on a weekly basis a group of prisoners with a few prison officers, other prison staff and volunteers for open Dialogue. Peter Garrett was a volunteer from the first session onward and, when Dave Parsons left the prison nine months later, Peter continued to run the group as an external volunteer. The Dialogue Group proved extremely popular and ran weekly for the next seven years. Peter kept notes of every session, and it formed the basis for all future Dialogue work in prisons.

Aims and Objectives

Dave Parsons and Peter Garrett were both intrigued by the potential of Dialogue as a means of social integration. The prison culture was fragmented and dehumanised, commonly resulting in violation and violence. The Dialogue Group was seen as an opportunity to break down the barriers between different prisoner groupings, and between prisoners and staff. Prisoners were on long sentences (typically from 12 years to natural life), in single cells on a block that was full to capacity. The prison at that time was struggling to keep order and discipline, and suffered staff and prisoner assaults, hostage-takings, murders, minor rioting and an escape. The management accepted Probation's proposal to make use of Dialogue as an intervention without much understanding of what was being proposed.

Method: Activity, Participants and Duration

To start the group a poster was designed with the slogan "When you fight with monsters, take care you don't become a monster yourself". This was intended to refer to the aggressive stand-off between different groups of prisoners, and between prisoners and staff. It attracted a starting group of around 12 prisoners, which quickly increased to an average of 17 prisoners plus six others (limited by the capacity of the meeting room), of whom two were the security staff detailed to attend each group. Other prison staff involved over the years included all grades of personnel, including Governors, Probation, Psychology, Chaplaincy and the Board of Visitors (now the Independent Monitoring Board, or IMB). Other visitors included staff from Prison Services headquarters and both the Cambridge and Texas Institutes of Criminology. From the first session volunteers interested in learning about Dialogue were invited from outside the prison. The intention was to include a cross-section of participants based on the notion that 'everybody learns but nobody teaches'.

The group met weekly for at least two hours on Tuesday mornings for 45 weeks of the year (three terms of 15 weeks each), convened by Probation and facilitated by a Dialogue practitioner. There was no agenda or preset theme to sessions, and people talked about whatever mattered to them. Each session started wherever it started, and the facilitation sought to encourage enquiry into what had been said, rather than an argument. No subject was prohibited, but the putting down of individuals not present was not allowed. Attendance was voluntary, and there tended to be a mixture of regulars and newcomers at each session. It was not an advocacy group, but one where issues were explored in depth and contributed more indirectly to their being resolved because people thought differently about those issues. It established a way of working which participants explained to newcomers at the outset, and eventually included a check-in and check-out (a round of comments at the start and close of each session).

Sometimes the topic was very personal (about individuals' life experiences), sometimes political (IRA Catholics, Protestants and British Army participants engaging one another), sometimes organisational (the impact of sniffer dogs on visitors), sometimes tragic (acknowledging the suicide of a participant), sometimes triumphant (a participant finally winning his appeal after 18 years in prison), sometimes humorous (competitive joke-telling sessions), and sometimes spiritual (about the experience of different qualities of love).

Participants signed an attendance register, detailed records were kept of every session by the facilitator, and a four-page typed report was written after every 15-week term, agreed by the group and then distributed around the prison. The aim was to encourage the prison to think about the issues being discussed without naming individual participants or making them vulnerable by quoting them.

Outcomes
The prisoners, who had generally received a limited education, showed a significant increase in their vocabulary, their ability to reason and reflect, and their skills of social engagement. They not only supported and challenged each other but proved more than capable of taking on visiting Professors of Criminology about the validity of their research. They also began to view their own lives as a journey or story that they could author rather than suffer. This led strongly resistant offenders to participate in rather than reject what was on offer in the prison, including therapeutic treatment courses and education. Prisoners and staff were surprised to find each other to be intelligent and compassionate. "That is the first time in my life I ever heard that prisoner say something intelligent!" was a typical quote from a new security officer after first attending a Dialogue Group. The prison benefitted from a forum for social interaction. Even after minor rioting, when the entire prison was locked down, the Dialogue Group still ran. There are too many changing factors involved in policy, practice and resourcing to find a statistical correlation, but incidents did dip markedly on Tuesdays and reduced during the life of the Dialogue Group. Prison Dialogue gained experience and reputation, and had a regular setting for the development of dialogic facilitators.

Learning
Prison Dialogue empirically realised a set of Dialogic Practices (Voice, Listen, Respect and Suspend) without which good quality conversation is not possible. In a setting where violation and violence are commonplace, respect is fundamental to people listening to each other, speaking genuinely and loosening their certainty that they are right and others are wrong. This formed the basis for the Dialogic facilitation. The Prison Dialogue facilitators also were intentional about making accessible to others their facilitation skills, thereby moving towards becoming redundant. This involved a deliberate transparency, whereby the facilitator explains why and how they are facilitating in a given way. Over time many of the prisoners, some officers and some volunteers gained good facilitative skills. Finally, the Dialogue Group provided an excellent research forum for the Cambridge Institute of Criminology, significantly aiding their work as the group made available thinking that is not normally accessible. This opened the door to Dialogue as a research methodology.

HMP Dorchester Prison Turnaround

This case study illustrates the value of Dialogue in helping to turn around prisons which are struggling or failing. It's clear from what we see in the media, and from the data available, that many prisons in the UK – and elsewhere – fall into this category. So often the only solution that is offered to these situations (both by the authorities and by critics of the prevailing circumstances) is to throw additional resources at them. But even where more resources are needed, they still have to be employed effectively, so this is at best only a partial solution. The Dorchester example shows how Dialogue helped to effect meaningful and sustainable change in a complex and contentious environment – and why it has much wider application against the background of so many failing institutions.

Context

In 2003–2004 Dorchester was almost the lowest-ranked prison in England and Wales, ranking 135th out of 136. This resulted in the prison being subject to a 'Performance Improvement Plan' and given 18 months in which to demonstrate significant improvement or face the likelihood of being privatised.

The prison was a local institution serving the courts in Dorset and South Somerset. It was built in around 1880 and housed 250 male prisoners. In 2002, the Prison Governor, Steve Holland, articulated his vision for the prison as a Centre of Excellence for Resettlement, with a healthy and happy staff group surpassing expectations for local prison work. Progress was hampered, however, by the attitudes and perceptions of staff combined with a lack of shared vision of what the prison could be. Staff were not involved in important decisions affecting the establishment, and there was much resistance to change. The way the Senior Management Team operated was ineffective, with the Governor as the hub and each of his reports relating to him like the spokes of a wheel. This meant that the Governor was involved directly in every decision, which filled his days and left him little time to plan and manage strategically. The Governor had worked previously with Prison Dialogue, and contacted them to help him achieve his vision.

Aims and Objectives

Soon after his appointment, the Governor identified four areas of special focus to turn round the prison: performance; labour relations and staff culture; resettlement; and the Senior Management Team (SMT).

Without reforming the SMT, the Governor could not make his vision into a reality. He realised he needed to change some SMT members and recruit new people with the right experience, skills and style. He saw that he needed to change the roles of others and to improve their capacity and skill levels in order to create an effective decision-making team, and give him the space to lead more strategically.

The Governor and his SMT needed to develop a working vision to address the poor levels of operational performance in many areas across the prison. They then needed a strategy to actively engage the staff to make the necessary changes to the operational practices if the prison was to improve to meet the requirements of the Performance Improvement Plan.

Method: Activity, Participants and Duration
Once the Governor had assembled his SMT team, three off-site meetings were held for them at the Prison Dialogue offices, and ongoing coaching support was provided by Prison Dialogue to individual team members between the sessions. In the first session, team members took stock of their history, current situation and the future they wanted to create. This was done by together creating a Wall History of Dorchester on flip charts. The first member of the team to work at Dorchester started telling the history at the point when they arrived, describing the situation and their experiences along with key incidents at the prison and in the Prison Service. Newer members joined in chronologically until everyone had added to the story, the most recent being the Deputy Governor who had joined Dorchester a few weeks previously. People signed the Wall History to signify 'signing into' the story at the time they joined the prison. The activity provided an opportunity to share knowledge, understanding and experiences. It bound the team into a common story and helped them to understand why the staff they were leading behaved the way they did. One of the Senior Managers later reflected, "The SMT awaydays . . . gave me a real feel for Dorchester past and present . . . The result was that I had a clear vision for where the whole SMT and the whole prison wanted to be".

The second off-site meeting involved creating a simple but profound strategy. Although many areas were underperforming, others were doing well, and it was difficult to get clear about what needed to change where. The four-step strategy for progress was 'Comply (without which the prison was penalised), Perform (do what is expected to the highest possible standard), Serve (work in the service of others and of the community) and Shine (be a beacon – the best-in-class across the prison service)'. Areas were then defined as to where they were on this progression, and what was needed to take them to the next level.

At the third off-site meeting at the Prison Dialogue office the group analysed the different staff configurations, which enabled them to take different approaches with different groups of people. This identified and shifted one particularly cynical group of uniformed staff, and that accelerated the overall recovery.

The team recognised that achieving whole-prison change was a long-term project. Throughout the period 2003 to 2006 Prison Dialogue was present at Dorchester for at least two days each month, and also worked with staff and managers between sessions by phone and email. The first phase was assessment, and from six months from October 2003 Prison Dialogue worked with the Governor and a steering group of 12 staff representing all areas of the prison. They focused on how staff communicate, their experience of working in the prison and what they would like to change about the prison. As one prison staff member commented, "Communication in Dorchester isn't all good. It's only brilliant because we deal with prisoners without challenging them; good can mean complacent". Prison Dialogue interviewed and shadowed 35 staff, and held regular discussions with groups of staff. They also met regularly with the Resettlement Team, and worked with them to draft the new Resettlement Plan. This led to the development of a long-term strategy which ran until 2006. It focused on the staff development journey, along with leadership and support. Alongside this was the Prisoner Resettlement Journey, focusing on reducing re-offending. Fundamental to the cultural change in the prison was the development of a shared vision that could be achieved through jointly agreed strategies and plans, and a series of dialogic forums where all and any aspect of the change could be talked about.

Outcomes

In April 2004 Her Majesty's Inspectorate of Prisons echoed the need that Prison Dialogue had identified for an integrated approach to the resettlement of offenders. "There was not yet a whole-prison approach to resettlement", the report stated. "The Governor recognised the major challenge of trying to introduce new ideas to the reluctant staff group. However, he had developed a strategy to achieve the aim of a whole-prison approach to resettlement. This involves working with Prison Dialogue, a small group with experience in improving communication".

The SMT shifted identity from dominantly operating as individuals, to working as a team as they externalised the problems they faced, to having a shared ownership in shaping the future of the prison. As one SMT member said, "We have a stronger and more cohesive SMT approach".

Developing a working vision enabled managers to set a measurable, progressive path to address the variable levels of performance across the prison. The Comply, Perform, Serve and Shine progressive strategy began to be used extensively. As one SMT member said, "I feel I am part of an organisation that's serious about developing its future; it's good to be part of a system that has a sense of pride and a much sharper focus on quality development, moving the prison forward".

Significant performance improvements were achieved, and the prison moved from its near-bottom-of-the-list ranking in 2004 to being 35th of 136 in 2006, the highest ranking it could achieve as a local prison. Also in 2006 the prison achieved outstanding outcomes in the independent survey: the Measure of the Quality of Prisoners Life (MQPL). Dorchester was ranked either first or second in the country across all the 12 areas measured. Audit success rates across Standards were up to 93% from 69%, and Security from 68% to 86% in 2006.

Acknowledging this enormous improvement, in 2006 the prison Governor said: "The Director General called me to pass on his personal congratulations for what was seen as an extraordinary shift in the prisoners' custodial experience. Staff satisfaction with their working lives, as measured by the National Survey, has also improved dramatically. Only two other prisons [out of the full 136] returned more questionnaires, and the levels of satisfaction were so high that I was contacted by the survey team to find out on behalf of the Prison's Board what has been happening at Dorchester".

Learning

A member of staff summed up the changes felt by many: "It finally feels like we're getting somewhere at last. Dorchester was in a time warp and needed a shaking. Some staff had been here a very long time and it's harder to change the longer you are in the service. Attitudes have changed, no longer is the prison so dominated and owned by the few".

For the first time, Prison Dialogue started working closely with staff and managers from across the prison to address needs that they believed were important. Also, Prison Dialogue recognised that to achieve culture change there was a need to review the ways the SMT worked, to coach them in their engagement and communication skills, and to review their roles and responsibilities.

This was the first time that Prison Dialogue had worked with a whole prison and worked exclusively with staff and managers to address their needs. The cascade model started with the Governor and then his SMT. Looking back, one SMT member said, "There's a much greater understanding of why change is needed now, although there's still some resistance. We're certainly going forward with much greater confidence".

Having the sponsorship of the Prison Service Area Manager (the Governor's line manager) provided Prison Dialogue with additional status and authority to affect the situation. This was established in the first meeting Prison Dialogue had with the Area Manager and the Governor working together. And although Dorchester has since closed, the introduction of Dialogue profoundly changed the relationships and sense of potential among those who worked and lived in the facility.

Bournemouth and Dorset Threshold Dialogues

This was another groundbreaking piece of work involving the use of Dialogue across multiple organisations to reduce the fragmentary nature of the process of releasing prisoners and make it more coherent and therefore more effective. Settling back into normal society upon release has been shown to be a stressful and challenging activity even in the best of circumstances, but the way the process is organised often makes this even more difficult. This initiative showed how Dialogue between all the different parties in the process could help ease the 'prisoner journey' across the 'prison threshold' and increase the likelihood of a successful outcome. In fact, given the degree of fragmentation which characterises it, it is hard to see how the process can ever be as effective as it needs to be without an enhanced degree of Dialogue between all the participants involved in it.

Context

In January 2006, Prison Dialogue launched the Bournemouth Threshold Dialogue pilot, an innovative inter-agency intervention based on Dialogue, to support high-repeat offenders leaving Dorchester and returning to the community in Bournemouth. The aim was to reduce reoffending. Over the next five years this developed into the Dorset Threshold

Dialogue, with a network of Threshold Dialogues in three prisons and three community centres, a multi-agency team of trained facilitators, and an integrated inter-agency Operations Group and Governance Board.

In line with national policy, Dorset Criminal Justice Board was establishing projects for Prolific and other Priority Offenders (and some High-Repeat Offenders) who were responsible for committing the majority of crime in the area. Many of them experienced problems with drugs and alcohol, mental health issues, unemployment and homelessness, and were trapped in a revolving door in and out of prison, but never serving a long enough sentence to benefit from meaningful intervention work in prison. Bournemouth Threshold Dialogue was ideally suited to work with this particular group of offenders because it could continue to work with them seamlessly as they moved in and out of prison. The Dorset Criminal Justice Board provided some basic grant funding, and Prison Dialogue secured additional funding over the following years from the J. Paul Getty Junior Charitable Trust, Mulberry Trust, Tudor Trust and Dialogue Associates Ltd.

Aims and Objectives
The aims of the Threshold Dialogue were to reduce re-offending and to improve relationships and understanding between repeat offenders and those charged with their management so that they could work more effectively together to do so. In addition, Threshold Dialogue aimed to:

- Engage with the offenders whilst in custody to help them to prepare for release
- Support the offender in their transition back into the community and once they were resettled
- Enhance the resettlement opportunities that were available
- Develop staff awareness of the needs of offenders in resettlement
- Promote closer partnership working between agencies and enable joined-up practice

Method: Activity, Participants and Duration
Threshold Dialogue was based on the extensive use of Dialogue as a forum for prisoners and the agencies involved in resettlement and crime reduction to come together to think through what was needed to make resettlement a success. These Dialogue forums were based in prison and the community. They followed the offender on their journey across the 'threshold' of the prison gate, hence the name Threshold Dialogue. Offenders often crossed the threshold with intentions not to return to prison but did not seem able to sustain the transition into an offence-free life.

There were three phases in the development of Threshold Dialogue in Bournemouth and Dorset. The first phase ran throughout 2006 and was evaluated by Coventry University. In total, 41 offenders from Bournemouth, who were defined as Prolific and other Priority Offenders or High Repeat Offenders, took part. Prison Dialogue facilitated two cycles of Bournemouth Threshold Dialogue in the Dorchester prison and in Bournemouth town. The sessions ran weekly, both in the prison and in the community. Prisoners were awarded certificates for completing the whole programme. Agencies came into the prison to take part in the sessions, including Police Officers and agency staff. Previously Police had only come into a prison in order to investigate a criminal offence, and it was unheard of for Police in uniform to come and meet and talk at length with a group of prisoners. The prison staff were so nervous about walking them through the centre of the prison that they instead took a back route to the meeting room. On the other side, Prison Officers attended community-based meetings with ex-offenders whom they had known in prison, and worked closely with the community agencies. Some prisoners were granted Release on Temporary Licence to attend Dialogues in the community before their release, engaging with the Probation and agency staff who would be supervising and supporting them and the Police from their community who would be 'keeping their eye on them'.

The second phase extended the Threshold Dialogue network based around Bournemouth and, in doing so, established the Dorset Threshold Dialogue. Dorchester was a local prison (housing short-term prisoners and those who have been convicted but not yet been sentenced, like a jail in the US) and prisoners were moved on from there regularly to nearby HMP Guys Marsh, a training prison set up for sentenced prisoners to engage in purposeful work, training, education and programmes. Following the offenders' journey, Threshold Dialogue was introduced at Guys Marsh next, and then later into the Young Offender Institution (HM/YOI) Portland. In the community, Threshold Dialogue was established at two sites in Bournemouth: at a supported Housing Unit that offered accommodation to prisoners on release, and at a direct-access hostel and day centre for people whose lives were more chaotic. It was also established at one site in the neighbouring Borough of Poole.

More agencies became consistently involved, including Police, Probation, Bournemouth Borough Council, Drugs and Alcohol Services – especially Crime Reduction Initiatives – and accommodation providers – particularly the Bournemouth Churches Housing Association. At the same time, an inter-agency Operations Group and Governance Board were set up to provide local leadership and integrated ownership for the initiative. A team of facilitators was trained so that Threshold Dialogue could be sustained without Prison Dialogue's long-term involvement. Key to this sustainability was the case that Threshold Dialogue was an effective and efficient way for all of the agencies to carry out their 'day job' and it was a valuable way for staff to apply their time. For example, the Police recognise that engagement with local offenders is an effective way to improve policing and a Police Officer could achieve over 20 hours of high-quality engagement with local offenders in a 90-minute Dialogue with 15 prisoners.

The third phase of Threshold Dialogue was the handover of Dorset Threshold Dialogue to the local agencies at the Line of Sight Workshop in November 2017.

Outcomes

In 2007, one of the practitioners was a Team Award Winner for the Dorset Justice Award for the Partnership of the Year. Genuine effective strategic and operational partnership was significantly improved among the agencies. There was progress towards shared ownership and an integrated approach to reducing re-offending. A shared understanding of the offender journey and a wider knowledge of the range of support services – and the gaps between them – greatly enhanced the resettlement opportunities and successes for offenders. On a day-to-day basis at the front line of offender services there was far greater inter-agency cooperation and collaboration, and the programme made a firm contribution to enhanced community safety.

As in Bournemouth, Threshold Dialogue in Dorset provided an opportunity for the agencies to see the offenders in another environment and to work effectively in depth with a large group of offenders through the dynamic of Dialogic group work.

Threshold Dialogue recognised the crisis that offenders have to manage on release from prison, and it helped individual offenders manage that crisis and successfully make the transition. In prison most offenders have the majority of decisions made for them: when they are locked up, when they have association with others, when they eat and, in some cases, what they wear. During resettlement in the community, they have to think for themselves and manage their own lives, which can be stressful and challenging when support seems hard to access.

The Bournemouth Borough Council changed its policy on Anti-Social Behaviour Orders as a result of engaging with offenders in Threshold Dialogue and understanding the counterproductive implications for ex-offenders of some of the terms imposed.

Learning
Despite years of experience and the quality provision that the agencies already provided, prison staff realised that they could learn more about the needs of the offenders they worked with, and about different ways in which they might do their work to prevent re-offending. Agencies learned more about each other, and about how they could work together more effectively. Through-the-gate thinking was really embedded in the mindset of Bournemouth services. People have to make numerous transitions to move from dependence to independence on their resettlement journey. Each transition has its own potential stumbling blocks and crises, and each area of one's life has many transitions (employment, housing, health etc.).

Prison Dialogue learned how to train agency representatives to facilitate Threshold Dialogue. Dorset Threshold Dialogue was an integrated service based around the whole offender journey – from the community into prison, back through the prison gate into the community again. Prison Dialogue learned about the fragmentation of the Criminal Justice System close-up, and the challenges of integrating the system. Typically, each agency only owns 'their part' of the activity and there is no ownership or leadership for the whole system. Threshold Dialogue establishes the premise that the community should 'own' its offenders, and the community should require agencies to provide effective integrated support for offenders to resettle and become contributing members of society.

HMP Oakwood Personal Officer Learning Circles

One of the biggest challenges facing the adoption of Dialogue in prisons has been to embed it as a core feature of prison activity, rather than it being treated as something of a discretionary add-on. As a result, despite the clear evidence of the value of the approach, once the Dialogue facilitators are no longer present, experience shows that its use begins to diminish. This case study provides a practical illustration of how Dialogue can be integrated into the ongoing routine of prison operations. Despite this, the initiative ultimately fell foul of another consistent threat – namely a change in prison leadership before it had become fully embedded. Even so, it shows that ways of genuinely embedding Dialogue into the fabric of operations can be found if there is genuine intent to do so.

Context

As mentioned, it has often proved quite hard to sustain some Dialogue initiatives after the departure of facilitators or supportive prison leadership, particularly where Dialogue is seen as something of a cost-prohibitive luxury. To this end Prison Dialogue is currently pursuing two new projects which present the opportunity to embed Dialogue as a core part of prison activity and routine. The first of these involves the newly-built HMP Oakwood in the West Midlands, which is being operated by G4S, where all prisoners are required to participate in fortnightly 'learning circles'. These are linked to mandatory work with a Personal Officer (as described below) and are formally scheduled into the prison's 'Core Day'. Each of the sessions involves one prison officer and six offenders. Prison Dialogue is providing advice, training and ongoing support to the learning circles, so that these are conducted as genuine Dialogues.

Oakwood was opened under the management of G4S in April 2012. The private prison provider won the contract to run Oakwood under the then-Government's new privatisation programme. Prison Dialogue had worked closely with G4S on a number of projects, and assisted them in the bidding process with a view to creating a more sustainable and better-resourced programme of Dialogue input to support the way the new prison was run.

The new Director, Steve Holland, who had previously worked closely with Prison Dialogue for almost 15 years, and Prison Dialogue saw a way for all prison staff and prisoners to engage in Dialogue through what is termed 'Personal Officer Work'. In the UK, prison custody officers are expected to fulfil a dual role of security and prisoner rehabilitation, motivating and encouraging prisoners to engage in prison activities, supporting or challenging their behaviour, and using authority and discipline. As well as this general responsibility to every prisoner, they are Personal Officers to a small group of prisoners (usually 10 to 15) on the unit where they are based. They are responsible for knowing more about the individual circumstances and character of these prisoners and addressing some of their needs and opportunities. The reputation in most prisons is that Personal Officer work is at best patchy, depending on the motivation of the individual officer, and staff complain that there is not enough time to do the work.

As an attempt to address this complex set of responsibilities, learning circles were introduced as a group forum based on Dialogue for Personal Officer work at Oakwood.

Aims and Objectives

As designed, learning circles would offer high-quality Personal Officer work to prisoners, create good staff prisoner relationships, provide regular communication channels between prisoners and staff, and embed the vision that the prison had set out as 'the Oakwood way'. They would help support a smooth prison opening by providing a forum for prisoners to talk, be listened to and release their frustrations. Policies, procedures, training and advice to staff would be required to sustain learning circles as part of the regime.

Method: Activity, Participants and Duration

Before the prison opened, the process to run learning circles was agreed and a draft policy and Prisoner Compact written to support their introduction. Each Personal Officer would run one learning circle each week. They divided the 12 prisoners they supervised into two groups of six each and met with each group on alternate weeks. Although there were only two officers on each housing unit, this was possible because during the day, when prisoners were at work, one officer was detailed to Personal Officer work when they would run their learning circle, while the other officer supervised the unit. The learning circle lasted one hour, after which the officer submitted a report (via computer) to their manager showing the names of the participants, up to three dominant themes in the Dialogue, and any prison communications that were passed on. They could then record Personal Officer comments on the record of the individual prisoners about how they engaged in the session, issues raised, progress made in their sentence planning and any safety or security concerns. This was a more thorough report than is usual for Personal Officer work. Documented, purposeful activity hours were recorded for the prison, which form part of the contract targets, or goals.

A half-day introductory training for learning circles was provided to every prison custody officer. This included the Dialogue Modes, check-in and check-out processes, why learning circles were important, how they were intended to work, ground rules, reporting, guidance for making Personal Officer entries, and a role play of a learning circle. Guidance was also provided for setting the themes for more than 20 sessions.

A learning circle Development Team (LCDT) of Pioneers helped to steer the set-up process and support less-confident colleagues, and they met monthly long-term. A group of prisoners was recruited as learning circle Mentors and, at the time of writing, 12 of them are waiting to be trained. The aspiration to provide more in-depth Dialogue Skills Training to staff to develop their skills for learning circles was not achieved. The prison had contract targets for other training that took priority. Prison Dialogue and the prison are looking into education funding to resource Dialogue Skills Training for learning circles for both staff and prisoners.

Outcomes

Learning circles have been successfully piloted at Oakwood to show an efficient way to provide high-quality Personal Officer work. Organisational structures, policies and training were put in place to embed learning circles in the Oakwood regime. Delivery during the first year has been patchy as the prison has managed the ups and downs of the opening. In places, with certain officers, they have proved highly effective. One prisoner said "because I know [the officer] now and know I can discuss my problems with him. I couldn't knock him out. In other prisons I would have knocked them out".

The performance management work is ongoing to realise the value of the structures that are in place. A learning circle newsletter is circulated to all residential staff by the LCDT every week giving ideas and current information to stimulate the sessions.

Learning

Group Personal Officer work is effective and can be embedded in the prison policies and regime to be delivered across a whole prison system in support of a purposeful and rehabilitative prisoner culture. Once the structure is in place it can be used to integrate the different activities that affect a prisoner. For example, Programme staff could attend learning circles so that their efforts are integrated with Personal Officer work. As such there is great potential to develop this initiative into a large-scale Threshold Dialogue process.

Conclusion

As part of my role as a Trustee of Prison Dialogue, I've now had the opportunity to visit many different prisons and speak to numerous prisoners and prison staff. One conversation stands out in particular. It was with a prison manager at a private prison in Wales that practised Dialogue. He was a former soldier and had moved to the private prison from a public sector one. He told me that when he arrived at the private prison, he was amazed and somewhat intimidated by the ratio of staff to prisoners, which was much lower than he was previously accustomed to in the public sector. But he said that it made him realise that to maintain safety and security in his unit, he could not rely on his baton; instead, he needed to get to know the prisoners and build some form of relationship with them. Over time he came to recognise that this was a more effective and less expensive way of maintaining security, because even with a much higher ratio of staff to prisoners, the prisoners will still almost certainly outnumber the officers. Moreover, Dialogue represents a much better way to encourage in prisoners a healthier relationship with authority, which is likely to be far more effective once they are released than one based on antagonism and resentment.

Notwithstanding the many other ways in which Dialogue can be beneficial in the context of prisons and criminal justice, for me, these words of wisdom sit at the heart of why Prison Dialogue really matters in this setting. Through Dialogue, prisons can become more effective institutions both in terms of ensuring the safe and secure incarceration of the prisoners in their care, and in terms of helping to equip prisoners to return to society as law-abiding citizens.

Conference Session Extracts

From conversation with 20 participants considering the paper with the author

When we introduced dialogue, our staff was like, "Oh, here's another staff-offender relationship skill!" I'm like, "No, this is about communication among staff. This has nothing to do with the crime itself". So that sparked an interest. There's been some managers that ran their meetings different. We've even done a check-in and check-out with our administrative staff, our assistants. And they felt more involved in the meetings. So now, people have a taste of what it is. So now, they can hope.

You include some case studies in your paper, that almost said people should see what's in it for them, and then when they start to see how this will make a difference people realize it made a difference to their family life as well, because it affected how they talk with the family.

Sure.

Then they start to be convinced and want to be part of it.

Right.

So perhaps need to be more simple, sometimes, in the stories that we tell.

Yes.

I could speak to that. In my community, there's a returned citizens' organisation. And so we had a meeting, the community and the people who represent them and some lawyers, to have a sort of community approach to helping these returned citizens. To be able to get jobs again, and erase their record, and things like that. And I thought that was extremely helpful, because it not only engages [them] and they felt that they could be part of this community, but the opposite was also true, that we're aware. Everybody's aware now, about that. So part of it, the system of the movement, could be also community-based, because communities are aware people actually know each other, and they can care more about this. Whereas if they go back all by themselves into a community where there's nobody involved, and enabling them to not to get into trouble, and all that kind of stuff, but the community itself becomes more contributive, which is really helpful to the rest of the community. So there's a role to play with returned citizens, that would enable them to want to make sure that the systems that we have address some long-term change in the system.

I was thinking about my wife. My wife's name is Julia. And with Julia, I introduced dialogue in the school system. We worked with the children and their teachers – puberty. And we noticed that it's very successful. It's very good. And when we had this experience, I became very interested and said, "We have to spread the word. We have to bring it into the system, and we have to get the – how do you say – the directors", and so on. And my wife said from the beginning, "Don't do it. Just keep quiet. And we will just only work when we have one question of one teacher – we can react and work with, and we can have a dialogue. And then, we wait for the next question". Now, I have tried to bring it into the system with brochures, with information, with talk. Over eight years, I was not successful. But when we waited for the questions, you saw a very slow increase of interest in school dialogue.

Postscript

The author's reflections written some months after the conference

I was keen to write a paper for the conference on behalf of Prison Dialogue, because I saw it as an excellent opportunity to showcase some of the tremendous dialogue work that Peter and Jane in particular have undertaken over the years in prisons and the Criminal Justice System. There is no question in my mind that 'Criminal Justice needs dialogue', and that their work demonstrates how valuable dialogue can be in the sector – especially in light of the huge challenges facing prisons and criminal justice not just in the UK but throughout the world.

This said, obtaining support for the adoption of dialogue from those who have authority over or influence upon prisons or probation or other aspects of the system remains hugely challenging. Despite the excellent work that's been done over a period of some 30 years, despite the evidence of its value, the awareness of this among Criminal Justice professionals remains restricted to individual converts and narrow pockets of interest. And so it is absolutely critical that we find ways to publicise and promulgate to a much wider audience what has been achieved, and the benefits delivered. I see this as the core role of Prison Dialogue as a Charity: we don't need to do more work to prove the value of dialogue; what we need to do is 'spread the word'. Writing a paper was one – small – way of doing this. In keeping with this, the paper is really targeted more at prison and criminal justice professionals than it is at dialogue practitioners.

Leading up to the conference, it became increasingly apparent that the question of how to persuade a reluctant world to embrace dialogue more fully was an issue which was relevant everywhere, not just in the case of prisons. Clearly, great dialogue work is being done in all sorts of different situations in any number of geographies, but these are all single-point interventions, rather than coalescing to form a broader 'movement'. The challenge for the Academy is in many ways similar to that facing Prison Dialogue. Given this, I tried to position the dialogue around the paper at the conference as something of a reflection on this topic. In practice, for me the dialogue that transpired was somewhat disappointing – partly because only a minority of attendees at the session had actually read the paper. This said, there was a clear recognition from some of those who participated of the difficulties that need to be negotiated, the need to continue doing great work and finding ways to share this with an ever-wider audience.

Section Three

Healthcare Needs Dialogue!

Dialogue as a Whole-System Healthcare Intervention

Beth Macy

The dialogue intervention I'll be describing in this paper consumed a year out of my life and went deeply under the surface of my own consciousness with an impact that still reverberates. It was an intense, whole-system engagement focusing on dialogue within a long-term healthcare facility. Although the intervention was conducted almost 22 years ago, it offers a perspective that is still relevant today, as it focuses on the intensive use of dialogue, eventually taking in a whole organization. In using dialogue extensively in ensuing years since this experience, I've found that many of the issues and the aspects of this intervention remain constant across the various types and depths of interventions.

Context for the Intervention

At the time when this dialogue intervention took place, I was the administrator of a large US healthcare system that served about two thousand patients. Having participated in dialogue training with Bill Isaacs, then-director of the MIT Dialogue Project and originator of the consulting firm Dialogos, I was having encouragingly positive results in conducting leadership team meetings utilizing dialogue. My request for a colleague (I'll call her "Lynn") from one of the system's long-term care facilities and myself to participate in Isaac's Practitioner Development Program was approved by the leader to whom I reported, and the two of us then sought an opportunity to put our new skills to work.

At the same time, one of the long-term care facilities stood out in its degree of administrative and other challenges. Key was a longstanding high level of absenteeism. Nursing was overstaffed by almost fifty percent in order to maintain minimum staffing on each shift. It was referred to as the call-in problem. That is, a nursing staff member would call in absent shortly before his or her shift was to begin, forcing someone at the end of their shift to stay over in order to maintain adequate staffing. For the nurse who needed to cover for his or her colleague, this meant working a 16-hour shift. HR folks already had applied all of their remedies – focus groups, restrictions, incentives, punishments – in an attempt to bring absenteeism within an acceptable range. Nothing seemed to work.

Various changes at that facility were anticipated, adding to the sense of malaise among staff. An organization-wide reorganization was anticipated, the facility was thinking about embracing a new philosophy for providing care, and a shift to a more participative leadership/management style was being considered.

Last, but significantly, the culture of the facility was unhealthy. While individuals exhibited strong caring for their patients, the units were competitive with each other, the various professional disciplines squabbled among themselves, and the general tenor of communication among individuals and among levels of the organization was cynical.

The administrator and the director of nursing from that facility suggested their site for a pilot implementation of dialogue, hoping to improve the ailing culture and to develop resilience among staff for the changes to come.

The Intervention Purpose

As described to staff of the healthcare facility, our purpose in bringing David Bohm's process of dialogue was to create a high level of trust, common ground, and skill so that all staff could talk, listen, inquire and *think together* about what really mattered to them about their work. We hoped to lay the foundation for a healthy and productive work culture in which staff could use dialogue skills to resolve many of their own workday issues. Though the intervention was not intended to be the problem-solving mechanism for challenges named during the sessions, we hoped the dialogues would penetrate deeply enough into persistent issues to illuminate the real under-the-surface problems that prior methods had been unsuccessful in resolving. This was a whole-system intervention, and so the design of it needed to encompass the totality of that intention.

To begin the intervention, we brought into the project planning process the key administrators who would be affected. This began in November and December. In that process we engaged with the administrator and director of nursing, in particular, who had volunteered to be the local sponsors for the project. With them, we laid out some initial thoughts for the project's design.

At the recommendation of those sponsors we planned to train everyone in the facility on dialogue and then to go forward with a group of volunteers after that initial training to do the long-term dialogue project.

We began with one-day training sessions for every staff member in the facility. There were 165 members of staff at the facility, which translated into six, day-long sessions with 25 to 30 people in each session. We made the training mandatory and, as you can imagine, that didn't sit well with some. In the end, however, the breadth of staff exposure to dialogue paid off in giving a deep foundation for the work that went forward. Those sessions were a combination of training and practice in dialogue, focusing on listening, balancing advocacy and inquiry, and suspending judgment.

Following the one-day training we asked for volunteers from across the facility, hoping to gain about 30 participants from various disciplines and levels of the organization. Much to our surprise, however, 53 volunteered in addition to the 27 management staff. In all, that meant close to half of the facility's employees would be engaged in dialogue programs for the rest of the nine-month period. The unexpectedly large number of participants required a redesign of our original plans, and approximately 80-plus people were involved in various parts of the dialogue intervention.

Participation was also mandatory for management team members. Having that group fully engaged would allow for a more effective follow-through, both during and after the intervention. Two full management team training/dialogue days were scheduled and, in addition, all management team members participated in one of three cross-sectional and management dialogue groups, so that each participated in a total of seven training/dialogue days throughout the intervention. Each cross-sectional group included individuals from most disciplines, departments, shifts, and levels of the organization, so that each represented a microcosm of the whole system, a diagonal slice through the system.

In addition, several open dialogue sessions were held, to which all employees were invited. Different from the other groups, these sessions were purely dialogues with no additional training offered. The open dialogues were not recorded or transcribed, as were the six-month volunteer groups.

Finally, at the end of the six months of the various dialogue groups, the facilitators and management began considering the learnings of our experience with dialogue, and what follow-up would further embed the practice of dialogue into the organization's culture.

Teaching Methodology, Skills Learned, and Dialogues
The One-Day Training Sessions for All Staff

The content of the one-day training/dialogue sessions included an overview of dialogue and how it works. We began with a description of dialogue and guidelines for participating in it.

The main dialogue skill training skills/tools came from Bill Isaacs' Practitioner Development Program in which both of the facilitators then were engaged. Many of these teaching methods are documented in *The Fifth Discipline Fieldbook*. We focused on the skills of listening, balancing advocacy and inquiry, ladder of inference, suspending judgment, and then conducted a dialogue practice.

Cross-Sectional Dialogue Groups

The three follow-up cross-sectional and management dialogue groups gave the opportunity to focus on the same skills as the initial one-day training, but with more depth and practice, and we added David Kantor's Four-Player model and dialogue. To supplement the training, other teaching exercises were added from our own repertoires to ensure that the skills were approached from multiple avenues and that ample practice in the small-group sessions were provided. As well, the dialogue sessions focused on many of the issues that had arisen during the introductory trainings, though these sessions tended to get much further below the surface.

Generally, those sessions followed this format:

- Opening check-in
- Morning dialogue skill-training in small groups
- Morning dialogue
- Afternoon skill-training in small groups
- Afternoon dialogue
- Check-out

In the following pages, the participant feedback and skills update have been combined for the initial one-day training for all staff and for the cross-sectional, five-session dialogue groups.

Skill Training: Listening
Participant Feedback: In both the one-day and the longer-term portions of the intervention, feedback from participants gave the highest impact of teaching and practice to the listening exercise, and it seemed to be the most effectively absorbed of all the skills.

Several people commented that they were amazed at how poorly they generally listen to others, which was especially weighty in their reflections as all were engaged in a health/helping field of work. Some commented on how difficult it was to keep still and only listen, noting that it was a surprising experience to notice the disruptiveness of their internal dialogue. Most found the experience of being listened to so intently as was required by the exercise very valuing, pleasant, and out of the ordinary.

In regard to the impact of listening, one person shared that she had seen her listening exercise partner daily for 12 years in the hallways yet had never had a conversation with her. From the ten minutes together in the listening exercise, they developed a strong sense of commonality. Others noted how the exercise would change relationships back on the floor as they bumped into their exercise partners, feeling they now had a sense of who the other person was. Many people said that this was a skill that they would take home to their personal lives as well as use it in their work relationships, and sometime after the one-day trainings, a participant shared a touching story of her having stopped to listen to her teenage son, and in the process was able to guide him through an attempt by his peers to induce him into drugs.

But not everyone liked the focus on listening. One woman said she knew she was a bad listener, didn't care that she was a bad listener, had no intention of changing, and was just waiting till five o'clock so she could be out of there!

Incorporation of Listening Skills: Throughout the nine months we saw various indicators that listening was impacting both the dialogues and the relationships on the work floor. The first of our dialogues were what I called "popcorn," with various people in rapid succession blurting out a comment that either echoed a strongly held and negative view in response to something someone else had spoken several minutes back, or others randomly broaching totally new topics. There was little flow, but rather individual comments just popped, lacking relevance to what had preceded. Listening, if it was happening, was in short supply. But, by the latter dialogues there was a much greater frequency of the groups engaging in a flow of conversation, building upon each other's comments and sometimes reaching deeply under the surface.

As the sessions proceeded, another indicator of listening skill uptake occurred as individuals took more initiative to slow the conversation so that they could better understand others' points of view, sometimes going back to a comment made earlier in the dialogue that had not been fully addressed and thus indicating that they had listened and had been impacted by what they heard.

Outside of the dialogues, people also reported successes. Contentious interpersonal relationships between peers or between employees and managers were reported to have improved during the intervention, particularly through the listening aspects of training/dialogue. One person said, "There is a person in this group that I can't work with that I have very strong negative feelings about. After listening to that person today, I know that I can't go back and feel the same way about them."

Throughout the intervention, we were impressed by how infrequently people felt deeply listened to or understood and how much they valued that experience in the dialogues. Said one participant, "I'm very happy that people listened to what I had to say, whether they agreed or disagreed." Many felt their life-outlooks and feelings of adequacy to address life was enhanced by having participated in the dialogue effort, particularly the skill of listening.

Skill Training: Balancing Advocacy and Inquiry
Participant Feedback: The balancing advocacy and inquiry exercises received a mixed response. Participants commented that they were encouraged to hear their peers' questions during the exercise because they all seemed to share so many of the same worries and hopes. Some commented that they never considered the value of inquiry and noticed how rarely they inquired, and conversely how much more common it was to throw out judgments and opinions without ever querying others, or even being queried themselves. Some found the concept of questions puzzling and thought the exercise was very difficult.

Incorporation of Advocacy and Inquiry Skills: Advocacy seemed to come naturally to our participants . . . as it does to all of us! It sure didn't seem that people needed any augmentation of their tendency to advocate, though a more skillful manner of advocacy was desirable. Our intent was to help folks recognize how skewed their communication was toward putting forward their own position while leaving little room for another person's differing view, "I'm right" being the dominant communication strategy.

In retrospect, we spent more emphasis on listening and inquiry than on the other skills, and that showed in participants' comments at the nine-month completion. As one participant said, she had begun to listen below the surface of a conversation to the "why" level, and to ask deeper questions before trying to find a resolution. It helped her understand the real problem before jumping to solution. Another spoke eloquently about the perennial call-in problem, saying that everyone needed to stop blaming those who called in, and rather to ask "What's causing us to call in so much? There has to be a reason, and just blaming isn't getting to the core of it."

Skill Training: Suspending Judgment
Participant Feedback: Almost of all the participants were able to understand and work with the ladder of inference with a few needing coaching or additional examples. In the debrief many came to the intended awareness that we add a great deal of interpretation to what is really out there, noting how often they interpreted that an apparently negative behavior on the part of another person was meant to hurt or offend them personally. A commonly held interpretation was that our need to protect our identity and self-esteem often guides the information we add to the raw data of our environment.

Incorporation of Suspension of Judgment Skills: In their small working group sessions, participants developed their own suggestions for how to support peers when a judgment appeared to be worthy of challenge. I share some of these suggestions here because they have proven valuable to many dialogue groups since this intervention:

- Ask questions instead of confronting the person
- Affirm their perception before offering your suggestion
- Clarify the other's point of view
- Question yourself, your motives and assumptions
- Ask, "would you mind if we do a ladder of inference for this question?"
- Ask, "What other conclusions might you have made?"
- Say, "In a similar situation, I came to a different conclusion"
- Ask, "Could you say more about that?"

Suspension, or setting one's assumptions out in front of oneself and the group in order for the individuals to perceive them fully, was a harder skill for participants to incorporate. One participant shared how the making of unfounded judgments affected the feeling tone of her work environment, expressing the hurtfulness she saw and experienced as peers made unfounded judgments about others. In her own words, "They really don't even know what that other person is supposed to do or whatever the job is. I see this a lot, and it's very hurtful when somebody is out there making those assumptions and judgments."

Though this was a harder skill for participants, there were indications that the impact of unexamined judgments had become part of their repertoires. Though I would be remiss if I overstated how well the concept of suspension penetrated for all individuals, many did report its importance to them.

Skill Training: David Kantor's Four-Player Model
Participant Feedback: In check-outs and formal evaluations of the overall dialogue intervention, few comments were made about the Four-Player model.

Uptake of The Four-Player Model: This skill was the least stressed of all the skills, and least taken up as a consequence. Move, follow or oppose were natural tendencies, though unconsciously and unintentionally used, whereas bystanding was foreign to most participants. As facilitators we could see quite a difference between silent bystanding and silent uninvolvement, though sometimes being surprised when someone who had been quiet throughout the whole dialogue would share an articulate bystand comment during the check-out, and we would be humbled by our misperception about the reason for their silence. But that was not the norm.

Skill Training: Dialogue
Dialogue sessions lasted from an hour and a half to two hours. In the initial one-day training we seeded various questions to get the dialogue started, picking questions from themes that had occurred during the morning sessions. Here are some of the questions that we used in the various groups:

- How can I create a safe work environment?
- How does trust get created at work?
- How does gossip affect our sense of the work environment being safe?
- What about our work has heart and meaning?
- What's power and who's got it?

Although the questions proposed at the start of the dialogues were unique to that day's conversation, the conversations quickly reoriented to themes common across all of the groups, i.e., they were systemic. I'll be exploring them in the pages that follow.

The Experience
The Emotional Tenor and Overall Progression of the Dialogues

In each of the three groups, Session One and Two dialogues were somewhere between difficult and raw. The opportunity to talk about "what really matters to us" turned into what some called "bitch sessions." We had expected that the first sessions would include a lot of venting and, clearly, they did.

Two of the groups became much more coherent by the third session, while some in the third group were still venting at the very last. As one participant in that latter group put it, she had a lot of anger as did other people in her work group, and they all thought that dialogue was a safe place to vent what they couldn't say safely in their workgroups. That anger ate on people and affected the atmosphere of their work environment.

One reason cited for participants' anger was what some considered the threat of repercussions for speaking their opinions during a dialogue session. We in administration could say the dialogues were safe, but "a lot of us don't want to say nothing because we know there's going to be something, something is going to happen further down the road because of repercussions, if we speak our piece." More poignantly, another person said, "I thought we were able to come here, speak our opinions and be comfortable with that, and there's an old expression that manure rolls downhill, and I felt like I was getting buckets of it. That's how I feel about it, and we shouldn't [feel like that] with dialogue." Though the concern about repercussions emerged several times, our follow-up attempts didn't give evidence that the opinion carriers' suspicions were correct.

Closely related to the anger was resentment at the dialogue occurring . . . period! It had no place or positive effect at all, in the opinions of a few who propelled their resentment into the circle. Said one afterward, "We need to get back to fundamentals of working and stop this talking!" To this person, talking was a waste of money. Another felt that back in '59 when he was hired it wasn't to sit in meetings, but to produce! Yet another worried that all this talking would bring people closer together and then they would want to express their emotions. What then would happen if, as a male, he hugged a peer? Would he then be subject to a complaint?

The negativity and the unveiling of many organizational issues were particularly difficult for the facility administrator and for some top managers. In fact, I had created a structural trap (to use a term learned from Bill Isaacs) in wearing two hats. First, I was the administrator's boss and second, I was the lead consultant and co-facilitator. Certainly, regardless of the fact that the administrator had willingly invited dialogue into his facility and had helped plan the intervention, he was in a box. During one of the dialogues he said, "My biggest risk is all of you who are sitting here talking about the negative things in front of my boss. That's a risk for me."

The victims of the venting included those in supervisory positions. It seemed that anything and everything that didn't work was the fault of the supervisors, and participants expressed very little empathy toward them. That was hurtful to those in administration who took their work seriously. A nurse manager tearfully shared her experience of never being able to satisfy those who worked for her, their expectations of her being so far beyond what anyone could ever satisfy.

As facilitators, Lynn and I were not immune to the emotionality of the group. To stay in the role of neutral bystanders when our own values were challenged, or as individuals spewed out their negativity in a way that contradicted what we believed to be so from our broader organizational vantage points, was tough. I would find myself ruminating days later about something that had arisen during a dialogue, the emotions and projections still bubbling and bouncing around in my head. We sometimes would be overwhelmed at the depth of feeling expressed during the dialogues and at the difficulty of letting it discharge afterwards.

But in spite of the venting, the anger, the suspicion of repercussions, the dislike of dialogue interrupting individuals' ways of doing their work, and the dumping on people in the hierarchy – in spite of all that – the overall positive emotional tenor and impact of the dialogue sessions ramped up throughout the course of the intervention. It was a big lesson for me about how deeply embedded an attitude of "don't change" can pervade an organization, even when espoused by just a small but vocal minority, but not to let that block the higher intention. As the facilitator I must be able to stay present and to hold the space in dialogue in order for the coherence of the field to emerge.

A major turning point in most dialogues came as individuals became more self-reflective, a relief for us facilitators, as the many small group processes had aimed to gently guide participants into bystanding their own ways of thinking and participating. As well, when one individual shared his or her reflections in a self-revealing way, the group softened, and others began sharing. The self-reflectiveness and self-disclosure had an underlying aspect of honesty and authenticity, and along with it the willingness to risk sharing with a sense of vulnerability.

Humor was an additional indicator that dialogue was sinking in. In one group, someone told the story of their first encounter as a new employee with a former staff person who had been a practical joker. Then someone else told a story about that person and then another. More stories tumbled out about funny first experiences as new employees, opening the space for comradery and relief of the frequent tension.

Overall, the final evaluations participants gave of their experience of dialogue were positive. One person summed up the positive feelings that she held of the dialogue experience: "I guess I'm just in awe, you know, there really aren't words about where we were and where we are today. It's kind of awesome. I guess the insights that are common, is just pretty neat."

Another Structural Trap: Dialogue, Problem-Solving and Changes

From the beginning we had stressed that dialogue is not about problem-solving and that no decisions were to be made in the dialogue sessions. The purpose was exploration and learning. Yet we asked participants to dialogue about the topics that mattered most to them. Of course, by flushing workplace problems into the open, employees wanted resolution. Another structural trap! While most were willing to go along with our insistence that we not problem-solve, they did expect to see resolution outside of the dialogue circles.

Behind the scenes, the administrator and management team had triaged the issues arising out of the dialogue sessions along with the long list of issues they already faced but, of course, the behind-the-scenes efforts were not visible to the full staff. In that gap, it appeared to participants who had raised issues that their concerns were falling on deaf ears or had become the management issue du jour, to be dropped as soon as they had been taken up. Said one irritated participant: "We hear this and we hear that, and it's thrown around for a month or two, and then it's gone. And then something else is put in its place, and that's run around for a month or two, and it's gone. And then something else. Nothing is ever carried through from the start to the finish." Others disagreed with this cynical attitude. Such an attitude was much too simple, they argued. It was a complicated place, and change takes time. I was thankful for such armchair philosophers who at times had a palliative effect on the group.

During the course of the nine-month project, the dialogues added to the depth of understanding of the call-in absentee problem, perhaps the hottest topic in the system. The administration worked with the head office on a policy regarding the use of sick leave to address the problem. Given the polarized opinions about the reasons for the problem, a policy that would meet with everyone's acceptance was unlikely. That the issue was being dealt with meant to some that the concerns raised during the dialogues were being heard and acted upon. But others realistically voiced the thought that, whatever action was taken, lots of people would wrongly say that a new policy would be evidence of repercussions. There was no way to please everyone.

Personal and Culture Changes

In the beginning our assessments of participants' personal attitudes ranged from healthy to malignant. Early on, an unexpected focus presented itself. From the first of the dialogues, participants began beating a path to Lynn's office, some still stirred up about the dialogue conversations. Yet – of much greater concern to us – several participants came to Lynn because of her mental health profession. Things had popped into their minds as they sat in the dialogue circle, some things they usually kept out of their conscious thinking, and some things that they long ago had pushed way down under the level of awareness. One had an abusive husband who was likely to berate or beat her as she left her shift and went home. One had sat quietly during the dialogue with memories of a difficult divorce between her parents when she was a small child. Another had visions of being sexually abused by her father as a little girl, something she had never before recalled. And others.

As facilitators we were shocked! What had we done during the dialogue that would arouse such memories to bolt into participants' awareness? An answer to that question was illusive, and one that became a driving curiosity as now, twenty years later, I have been tracing the history of dialogue. But in that time, Lynn carried a heavy load, vetting the long line of participants and their issues, some just continuing their venting and some in need of professional help. How many times did I say, "Thank God my co-facilitator is a therapist!"?

Fortunately, the number of participants who really did need professional help were few, and we were able to refer them to the help they needed. The ones who just wanted further venting were more prevalent, and most participants went along their way, incorporating the experience of dialogue.

Though negativity continued for some, many loosened their previously tightly held assumptions. An example came from a conversation in which the group dialogued about the manner in which they felt rewarded for their work. After a few comments about the need for administration to express more appreciation to employees, a couple of participants differed. Said one, "I think most of your true worth has to be when you've done something for the patients, to observe their behavior and their reaction and see if there's an outcome for them that's been accomplished and feel good about achieving it."

As the trend toward a more positive outlook progressed, we also observed a shift in participants' descriptions of their interpersonal relationships. At the beginning of our dialogue project, such descriptions were very self-defensive. One participant, for example, described her attitude toward her peers as "I can forgive, but I won't forget because you're not going to burn me twice. I'll accept their apology if they give me an apology, but it doesn't mean I'm going to be suckered in twice."

Early in our dialogues, another participant described the converse of the Golden Rule that she felt operated in her work area: "I noticed in my department, the old Golden Rule – do unto others. It's more of how can I get out of doing this because somebody else will have to do it. It's going to have to get done, but it doesn't necessarily have to get done by me."

Those comments reflected our starting point, but throughout our deep dives into the dialogic field the trend toward more supportive interpersonal relationships was encouraging. Some units reported that they had begun their own dialogue sessions in addition to those we sponsored. After one such self-run dialogue, a nurse gave her account: "We talked, and we talked, and we talked. Everyone had their say-so. By the time we were through, some of us got pretty teary, and some pretty loud. We had problems, we had tears, we had anger. We just kept talking until we kinda decided, okay, this is the way it is. When we left it was fine. We worked it out, and we felt much better."

These comments reminded me of something Patrick de Maré, who heavily influenced David Bohm's development of the dialogic method, had said about the intent of dialogue. "We are concerned in large groups with humanizing the group as opposed to socializing the individual." I think our dialogue project made great inroads in humanizing the culture of this facility.

Empathy was a word that group members used: "I have a lot of empathy for the ones that opened up this morning. It was great, you know, because they had feelings that needed to get out, and a lot of the emotion was there, and I can understand their situation. And, I feel very comfortable in this group. I don't think that there is anything that I couldn't say in this group that in some way or another they wouldn't help me." Another felt the safety to speak her mind: "We've gotten to know each other. And I feel very comfortable that if I've got something to say, to be able to say it. The fear isn't there anymore. I know people understand where I'm coming from, you know. And that's good feeling."

Along with the comfort was a sense that the "container," or shared group context, was now resilient enough to bear difficult conversations. Individuals reflected at the end of the intervention about the change their groups had experienced. Whereas some of the first dialogues had felt explosive, some commented that they were struck by the fact that the issues dealt with in the last dialogues were certainly no easier, but the group was beginning to look underneath the surface. They were able to do so without becoming so defensive and were able to explore assumptions. A nurse put it poignantly:

I feel that we have opened up many, many new wounds, and that for us to grow, the opening up of the wounds was highly necessary, that if we hadn't opened them up, we would not have changed, we would not have grown. But, that this is just a beginning, that the hard, hard work is still yet to come, but without continuing to work on the skills that we've gotten from dialogue, we won't make that jump. Without continuing commitment from every employee here, be it management or if it's all-inclusive, we won't jump.

The Call-In Problem

Addressing one of the original reasons we engaged in the dialogues, the absentee call-in problem, surfaced some of the deepest, most significant and unexpected realizations in the group.

As the group gathered for the day's dialogue, one of the maintenance men sat down looking very gray and distressed. We asked if he was okay, as his demeanor was so out of context from his usual stoic, quiet self.

"Mr. Jones [a patient at the facility] died last night, and I just heard about it before I came here." He choked back the tears as he spoke. "He was like a father to me. I visited him every day for that last many years. And he died . . ."

Silence engulfed us all, feeling the welling up of tears in our own eyes. Finally, one of the nurses spoke. "I know just how you feel. Sometimes I leave my shift, and I say to myself, 'I wonder if [so-and-so] will make it through the night.'" And another: "Some days I pull into the lot, put my car in park, and sit there with the engine still running. I wonder who's died since yesterday, and it's all I can do to keep from putting my car back in drive and going home to call in sick." A housekeeper added, "I'm the one who comes to pack up the clothing and belongings after a patient dies, and it's like there's an unfillable hole left behind." And slowly, others spoke as well, all sharing their sentiments toward death as a frequent visitor.

We had tried new regulations, inducements to show up for work, punishments for not showing up, but none of us had considered the weight of human grief staff carried as patients who had been the focus of their efforts for months and years died. The pain to the human hearts of all – the care-givers, support staff, and administrators – when patients they loved had died was core to the care-giving they themselves needed.

We began offering grief therapy.

Observations and Learnings from the Dialogue Intervention

By the time this intervention had ended we had clocked at least 25 full-day sessions and, within those days, most involved two dialogue sessions. Then came the ultimate question: Did it work?

Our intent had been "to create a high level of trust, common ground, and skill so that all staff could talk, listen, inquire and think together about what really mattered to them about their work." As I mentioned at the beginning of this paper, we had wanted to lay the foundation "for a healthy and productive work culture in which staff could use dialogue skills to resolve many of their own workday issues." And though we knew the sessions wouldn't a problem-solving mechanism in themselves, we hoped the dialogues would shed light on real, under-the-surface issues that our prior methods hadn't been able to resolve. As the saying goes, we wanted to teach them to fish for themselves.

Perhaps the best way to describe the end state of the dialogue intervention is through a series of pictures drawn by one of the small groups on their last day together. They had been asked to draw something in whatever form they chose that reflected their sense of where the group had started, where it was as we completed the intervention, and their hopes for the future of the facility's culture.

The various groups' pictures were quite consistent with one group's image. They first depict a large wall that separates people. Dark clouds are in the sky on both sides of the wall, and people are frowning. In their representation of the "present" they had begun tearing chinks out of the wall, but the wall is still there with only an opening. People on either side are less negative than in the past. The clouds are beginning to be less dark, and on at least one side the sun is poking through. The "future" picture shows the wall gone and the bricks tossed to the sides, the sun bright and people smiling, people holding hands, and bringing the patients into the picture as well.

At the close, at an individual level, personal reactions ran the gamut, with a few people expressing polar extremes. Said one: "I thought that when we came to dialogue it was a safe place and what was said would stay in our group and nothing would happen to us at work. But it was a lie." This was counterbalanced by another: "In the beginning I was negative and didn't think it would be a lasting thing and any more than a bitch session, but as we have gotten into it, I do believe I have myself learned there are choices that can be made and only I can make them; that there are better ways of communicating than just getting angry, so you can be heard. I also realized that there is much more to listening than I had thought. Taking time to respond is not negative, it means they may have listened and are thinking their thoughts through."

So, was it a success or a failure? I think some of both, and I'll share some observations, realizing that both the positive and the negative left their marks on individuals as well as on those of us who organized and facilitated the sessions.

Incorporating Training in the Dialogue Intervention

Within the general field of dialogue there exists a difference in opinions about the best way for individuals to learn dialogue. One camp says that the method is solely through participation in the dialogue circle so that learning will occur experientially. The other holds that it is important to incorporate additional learning processes that teach and practice the various skills of dialogue. In this whole-system intervention, we chose the latter, putting almost equal focus and time on learning and dialoguing. Looking back, I think the focus on a learning component was vital to the individuals' capacity to participate as successfully as they did in the dialogues.

Now, after 20-plus years of experience with dialogue, I still think that skill-building makes for much deeper and easier uptake of the dialogue capacities regardless of participants' educational background or comfort in dealing with abstract concepts. Literally all of the individuals, regardless of background or position, were building new skills from scratch, and in that sense they all started from a common point.

The Value of Small Groups

We broke the intended dialogue skills into simple and single components that could be practiced in the small groups which served their intended functions as a locus for skill-building in a more intimate setting that encouraged individuals to practice without the risk of "looking stupid" in the full dialogue group. Breaking the skills down into palatable chunks that participants could grasp and practice brought the skills into much better conscious perception and integration.

In addition, the smaller groups allowed individuals to see a few of their peers in a different light than happened on a day-to-day basis. Rather than being seen as position-holders, their peers became people with lives and worries much like their own. Having worked together for many years, individuals carried deep history and harbored resentments and judgments about their colleagues that, for some, were dissolved by their shifting perceptions of them as people.

Culture Change, Personal and Group Attributes Affecting Skill Uptake

The existing culture was powerful, and as we started we were idealistic about what we could accomplish in the timeframe. Perhaps transformation of the culture was too lofty of a goal and needed a longer time for dialogue to become habit. Participants got "baby steps," a taste, as my co-facilitator opined.

As facilitators we pondered at the end whether we would have been more effective taking alternative approaches. Perhaps we could have worked with the management team for an extended period first to insure we had those people's support. Or, maybe we could have worked with one group of 30 or so folks from across the facility, given them more frequent sessions and deeper skills, then proceeded to a whole-system approach. But, these alternatives would have lost the cross-sectional, full-system effect which, though the sessions were a month apart, at least gave more employees access to the attempted cultural change.

Our conclusion was that the whole-system approach was sound, but it needed a much longer time for significant uptake. Culture change would require many more months, if not years, to take effect.

Dialogue or Psychotherapy?

While appreciative of folks who did learn and shift their orientation through the intervention, I was personally struck by the issue of "difficult" people in a dialogue setting. We had wrestled with the question of whether the challenging behavior that occurred in the dialogues reflected a difficult work environment or whether it was due to individual history of abusive or problematic childhood or life experience. Clearly, there was reason to suspect the latter as individuals needing professional mental health support had come forward. Were the others who were difficult also exhibiting psychological difficulties? What were we to do with the "spoilers" whose venting in the dialogue circle turned off the potential for real conversation?

Even more troubling was the question about whether we were doing dialogue or psychotherapy in our intervention. That question of psychotherapy versus dialogue has been haunting me for years, and as I have researched the background of Bohm's dialogue, I have found that it takes key elements from Bohm's interactions and psychotherapist Patrick de Maré, one of the early developers of group psychotherapy.

I still don't have a good response to that problems difficult people or of the overlap of dialogue and psychotherapy. But, one of my learnings is that in an ongoing deep dialogue process, I want a "Lynn" by my side or available for referral if the need arises. If I have doubts about the depth to which my proposed design might take participants, I ask a licensed mental health professional to review my design with me and to help me keep within the bounds of my own unlicensed capacity.

Authority and Importance of the Sponsors

Our conclusion at the end of the intervention was that having clear agreement, endorsement and support of the uppermost levels of authority is essential. In our case, I had cleared our intervention design with the leader above me, and then had the invitation and participation in planning by the facility administrator and the director of nursing. All that paid off as the dynamics of the intervention played themselves out.

In retrospect I see that bringing dialogue into a work setting is an invitation to create concern on the part of employees who have no idea of the truths that might be exposed and the resulting implications. In our setting, people of all levels – management as well as line staff – were fearful of repercussions for speaking the truth or of having their truth exposed by others. We perceived all manner of resistance, resentment, and sabotage just because dialogue was occurring. At one point, one of the top leaders of the facility went to our corporate office without my knowledge, complaining to the finance director about the amount of money I was wasting on this dialogue process. Thankfully, the finance director and I reported to the same leader, the one who had originally approved and paid for Lynn's and my dialogue training with Bill Isaacs. That leader had wanted to bring dialogue into our overall organization. Without that initial concurrence, we would have been sunk.

Dialogue Versus Problem-Solving

We had emphasized over and over that dialogue was an explorative approach to teasing out the collective attitudes that interfered with effective relationships. People bought that, but it wasn't enough to satisfy. The dialogues did the job of digging up the collective "stuff" that, as one participant had emblazoned in our minds was "like the [stuff] she dumped out of the bedpans." Well and good, but just dumping them left its sensory impact in the center of the dialogue circle, and along with it the frustration of employees and management. To raise the issues and leave them unsolved was not enough.

In retrospect, a pervasive design such as we implemented needed a parallel process to which the identified problems could be referred for problem-solving. True, the management team of this facility did some of that, but it already had a big load with its day-to-day issues and with other organizational changes in the planning. The huge tranche of difficulties unearthed during the dialogues was too large for the management team to integrate. My advice to myself has been to right-size the intervention with the capacity of the organization to respond. I'm reminded of one of my favorite organizational theorists, Stafford Beer, who had a rule to not ask for input if there wasn't capacity to integrate it and to respond to it.

Turning Points in the Dialogues

Reading back through the dialogue transcripts has given me a fresh sense of the behaviors that preceded turning points in the dialogue, things I know now to watch for as indicators the conversation is about to shift.

Most blatant were the blunt, unfiltered comments such as those documented in the dialogue excerpts. Who can resist the temptation of tuning one's attention to what's going to happen next when a really impassioned, evocative statement has been tossed into the middle of the circle? Such openers invited the next person with a likewise pent-up disgruntlement or truth to jump into the game, and then the snowball was rolling down the hill. The comments presented a paradox. On one hand, comments like these were highly emotionalized, which made them irresistible. The issue clearly galvanized the group's attention. But that emotionality could take a turn for resistance to "listening for understanding," and further entrenching the already hardened assumptions.

But, emotionality didn't always carry the group in a downward spiral. At times it served as the call to attention that drew participants in to listen. It brought out the commonness of humanity, each of us more able to feel our own likeness to the emotional speaker. On the other hand, those who spoke with distance and over-intellectualization flattened out the conversation.

Closely related, those who shared their self-reflections and spoke through self-disclosure opened up conversation by a tacit invitation for others to open and lessen their defensiveness. Those conversations tended to open the space for further vulnerability, honesty, authenticity and risk-taking.

Humor was a great asset to building the strength of the container. With so much venting that had occurred, when someone told a funny and the group could laugh, the possibility was there for a change of direction or of depth in the conversation.

A final turning point I noticed was what seemed to be a shift that came from the group's ability to tolerate depth of conversation. A dialogue would progress to a rather deep level and, suddenly, someone would make an off-hand comment that was mundane and irrelevant to the topic. Such a comment bounced the whole group out of the dialogic mindset. Thinking back now with that insight, I can remember that phenomenon in other dialogue groups. I wonder if the container needs to be tempered both by difficult situations and by depth of dialogue in order to become strong enough to sustain a length of exposure time to the underlying dimensions.

In Retrospect

As Dorothy in *The Wizard of Oz* said, "Toto, I don't think we're in Kansas anymore!" At the end of this year of an intense organizational intervention, a tornado had picked me up in the Midwest, taken me to see the dialogue wizard, then plunked me down in Texas! What happened?

The dialogue intervention had consumed a year out of my life that went deeply under the surface of my own consciousness with an impact that still reverberates. At times during those days I ruminated on words spoken, emotions vented, fissures erupted or mended – all ricocheting in my awareness. I felt that I had absorbed and carried the various emotions that the groups were trying to expel from their inner beings, as if I were a sponge for the facility's shadow, a projection point into which the expressed emotions penetrated. In retrospect as I think of David Bohm's enticing promise about dialogue, to a large degree I think that as a carrier of the group drama, I also became a deep well within which changes occurred, some that felt like the churn of Dorothy's tornado.

As we completed the dialogue intervention, I left my supposed life-long partner of many years, much to his surprise. I left my profession as a leader in the field of healthcare, and I moved from the Midwest to Texas where I became an internal organizational development consultant in the energy industry. On one Friday I left a job in which I had 2,000 employees and 2,000 patients. On Monday I was a solo performer in a global company with a wise leader who valued dialogue. That seemed to be the one and only constant with me before and after, the red thread of dialogue.

Now, 25 years after my first introduction to dialogue, the red thread of dialogue continues to hold me in its grip. As one of my colleagues commented, "You're not interested in dialogue, you're *compelled* by it."

References

Senge, P. (1994). *The Fifth Discipline Fieldbook*. New York: Doubleday.

De Maré, P., Piper, R. and Thompson, S. (1991). *Koinonia: From Hate, through Dialogue, to Culture in the Large Group*. London: Karnac Books.

Isaacs, W. (1999). *Dialogue and the Art of Thinking Together: A Pioneering Approach to Communicating in Business and in Life*. New York: Currency/Doubleday.

Conference Session Extracts

From conversation with 20 participants considering the paper with the author

As a young physician, I worked with a psychiatrist who said something I've never forgotten: in order to really help someone, you have to go for the affect first. Unless you deal with the emotional aspect of what a person is bringing, and your own affect if it happens, what's being dealt with will push buttons.

In a dialogic process, affect is one of the languages. I think we really have to feel it, because that gives you more strength.

And yet, the medical establishment has spent a lot of time pathologizing emotion – take a pill, feel better, the opiates that are really repressing the emotion.

So we have had lunch, and we're very comfortable, and we can get to it and we're excited about it. But when you take it into the workplace, I don't know how other people find this, "Oh, I have to go to this thing this afternoon where we have to sit around in a circle." And right there [laughter], that talk about a hidden curriculum that devalues. You have a long way to get into container from that statement. So I think building the importance of what we're doing and getting buy-in from the constituents is really, really valuable. I think you can spend the first session, for sure, getting buy-in to the process.

And it takes time. One thing I think about container-building in every way that I've seen this, especially when you start with people who are the product of that hidden curriculum, if you will, who are cynical and feel pressed for time. You have to bring people together, so that container forms gradually.

And it really doesn't form until somebody shares a first-person story. We had one group of physicians, nurses, and administrators in the work we did. It was two or three months into a six-month process, meeting twice a month for six months, and we would have dialogues after talking about some techniques, but then we would have a sit-in-a-circle dialogue. And one day, somebody told a story about how he had been wounded in the course of his work, he was an administrator, and how he'd been demoted, and how the organization had not treated him very well. And he said, "I just want to share this."

What was demonstrated that day was that the container had formed because he was able to say that, and people were able to hold that tension and then work with it. But that was two or three months in. That wouldn't have happened on the first day when we got together. So I think one of the things that that frustrates people about dialogue is that, well, why isn't it immediate gratification? Okay, we sat for an hour, what are we accomplishing? I used to look at people when I would set circles up and in my world, after about 12 minutes, everybody's looking at their phone like, "What are we doing?" Well, you're not going to really accomplish much when you're expecting something in 12 minutes. At least you're not going to accomplish a dialogic thing. So I think one of the things is time and being willing to commit and spend the time. I don't think you can rush it.

Postscript

The author's reflections written some months after the conference

Having had the time and conversations to soak into the experience I shared at our Roffey Park conference have added immeasurably to my own assimilation and deepening of the process of dialogue. Of course, it's an honor that people would participate with me and, in doing so, evolve the work I first brought forward. Here are a few learnings that have emerged through the dialogue during the Roffey Park conference and through the three online meetings of the practitioner circle following it.

Multiple interventions into outstanding problems at the institution described in my paper had failed. At the time I was convinced that additional attempts also would fail unless the context of the problems were addressed first, the context being a fragmented, refractive culture. Looking back, I still concur with that judgment. Since then I've noticed that many OD interventions fail because they are attempts to "put new wine in old wineskins." And I have seen that successfully healing a sick work culture is a long-term and essential prerequisite to, and concomitant aspect of, an overall intervention.

In retrospect I must acknowledge my own naiveté about how dialogue would play out in this whole-system approach. Given, it was an early use of dialogue as an OD technique. Yet, being forgiven for the technique's newness, I didn't foresee how much consternation would result in the client system from not having a problem-solving component attached to the dialogue intervention. My learning: insure provision is made to address problems issues surfaced during long-term dialogic intervention.

These dialogues often were emotionally volatile after decades of unresolved differences and disagreements having been shoved under the corporate carpet. The invitation for staff to talk about what mattered most to them in their work was met with a deluge of emotions. We facilitators held the line on safety and respect, and yet even when participants spoke with respect, for all of us it was tough coming face-to-face with the rawness of the organization's under-the-carpet sweepings. The most significant breakthroughs almost always were birthed by an emotional outburst, and most often it was the front-line staff who blasted through the years of corporate restraint to say out loud in the presence of all what was really so.

An OD intervention is structured so that representatives of every segment of the organization, including professions, shifts, levels and functions, are simultaneously engaged in dialogic groups and so are learning together the reality of the whole system's "what's so." Participants, regardless of their position or location in the structure, together hear the same stories about what it really means to work there. If this convergent and simultaneous approach is not constituted, accountability for "what's so" slips and slides out of uncomfortable awareness. Having the whole system represented in this way is a prerequisite to landing the otherwise unspeakable issues.

Teaching and Using Dialogue in an American Academic Health Center

James M Herman, Alan Adelman and John Neely

Why Academic Medical Centers / Medicine Needs Dialogue

Medicine in the United States is generally fragmented as a profession, as are Academic Medical Centers as institutions. Academic Medical Centers (AMC) typically consist of a College of Medicine with its affiliated University Hospital. The University Hospital often has a closed medical staff, meaning that only the faculty members of the medical school are able to care for patients in the hospital. Community physicians who are not faculty members are typically not allowed to manage patients or to perform surgery in these institutions.

An AMC has four missions: teaching (medical students, residents, fellows and other health professionals); generation of new knowledge (research); provision of medical care; and service to the medical school, hospital and community. These four missions often clash with each other in real day-to-day situations. Several examples include: 1) teaching medical students or residents may be disruptive to the timely (translate as "profitable") provision of medical care by the teacher; 2) researchers (both MD and PhD) may feel pulled away from their research by teaching or care obligations; and 3) missions become unbalanced as faculty face "publish or perish" demands.

The profession of medicine is also fragmented. Medicine is becoming more and more specialized. There are physicians who take care of only individuals with liver disease or do just joint replacements or see only women or children. Specialists are usually favored by AMCs because of their clinical expertise. In addition, more highly specialized care is also more remunerative in the American health payment system. Only one specialty is not limited by age or gender or medical condition: Family Medicine. However, family physicians often prefer to practice in a community-based practice rather than an Academic Medical Center, for many of the reasons stated above. In many situations patients see a series of specialists without anyone coordinating their care in a continuous fashion over time. This type of fragmentation can lead to over-diagnosis, unnecessary testing, and drug-drug interactions, when each specialist only looks at their part of the patient and not the entire patient. Family physicians often comment about fragmented specialty care by employing the Abraham Maslow saying, "When all you have is a hammer, everything looks like a nail" (Maslow, *The Psychology of Science* 1966).

Chapter Road Map

In this chapter each of us – Jim, Alan and John – will describe how our journey with dialogue began. We will then describe how dialogue was applied in a single department of an AMC, the Department of Family & Community Medicine, over a decade or more. Next, we will discuss how we impacted the entire Academic Medical Center and, to conclude, we will each discuss how dialogue has contributed to our careers after the time period described in the earlier sections.

Beginning the Journey

In the 1998-1999 academic year Jim participated in the yearlong Leadership for Collective Intelligence (LCI) program hosted by the Dialogos organization and coordinated by Bill Isaacs, Peter Garrett and Michael Jones. At Jim's suggestion, Alan and John followed the next academic year. Jim had taken a three-day introduction to Dialogue course some years earlier, and had put many of the practices learned to use in his day-to-day position as Chair of the Department of Family and Community Medicine at Penn State's Milton S. Hershey Medical Center in Hershey, Pennsylvania. This department consisted at the time of about 30-40 faculty family physicians working in ten primary care practices. These faculty members also taught medical students and residents, conducted research and served on numerous medical school and hospital committees. The practice sites were dispersed in the south-central region of Pennsylvania. The nearest practice was approximately one mile from the University Hospital in Hershey, while the furthest was 90 miles away in State College, home of the main campus of Penn State University. Most of the practice sites were within 20 miles from Hershey.

Faculty meetings were set up on a dialogic model each month: Chairs were arranged in a circle without desks, a check-in and check-out format was included, and agendas were based on important questions of the day rather than reading reports. The first change that we noted was that moving to a dialogic format increased participation by faculty members. A majority began to attend each meeting, necessitating several changes in venue as participation increased and the overall number of faculty members expanded. Faculty members reported that they came because they felt that the conversations were important and that they didn't want to miss something important.

Dialogue in the Department of Family and Community Medicine

Two events clearly demonstrated the power of dialogue during these meetings. First, an unintended consequence of the decentralized structure of the department was increased fragmentation. While the department had a physical presence at the AMC, the faculty was spread across the region in ten practice sites where they spent the majority of their time providing medical care to patients and educating medical students. Faculty members split their time between the practice sites and the AMC where they might care for hospitalized patients, teach medical students and serve on committees.

Practice sites were administered by a dyad of an office manager and medical director. While the medical director understood the multiple roles that physicians played, the office managers often did not. This led to friction because the office managers would complain about the inability to run their practices when clinicians were not present to see patients in the office all of the time. They questioned why clinicians "were being taken away" from the office. They were unaware of the multiple roles that clinicians serve in an AMC. Office managers were also isolated in their own offices and not aware of the multiple and shared department goals and could not share their concerns with other office managers.

To reduce the fragmentation due to multiple practice sites and strengthen the dyad of each medical director and corresponding office manager, a monthly meeting was formed that brought together the senior leadership of the department as well as the office managers and medical directors. The participants sat in a circle to discuss their issues. Initially the entire group discussed the multiple missions and goals of the department. Through this discussion of the four missions of the department, participants felt empowered by knowing where their role could contribute to the multiple missions. The group became aware that each individual faculty member did not have to contribute to all of the missions.

To strengthen each dyad and reduce fragmentation, each office dyad was tasked with identifying an issue of concern at their office. They were also tasked with generating an action plan to address their issue. Each month each office manager/medical director team would present their issue and progress made to address the issue to date. From this approach we learned that 1) Many issues were common to more than one practice; 2) As the container of the group strengthened, the offices were able to tackle more tasks that required the coordinated effort of all of the offices; and 3) The dyads were able to take on more difficult tasks as time progressed and the group experience deepened. Furthermore, this led to major initiatives being completed by the group, and the inclusion of other primary specialties joining the monthly meeting.

The second event that demonstrated the power of dialogue centered on the role of pharmaceutical company representatives in the department. In the late 2000s it was common practice to have pharmaceutical representatives come to office practices to provide samples of medications, provide food for clinicians and staff, and provide advertisements in the form of pens, notepads, and calendars. In some situations they would also provide monies to travel to pharmaceutical-sponsored continuing medical education. Finally, they would hire clinicians as speakers for their continuing medical education programs.

While many clinicians took advantage of these practices, there was growing data that indicated that these practices influenced the prescribing practices of clinicians. There were many faculty members who felt that these pharmaceutical representative practices were leading to prescribing more expensive medications which were either not indicated or where less expensive and equally effective alternatives were available. Despite these growing concerns there were no policies to change these behaviors. In our department, about half of the clinicians defended the practices and stated that their prescribing behaviors were not being influenced. Their office staff appreciated the free food, and providing sample medications benefited their patients. The other half felt strongly that the practice should be completely stopped.

In this conflicted environment Jim, the chair of the department began a series of dialogues at the monthly department meetings with this issue as a topic. In addition, a group of faculty members were asked to research the issue. As already described, initially the faculty was polarized around this issue. It was necessary to develop and maintain a strong container that persisted over a period of at least six months. This container needed to be strong enough to "hold the tension" that the faculty felt arising from their fundamental disagreements.

Over time the conversation centered on the assumptions that each group was making in determining their opinions. The "aha" moment came when a faculty member asked about the effect that the presence of the pharmaceutical companies in the practices was having on medical students and other learners, and if this was what we really wanted to "teach" our students?

Following this, and through dialogue, a consensus emerged. The department collectively decided that pharmaceutical representatives would not be allowed to provide food at the offices, nor would pharmaceutical samples be available in the offices. In addition, no other forms of advertisement such as pens, notepads or calendars would be provided to the offices. No vote was necessary. The faculty members who began the conversations intending to continue the practices were genuinely willing to adopt the new set of policies.

Interestingly, our department was the first group of clinicians at this Academic Health Center who made this policy. Shortly after our decision was made, the entire Medical Center instituted a similar policy.

Dialogue at the Medical Center

In 2004 it was decided at the Medical Center that a leadership center would be developed and a series of courses on leadership would be offered. Jim was on the steering committee of this center. Four courses were offered. The three of us took what we learned and, with the help of Peter Garrett, formed a course entitled "Leadership, Dialogue, and Sustainable Change" in which we enrolled senior leaders at the Medical Center (physicians, nurses and administrators). The course took place two afternoons per month for six months. We were able to sustain this effort over five successive years during the 2000-2010 decade.

Participants learned the essentials of container building, structural dynamics, systems thinking, dialogue, and dialogic facilitation. Each four-hour session included a set of didactic materials and a 90-minute dialogue. The didactic material also included poetry, music, and videos – all uncommon pedagogies in an academic setting – where the usual mode of learning is strictly cognitive.

Participants completed a "Change Project" in which they chose a problem in their work environment that was thought to be not solvable, applied dialogic principles to re-analyze the problem and develop a working intervention to see if the situation could be helped by this process. The results of many of these projects were truly transformational in that these "not solvable" issues were moved along towards resolution. One common phenomenon that we discovered was that our learners discovered that what they often thought was the problem was not, and that there was a deeper set of issues (often not discoverable by the operating politeness of the system) that had to be uncovered and worked through first.

This course demonstrated three important issues for the three of us as we reflected on our progress and the progress of our participants:

First, the course demonstrated the fragmentation, or silos, of the Medical Center. We discovered that a large organization really consisted of a set of "microclimates" in which employees functioned, and that people working in close proximity to others could be part of very different microclimates. These zones were determined by the rules of politeness and the way the rules were interpreted by the "boss," and the predominant language used by the group, usually the language of power from above.

One assignment that we repeated yearly was to have participants draw a map of the Medical Center and where their unit fit on the map. A common drawing depicted their unit separate from the rest of the Medical Center. They felt that their unit was not well integrated into the Medical Center. Participants also stated that they felt separated or isolated because they weren't doing their tasks the "Hershey Way." Year after year, the groups defined "The Hershey Way" in amazingly similar terms: *extreme organizational politeness* (so difficult conversations were frowned upon) and *false empowerment* (in that people were told they could make decisions, but were usually chastised for not following unspoken traditional rules of "The Hershey Way").

As these maps were shared within the group in class, deep conversations evolved through common understandings. The group "aha" moment came about in dialogue with the realization that, while individuals often say that there was a "Hershey Way" of doing things, in reality this was a false (but powerful) barrier.

Second, we discovered how the power of dialogue could change the way we look at ourselves and others, and could have a profound effect on microclimates and on the organization as a whole. For example, after a while people would comment when they came into a room where the chairs were in a circle "Oh, Jim must be in charge of this." In another example, one of our course graduates brought a dialogic approach to a curriculum committee, which changed the functioning of the group substantially, in that bystanders and more introverted members found it easier to speak through the use of the check-in and check-out.

Third, we noted an occurrence that happened each year after reviewing David Kantor's concepts of Move-Oppose-Follow-Bystand. Participants were asked to divide themselves by how they view themselves in conversations. To add another dimension, we included archetypes that further defined the positions and mirrored the concepts of Move-Oppose-Follow-Bystand: Sovereign-Warrior-Lover-Magician. Students were then asked which position/archetype they most identified with, and which position/archetype they felt weakest in.

Students gathered in one of four corners of the room corresponding to their position and, as a group, discussed how their preferred archetype shaped their role in conversations and what they felt about the other positions/archetypes. Before each group was to report out to the class, we took a break. During the break the three of us discussed how we as the facilitators would proceed. John suggested that we ask the Followers/Bystanders to report out first since they typically were quiet. We were surprised by the pushback from the Sovereigns and Warriors. They felt that they should report out first. This led to a very interesting dialogue that day. We learned that Followers/Lovers and Bystanders/Magicians often felt trampled by Movers/Sovereigns and Opposers/Warriors, who thought and spoke more quickly from a presumed position of more authority. Meetings would often devolve into fast paced ""Move-Oppose" volleys. Followers and Bystanders reported that by the time they got their thoughts together about a topic, the Movers and Opposers had indeed moved onto something else. Meetings had no opportunities to benefit from the measured thoughts of the Followers and Bystanders.

After five years, unfortunately, a new senior Medical Center administrator effectively closed the center and stopped our course from continuing. His statement was, "If people have time to attend your course, they are not working hard enough."

Dialogue Course Participant Responses

We recently polled graduates of our course. Unfortunately, many have moved or retired from the Medical Center. Those who responded felt the course was a positive experience. Several themes emerged:

Better Communication Skills
- *I gained an appreciation for the complexities in our communications and have become better at navigating around the roadblocks.*
- *I became more aware of the dynamics occurring in my communications. I try to change strategies when communications become stalled.*
- *Recognizing this, I plan my communications around the group meeting and have gotten better results.*
- *There are times when I'm engaged in a deep conversation and recognize it because of that course.*
- *It did change the way I communicate. I'm a better listener.*

Change Management

- *I do know one thing and that is we learn to embrace change no matter what direction we move forward in. While we don't always like change, I think we tend to adapt to it over time and a new direction is then formed. I guess the course helped me to embrace change. I hope you are successful in gaining information from others who were in the class as I don't feel like I have that much to offer.*

General Comments

- *Remember the course well. I think it changes your life significantly.*

We believe these responses, although a limited sample, demonstrate the lasting impact that the course had on our participants.

Leadership Retreats

In addition, the three of us coordinated leadership retreats using a mixed dialogue/World Café format in several high-stakes situations including: 1) the difficult responses of our residents to moving the location (hospital) of their training from a small community hospital to the academic health center in Hershey; 2) a retreat of 40-50 basic science researchers unhappy with their involvement in Medical Center leadership; and 3) a leadership retreat of faculty members at the OU-TU School of Community Medicine in Tulsa, Oklahoma.

These were usually one-day experiences in which we tried to bring issues that were lying "under the table" to the forefront in a safe way, and to determine the beginnings of a way forward to a different future. Our residents found the day to be quite helpful, and the process began a lengthy process of healing. The basic scientists were energized, but the energy of the group was dampened by the presence of a CEO that found the process threatening. The faculty in Tulsa, under new leadership, learned about themselves in a way that they had not before.

Afterword

Jim: After 24 years as chair of Family and Community Medicine at Penn State, I departed to become Dean of the University of Oklahoma School of Community Medicine in Tulsa, Oklahoma. I have been in this position for three years. One of my reasons to take this assignment on was to see if a dialogic approach to leadership would be functional and successful in an entire school atmosphere, including many physician specialties, instead of in a single department. This involves family physicians, internists, surgeons, gynecologists, etc. I have a weekly meeting of my leadership team which I run using dialogic principles. In addition we meet monthly with all specialty department chairs using the same format. To date this is working well, with increased participation, common goal-setting and performance and less passive aggressiveness between and among the departments. We have set large goals that many thought not possible and have made significant progress.

Alan: Dialogue has made a huge impact on me. Since the LCI all of my interactions have been framed by what I have learned. Dialogue forms the basis of how I view all my interactions. I recently stepped down from the Curriculum Oversight Committee for the College of Medicine. For three years I chaired the committee. I always tried to make sure that all participants voiced their opinions. I often inquired why they took the position they did no matter what my own thoughts were. I think that I brought the same approach to all committees I served on whether or not I was the chair. Recently I had the experience of listening to a presentation on leadership. The speaker presented the best type of leadership. They were at a loss when I raised the possibility that there are different styles of leadership (the four-diamond leadership styles) and how different situations may call for different styles.

John: After spending over 30 years in standard academic medicine as a leader in Pediatric Cancer Care, as well as stints as Chair of Pediatrics and Medical Humanities, I am now splitting my time between teaching the principles and practice of Pediatrics and new frontiers of medicine attempting to address the fragmentation in our healthcare system. Addressing the frontiers, I teach and practice a field called "Functional Medicine," which addresses health through imbalances in vital functional systems (energy production, digestion and absorption, immune defense and repair, environmental exposures, and so on) – very systems-thinking medicine! I practice and teach this field, utilizing dialogic and systems thinking principles, to better understand patient and family issues in health. I also have an active consulting practice for organizations (primarily healthcare) with difficult transitions, utilizing World Café and Dialogue to teach organizations how to self-heal.

Conference Session Extracts

From conversation with 20 participants considering the paper with the authors

Physicians are very cognitive. They're very intellectual. All their life, they've gone everywhere and gotten everywhere by taking exams. And so developing a capacity to be more than just intellectual but to assess all the capacities, be they affect or spirituality or all different things and to apply that, does not come naturally to most physicians, and it doesn't come naturally to most people in healthcare in the United States, where it's very fast and results-oriented. So, just the idea of gathering together and slowing down is a very foreign concept.

I mean, the doctor-patient relationship, in my mind, is an example of a container. It's dyad, but it's still a container, and then it expands from there to being members of the team. There's a whole host of containers that, if you're going to be successful, you have to negotiate, be part of, and practice it.

I have a comment and a question, and it has to do with the mental construct within which doctors are listening, right, that is part of the system, at least in the United States. I can't speak for other healthcare systems, but it seems to me that what I've noticed is that there's a construct that the patient doesn't really know anything, and it's reinforced by the fact that, for so many years, and even now, it's kind of token, there hasn't really been an emphasis on me knowing me, taking responsibility for my own health, and that's only just beginning to kind of come in, right? And it hasn't made inroads.

So, therefore, I don't really know what I'm talking about, and for the most part, patients don't really – they don't take a lot of responsibility; they just look to the doctor, so it reinforces that whole system. So listening is also happening inside that construct, and it's being reinforced for the doctor and for the patient. So people are existing in a system that's also reinforcing their behaviour. So I'm curious how do we begin to engage that.

My sense, particularly having worked in healthcare, most people and particularly most physicians have never operated in a healthy group. A healthy group is something that's a new event for most of us, but particularly for all the things that I think the medical profession has to protect.

I was with a medical student, a third-year medical student, a couple of weeks ago, and we were seeing a woman with a terrible condition that could be fixed surgically. She and her daughter were so happy – we didn't know this, but, well, what happened was they started weeping. The medical student looked at me in a panic and motioned to the door, and we walked out, and she said, "She's crying. What do we do [laughter]?" And I said, "Well, let's be human beings. Let's try to find out what's going on [laughter]." So it turned out the woman was crying out of joy. But the point is affect. Self-disclosure moments, especially when they're truly affectual. It's not just self-revelation; it's self-revelation with affect. Genuine, like, "This is how this has made me feel," can be an amazing moment.

I do really appreciate the stories. I just think the stories are the transformative ground that helps people in.

Postscript

The authors' reflections written some months after the conference

The group assembled for the dialogue on our paper had a mix of experiences. Some had extensive experience in using dialogue in medical settings, while others worked in healthcare advocacy. Some had no experience of dialogue in medical settings, but had experiences as patien ts or family members seeking medical attention.

Our initial discussion served as a review of our experiences of dialogue in a medical setting, and further expanded on our paper by adding context. Others added their own experiences of using dialogue in medical settings and in advocacy for challenged populations in seeking healthcare. Still others provided some of their own experiences with the healthcare system. We also discussed the need for support in large organizations in order for dialogue to flourish. There was no overall theme or thread that emerged from our dialogue.

Dialogue and Communities of Practice in American Graduate Medical Education

Beth K Herman

As the Director of Graduate Medical Education (GME) at an academic medical center, I oversee the requirements of the resident physician training programs. Resident physicians (residents) are in the final phase of medical education. They are learners who have graduated from medical school and are training in their selected medical specialty field with supervision. At the completion of residency training, these physicians are eligible to be licensed, board certified, independent practitioners.

I have worked with residents in GME for 31 years. My training in dialogue began in 2005, when I enrolled in the Leadership and Collective Intelligence class at Penn State Hershey. I immediately began to put the principles of dialogue to use in my conversations with senior physicians, residents, administrative leaders, nurses and others with whom I interact on a daily basis. I began to arrange meetings where participants sat in a circle, and included a check-in and check-out for all meetings. I observed that this had the effect of reducing hierarchy when applied to difficult situations arising from the complex and experiential nature of residency education. For example, it was desirable to have residents included in ongoing quality improvement activities within the hospital infrastructure. However, integration of residents into this process was difficult due to perceived differences in power and hierarchy between residents and other staff members. The implementation of a dialogic approach to these meetings ensured that all voices were heard and lead to a superior outcome.

Residents are unique in that they are performing a service as employees of a large hospital and are learners engaged in becoming certified specialists in a given medical field such as surgery, family medicine, or obstetrics and gynecology. They learn in an atmosphere which includes great responsibility in the provision of high-quality patient care, time pressure, and the need to develop a professional identity. The fragmented nature of the American healthcare system includes such factors as specialization, uneven distribution of resources such as health insurance coverage and ego-driven behaviors on the part of many providers. This fragmentation creates a system in which learning is made more difficult. In addition, residents must successfully navigate a learning environment in which there are hierarchies of power, control, and supervision. In order to accomplish this, residents join communities of practice, both formal and informal, as they progress. These are essentially groups of colleagues who have more or less knowledge than other participants about the actual practice of healthcare. This is learning from each other's actual experience as against the knowledge that is written in a book.

Road Map

In this paper, I will describe the theory of dialogic communities of practice, which is a well-established paradigm within adult learning and knowledge management. I will describe, for the first time in the literature, the deep connection between the principles of communities of practice and the essential Dialogic practices of Voice (to speak authentically and genuinely), Listening (to hear what is said and understand what is meant), Respect (regard for the person, their history and their situation) and Suspension (revealing one's thinking so that assumptions and logic can be confirmed or corrected). Included in this paper will be examples from my own experience working with residents and as a dialogic practitioner.

Communities of Practice

In the academic residency context, communities of practice are groups of residents who come together informally to learn and practice. Communities of practice are an integral part of the daily lives of residents. Although they are informal and pervasive and rarely come into explicit focus, they are recognizable in all facets of professional life. Most of these communities of practice do not have a name and do not issue "membership cards." Collectively, the communities determine a culture that develops in which the residents' professional identities are developed. There is a strong connection, previously undescribed, between the four practices of Voice, Respect, Listening and Suspension, and the successful development and maintenance of a community of practice. Even further, the dialogic principle of building a strong container essentially describes what is necessary for a community of practice to function over time. Since my training in dialogue, I have witnessed this essential connection many times. For example, a hospital which supports residency training is required to have a Graduate Medical Education Committee (GMEC). This committee must include faculty members, residents, and administrators and is responsible for the ongoing maintenance of essential requirements for GME. This group functions as a de facto community of practice, with members rotating on and off regularly. I have contributed to this community by introducing concepts of dialogue and ensuring that steps are taken to maintain a strong container on a longitudinal basis.

Medicine, as a whole, represents a community of practice that resident physicians wish to join. More specifically, residents share knowledge within smaller communities of practice, based on who they work with at a given time. As part of this process, residents share resources, organize their workloads, coordinate their patient care activities, and develop relationships to support their everyday activities.

Being included in what matters is a requirement for being engaged in a community. As younger members of a specialty, residents enter these communities from the periphery and, through increased participation, move to the center over time. Individuals construct knowledge through their social environment, where they make meaning by process. A shared repertoire begins to be adopted as they socially construct knowledge together.

Resident physicians come together to learn in a clinical setting and become part of a community of practice within the educational setting. The residents develop a shared language and set of tools that become part of a common repertoire that they use to communicate with each other and practice within the scope of their specialty. In the dialogic framework, an effective community of practice is similar to a strong container. It is a place where people can talk openly and genuinely about their work, their skills, their successes and their failures. For example, in Oncology, groups of residents and supervising attending physicians regularly share experiences during conferences relating the difficulties in their practice. Another example occurs in surgery, where departments have monthly Morbidity and Mortality Conferences to review good and bad outcomes and to develop professional abilities of learners.

The development of strong containers is described within the literature of communities of practice as having three major components: mutual engagement, joint enterprise, and shared repertoire. I will describe each of these with particular attention to how their effectiveness depends on good dialogue skills, and in relation to the four Dialogue practices essential to creating a strong container.

Personally, I am a member of several communities of practice within my profession. One important community of practice is the Graduate Medical Education Network (GMEN). The group includes 44 members, which is rather large. Membership in this community is voluntary, but the goal is to work together to share common work practices and assist each other. The group generally meets monthly, but there is also an online component. Working collectively, the GMEN group has completed several significant tasks, including rewriting various job descriptions, implementing a new career ladder and developing a mentorship program. Individually, this work would be overwhelming; however, when working collectively in a community of practice the work is manageable. Members learn from each other and share values and goals.

Mutual Engagement: Respect and Voice

Mutual engagement is the perception of mutual involvement and commitment (Wenger, 1998). The coherence of a community is the mutual engagement of the participants (Wenger, 1998). People are engaged in actions whose meanings they negotiate with one another. Learning within communities of practice does not reside in books or lecture halls, but rather as experiences and situations that occur through mutual engagement among the members. Residents work closely with each other over long hours. They must negotiate the "rules of engagement" with each other in order to survive. Residents must participate equitably with a shared workload.

For these negotiations to be successful, participants must develop their sense of respect and voice in the dialogic perspective. Respect is taught via the "hidden curriculum" and is taught by example and role modeling. Encouraging residents to find their voice is essential in a learning environment. A community of practice will allow residents to build confidence and find their authentic and genuine voice. An important topic currently in graduate medical education is the development of a culture of respect between and among learners and teachers. There is a long history of members of different specialties "bashing" colleagues in different specialties. For example, a surgeon may describe an internist as a "flea" in front of a learner, meaning "the last thing that leaves a dead body." Also, a subspecialist may describe a primary care physician as "a person who only treats runny noses and not real disease."

In a particularly vivid example, a first-year resident sat in my office upset because she was publicly humiliated during morning rounds. The senior resident had asked her a question in front of the entire team, and she was a bit unsure of the answer. When she hesitated, the senior resident picked up a book and said, "Do you know what this is? It's a book. See these things inside the book? They are pages. See the things on the pages? They are words. I suggest you learn to read the words if you are going to be a doctor."

Many residents fear this type of retaliation if they ask a question. Bringing residents together as a group, having them sit in a circle and voice their concerns without fear of retaliation has helped many residents. Hierarchy is significantly reduced when seated in a circle. Questions such as "Who was your most challenging patient this week?" are asked and answered.

As a recent example, in the Family Medicine/Sports Medicine residency I witnessed residents voicing an issue with a faculty member who, in their perception, was quite harsh and critical in providing feedback to them. The program director, trained in the principles of dialogue, allowed for the development of Voice among the residents and maintained a respectful atmosphere in which the issue could be discussed and adjudicated. As a result, the faculty member was more respectful in how he spoke, and the residents appreciated the feedback they needed to hear. The outcome was successful, in major part due to these dialogic skills. Similarly a new program director was inexperienced in dealing with a group of subordinate residents. Through the Dialogic practice of Voice, he was able to find his sovereign voice.

We introduced the Exceptional Teacher Initiative at Penn State Hershey. Our direct focus on problem behaviors, though only attributable to a small proportion of teachers, had the unintended consequence of minimizing the visibility of the excellent teaching provided by the majority of our faculty. Dialogue has rebalanced the conversation about mistreatment. Now we see that the conversation about learner mistreatment at all levels appears to be improving. Faculty and students alike express appreciation that there is an effort to highlight the positive. All indications are that the needle is currently moving in the right direction. The importance of creating a respectful learning environment must be a top priority in today's academic health systems, just as it is necessary for effective dialogic practice. The evidence for its impact on patient safety and on learning is compelling. The discussion continues to emphasize the institutional imperative for a respectful learning environment while contextualizing the distribution of the mistreatment problems more appropriately. Exceptional teacher initiatives also have the potential to spread innovative teaching techniques when student descriptions of excellent teaching, especially when paired with specific examples of what worked well, are broadcast across the institution.

Joint Enterprise: Suspend

The second component of a community of practice is the negotiation of a joint enterprise. The joint enterprise is what keeps the community of practice together. The joint enterprise is the result of a collective process of negotiation that reflects the complexity of mutual engagement (Wenger, 1998). It is defined in real time as it is negotiated by the participants and belongs to the members, in spite of forces that are beyond their control. The joint enterprise creates mutual accountability among the participants who become an integral part of the practice (Wenger, 1998).

To form a joint enterprise, it may be necessary to suspend the assumptions that you bring to a joint conversation long enough to develop potential new ways of thinking. For example, a family medicine resident and an obstetrical resident recently were working together. Initially, the obstetrical resident believed they knew more about the care of a specific patient than the family medicine resident. However, after suspending assumptions and talking with the family medicine resident about the complexity of the care, the two formed a joint enterprise and they were better able to care for the patient. Although the obstetrical resident had had more time to learn the skills of obstetrical medicine, by suspending assumptions, it became clear that the family medicine resident also had knowledge to teach the obstetrical resident in other fields beyond obstetrics. In one recent case, a patient in labor became suddenly short of breath. The family medicine resident was able to diagnose a pulmonary embolus more quickly than his counterpart, and to institute life-saving treatment because he had had more experience with this disease than the obstetrical resident.

On hospital rounds, communities of practice are visible. Rounds within the hospital include various members of the healthcare team. Historically, rounds are extremely hierarchical. However, using Voice, Listening, Respect, and Suspension, rounds can be a valuable dialogic learning forum. Suspending assumptions can allow others to see that there are many ways to accomplish a task.

Shared Repertoire: Listen

The third characteristic of a community of practice is the development of a shared repertoire. The repertoire of a community of practice includes routines, words, tools, ways of doing things, stories, gestures, symbols, actions or concepts that the community has produced or adopted in the course of its existence and which become part of the practice (Wenger, 1998). The shared repertoire within a residency program is easily identified when attending physicians conduct morning rounds. During the rounds, residents use shared definitions and code words for procedures, people, and practice tools.

Learners must be able to invest themselves in communities of practice in the process of approaching a subject matter. When the learners have committed to the joint enterprise and the shared repertoire, the members move from peripheral participation to a member with greater involvement. Participants in communities of practice participate in a variety of interdependent ways. In order for a shared repertoire to develop among residents, they must listen deeply to one another to understand what is communicated. For example, when a given resident's shift of work ends, he or she must deliver the state of a patient's care to the next resident on call.

Despite the importance of this skill, residents are not generally taught how to listen during their education. In my work, I have discovered that most physicians do not listen deeply to others, often due to time pressures and the need to get on to the next task. There is also the tendency to "reload" or spend time thinking of their next response while the patient is speaking, rather than genuinely listening. The reloading factor often causes physicians to interrupt patients quickly as patient begin to tell their story.

Understanding the importance of dialogic listening skills, I teach residents to actively listen. One tool that I use is to play an excerpt of a short conversation – not a video, but a voice recording that is maximally 15 to 20 seconds in length. I play the recording and have the learners write down what they think they heard. Most find it very challenging to reiterate accurately what was played. I repeat the process several times. In my experience it is often extremely tiring for an individual to listen and correctly repeat exactly what someone is saying. Although a critical skill for patient care, most are not proficient listeners.

In one instance, after training a group of residents to really listen and not "reload," I received the following comment from a resident:

> *The patient had my full attention. And the patient knew he had my full attention, for just five minutes – maybe that's all it was. But the patient knew that – that I was his doctor, and he had my attention. And, I knew in a short amount of time, that I was able to transmit to the patient that the patient had my attention, and I am really there for them. And, that's what I try to be. No matter how rushed I am, or how many multiple things going on, I want every single patient, when I walk into the room, to feel that I am there for them. When things get crazy and busy – and maybe I'm thinking "why is this patient here, why are they wasting my time?" – but then I say, no that is not how I want to behave. I want to listen. I'm a better listener.*

Professional Identity Formation

Professional identity formation occurs most powerfully through participation in communities of practice within the resident's work by observing how others behave and how they embody the values and behaviors of the profession. (Lave & Wenger, 1991). This is a gradual socialization into the clinical/professional role through increasing participation in a community of practice (Wenger, 1998).

Although educators cannot force a professional identity upon learners, they can contribute to the production of an environment conducive to its development through the use of dialogic practices and actual dialogue during rounds, conferences, and conversations. Professional identity develops in a nonlinear progression, understanding there will be highs and lows in the process. Effective morning reports, where the on-call resident reports about events of the previous night to members of the team who are arriving in the morning, rely on a system of check-ins.

Role modeling supports professional identity development and communities of practice. A role model is always modeling, whether consciously or unconsciously. Residents will experience role models in very different ways and will frame the role model in light of their own values, goals, and experiences. Attending physicians are important role models, but it is by virtue of their membership in the community of practice that they teach other members. Successful role modelers use respect and listening skills, and allow learners to develop personal voice and suspension skills. For example, a role model will handle "specialty-bashing," if and when it occurs by demonstrating an alternative approach to dealing with stress. One exceptional teacher recently said,

You want to surround yourself with people who want you to do what they do because they love what they do. I can talk forever about why someone should do family medicine – forever – and it's never about why they shouldn't do another specialty. It's only about all the positive things that I see coming out of why I did what I did. And so, for me that becomes the key. That's how you demonstrate to students.

Conclusion

Communities of practice are an important practice in adult learning. In this paper, I have attempted to demonstrate the fundamental commonalities between these communities and the essential practices of dialogue, using the lens of my experience as an educator and administrator in American Graduate Medical Education and as a dialogic facilitator. I have found that effective learning and professional identity formation are best served in a dialogic environment. Masterful teachers might possess these skills innately or they may need to be educated in their use – but when they do have the skills, fragmentation in the educational process, and thus in the healthcare produced, is reduced.

An Afterthought about the Academy of Professional Dialogue

There may be an interesting correlation here with the developing Academy of Professional Dialogue. Dialogue facilitators and practitioners applying to join the Academy may have read the literature and done a range of dialogue trainings courses, but they may not yet be professionals in their dialogue practice. The residents come to us at Hershey with significant knowledge, having already graduated from medical school, but it is the experience of practice, significantly aided by the various communities of practice they participate in, that leads them to develop the identity of a professional in their particular specialty. This means the skills, attitude and values have been internalized in a way that results in a different stance – the stance of a professional. It is my hope that the Academy helps to cultivate the kinds of communities of practice, perhaps through the Practitioner Circles, that establishes Dialogue as an internationally accepted and useful profession. The Academy is only going to move forward if they are successful in developing communities of practice.

References

Lave, J., & Wenger, E. (1991). *Situated Learning: Legitimate Peripheral Participation.* Cambridge, UK: Cambridge University Press.

Wenger, E. (1998). *Communities of Practice: Learning, Meaning and Identity.* Cambridge, UK: Cambridge University Press.

* **Editor's Note regarding Conference Session Extracts for Beth's dialogue:** Unfortunately, there is no recording of Beth's session, so there are no excerpts from it.

Postscript

The author's reflections written some months after the conference

Since the *World Needs Dialogue!* Conference in October of 2018, I have continued my work in dialogue within graduate medical education. In the United States, much of the professional learning that takes place occurs via communities of learning and practice. Dialogue within graduate medical education encourages reflection in action within these communities. Unfortunately, education is primarily structured around a standardized teaching curriculum, as opposed to a learning curriculum. In a teaching curriculum the teacher is the center of all instruction and learning, and the setting is generally used to instruct novices or newcomers. On the other hand, a learning curriculum is learner-based and uses experiences and everyday interactions to build a base of knowledge within the learner. Dialogue assists the learner-based curriculum by promoting and stimulating learning and thinking together in groups.

In the spring of 2019, I completed my doctorate in education and defended my dissertation entitled "Teaching Professionalism in Medical Residency Programs, Exemplary Educators, Role Modeling, and the Influence of the Hidden Curriculum." My research emphasized the experiences of the learners and social connections within their communities of practice. Learning often involves a shift in attitudes in addition to the acquisition of skills. Changes in attitude often do not happen easily or quickly. Learning is a complex fabric, woven over time, which is particularly evident in a helping profession, such as medicine. I was fortunate to have studied positive teaching, learning, and role modeling. I plan to continue to conduct research focused on the hidden curriculum, professionalism, professional identity formation, and communities of practice.

In closing, I believe the attendees at the *Communities of Practice in American Graduate Medical Education* session held during *The World Needs Dialogue!* Conference in October of 2018 arrived with varying expectations. Some of the participants worked in the healthcare field, while others were curious about the topic of communities of practice. Although it is always challenging to manage expectations, the session addressed ways in which dialogue has been applied to bring about change in graduate medical education. I trust that my work with the unfolding practices of dialogue will add value to the teaching and learning of professionalism of resident physicians and will prepare physicians to be caring and competent physicians.

Section Four

Society Needs Dialogue!

Dialogue, Politics and the Search for Global Solutions

Claudia Apel

International development is concerned with complex global problems such as climate change, urbanisation, poverty and migration. International development actors worldwide are becoming aware that seemingly simple solutions might have short-term, localised effects, but often create more drastic problems in the long run. Solutions that look good at first sight often reproduce effects similar to those that they were meant to counteract. Over time, this leaves many people disillusioned and doubtful that real change might be possible. Why do so many seemingly great ideas never alter what really matters to us?

One answer lies in the way in which we approach the search for solutions. In most cases, solutions are developed and implemented on the basis of the same patterns of thinking and implicit assumptions as the problems with which we are dealing. These are assumptions about how humans are, how societies work, and many more. Rooted in the fundamental values and beliefs of the systems we live and work in, they are so natural to people that it becomes almost impossible to realise that they are indeed assumptions, and not 'the' reality.

The fact that we hold such culturally shaped assumptions and beliefs about the world is not inherently bad, as they grant us orientation, guidance and the capacity to act within organisations and systems. However, since they lend stability to a system, they can become hindrances when we are trying to achieve change. In the search for new solutions to complex challenges, our unquestioned assumptions about the world narrow our possibilities and blind us to untried, different ways of approaching change. Viewed from a positive angle, this means that once we learn how to identify and question our own assumptions, we will be able to develop new ideas for dealing with complex challenges.

Among the many means that can help foster new solutions to pressing global challenges, communication and an exchange of perspectives with the aim of a better mutual understanding seem crucial. The formats for exchange that international development policy-makers and practitioners often rely on – conferences, study trips, trainings, round tables – do not seem to be able to fully address the challenges arising from complex problems and silo-thinking. There is a need for new spaces that allow for a collective search for new approaches and initiatives – spaces for personal and collective development, for listening and strengthening mutual understanding, building trust to break institutional silos and sparking new actions to address the global challenges of our times.

The Global Leadership Academy

The United Nation's 2030 Agenda, with its Sustainable Development Goals, guide many of the activities in the field of international cooperation and development. They re-emphasise how interrelated and inseparable social, environmental and economic issues are.

The Global Leadership Academy, commissioned by the German Federal Ministry for Economic Cooperation and Development (BMZ), is an international development programme carried out by the German Development Cooperation, or Deutsche Gesellschaft fuer Internationale Zusammenarbeit (GIZ). The German government and in particular the BMZ acknowledge that, in order to meet global challenges, international and development cooperation needs to look beyond its traditional bilateral, regional and sectoral boundaries and follow the trend of dissolving conventional stakeholder patterns such as those of donors and recipients. It realises that long-lasting progress can only be achieved based on mutual respect and collective action. Therefore, it is interested in fostering innovative forms of cooperation, joint understanding and commitment, based on partnerships between equals and on mutual learning.

Founded in 2012, the Global Leadership Academy is mandated to conduct international dialogue processes for leaders and change agents from around the world on issues of global relevance. Currently working in a small team of six people based at one of GIZ's head offices close to Frankfurt am Main, our practice has been continuously evolving over the past six years. As a team, our daily work is oftentimes characterized by the experience of polarity between being a programme in a government agency, with its bureaucratic processes and mandates and the elements required to hold creative and open spaces, where different actors meet as peers, as well as working flexibly and sensitively with power dynamics and process, and of attending to and following what emerges in the diverse groups.

What We Do

Our dialogue processes – we call them Leadership and Innovation Labs – are designed on the basis of the Social Lab Methodology. Social Labs represent a format that enables groups to tackle the kinds of complex challenges that no actor can successfully solve on their own. They have a distinctive multi-stakeholder nature, meaning that experienced representatives from government, civil society and the private sector gather and converse at 'eye level' and with equal responsibilities. Importantly, Social Labs use an experimental, or so-called emergent approach, which does not prescribe outcomes but rather facilitates and fosters the knowledge, potential and opportunities that a group holds. Social Labs are known to create deep ownership and enable the collaborative development and implementation of new ideas and solutions. Subsequently, Social Labs enable results and impact on different levels: new impulses and lasting changes go beyond individuals, to the level of the group and network, to participants' organisational contexts and, ultimately, to a systemic level. Finally, they are often characterized by a specific intervention architecture, entailing multiple face-to-face meetings as well as active phases of reflection and collaborative implementation of new ideas in participants' home contexts, supported by professional coaches.

At the Global Leadership Academy, our expertise is the conceptualisation, set-up, management, co-facilitation and evaluation of Leadership and Innovation Labs. The Labs we have worked on – 13 individual processes since 2012 – address different topics relevant to international cooperation and development. These include reconciliation, urban development, ocean management, diversity and migration. We implement them together with partner organisations that bring topical expertise and/or in-depth experience in facilitating large and very diverse groups.

Our Labs span a period of six to 18 months, with two to four face-to-face meetings, each about three or four days long. A selected group of 25 to 30 decision-makers and opinion leaders from different world regions and societal sectors (government, civil society, private sector) meet in inspiring locations that allow for further exploration of the Lab's topics. The process will be described in further sections below with the help of one concrete example.

What Do We Mean by *Dialogue*? How Do We Employ It?

With the aim of advancing leadership and innovation capacities, our Labs are rooted in a dialogical understanding and employ dialogical methodologies and formats.

Dialogical philosophies and practices have been at the heart of many indigenous cultures for thousands of years. In the 1980s, physicist David Bohm and later organisational change specialists such as Peter Senge and William Isaacs have recognised, expanded and scientifically underpinned the benefit of dialogue for modern societies and organisations. According to Bohm, dialogue is a free-flowing group conversation in which participants attempt to experience everyone's point of view fully, equally and non-judgmentally. Dialogue combines conversation with the concurrent observation of the accompanying thinking process, thus slowing down communication and inviting us to recognise the borders of our comfort zone and their limiting effects on learning and understanding. The approach is ideally suited to enable individual and collective learning about deeply held assumptions and patterns of thinking of those participating in the dialogue.

Our Labs build on many aspects of Bohmian dialogue: we work with what emerges in a group process and we use dialogue for deep reflection, deep listening and the collective emergence of new perspectives. In contrast to Bohm's work, however, we use dialogue as a way of directly addressing practical issues. Our Labs are designed around specific topics, with an explicit intention to lay the groundwork for enabling change through the development of concrete change initiatives. Sessions are guided by a facilitator who accompanies the group and holds the space.

In the Global Leadership Academy's programmes, we employ dialogue to:

- Enable personal transformation and foster leadership development
- Use the diversity of perspectives for a deeper understanding of complex challenges
- Strengthen networks and build cooperation across organisations and sectors

We believe that the experience of dialogue and the nurturing of the corresponding mindset enable leaders to go beyond solutions that recreate the status quo – enabling innovation and the initiation of sustainable and inclusive change.

Methods and Instruments of Dialogue

Moving from debate and discussion to dialogue is the transformation towards an inclusive learning culture. As Glenna Gerard, Linda Ellinor, Peggy Holman and Tom Devane have pointed out, dialogue invites all members to free themselves from established perceptions and roles, to be able to see the whole issue rather than parts of it, to recognise connections and relationships, to explore assumptions, to learn through exploration and disclosure, and to let go of the fixation on a specific predefined outcome of a conversation. This collective search for something new to emerge can initially be an unusual experience that requires letting go of learned habits of relating to others. As the dialogue process proceeds, initial caution often gives way to increased curiosity and creativity. New ideas and solutions can emerge, to be shaped and turned into approaches for action.

While some of the Global Leadership Academy's programmes have been designed around one particular dialogue method (e.g., our Global Wellbeing Lab is based on Theory U, the Power of Diversity Lab is based on Deep Democracy, and the Migration Laboratory is based on Professional Dialogue), other initiatives have drawn on a variety of different methods (e.g., the Mandela Dialogues on Memory Work). These methods differ in many ways, yet they all serve the purpose of enabling deep listening, an open-minded, open-hearted exchange, the questioning of individual and collective assumptions and the generation of new perspectives.

The Migration Laboratory

Human mobility is an increasingly important global reality that affects the future of all countries across the globe. According to the 2017 International Migration Report, there are an estimated 258 million international migrants, the majority of whom move across countries in a safe, orderly and regular manner. However, a considerable number of international migrants find themselves in situations of forced labour and other forms of irregularity.

The following section is a description of the Migration Laboratory, and it includes a part of the invitation that potential participants of the Lab received:

The Migration Laboratory brings together 31 participants from 18 different countries to enable new perspectives and to facilitate the co-creation of ideas and innovative practices. It aims at going beyond 'us' and 'them' and towards a migration that benefits all actors in society. This multi-stakeholder dialogue process enables mutual understanding and builds bridges beyond institutionally and sector-specifically defined responses. It aims at providing opportunities to explore critical challenges and stakeholder relations in the field of migration and development, allowing for a new and systemic understanding of the issue.

The Migration Lab fosters profound reflection, experiential learning, and tangible action to empower participants to significantly further their work and that of their home organisations. Peer-circles enable reciprocal support to participants in relation to their own specific challenges within their work, organisation or region. The whole process is geared to promote and enable change. Between the three face-to-face Lab meetings, professional reflection sessions enable participants to review lessons learnt from the meetings and explore how these insights can grow in their contexts and be transferred into their work. Participants are further encouraged to cluster regionally and to undertake self-led learning journeys into migration and development-related initiatives in their countries, exploring parts of their own field of work that they are least familiar with, thereby uncovering blind spots and making space for innovation.

The Migration Lab was designed to provide a space for dialogue, experimentation and collaboration targeted at five key objectives:

1. To engage critically with the challenges and potentials of ensuring that migration is beneficial for all actors in society
2. To bring diverse interests in the migration system into dialogue and support a better understanding of mutual perspectives
3. To encourage cross-sectoral collaboration and new forms of cooperation on concrete change initiatives tackling critical issues in the field
4. To foster a global network of change agents
5. To impact national and global discourses on migration

The Global Forum on Migration and Development (GFMD) is an initiative of the United Nations Member States to address the migration and development interconnections in practical and action-oriented ways. It is an informal, non-binding, voluntary and government-led process. In view of the societal implications of these issues, civil society and business representatives have been involved from the outset in this process. Within the framework of the GFMD and on behalf of the Federal Government of Germany – as Co-Chair of GFMD in 2017/2018 – the Global Leadership Academy and the Sector Project Migration and Development of GIZ launched the Migration Laboratory.

Initiation and Preparation of a Lab

Several steps and processes are at the core of the initiation and preparation of any Lab that we set up. Taking the necessary time for these preparatory processes has proven to be one of the success factors of the later dialogue.

A global issue relevant to human coexistence around the world is the focus of each Lab, and pools the passion and sense of ownership of participants. The global issue – in this case migration and its development potential – is at the heart of all subsequent steps, from building a strong hosting team, to selecting participants that share a passion for finding solutions to this challenge, to developing a tailored intervention design with the appropriate methodologies. Importantly, it serves as a prerequisite for the building of the network among participants that in most of our Labs lasts well beyond our intervention. On the basis of the global issue, we formulate a strategic question for the Lab that provokes people's interest and attention, in the case of the Migration Lab: "How can we act together across sectors so that migration is beneficial for all actors in society?" This strategic question is important, because within a Lab, we are acting as adaptively as possible to the dynamic social process of the Lab group – while the question and the objectives we derive from it (see above for the objectives of the Migration Lab) provide the barriers of the corridor we act in.

We host Labs collaboratively together with other organisations or organisational entities – in the case of the Migration Lab together with another entity of GIZ, the Sector Project Migration and Development. All important decisions during the preparation and implementation of the Lab are taken together in this partnership. Our cooperation partners complement our expertise in a variety of ways. They may bring in particular technical experience, knowledge of a sector, geographical, or cultural insights, methodological know-how, funding – or a combination of these aspects. We choose this cooperative approach to convening and facilitating our Labs because we firmly believe that, in order to create and host a successful Lab, we need the same diversity of perspectives, skills, experiences, and views that the Lab group itself needs to generate new insights and innovative ideas for change. At the same time, co-hosting comes with many challenges that shared ownership brings. It means navigating diverging institutional interests, managing different roles during the Lab process, facing conflicts, and letting go of control over the process while allowing for an emergence of new ideas. In that sense, the hosting team is a 'microcosm' of the entire Lab group. The premise that sustainable change is achieved through dialogue and cooperation needs to be embodied by the conveners who themselves experience the advantages, opportunities, difficulties, and conflicts of working collaboratively in shaping change.

In the Migration Lab, the fact that two entities from within GIZ were partnering made not all, but many things easier – the restrictions each one of us was facing were well known to the other. We also brought on board Dialogue Associates, represented by Jane Ball and Peter Garrett, as a methodological partner. At the end of a long, and on all sides arduous, tendering process, we finally met with all three partners together for a first design workshop in Berlin, about a month before the start of the Lab. We clarified strategic objectives, activities and roles and worked towards a common understanding about where all of us came from and what we wanted to achieve with the Lab. Some prior virtual calls had prepared us for this coming together.

In order to make the work of Labs sustainable, we aim at creating institutional linkages or at anchoring them in higher-level international policy processes. The Migration Lab was implemented in the framework of the GFMD, which itself provided access to a lot of high-level actors and visibility and came at a decisive time for the global community concerned with migration and development: the first Global Compact for Safe, Orderly and Regular Migration (GCM) was being negotiated during the Lab's active period and is going to be adopted at the end of 2018. With the help of our partners, Dialogue Associates and the Sector Project Migration and Development, which supports the Migration Policy unit at BMZ, we created an understanding of how the Lab would fit in with these international processes and actors. In doing so, we were able to communicate clearly about its role and potential and create spaces for exchange and synergies between other actors and the Lab. This understanding helped us as a hosting team to take a strategic approach to designing and implementing the Lab's activities, so as to maximize its impact and outcomes and strengthen its role as an actual intervention into how greater political systems and processes work.

When identifying participants for a Lab, we pay attention to the diversity of the group in terms of experience, age, gender, societal sector, cultural and professional backgrounds. The success of a Lab largely hinges on the identification of participants who are passionate about the issue at stake, open to new ideas and impulses, able to engage in dialogue and willing to reconsider personal attitudes and deeply held assumptions. Our Labs not only seek to facilitate conversation but also to enable change. While acknowledging that official rank is not a prerequisite for the implementation of change initiatives, the capacity to exert influence matters – be it through institutional standing, networks, or opinion leadership. Because of the political nature of our field of work, sometimes, as in the Migration Lab, we do not have full freedom in the selection of participants. Here, those participants coming from the government side had been mandated by their own institutions. Hence, we haven't had telephone selection interviews with them, as we generally do with all potential participants, but still have tried to have 'onboarding calls' in order to prepare them for this somewhat new experience awaiting them.

We believe that the first interactions during a Lab – including those with the hosting team in the preparation phase – are vital to set the tone for dialogue with and among the participants. Leaving habitual patterns of thought and action doesn't just occur by chance or by introducing a few tools; it requires a setting that allows us to step out of our typical roles. A setting does not just refer to a physical place, but rather includes a space or 'container' where meaningful conversations thrive. We initiate this kind of dialogical setting when we solicit participation in a Lab. In our first conversation with prospective participants, we not only try to understand their passion and viewpoints with regards to the set Lab topic, but also clarify the Lab process, generating an expectation for dialogue and novel experiences to take place in the Lab. Thus, most participants arrive at the first meeting with a clear intention to engage in dialogue and are open to the idea of using dialogue to generate new perspectives on a complex issue that holds meaning to them.

Together with our partners, we create a tailored intervention design for a Lab to fit its objectives and the needs of participants, including decisions on the overall duration, number, and location of Lab meetings, accompaniment such as coaching, working with individual or collective change projects and platforms for online sharing and exchange. The Labs involve multiple Lab meetings and accompaniment/coaching phases. This iterative process design increases the long-term absorption of new experiences and insights, as everyday routines are broken up at several time points and the learning effects of the Lab meetings can resonate at different times during individual and institutional development. The complementarity of Lab meetings and participants' work in home systems enables them to engage in novel and daring thoughts in the enabling space of the Lab, while repeatedly returning to their home systems to rub their new ideas against the rough skin of reality.

The transfer of ideas from the Lab meeting, with all the excitement generated there, to participants' home systems is probably the most sensitive, difficult, or even discouraging part of the Lab process. We support participants in this process in different ways. During Lab meetings, participants can reflect the current framework conditions in their sphere of influence; taking the perspective of those who oppose change helps to identify and understand the leverage points change agents have at their disposal. Between Lab meetings, we accompany participants through coaching calls (individually or in small groups) and other forms of contact. Often, the greatest encouragement in managing the obstacles and frustrations of initiating change is the Lab group itself, which we frequently see turning into an active network of peer support. Exchanges among Lab peers often take place through social media and other online platforms that provide a virtual space for co-creation, communication, and knowledge sharing.

Architecture of the Migration Laboratory

The Migration Laboratory was designed to entail three face-to-face meetings, which took place between October 2017 and May 2018. The meeting locations were chosen strategically to ensure political support and attention as well as access to important local actors. The first Lab meeting took place in Berlin, Germany, the home country of the commissioning ministry BMZ. The second meeting took place in Rabat, Morocco, securing the on-site political support of the Moroccan Co-Chair. The third meeting took place in Quito, Ecuador. The decision for the last location had been left open and handed over to the Lab group, who defined criteria that ultimately led to the selection of Ecuador on the basis of the Ecuadorian Lab participants' invitation and Ecuador's potential role as a future GFMD chair in 2019. Personal and group accompaniment in the form of virtual calls with the facilitation and convening team were offered and encouraged throughout the process to support individual learning and the co-creation of tangible change proposals. The Migration Lab itself was later presented as 'a different way of working' together with the eight project proposals it developed, at the GFMD Summit in December 2018 in Marrakech.

The Process and Content
The First Lab Meeting: Berlin, Germany

The first meeting of the Lab took place in under the theme 'together understand'. It was designed to introduce the theme, the facilitators, the Lab methodology, and the participants to each other. Furthermore, it was conceptualised to explore different perspectives and interests held in the field of migration and development and to facilitate dialogue between stakeholders with different viewpoints. This first meeting was set up along a migration journey and the six themes of the Modalities Resolution of the Global Compact on Migration.

The facilitators introduced the Professional Dialogue approach, first giving an example for a typical monologue, then initiating a debate on the notion that migration is not beneficial for all, followed by a discussion on the Lab location for the third meeting, then conversations in small groups exploring a common interest and finally a dialogue on the potential of these eight months Migration Lab. In the end, the concept of a generative dialogue was explained.

The key learning of the event's first day was that different modes of talking and thinking together engage people differently. All are needed, but at different times for different levels of engagement and for different purposes. Furthermore, the complexity of grasping migration phenomena, even among experts, was highlighted. In this sense, the first dialogic group sessions ended with the two questions that many participants continued pondering: What can the Lab do to impact on the global narrative of the potential of migration? And how can the Lab foster political will for the pursuit of a migration that benefits all?

In the evening, the Lab participants attended the musical *Hoch hinaus* (*Flying High*), a co-creation of an American composer, German teenagers and refugees living in Germany who have been working together for several months to make the musical happen. We purposefully looked for such extra activities which relate to the Lab's theme on a content level but at the same time enable a different experience for many Lab participants: one of experience and emotion, rather than of thinking and concepts. The visible friendship and solidarity between the German and the refugee teenagers were considered a moving and encouraging experience by many Lab participants. Using the newly learned approach of Professional Dialogue as a basis for understanding migration together, the second day under the theme 'together understand the drivers of migration' was guided by the questions: What do migrants think as they leave their home countries? What leads them to think and feel that way? In order to address these questions and to make use of the different geographical backgrounds, the group divided into six sub-groups according to their interest in working on the perspective of countries of origin, transit or destination, respectively. After the conversations, the groups placed themselves according to a 'typical' migrant's journey, starting with the country of origin, transit and destination. Despite the long and rich experience of the participants in the field of migration, walking along the migration cycle set the basis for a new understanding of the complexity as well as the variety of drivers of migration. In addition, the fact that migration links origin and receiving societies and migrants themselves made it obvious that honest cross-national and sectoral partnerships are crucial for ensuring that migration is beneficial for all.

Afterwards, Lab participants went on 'learning immersions'. These visits allowed them to get to know the perspective of refugees and migrants arriving in Germany and their drivers for migration: talking *with* rather than talking *about* migrants, and hearing the first-hand accounts of their experiences and situation. Two initiatives were visited: Interkular, a social enterprise that finds and promotes the potential of young people of all origins by cooperating with local offices, employers, neighbourhoods and the civil society; and Bantabaa, an integration project that serves as a meeting point for refugees around Görlitzer Park in Berlin Kreuzberg, and focuses on education and jobs in the catering sector. Coming out of these encounters, many participants were deeply moved and spoke of emotions such as awe about their conversation partners' courage and strength, as well as feelings of shame at the realisation of a harsh lack of human-centred policymaking – allowing for a new depth, emotional openness and bonds in the participant group.

The third day contained a 'policy immersion' at the office of the commissioner for integration and migration of the City of Berlin. The theme of the policy immersion was an enquiry into good practice for successful integration of migrants into the local community with speakers from different German parties and authorities. In the subsequent discussion, the participants appreciated the honesty and openness of the speakers, while some participants also brought to the table their frustration about some of the statements having been very 'political' and not enough 'to the point'. Some seemed to get argumentative and stuck in criticizing roles. As a hosting team, we tried to tie this observation not only to the content perspective, but also to the constraints and the atmosphere in which policy and administration actors – and civil society actors, respectively – are working in order to make change happen.

In the afternoon, participants engaged in a dialogue on the different migration pathways and the choices and experiences involved. The results of the dialogue included different findings – for example, "there is a lack of legal pathways for low-skilled migrants" or "shared responsibility is the precondition for migration governance".

On the fourth day, participants held a dialogue on migrants' contributions. It ended with the conclusion that the perceived value of a migrant's contribution depends on different perspectives. Contribution to whom? State? Migrant? Host community? Family? In this sense, contribution would need further defining, which is why the participants agreed that fostering an enabling environment that allows migrants to contribute is more important than predefining positive contributions on behalf of migrants and raising false expectations. In addition, as with the example of 'expatriation versus migration', the use of language often discloses embedded power dynamics in the field of migration policy making.

Afterwards, we introduced the bridge period between the meetings in Berlin and Rabat. We proposed to participants that they make use of this time to engage and involve people locally, to organise local immersions in order to understand different perspectives and/or to hold dialogues with mixed groups about migration of benefit to all and note the different narratives.

The first Lab in Berlin ended with a check-out session that invited all Lab participants to sum up their experience in one sentence.

The Second Lab Meeting: Rabat, Morocco

The second meeting of the Migration Lab took place in Rabat with the theme 'Together initiate proposals'. Based on the first meeting's topic, 'Together understand', the second meeting's objective was to enable participants to further develop their thinking on specific topics in the context of migration and development before eventually developing proposals.

The meeting started with sleepless nights for some of us in the hosting team and external helpers. It had proven very difficult to obtain the visa to go to Morocco for some of our participants from countries such as Moldova, who had to travel in person to an embassy in Romania. All our prior efforts to support this process had failed. But with a small group of 30 participants, and oftentimes only two or three participants per country, every single person counts. With the emergency help of government colleagues of our Moroccan Lab participants, we managed to get a last-minute visa to secure entrance for our Moldovan friends – as they were already in the air approaching Morocco, after having decided that they would board the plane trusting that we would sort out the situation!

The first day of the Lab meeting was kicked off by welcome speeches by officials from Morocco and Germany. They highlighted the current window of opportunity in the field of migration policy that is characterized by the negotiations on the GCM, underlining the importance of formats like the Migration Laboratory and its opportunity to contribute to the GCM process and beyond.

After this official welcome, the Migration Lab participants started the sessions with a check-in, aimed at surfacing how it felt to be back together, which immediately brought back the energy developed during the first Lab meeting. Several participants voiced their surprise about their own feelings of immediate familiarity, trust and closeness in the group. The atmosphere felt very light, positive and full of energy to 'get to the work' – conditions that smoothly moved us into short inputs revolving around what individuals had learned during the bridge time.

The facilitators introduced the Dialogic Actions as developed by David Kantor: Move, Follow, Oppose and Bystand. The Dialogic Actions laid the basis for working together on initiating proposals. A balance of all four actions makes up a functional conversation and is important for rigorous decision-making processes within a group of people. The participants tested the Dialogic Actions in small groups and acquainted themselves with the conscious use of these dialogic skills. Thanks to the trust already gained in the first meeting, most participants were very open to embracing this new experience, and the engagement felt light and full of laughter – a fruitful atmosphere for learning.

The second day's aim was to concretize the areas of interest and concern on the way towards initiating a project proposal that would make a real difference in the world 'out there'. The activities resulted in preliminary cluster groups, which were slightly modified in the course of this second Lab meeting.

On the third day, the participants had the opportunity to go on learning 'immersions' once again, visiting organisations and encountering migrants and refugees in order to better understand migration from a local Moroccan perspective. One immersion at Fondation Orient-Occident enabled participants to get to know migration from the perspective of Sub-Saharan migrants, and to gain knowledge in the field of community development and integration. Another immersion at MAScIR (Moroccan Foundation for Advanced Science, Innovation and Research) and the Université Inter-nationale de Rabat was set up around the topic of return of highly skilled migrants. The third immersion at the PME Business Incubator focused on the topic of business, entrepreneurship and development in the context of return and reintegration of diaspora. All three immersions enabled participants to get to know Morocco's migration reality on the ground and gain first insights into Morocco's ongoing transition from a country of origin and transit to a country of destination.

Back at the Lab venue, the subsequent session dealt with refining the proposals made the day before. The proposal groups were divided in two. One half presented their proposals and was coached by the other half. This was done by means of focusing on three of the four Dialogic Actions – follow, oppose and bystand – to encourage participants to support each other in order to think constructively and practically rather than giving advice. Additionally, the facilitators introduced the Coaching Pattern to support these aims. The goal of this exercise was to make use of the Lab participants' expertise in the field of migration and development, allowing for a further development of the preliminary proposals. Some participants came out of this session in a very thoughtful mode, after realising their own – and their comrade's – apparent difficulty in holding the intention not to give advice but instead to follow, oppose or bystand.

On the morning of the last day, the proposal group that had previously coached had the chance to be coached themselves. Ultimately, each group prepared and presented a final flip chart outlining their proposal's major objective, the team members and planned activities. The Lab participants came up with eight proposal groups, on which more detail will be presented in a later section.

The final dialogue dealt with planning the next steps for the second bridge and with the future of the Migration Lab. The Lab meeting in Rabat again ended with a check-out session that invited all Lab participants to sum up their experience.

The Bridge Between Rabat and Quito

The bridges between the Lab meetings, as outlined above, have an important function in enabling the transfer of insights from the 'safe space' of the Lab meetings into participants' reality. They also serve to enable ideation of project ideas that have been sparked in the meetings but need time to grow and possibly get redirected. In this second bridge, as in the first one, we requested participants take part in the accompaniment calls we offer. Their main counterparts were the facilitators, providing guidance through questions and inputs. We had a lot of work getting people from a number of different time zones around the world to agree on dates and times and to actually attend these calls in the midst of many pressing duties from their high-ranking jobs. When they did so, however, most of them strongly acknowledged the inspiration that came from the calls, the energy they brought back to continue refining their proposals, and the joy of talking to the peers that they so appreciated spending time with in the Lab meetings.

The Third Lab Meeting: Quito, Ecuador

The theme of the third, four-day meeting was 'Together support and track' – referring to the implementation progress of proposals. Building on the first two meetings, the Lab session in Quito allowed participants to concretize their proposals and to think ahead on their implementation. Moreover, the future of the Migration Lab was a topic raised and discussed by the participants throughout this third Lab meeting.

Participants developed common criteria for their project proposals. To keep the balance between being innovative and radical but at the same time not 'reinventing the wheel', three main criteria were agreed on: 1) meet the goals of the GCM, 2030 Agenda and the New York Declaration; 2) reflect and actively include perspectives from all three sectors (civil society, private sector and government); and 3) be viable, practicable and feasible.

On the second day, in the form of an immersion, the Lab visited the Department for Human Mobility of the Province Pichincha and the Mayor's office of the Pedro Moncayo Municipality in order to engage in dialogue with local migration experts and practitioners and to gain insights into the Ecuadorian migration reality and inspiration for their work and proposals. One participant summed up the feeling of many: "The immersions were really touching, as we were in small groups with almost the same number of migrants and refugees. I think to me it was really good to be exposed to the situation on the spot and, at the same time, to see how government reacts on the situation. How can I feed in these learnings and how will they alter my policy recommendations?" Most of the participants described the immersions as an important 'reality check' on their own situations.

The third day focused on refining the proposals by discussing their purpose and value in view of the GCM as well as the 2030 Agenda. An open dialogue followed, aiming to explore the future of the Migration Lab. There was great consensus – for some, offered enthusiastically, and for others, cautiously – that this experience needed to be continued and enlarged, as it was outstandingly meaningful.

On the fourth day, the groups further worked and modified their proposals to find a way to connect all proposals and the appropriate language for their respective audiences. The groups underlined that all proposals are interconnected and that their concretization will unveil how to link them.

This third and final Migration Lab meeting ended with a check-out ceremony, allowing each participant to acknowledge one another. Each participant received comments of acknowledgement by Lab colleagues and then had the chance to say a few words on the Lab process and his or her own development within it. Many participants were deeply moved by the very warm and personal appreciations they received from others, some allowed their emotions to show – there were laughter, hugs and tears. Some voices and reflections capture the feeling of the time:

- *I think this is a unique opportunity to really bundle the expertise of the different sectors.*
- *I learned how to have a true interaction and meaningful conversation.*
- *I think this is the highlight of my career. I am so grateful to have been part of this experience.*
- *The Lab was like a healing process for me.*
- *At the Lab, I see a potential by which things can be done. I see a group that can actually break away from the norm and put things into action.*

Outcomes and Impact

Social Labs, designed on the basis of a dialogical approach, create impact that can take different forms on a number of different levels. One way of looking at this impact is through the lens of individual capacities, social capacities and physical capacities. Individual capacities developed through the participation in a Lab include knowledge gains, listening skills, leadership, facilitation and innovation skills and attitude changes that are favourable for collaboration. Social capacities refer to relationships and an increased trust and capacity for collaborative action, including with partners from other sectors and unlikely allies. Finally, through the professional support in developing tangible change initiatives, and building on the transformations on the individual and social level, participants develop tangible new products, infrastructures and services. In the case of the Migration Laboratory, these include eight multi-stakeholder project proposals that have been made available to a range of international and regional actors through publications and events, with the aim of getting broad support from diverse stakeholders to ultimately enable the full implementation of these projects.

The Experience of Dialogue Changes People

Early in this document, we referred to the experience of dialogue sometimes feeling uncomfortable for those in it, and to the necessity of moving people out of their comfort zones before an understanding of the potential of this kind of coming together emerges. The following comment of a participant from Germany, given in an interview at the end of the last Lab meeting, illustrates this experience: "Coming together in Berlin for the first time was weird, because there were so many very important people who I know from policy papers, from international politics processes. We were brought together and there was nothing we had to do. There was just room and space that we were about to fill – but not with content, rather with process. It took a couple of days for me to familiarize and to realise what's happening – that exactly this kind of trust building was needed."

Similarly, as mentioned above, we use dialogue to enable a new and more holistic understanding of the issue at stake, and to help people realise how their opinion is not 'the reality'. This is mirrored in the reflections of a Moroccan participant: "It helps us to get a deeper grasp of what's going on in migration – because everyone has their own particular perspective. Here, we start to understand the complexity of migration issues and we become a little bit more humble about our own opinions."

Another intention for our dialogue practice is to enable personal transformation and a questioning of assumptions. This was appreciated by a Mexican participant: "Once you are out of your comfort zone, everything changes, because you have to really make an effort to listen and acknowledge before you talk. You have to question – what is the drive that makes you think a certain thought? That is why I think the Lab actually helps to understand issues of migration and also the actors themselves."

Finally, we use dialogue to spark new ideas that will make a difference, and to identify new leverage points for change in participants' home contexts. The same Mexican participant noted: "I am lucky, because I got to know people who come from different backgrounds – and sometimes that helps you to explode your own creativity! I need that, because I have to design policies for protection and integration. When you have different perspectives, you can imagine different things. And think that, what you were proposing is not what is needed."

In the Migration Lab, we have seen stuck opposers and forceful movers turn into highly supportive followers, and sometimes even bystanders. One participant from Germany described her transformation as follows: "I'm willing to understand the 'other' a bit more than I used to, because as an NGO representative with a human rights perspective, I have high standards that I want to see realised. I could not understand why anybody else would not have the same perspective on these things as I do. So maybe now I'm a little bit more sensitized to the interests of the other – and that it's not about compromising, but finding other solutions. It's a willingness to open up and not have a result already in mind, but to move together." This illustrates very well how the experience of dialogue creates capacities for people from very different walks of life and institutional backgrounds to collaborate and get to collective action.

Tangible Change Projects and New Physical Capacities

Through concrete cooperation across sectors over the course of the Migration Lab, members have developed proposals that tackle critical challenges in migration and development, thereby creating new physical capacities. Eight cross-sectoral groups have arisen, proposing projects on topics such as reintegration, the inclusion of private sector actors, and the protection of particularly vulnerable migrants. The projects are designed to contribute to the achievement of the objectives of the Global Compact on Migration and migration-related Sustainable Development Goals. Laboratory participants are continuously working to realise all eight projects, which have been published in *"A different way of working – Multi-stakeholder dialogues to implement global policy frameworks on migration and development"* (available here as a pdf: https://bit.ly/2MXVYrW).

Personal Reflections and Lessons

The work in the Migration Lab has taught me many lessons and has beautifully confirmed some things that I held to be true. One aspect most important to me is the collaborative hosting and steering of a Lab. None of us in the hosting team – the Sector Project Migration and Development, the Global Leadership Academy, or Dialogue Associates – individually could have ensured the success of the Lab as we all could in collaboration and appreciation of each other's strengths and knowledge. This is not only a demonstration of success of the collaborating entities, but also of the individuals involved. Our working with each other and learning from each other was not without friction around our different needs, as well as our communication and working styles. However, our process almost always was based on the openness and mutual respect one would expect from a team working on and with dialogue.

I have learnt particularly from the simplicity of the dialogue tools introduced in the Migration Lab, and how great their impact for participants was – minor interventions making them aware of communication and thinking patterns enabled significant increases in consciousness and subsequent impact in this regard.

I have found it to be very important for the success of a dialogue that those hosting it embody a dialogic mindset. For me this means, amongst other things, being able to see every comment and behaviour as part of a greater whole which is needed to move the process forward and welcoming it, while also giving productive direction. This is a balancing act that I have learnt a lot about through the expertise of our facilitation team of Dialogue Associates, who welcomed unexpected comments with humour and clarity and helped keep the group on track through helpful explications, integrating what we were doing into a larger context. Humour is and was probably one of the most transformative elements of the Migration Lab for me – both in the hosting team as well as in contact with the participants. I have learned a lot from the experience of lightness and openness that was enabled through giving space and time for humour in professional situations – it has brought a human and sane dimension that helped move things forward and connect with others more deeply.

Some further crucial attributes of a dialogue professional, to me, are being aware of one's own trigger points, being open to facing one's own blind spots, and being conscious of one's own rank, resulting from individual attributes and one's role in the dialogue. We wouldn't be human if we were able to live up to these all the time, and to aim for it means continuous and sometimes painful work on ourselves, yet we earn to become even more effective in what we are doing.

For this paper, I was asked to reflect on why this work matters to me. I was reminded of this in the closing session of the Migration Laboratory's last meeting. I looked around, into this group of women and men from all parts of the world, and thought of all the constraints I knew they were facing in their work every day, when trying to make experiences of migration just a little bit safer and more positive for all those involved. I thought of the passion, feeling and professionalism I had seen them bring to their work. In that very moment, I was reminded of a quote by Oscar Wilde: "It takes a great deal of courage to see the world in all its tainted glory, and still to love it". This courage to love the world and fight for its better, no matter what, is what I see in the participants of our dialogue processes. To be able to work together with such groups and individuals and to support them in connecting, becoming more aware and more effective in what they do, is what I am incredibly grateful for – it is, and continues to be with every new encounter, touching, inspiring, and humbling.

Kind acknowledgements for their contributions to this written work to Camilla Lovrek, Maksim Roskin and Yamina Ouldali, as well as the Global Leadership Academy team who have co-authored its publication "The Global Leadership Academy: Methodological Approach", from which excerpts have been taken and elaborated for this paper.

References

Bohm, D. (1996). *On Dialogue* (L. Nichol, Ed.). New York: Routledge.

Ellinor, L. & Gerard, G. (1998). *Dialogue: Rediscover the Transforming Power of Conversation*. New York: John Wiley & Sons, Inc.

German Federal Ministry for Economic Cooperation and Development (2015). Strategy for Development Cooperation with Global Development Partners. Available at https://www.bmz.de/en/publications/type_of_publication/strategies/Strategiepapier354_04_2015.pdf.

German Government (2012). Shaping Globalization – Expanding Partnerships– Sharing Responsibility. A strategy paper by the German Government. Available at https://www.auswaertiges-amt.de/blob/610644/ 49a58b5ecfd5a78862b051d94465afb6 / gestaltungsmaechtekonzept -engl-data.pdf

Global Leadership Academy (2017): The Global Leadership Academy: Methodological Approach. Available at https://bit.ly/2QoEunS

Hassan, Z. (2014). *The Social Labs Revolution: A New Approach to Solving our Most Complex Challenges*. San Francisco, CA: Berrett-Koehler.

Holman, P. and Devane, T. (1999). *The Change Handbook: Group Methods for Shaping the Future.* San Francisco, CA: Berrett-Koehler.

Isaacs, W. (1999). *Dialogue and the Art of Thinking Together: A Pioneering Approach to Communicating in Business and in Life.* New York: Currency/Doubleday.

Kovach, M. (2009). Indigenous Methodologies: Characteristics, Conversations, and Contexts. Toronto, Ontario: University of Toronto Press.

Senge, P. M. (1990). *The Fifth Discipline: The Art and Practice of the Learning Organization.* New York: Doubleday/Currency.

The Migration Laboratory (2018). *A different way of working. Multi-stakeholder dialogues to implement global policy frameworks on migration and development.* Available at https://bit.ly/2MXVYrW.

United Nations, Department of Economic and Social Affairs, Population Division (2017). *International Migration Report 2017.*

Conference Session Extracts

From conversation with 20 participants considering the paper with the author

I would like to say something. I've been wondering in all the sessions I've been in, where do they start? What's the first question? And you say, "On the basis of the global issue, we formulate a strategic question that provokes people's interest and attention". In the case of the Migration Lab, "How can we act together across sectors so that migration is beneficial for all actors in society?" I think that's a very pregnant question and very adaptable to a number of different kinds of situations, that kind of approach. So is it like leading – is it the question that invites people to come, is it the leading question in the first dialogue session, or does it inform the whole or the first – or is it the leading question for the whole process of the three, four-day sessions?

It's the leading question for the entire process. So when people are invited for it, they know that that's the leading question. And the process as such unfolds over a year or so in three different meetings and they always know that that's the overarching question.

And inside that, there are different questions?

Right.

I have a question that is coming to my mind now. I have a question. How much governments, when they force you to reshape and cut and resize everything, how much are they operating in silos? The government itself. How much do they need dialogue themselves? Because migration right now is a challenge for all Western societies, and it's going to grow as a challenge. Resizing means not seeing what's coming. It's not thinking ahead. It's thinking of the present. It's thinking about giving a response to the finance minister who is saying, "I need to fit this budget this year, and this is where I will cut". There are two big problems that all the world is facing right now, climate change and migrations, and they both interlink. Any cut in any ledger, in any budget, related to migration or climate change, is not wanting to see the big picture, and not thinking of the future of the societies they're ruling.

My experience in Sweden is that government organizations are only silos, the most outspoken examples of silos [laughter]. I was invited by the Social Democratic party to be part of a number of people they would invest in training for having political positions for the future. And the second seminar we had, there was a professor of political science who explained to me the governmental organization in Swedish governments. And then after that seminar, I say, "I won't go to be part of that shit". So absolutely, governmental organisations need dialogue, like all other organisations. And without talking politics and the aspects of different political parties, but what is happening all over the world with different aspects, there is a polarisation going on, and migration is one important, very strong force in that polarisation. And the only thing that, in my mind, can break that very destructive process is dialogue.

So if we can work on this, and we can find the language of money and power to show the impact that dialogue has on the affairs we're dealing with every day, then maybe that can also help the Academy and others in a certain way.

Postscript

The author's reflections written some months after the conference

In my paper I wrote about my work in the Migration Laboratory to illustrate one form of dialogue my government-owned organisation conducts. It quickly became clear that many who joined our session had experience working with migrants and/or refugees, and were interested in the topic of migration itself. Others were interested in the design of our interventions: who are the participants, how do all the parts work together and what are the outcomes? Finally, some were excited by the fact that our dialogue programmes are supported by the government.

I had been asked to think about my most burning interest and what I needed out of this session. I shared the sense of pressure our team experiences in having to prove the 'systemic' impact of dialogues after a relatively short period of time. I was interested in how my dialogue colleagues would deal with these pressures. Would they shorten the dialogues and include online elements, at the risk of putting their dialogical nature at peril? How would they communicate impact so that government decision-makers would be convinced that it is valuable to continuously invest into these complex projects?

Observing the bigger picture of the conversation, I came to realize that many of the different interests people were bringing into our conversation were deeply emotional. The time allowed for this depth of voices, opinions and emotions was very limited. To both enable this space *and* receive concrete responses to the question I had presented was challenging. At the same time, what I did feel very clearly, was a level of support, interest and connectedness that was extraordinary and of itself significantly helpful in supporting me in my work.

Thinking about my prior question and need, I found it reflected in other comments by colleagues throughout the conference: the pressure so many of us face to 'sell', 'defend' and quantify the impact of our dialogues, particularly in environments that prioritize the value of proving investment results. How do we reconcile the views and values of generative dialogue with the world view prevalent in our current economic and political systems that seems to demand justifying a 'return on investment'?

In our dialogue, some ideas and opinions were brought up which became starting points for fruitful further thoughts on my questions. What stuck with me more than anything else was the notion of really entering into a dialogic relationship with those decision-makers who have the power over the initiation, continuation or termination of our dialogue projects. Bluntly said, to really 'trust' dialogue as an approach to solving tough challenges. It reminds me of the fundamental intricacies of embodying dialogue when being in the role of those with less rank in a hierarchical, fast-paced system, that might even penalise the attempt of behaving dialogically. This is not giving a lecture about dialogue. It is not facilitating dialogue for others to help them solve their challenges. It is entering into the conflict with all its threats, 'getting our own hands dirty', that is, bearing the uncertainty and vulnerability that comes with it, not only as an individual but also representing a team and an organisational entity, with all responsibilities this entails.

I'll be reflecting on these questions further, and will be suggesting topics such as these for future gatherings – and I offer the possibility that we might explore conversational modes other than dialogue as a means for mutual learning and support in a community rich in experiences around these intricacies.

Economics and Time Management as a Vehicle for Dialogue

Lars-Åke Almqvist

My route into dialogue has followed a path from psychology to union representation, and from consulting to my current work. I started in 1971 as a mental health worker at a major psychiatric hospital in Uppsala, Sweden. This led me to becoming a member of the Swedish Municipal Workers' Union – known as Kommunal, Sweden's largest union – where I soon became the trade representative and then president of the local union in 1976. In 1980, I was offered the position of ombudsman at the headquarters office in Stockholm. There I worked until 2009, when I retired at the age of 60.

Looking back, I see that my work with Kommunal was a key step in my movement toward dialogue. I had the privilege of working on several development issues over the years at Kommunal. When Kommunal started Komanco, its consulting company, I joined them as the business leader, facing complex and long-standing challenges we needed to address at the outset. Since the 1980s, leaders had been discussing the need for changes in the public sector, and it was obvious that organisations could not solve problems by simply adding more resources. Citizens were demanding changes in public services, and we knew that our job would be to develop new ways to use resources more efficiently. We faced the very real risk that Kommunal would end up on the defensive, saying no to all changes – common practice for trade unions.

Prior to the start of Komanco we at Kommunal had initiated a number of development projects with local employers in care and nursing, as well as in technical services. The purpose of these projects was to build cooperation between employers and trade unions, developing service quality and finding more efficient ways of using resources. Our idea was that changes lead to better results if everyone in the workplace is involved and influences the changes. We developed a training programme that we called *Come On*. The title offered an invitation to everyone in the workplace to join in and change their work setting. Our material did not build on any particular theory of organisational development, but was strictly focused on bringing about practical, concrete changes.

When we offered the programme to organisations, a number of managers and other chosen employees would first take part in the trainings, and then work together as 'conversation leaders' in the organisation. The programme consisted of trainings and workplace meetings with all employees between each session to discuss how to develop the workplace. The number of training days varied according to the organisation's needs, generally taking place over five or six days. There were about three to four weeks between each training day. After the last training day, the managers would draw up action plans for changes in the business. We challenged employers with the claim that "If you start a development project with us, you will be able to reduce costs by at least 10%!" This frightful marketing meant that we got a lot of assignments! Approximately 70,000 people throughout Sweden participated in *Come On* projects during 1992-2002.

In 1995 Peter Senge's book *The Fifth Discipline* was published in Swedish. It gave us a theoretical frame of reference that confirmed what we did. In 1996, Kommunal commissioned a trip to the US to study examples of how companies and organisations were trying to develop learning organisations. During our visit to MIT in Cambridge, Massachusetts, we met Bill Isaacs, who talked about his work with dialogue. Bill came to Sweden in early 1997. During his visit Bill commented that if there was any country where dialogue could spread, it would be in Sweden. He wanted us to start collaborating. This led me to the Leadership for Collective Intelligence (LCI) programme in 1997-98. Peter Garrett became my faculty coach.

Komanco and Dialogue

After I went through the LCI, I introduced dialogue to my former colleagues. We worked together for a whole week and conducted a large number of exercises to jointly seek to develop a common understanding of the possibilities of dialogue. There were mixed reactions in our group. Some soon saw the possibilities. Others were very negative. One colleague said, straight out: "I will never work with dialogue". (She later became one of our most enthusiastic dialogue practitioners.)

Based on our discussions, we developed a dialogue training. The programme generally covers three days, and it addresses the needs of managers and their employees. In one course, up to 30 people can participate. After each training, a number of follow-up meetings are conducted as half or full days. Scope and content is determined after dialogue with the relevant manager about the organisation's needs.

The education has changed over the years, but today it has the following basic structure: The days are carried as a process rather than as a collection of segments. Most parts consist of an introduction of an assignment, individual reflection, dialogue in small groups and a common reflection with theory review. Step-by-step, we walk through the basic elements of dialogue. During the exercises, participants work with the support of various tools that they can then use after the course.

We conducted our first dialogue training in 1998 for managers in Smedjebacken

Municipality. The evaluation from participants was very positive. As a result, we have offered a number of dialogue courses in Smedjebacken over the years. Since the municipality wanted to continue the dialogue and be able to do it with its own resources, we decided to develop a dialogue facilitator training.

Framework of the Programme

We train a number of people from the employer's employees to become dialogue facilitators. The intention is that the dialogue facilitators will then provide, through internal education, further training for staff in their respective organisations. As a complement to our educational material in dialogue, we have prepared a guide for the dialogue facilitators.

Components of the Training

- Human Dynamics training: two, two-day sessions
- Dialogue training: five days
- Dialogue facilitator training: three days
- Facilitator reflection conversations, examination and licencing: time as needed

Human Dynamics Training
The purpose of the Human Dynamics training, developed by Sandra Seagal and David Horne, is to help people become more effective and aware of their potential, both as individuals and as group members. This inspiring programme helps leaders develop latent abilities and provides tools to better understand themselves and others, thereby creating the conditions for shared job satisfaction. Human Dynamics training programmes concern many aspects of the interaction between us, including communication, conflict resolution, composition of work teams, leadership and personal development. The education is carried out in two, two-day sessions and can be conducted internally or externally. Human Dynamics is conducted in groups of 20-25 people with two facilitators from Komanco/Alamanco.

Dialogue Training / Facilitator Training
The dialogue facilitator training consists of training and follow-up days, which are distributed as follows:

- The in-depth dialogue training is five days, with two facilitators from Komanco/Alamanco.
- The training for future dialogue facilitators, including practice and application, is

three days, with a facilitator from Komanco/Alamanco.
- Examination and reflection conversations, including licencing and examination of prospective dialogue facilitators, is performed by two facilitators from Komanco/Alamanco. The number of days depends on how many dialogue facilitators should be licenced. Four facilitators per day are possible.
- At the end of the training period, those who underwent dialogue facilitator training become licenced dialogue facilitators. It is assumed by clients that Komanco/Alamanco practitioners have sufficient qualifications to conduct the dialogue training for licencing. The education is conducted in a group of about six-12 people.

Practice and Application Process

To complete the practice and application portion of facilitator training, two dialogue facilitator candidates partner to conduct a dialogue training for three days, with support from a facilitator from Komanco/Alamanco.

Ongoing Dialogue Facilitator Meetings

Those who become licenced dialogue facilitators each year undertake a two-day dialogue facilitator meeting for reflection, experience exchange and further skill development.

Scope and Reach of Dialogue Education and Dialogue Facilitator Training

Since the first education in Smedjebacken in 1998, approximately 30,000 people have undergone three days of dialogue training. A total of 221 dialogue facilitators have been trained and licenced. Today, 15 people are still active.

Komanco Becomes Alamanco.

I was the head of Komanco until 1997, when I was elected Vice President of Kommunal. I then left to become chairman of the company's board of directors. When I retired, my colleagues in the federal board asked me if I was interested in taking over responsibility to move Komanco's business forward. I felt I could not resist that challenge. We made an agreement which meant that I bought the rights to the concepts I had actually created myself, and started a new company called Alamanco. Alamanco took over responsibility for the customer orders for which Komanco had already signed an agreement. From the start, our company has consisted of five people. All of my colleagues had worked in Komanco, and in most cases we have worked together for 25 years. We work with assignments all over Sweden, primarily in municipalities and county councils, but we also take on tasks for private companies. The organisations that primarily contract us work with disability, preschools and care for the elderly.

Staff Right

Another important concept within Alamanco's business is a programme we call *Staff Right*. *Staff Right* is also based on dialogue as a method and a process. We began developing the concept in 2003 while I was still working in Kommunal. I led a project group whose purpose was to try to understand why part-time work and temporary employment are so common in many care and nursing activities. We understood from the outset that there would be no simple explanation; instead, many cooperative factors have created this situation.

We initiated a pre-study, commissioning some of the Kommunal investigators to conduct deep interviews with different actors who in various ways influence the situation in their municipality. We interviewed zero-hour contract workers (where neither employer nor employee are committed to a minimum number of hours), part-time employees, supervisors, business executives, HR managers, union representatives and politicians. The interviews were conducted in a cross-section of municipalities of different sizes and structures. The results of the interviews showed that, despite some differences between the municipalities, there was a common denominator – a long tradition of hiring people in part-time and temporary employment because employers believe that it leads to increased flexibility and lower costs.

In autumn 2003 we started a collaboration with the Uppsala Municipality, in Sweden's fourth-largest city. Politicians also had an interest in offering more employees the opportunity to work full-time and reduce the amount of temporary employment. We started a joint project to develop ideas about how this could become a reality. Care and nursing activities at the time amounted to one billion krona (about £85 million GB or about $109 million US). Together with the employer, we selected half of the facilities to be included in the project. The employer appointed an internal project manager. For the more comprehensive management of our work, I was in charge with Magnus Johannesson, the manager for care and nursing.

The work began with the creation of comprehensive data for our selected entities. We had access to information about the number of employees, kinds of employment, amount of sick leave and other absences, as well as data on overtime work, how absenteeism for regular staff was covered, etc. During the autumn, we held regular meetings with unit heads and municipal union representatives. Developed data were advertised, and we discussed what changes should be made. The work progressed during the fall and we had a meeting on Wednesday before Christmas weekend. Each meeting was always initiated with a check-in to allow participants to tell how the work went. The mood was gloomy. The managers said they did not really have time for the project. In part, they said that they already had been tasked with reporting out on their budget for the next year and justifying why they should again go overbudget. As they expressed this they looked at their boss Magnus, implicitly saying all of this was his fault.

I said that if it's not possible to see the relationship between the financial problems and staffing the business, then we might as well close the project. This statement prompted the participants to begin to reflect. I pointed out that 80-90% of their running costs are personnel costs, so new ways of understanding and managing these costs needed to be found. The meeting was increasingly characterised by openness and a positive desire to move forward. After the meeting Magnus and I reflected about how the meeting had evolved. I told Magnus: "I think the bosses and their employees need a basic education in economics to better understand relationships between employee costs and financial results." Magnus agreed and asked how we might fix the problem. I had an idea, as I'd previously collaborated with Paula Liukkonen, Associate Professor in Business Administration at the University of Stockholm, about health records in organisations.

After describing the situation to Paula, I asked her if she had any thoughts about how to arrange an education in economics. She showed me a few simple worksheets and pointed out which parts managers and employees need to take in order to make better decisions. We organised a meeting with the care and nursing management group, at which Paula presented her ideas. Her approach received a positive response and we decided that a pilot training would be conducted within the project. The training led to many 'aha' experiences among the participants. We saw that there was something basic to build on.

With Paula, we developed a Kommunal training programme called 'The Job Puzzle'. By this time Magnus had left as Head of Uppsala Care and Nursing. The new management was not interested in continuing to work in a dialogue process with managers and employees, so our collaboration was terminated.

We got in touch with another municipality, Nynäshamn. This municipality is located south of Stockholm and has 28,000 inhabitants. They had launched a project called 'New Times' in 2007, enabling employees to work full-time and create more secure jobs. There we were given the opportunity to test The Job Puzzle on a larger scale. We received positive feedback from the participants. Komanco carried out the education efforts in connection with The Job Puzzle, initially in collaboration with Paula. The concept received a large response from many municipalities, but also from Carema AB, which was Sweden's largest private healthcare company at that time.

When Alamanco started, we brought with us a lot of experience from offering The Job Puzzle. In The Job Puzzle, education in what we chose to call 'Staffing Economics' is an important element. As time went on, our experiences showed the importance of seeing more aspects of how an organisation works than the purely economic one. It is necessary to have a holistic view: to understand the organisational culture, how leadership works, the levels of cooperation, employee roles, etc.

Our Staff Right training programme, described briefly above, grew out of this work. It consists of a training booklet, a facilitators' guide and a web programme for Staffing Economics.

Staff Right Collaborative Model

This programme is built on a collaborative model between employers and employees. The aim is to create the best possible workplace based on the needs and conditions of an activity.

That a workplace is *good* means that it will be good for users/customers, employees and the organisation/company. The purpose of education in *Staff Right* is to:

- Develop a common understanding and common language between management and employees about how to analyse and manage personnel costs.
- Develop a follow-up for the business based on an overall viewpoint.
- Create a consensus regarding staffing, placement and use of working hours.

Partnership

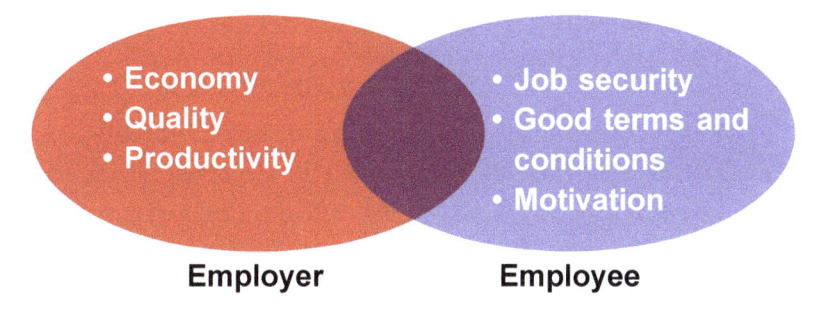

- Economy
- Quality
- Productivity

- Job security
- Good terms and conditions
- Motivation

Employer   **Employee**

The model is based on respect for the fact that there are natural, special interests in each organisation. The employer wants to have good economics and good quality, and to be competitive with other producers. Employees want to feel safe in their work, to receive a good salary, to feel job satisfaction and to be proud of their work.

There are also other special interests between managers and employees, as well as between employees and other employees. It's simply a fact that we all think, feel and act differently. We sometimes see this as a problem. Instead, we need to realise that it is natural that we work differently. It is a great asset if we learn to use our differences in a good way. We need to realise that we are not our opinion, but rather we need to learn to listen to each other and work together to create common solutions. This means that we do not have to lose face just because we acknowledge that a colleague has a better idea of how a problem should be solved. This is all fertile territory for dialogue as a practice ground for employees, employers and in organisations as a whole.

An important goal with *Staff Right* is to develop better collaboration. In order to do this, it is necessary to develop consensus on our work mission, and what benefit we will achieve for those we serve. In order for us to cooperate well, we also need a common understanding of what is needed to be successful, and agreement that we need to train how to work together. Much research shows that basically the same factors that enable us to cooperate better also make us feel comfortable at work, increasing health and work efficiency.

At Alamanco, we determine the effectiveness of an organisation by how well groups collaborate. The more complex work life becomes, the more important the working group is. More cooperation is required, and more and more tasks must be carried out by groups instead of individuals. Collaboration is the only way to perform complex tasks. They require too much knowledge and too many skills for a single individual to be able to perform them successfully. Operations running 24 hours a day and 365 days a year require work by different people, which requires collaboration. This occurs in the form of reporting and knowledge transfer. The knowledge explosion and complexity of our operations make it necessary to reassess how we organise our work. Employees to some extent can carry out their work in isolation. Teamwork, however, is necessary for organisations to be successful and effective. It is for this reason that the development of good teamwork is an important feature of *Staff Right*.

Why Are We at Work?

When we decide to develop our workplace, some things are easier to implement – and others may not affect us at all. In order to increase our potential for achieving the improvements we want, we need to find some common starting points. The most important issue we need to listen for in dialogue and agree on is "Why are we at work?"

Most people can easily describe what they do in their work. However, it is more difficult for most of us to describe *how* we do our work, and even more difficult to describe *why* we do what we do. It is something we less often reflect on. We do not have an easily accessible language or clear terminology to use to talk about these things. How and why we do our job usually involves what is called 'quiet knowledge'; that is, we know how to execute our work tasks, but we do not talk so often about them. What is the real purpose for what we do? What are our motives and driving forces? What attitudes, approaches and values guide us? These are fundamental questions that form the basis of the work of *Staff Right* and dialogue at its centre. In order to do better work and create a good working environment, we need to agree on why we are at work. Then we need to agree on how we will work together and what we can do in concrete terms for those we serve. It is in this sense that we need to think 'inside and out' to develop our workplace.

Developing a Consensus Between Management and Employees

The word *efficiency* is used with many different meanings in our daily conversations. As mentioned, in *Staff Right* we base our use of the term on a holistic view that encompasses economics, quality and the work environment. The most important resource is our total working time. How much value-creating time do we have? – that is, time for making things that create value for those for whom we are working. What daily tasks do we perform that really create value for them? How much time do we invest to create the right conditions for learning new things, evaluating work performance and developing the organisation? How much time is lost due to inaction, duplication and destructive conflicts?

HOW DO WE USE OUR TIME AT WORK?		
Value-Generating Time	Opportunity-Generating Time	Lost Time
Acting/Doing	Learning/Practising	Passiveness
Prioritising	Preparing	Doing the Wrong Things
Interacting	Planning	Duplication of Work
Communicating	Researching	Misunderstandings
Taking Responsibility	Evaluating	Conflicts
Correcting	Thinking/Reflecting	Jockeying for Position
Finishing/Finalising	Developing	Fussing

How efficiently the working time is used is mainly determined by the following factors:

- The level of consensus between management and employees about the organisation's/company's assignment, and the benefits it will offer to those the employees serve.
- The level of consensus between management and employees regarding staffing, allocation and use of working hours.
- The level at which organisational leaders work purposefully to create participation opportunities for their employees and to develop cooperation to achieve set goals.
- The level of skill for managers and employees.
- The values, attitudes and driving forces of leaders and employees.

Efficient organisations have clearly defined the organisation's mission, a point brought home by Susan Wheelan, professor of psychology at Temple University and useful resource in our work. These organisations focus on the benefits that are to be achieved for those who need its services, and on delivering benefits well and with efficient use of resources. *Staff Right* is not a 'savings initiative', though it recognises the importance of conservation of resources and attention to details. Clear structures have been developed to organise work, but also there is a preparedness for dealing with the unexpected. New ideas from employees about how work can succeed is encouraged and shared rapidly in daily operations. Employees across the organisation expect that all should be successful and achieve good results.

The results achieved by an organisation are highly dependent on its health – on how employees and the organisation as a whole feel. Employees, as is often said, are the most important resource of the organisation. Is there frustration, powerlessness, deprivation or many unresolved conflicts in the organisation that affect how the organisation works? In an efficient organisation management and employees are in consensus about how to staff, plan and use working time. This sense of spaciousness creates opportunities for employees to develop as individuals. Participation for employees is both a prerequisite and a result of developmental work. Good cooperation is cultivated based on respect for each other's differences, and the insight that we *are* each other's work environment. An open-communication environment develops where employees learn how to resolve conflicts in a constructive way and focus on how to solve concrete problems in daily work. In an organisation that works efficiently, management and employees agree about the division of responsibilities between the self, the team and the company/organisation, and what the relationship with the customers should look like.

The Development Process with Staff Right

Before we engage *Staff Right* in an organisation, we convene a dialogue with the management. Why are they requesting development work? What do they perceive as the strong and weak areas of the organisation? What do they deem to be the greatest development needs? Sometimes this leads us to do a preliminary study to further analyse how the organisation currently is working. Such a preliminary study means that we provide basic data about the staffing within the units of the organisation, based on a structure we have developed. These data are entered into our web programme for Staffing Economics. We compile reports for each unit. We conduct a number of deep, confidential interviews with a selection of managers and employees. Based on all these data, we prepare a report that we present to the management, and we describe our conclusions. Through additional dialogue, we agree on how the further development work will be carried out. In many cases, we have also assigned Alamanco employees the task of working as project managers for development work. We adapt our efforts to the needs of each organisation.

Below is a description of how our efforts are conducted. As we mentioned earlier, our materials consist of a training booklet, a facilitator's guide and a web programme for Staffing Economics.

As with the *Come On* programme, we train managers and a number of selected employees for five days, in a series of two days, two days and one day. There are usually four to five weeks between each training opportunity. The managers, together with their employees, act as conversation leaders at workplace meetings in smaller groups where all employees in the organisation participate. They facilitate a dialogue about the issues that are important to their respective workplaces, including what we call 'hard' questions about staffing and 'soft' issues like collaboration, attitudes and approaches in the workplace. In support of this work, they have been given our facilitator's guide, which provides tips and ideas on how to facilitate the dialogue.

By educating about 30 participant leaders, we can ensure that approximately 200-300 employees in an organisation are reached.

Framework for *Staff Right* Programme	
Days One and Two	
<ul><li>Introduction & Presentation</li><li>Content of the training</li><li>How do we create collaboration between management and employees?</li><li>Expectations and concerns for the work with Staff Right</li><li>How do we use our working hours? What is value creation, opportunity-generating time?</li><li>What is our mission? What benefit should we create for those we are there for? What are our strong and weak sides?</li><li>Review of the 'Golden Circle' (why, how and then what) and work with visual dialogue</li></ul>	<ul><li>Introduction for Staffing Economics</li><li>Presentation of web-based programme for Staffing Economics</li><li>Our staffing resources</li><li>Time accounting – worked time and absent time</li><li>Staff balance – How have we replaced our absence?</li><li>What is an effective team? Susan Wheelan's theory</li><li>Five key factors to create an effective team</li><li>Homework preparation</li></ul>*Two workplace meetings in about two hours are performed over a period of 4–5 weeks.*
Days Three and Four	
<ul><li>Reflection/Experience Exchange</li><li>Labour cost per hour</li><li>Labour cost in case of absence</li><li>Cost to replace absence</li><li>Distribution of salary costs</li><li>Distribution of hours worked bewteen different types of employment</li><li>Comparison between distribution of salary costs, budget and financial performance</li><li>How have we used our staffing resources? What do the concepts of flexibility, personal responsibility, co-operation and holistic view mean to us? Work with visual dialogue</li></ul>	<ul><li>How can we use our human resources more intelligently based on a holistic view, with better economy, higher quality and a better working environment?</li><li>How can we create new staffing models and new ways to use our working hours?</li><li>Each group produces at least five areas of improvement using Visual Dialogue</li><li>Homework preparation</li></ul>*Two workplace meetings in about two hours are performed over a period of 4–5 weeks.*
Day Five	
<ul><li>Reflection/Experience exchange</li><li>What is *KASAM*? ('sense of coherence' in English)</li><li>Presentation of Aaron Antonovsky's theory about Creating a Sense of Coherence related to Staff Right</li><li>Results evaluations. What requirements should we ask for? How do we set goals? What should we measure? How should we measure?</li><li>Develop draft action plans for some improvement areas</li></ul>	<ul><li>When and how do we follow up and evaluate?</li><li>Homework preparation</li><li>Course evaluation</li><li>Reflection and checkout</li></ul>*After the last day of the course, two additional workplace meetings are held, in which the preparation of the action plans are finalised.*

228 | Society Needs Dialogue!

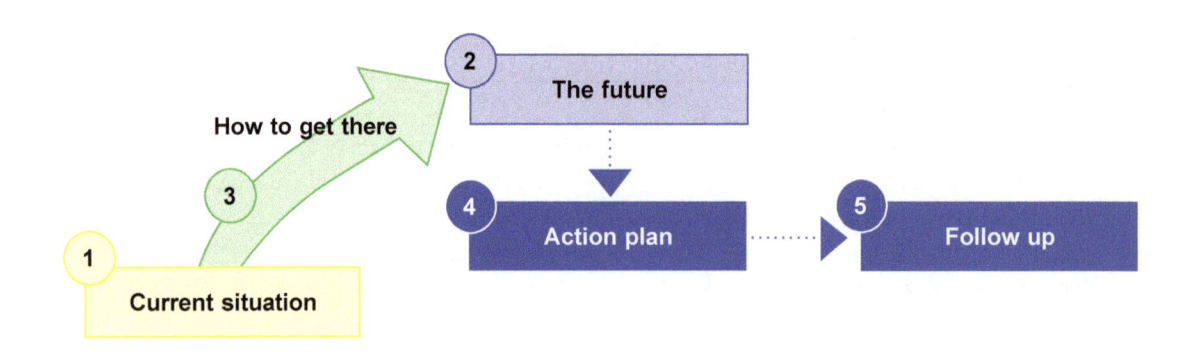

Staff Right is carried out in five phases:

1. **Current situation:** The group talks about the expectations and concerns for the work with *Staff Right*. They agree on what approaches should be taken in relation to each other during the forthcoming development work. The group talks about the group's mission, and what benefits it will lead to. The group also analyses how staff resources have been used during a selected measurement period. What are the strong and weak aspects of the group?
2. **The future:** The group creates a vision of how the future might look. What improvements need to be made? How should it staff its unit? How does the team allocate and plan its working hours? How should they develop collaboration? What should the group stop doing? What should they preserve in what they do?
3. **How to get there:** In order to achieve what the group wants in the future, what will be required of each person as an employee, by the group, and by the leadership and organisation?
4. **Action Plan:** The group draws up action plans for the priority improvement proposals. They formulate goals, decide on activities, responsibilities, time limits and evaluation. They assess what happens if nothing is done, and the results if the work succeeds.
5. **Follow-up:** After approximately four to five months of implementation of the action plan, each group performs a follow-up to evaluate what results have been achieved and what can be learned. An important element in the work with *Staff Right* and in our Dialogue Education is Visual Dialogue, a form of brainstorming and conversation.

The Westbay story

Västervik Municipality has 36,000 inhabitants. The municipality has decided that all employees who care for the elderly and disabled people should have the opportunity to choose the amount of employment in which they wish to engage, through a step-by-step process between employer and employee. The work began with Alamanco's commission in autumn of 2014 to carry out seven courses in *Staff Right* for all managers and a number of employees, for a total of about 230 people. As Social Director Jörgen Olsson pointed out as our work began, "We need to find a new way of thinking about staffing and use of resources. It applies to all levels of our organisation." The managers, together with their chosen employees, have served as conversation leaders at their respective workplaces for dialogues on how to create a consensus for staffing, allocation and use of working hours. One of my colleagues, Conny Ohlsson, was employed as project manager at the start of development work. In May 2016 the municipality forged a local work-time collective agreement with Kommunal on flexible working hours to support the introduction of the desired number of hours to be worked.

Through the agreement, employees can choose between different models for how to set their schedule. In order to support the development of good cooperation regarding staffing, placement and use of working time, all employees in the care for elderly and care for disabled people – a total of about 1,200 people – have completed Alamanco's three-day dialogue training.

After each training, we have facilitated a number of follow-up meetings in both full- and half-day sessions. The planning has been made through dialogue with the relevant manager. At these meetings we have worked with individual teams and their manager to resolve conflicts and develop cooperation. In some cases, these group meetings have touched all teams in one unit.

Disability care and care for the elderly in Västervik is organised in districts. Desired employment rates have gradually been introduced in all districts. The last district began earlier this year. Already the municipality has been able to monitor various data about changes made. In total, the desired employment rate has resulted in an increase of 30.8 full-time jobs if recalculated in hours for permanent employees. Translated into individuals, there are currently 110 more people working full-time compared to when the project started, addressing one of the original challenges we identified.

The Process

Annica Mässing, a District Manager, in charge of her area since 2001, describes the process in her own words:

We had already started working a bit with overstaffing at the Vapengränd retirement home. Directives had been given many times to keep down staffing. As a result, it has not been possible for people to support themselves. They may have had 75% employment and have struggled to get their hours. I thought it was amazing that we could offer full-time jobs. I have always been a little curious and that's why I put up my hand and said I want to join and do this.

Then we started to work. I began to read about other municipalities. How have they done? How did they succeed? We found that we have to work in a way that makes all people involved, to work with their expectations and concerns. In the home service, we had many part-time workers, high absence, many zero-hour contract workers. Users were always being visited by different employees. At Vapengränd we had already created a slightly safer personal situation.

Through Staff Right, the management's intention was to make employees aware of the economy and to be able to influence – for example, understanding how to use an increase in basic staffing. There were many concerns for choosing the working-time model, but we gave time for the employees for information, dialogue and participation.

We worked with different groups all the time. When you are worried you have to ask questions, sometimes the same questions several times and get answers. Then it will be fine in the end. I had come into contact with dialogue training already in the early 2000s. I realised that we would benefit from it in the work of the desired employment rate. We wanted to take advantage of all working hours. This gives you the flexibility to go in and work in another team. We had participants in each dialogue training from different working groups get to know each other. Through dialogue, employees are trained to open up to each other. It has helped in the process we have gone through.

Results

Again, Annica tells the story:

> Everyone has been involved in the process based on Staff Right and Dialogue Education to understand why we need to work in a different way. They have become aware of the economic relationships and how to work better together and how to better utilise their human resources.

When the Västervik Municipality achieved the desired employment rate and entered the new agreement in 2016, 79% chose fixed resource time and 21% variable time. More choose to switch to variable time when employees saw better how they could influence their working time. In the home services, more have chosen variable time compared to those at the Vapengränd retirement facility. Desired employment rate has meant an increase of 9.4 full-time jobs if recalculated in hours for permanent employees. Annica continues:

> The proportion could have been even lower if it had been possible to recruit more people with education. Today we could hire even fewer zero-hour contract workers if we could recruit more as regular staff. It is a big concern not only for us but for the whole of Sweden. We previously had many vacancies in the home service that we had to cover with zero-hour contract workers. At one point we were forced to take over many users from a private company that went bankrupt. It also meant that we had to quickly find staff, and it was often only zero-hour contract workers that we could hire.
>
> Sick leave continues to fall. Now, for example, home care has got better premises and thus a calmer environment when they need to meet. Desired employment rates have led to a safer operation. We have regular staff in place. It will be safer for our users. We have chosen to organise the work

with small work teams to create good continuity. Within the home service there are five employees in each work team.

The users are more pleased with our efforts today. It is a safer service. Our employees are also satisfied. They also feel more secure when they know what salary they receive each month and do not have to hunt for a decent salary. It's a calmer situation.

What Needs to Be Better?

We need to have better planning for filling free passes. If we get better, there will be plenty more to move over to variable time. It will be easier for employees to see which work passes are available in the future, and see more how to manage their working hours. We need to create space and time so that the work teams have the opportunity to think and plan ahead.

How is the Leadership Role Affected?

Desired employment rate is the biggest thing I have been introducing during my time as a leader. I think it's terrific that people get organised employment and a salary that they can live on. For my leadership, dialogue training has been very important. I spend a lot of time on reflection. I get a lot of feedback from our employees that we are working hard to build trust. We work with adult people and we try to create the conditions for taking responsibility in their work. In that work, dialogue training has been an important support. Through the resource time we have, there will be another way of working. We know we have people in place. We do not need to find emergency solutions as before and almost go out and get people on the street. We have a good order for the economy in our district.

Quotes from course participants in *Staff Right*:

- *We have had some tools that we can use in our ongoing work*
- *We feel part of an upcoming process*
- *To get an overall view of the organisation, we had interesting discussions with colleagues and managers*
- *Very good and useful to know what different things cost [that] you did not have a clue about*
- *Received information about what tools we can use to reach our goals*
- *Have started reflections all over the workplace, the group and myself as an individual*

Quotes from participants in the dialogue training:

- *Have more different ways of thinking when communicating individually and with a group*
- *To think before saying something to someone*
- *To be positive to your employees and to give feedback to each other*

- *Insight into myself*
- *You have come to know each other*
- *Reminded that dialogue is a very powerful tool both for good and evil*
- *Have many wise truths to bring in life*
- *Learned about my own role in groups and in everyday life*
- *Re-evaluate how I perceive and perceive myself/others*
- *The thought process is getting a fresh start*
- *Have a toolbox to use for all different interactions*
- *Awareness of own responsibility and opportunities for 'new thinking'*
- *To have these days together for reflection in peace and quiet. To not be at the workplace.*

As one manager put it, "I do not really know what you are doing, but I see that it works"

The Hofors story

Hofors Municipality has 10,000 inhabitants. The society is shaped by its large steelworks, Ovako, which is the largest employer in the municipality. At one time Hofors had an arrangement which made it possible for employees engaged in care and nursing to work full-time. However, the application of the agreement also meant, among other things, that conflicts arose among the employees and it was difficult to keep an eye on the economy. The working-time collective agreement that formed the basis for the model was cancelled by Kommunal in 2013. In 2014, Alamanco was commissioned to carry out a review of the staffing economy in elderly and disability care. Based on the report, the management of social services prepared an action plan.

We conducted a training with *Staff Right* for managers and employees in 2015. Alamanco's report and discussions during the training showed that there were a large number of zero-hour contract workers in the organisation and high overtime costs. Therefore, management decided to start an attempt to develop new staffing models within two operations: at Persgårdens, a care home for elderly, and at home services. As with Västervik Municipality, the aim was to enable employees to choose employment rates, reduce the number of zero-hour contract workers and gain better control over the economy.

Home Service

The Home Service has gradually introduced a new organisation. The new organisation has been created by all employees involved. We have had a large number of meetings together with the head of the municipality's home services and her conversation leaders. After these meetings, the conversation leaders led talks with their colleagues in the work teams. The new organisation means that the activities are conducted in small teams, which employees call 'bubbles'.

The work teams have a smaller geographical area where they are responsible for the care of their users. Each bubble consists of two employees who share responsibility primarily Monday to Friday. Several bubbles collaborate with each other in the field so that the resource time can be used effectively to cover absence and to manage nursing during weekends. The aim is to increase continuity between staff and users.

Employees have had the opportunity to choose their employment rate. Resource passes have been submitted to cover absences within an employee's own group or any other group. The first two groups started working in their bubbles in 2015. Other groups in central Hofors started in 2016.

At a meeting in 2016, 18 employees had raised their employment rate. A careful follow-up has been made of how the resource passes have been used. This has been done within the existing budget for staff costs. Initially, the development work created a lot of concern for the staff. It was uncertain what it would mean to work in smaller groups, always having to go to the same users. This fear was quickly reduced. It did not take long before positive effects were observed. During a meeting in 2016 with the conversation leaders, both positive and negative effects were openly shared and discussed. On the positive side, comments highlighted such factors as less stress, more fun at work, more control, more time with users (who are now happier and satisfied), better ability to read and follow care plans and less 'chatting behind the backs' of others. On the negative side, conversation leaders pointed out a number of factors, ranging from fear of changing 'bubbles' to high sick leave for some to continued scheduling difficulties in some areas. On average, about half of the workers increased their employment rate.

From 2015 to 2016, staff continuity has improved from requiring 16 different employees per user to an average of 11 employees per user over a four-week period. This represents an improvement of continuity by over 31%! It's hard to get this kind of increase due to schematic technical reasons. Development work has continued through 2017. Now all home services have an organisation with so-called bubbles. More resource passes have been introduced to further reduce the need for zero-hour contract workers. Home services will be divided into two districts by the autumn of 2018 to improve the conditions for supporting employees in the development of nursing care.

Persgården's Care Home

The activities at Persgården's care home are conducted in the form of three wards, one short-term care and two long-term care. Since Alamanco had reviewed the organisation's 2014 economy, we could see that there were high costs for zero-hour contract workers and overtime work. This led to a big overrun of budget. The pattern had also repeated in previous years. Because I like to challenge, I told the politicians: "You have to decide if you are going to make a budget for real or just pretend." They accepted the challenge. It made it possible to convert part of the costs of hourly paid and overtime to resource passes. Two full-time positions were introduced to each department, for a total of six.

The staff prepared proposals for new schedules in autumn 2015. The process was led by the conversation leaders. We had a number of meetings with them and their manager. This work also created concerns and contradictions among the employees. The work had been preceded by analysing how to use working hours – green, yellow and red time. There were many contradictory views on how to best plan the work. Eventually, a new schedule was agreed for each department. They entered into practice in November 2015. Resource passes would be able to cover absences on one's own ward or at another ward.

The unit manager, together with the other employees, had drawn up guidelines for how to use the resource passes. A new routine for planning the daily work of the wards has been introduced. The purpose was to create a clearer structure at work. We have had a number of follow-up meetings with the unit manager and employees. The meetings have been organised by ward, either half or full day. Despite the fact that everyone was able to influence the design of the rules on how to use the resource passes, there were contradictions and conflicts both within and between wards in spring 2016.

Therefore, we had a full day with each ward in June of the same year to try and figure out what the contradictory opinions were about. It turned out that too many people were unclear about the purpose of the resource passes. Many expressed a fear of sometimes having to go to another ward. Some thought that they were always understaffed. The unit manager had done a careful follow-up on how the resource passes were used week by week, and showed that they now often were more people in each ward than they were before. We agreed to continue with the resource passes the whole year when an evaluation was to be made.

A major change in employee attitude occurred in autumn 2016. It was decided to stop using the term 'resource passes'. The word had such a negative emotional meaning. Today, the staff do not use the word anymore without saying "we are our own temporary staff". A continued careful follow-up has been made for how the resource passes are used. On a significant number of occasions it has resulted in a strengthened staff in the wards.

Following the evaluation made by Alamanco at the end of 2016, the Board for Social Welfare decided to introduce another two resource passes each in the two wards for long-term wards. The purpose was to further reduce the number of zero-hour contract workers and reduce sick leave. A new schedule was applied from March 2017. Now there is an evaluation that covers development throughout 2017. It shows that absence due to illness has decreased both in short-term care and in long-term care. In short-term care, sick leave has been reduced from almost 9% to a little under 5%, and in long-term care from over 24% to 8%. The financial result shows a surplus of 321,224 krona (over £27k GB and $35k US).

A comparison of the total number of hours worked between 2016 and 2017 shows that Persgården reduced hours by a measure of two-years' worth of full-time worker hours in 2017. The conclusion of the attempt at Persgården is that ten new full-time workers have led to fewer zero-hour contract workers, a better continuity in staffing, which in turn greatly reduced sickness absence and resulted in lower costs.

The challenge for the municipality of Hofors is now to develop a budget model that gives the operations at Persgården the same stable conditions as today; that is, making a budget for real and not pretending. The municipality of Hofors has drawn up an action plan for 'full-time as a norm', where the experiences within the home services and Persgården will be an important foundation. This work will begin in autumn 2018.

Reflections on the Work with Dialogue as a Process

We live in a time when people are more interdependent than ever before, both in the big and the small. No single country can solve the environmental crisis, for example, on its own. The same applies to the refugee crisis. One can no longer unilaterally control an organisation from top to bottom in the same way as it may have been 20-30 years ago. People accept it to a lesser extent. This is especially true in Sweden. But it is also because the problems we need to solve tend to become increasingly complex. There is rarely a single obvious solution.

Often it is not enough to decide to do one thing or the other; we sometimes need to do two things at the same time. We need, for example, to:

- Lower costs while increasing quality
- Develop employee roles and leadership roles in a coherent process
- Provide for both employer *and* employee interests
- Decentralise responsibilities and competences while developing collaboration and a comprehensive view
- Allow for both self-interest and community interest
- Develop individuals while strengthening groups and developing teamwork

Expressed in another way, it is more necessary than ever to respect each other's differences. All people have the same worth. But we think, feel and act in different ways. It is a great asset if we learn to think together.

Conference Session Extracts

From conversation with 20 participants considering the paper with the author

I really like everything I've heard coming from you. And I really like the approach, I can relate to all of it. I don't see the dialogue yet. Where's the dialogue in it? Not dialogue as just exchanging, but dialogue in how I understand the Bohmian sense of something new emerging out the whole that we couldn't imagine before. Maybe I'm missing something?

What I'm noticing is that the approach to get people focused and working together as a way to have a more skilful conversation together, that would then lead to a dialogue.

So the answer is that they start to be able to discuss what their mission is together. Then they're bound together through the discussion of the mission, and the mission encourages, through all these sticky notes and groupings, a growing awareness of the value they're adding, and then they have a common understanding of their mission and value.

You showed us visual dialogue and I thought, "Well, is this dialogue? This looks like any tool that I would use as a consultant." And I'm sure it's what some would call team coaching.

Well, I'm really interested in this because I'm seeing that first of all, in doing that process, all the voices are heard, every single one. Secondly, the whole business of thinking about the value of what I do is a fresh thing. How many employees in organisations are ever asked about the value that they contribute? So that in itself is a change. Then, when they get to discuss this, the real dialogue could open.

You're talking about how the dialogue gives a common understanding, a connection between the individual selves, their inner self, and corporate purpose. That dialogue is good in that context.

Years ago I came across a Steven Covey story, when he has a glass beaker, and he asks his class to advise him when it's full. He starts with the large rocks and puts the large rocks. He says, "Please tell me when it's full". So he gets to the top and they say, "It's full, it's full". He says, "Maybe, maybe not". He reaches for another beaker of gravel. He puts the gravel in between the rocks and gets up to the top and they say, "It's full, it's full". He says, "Maybe." He reaches down for a beaker of sand. Pours in the sand. The sand falls in between the gravel, comes up to the top. They say, "It's full already, it's full!" He reaches for a beaker of water and pours water in between the sand. "For goodness sake, it's full". Water up to the top. Reaches for a salt shaker. Pours the salt into the water. He says, "What's the lesson here?" Somebody says, "Well, no matter how busy our schedule is, we can always squeeze in something". "No. That's not it". "No matter how organized we are, we can always reorganize our time and figure out how to be more efficient". "No. That's not it". He says, "What is it then?" He says, "Unless we start with the large rocks, we'll never have a chance to put them in later". So thank you for reminding us to start with the large rocks.

Postscript

The author's reflections written some months after the conference

There must be a number of conditions in order to achieve good cooperation between employers and employees. It is necessary, for example, to develop a basic trust and confidence in the organization, where everyone realizes that they all are interdependent. The big challenge is to introduce dialogue in a hierarchical organization. Therefore it is necessary to show that the work with dialogue as a process leads to positive results, both in terms of hard data such as economy but also soft data such as job satisfaction and a better work environment.

Someone or some people need to dare to invest their belief and energy to convince the management that using the dialogue as a process makes it possible to achieve results that one would otherwise not be able to achieve.

The purpose of working with dialogue is that all employees who will be affected by future changes can participate and influence them. This assumes that the work has a clear structure. A project organization should be created with clear leadership and where all important parts of the organization cooperate with a common purpose towards a common goal. The dialogue work should be carried out in concrete, practical forms of work that give all employees the opportunity to make their voice heard.

Dialogue deals with such basic issues as what, how and why we do what we do in our daily work. What benefit will it create for the society and those we are there for? The work with dialogue should train leaders and employees to respect each other's differences and to think together – to be genuinely interested in trying to understand how others think more than trying to convince others about my own way of thinking.

In order for work on dialogue to become sustainable, methods need to be developed to measure the result of the development work. This applies to data relating to the economy and how we use our work time, as well as quality, job satisfaction, sick leave and the work environment. The experiences that are made step-by-step should lead to the development of a common value document on what should characterize the cooperation in the organization.

Indigenous Affairs, Border Services and the Path of Dialogue in Canada

Peter Hill

For most of us, the term "border services" likely brings to mind protected boundaries, secured borders and the regulated movement of people and goods between nations. This would be true for the Canada Border Services Agency (CBSA) as well, but it would not fully encompass the emerging partnership between Indigenous Peoples and the Agency, nor the role I am proud to play as CBSA Champion of Indigenous Peoples. It also would not describe the central place of dialogue in our work.

Background and Context

I've been an employee of CBSA since October 2008, and have held a variety of positions, but have not been a Champion before. (Typically in other countries, a "Champion" would be comparable to an "Advocate." In my case, the Champion role goes beyond advocacy and entails direct responsibility and accountability to set a strategic direction and to deliver results and outcomes.) At a meeting in May 2015, my colleague read out a list of new Champion roles that were being distributed by the head of the Agency to each senior executive in order to address a range of critically important issues such as Official Language Rights, Employment Equity and Diversity, Next Generation Leaders and so on. I was a bit taken aback when my name was called out as Champion for Indigenous Peoples. I did not want to second-guess the depth of the challenge or the potential benefits a Champion could bring to this issue, but I had a very superficial understanding of Indigenous Peoples in Canada. Unflattering stereotypical images flashed across my mind.

I had two immediate thoughts. The first was a question: "How on earth am I going to carry this out?" The second was an answer: through dialogue. In that moment, I had a clear sense that the dialogue skills I first encountered in 2000 and had been applying since would be essential to any contribution I could possibly make. The work that has unfolded has exceeded anything I imagined, and it is all intended to help CBSA to deliver on the Government of Canada's commitment to Reconciliation, captured in the Prime Minister's statement that "*No relationship is more important to me and to Canada than the one with Indigenous*

Peoples. It is time for a renewed, nation-to-nation relationship with Indigenous Peoples, based on recognition of rights, respect, co-operation and partnership."

The vision we have crafted for the CBSA is to be a leading organization that partners with Indigenous Peoples in providing a workplace of choice and in addressing long-standing First Nation border issues. Our work has been inspired by Indigenous CBSA employees who have shared their experiences and stories as well as those shared by Indigenous Peoples based on their border crossing experiences. Long-standing border issues that have arisen In Canada are the focus of our dialogue. These issues include lack of full recognition of inherent mobility rights, which is contrasted by US recognition of the mobility provision of the *Jay Treaty*. Indigenous Peoples have reported friendlier treatment when entering the US, which is considered to be more consistent with Indigenous Peoples' understanding of their inherent rights as First Nations. Family and cultural connections are disrupted by current immigration and border management legislation, regulations and practices. Certain identity documents are not accepted at ports of entry. Some raise concerns about treatment by border services officers, including disrespectful or racist comments, and improper handling of cultural or spiritual goods and medicines. Trade and personal goods, including exchanges of game meat and fish for ceremonial purposes, are restricted. These are known issues. They have been well documented, such as in the *Report on First Nation Border Crossing Issues* by the Minister's Special Representative, submitted in August 2017.

Our work has also been shaped by the profound negative impacts of colonialism, which include severe socio-economic gaps between Indigenous and non-Indigenous Canadians, higher suicide rates for First Nations Peoples, significant over-representation of Indigenous Peoples in federal prison and endangered Indigenous languages. This is compounded by the traumatic legacy stemming from the church-run residential schools, reflected in the *Truth and Reconciliation Commission of Canada: Report and Calls to Action*. For over a century, the central goals of Canada's Indigenous policy were to eliminate Indigenous governments, ignore Indigenous rights, terminate the Treaties, and, through a process of assimilation, cause Indigenous Peoples to cease to exist as distinct legal, social, cultural, religious, and racial entities in Canada. The establishment and operation of residential schools were a central element of this policy, described by Indigenous Senator Murray Sinclair, Chair of the Commission, as "cultural genocide".

Our journey at the CBSA has only just begun to unfold. It has been heartfelt and assisted greatly by dialogue. For the rest of this paper I would like to share the role that dialogue has played in our ongoing process.

Overall Dialogue Context

I have been leading the dialogue work in partnership with the Agency's Indigenous Advisory Circle since June 2015. Gradually, I've been introducing, teaching and systematically applying some of the dialogue-based leadership models, concepts, tools and practices I have learned over the years. My key inspiration has been David Bohm and his seminal work *Wholeness and the Implicate Order*. The primary models and skills that I have used are the 'Four-Player Model' and practices for dialogue; the 'Fields of Conversation'; the 'Concept and Practice of Container Building'; the 'Flame Model;' and the 'System Design Spiral', each outlined below.

The Four-Player Model and practices for dialogue comprises Level One of the structural dynamics research pioneered by David Kantor and colleagues to advance a better understanding of the nature of human discourse and enable effective dialogue. The Fields of Conversation map, developed by Otto Scharmer, links particular qualities of behaviour and mindset, such as reflective and non-reflective energy, exchange, patterns, norms, pressures, rule-following and thresholds, together with a continuum encompassing monologue, discussion, conversation and dialogue. The Concept and Practice of Container Building comprises a set of key competencies to create a context through a pattern of relationships where a structurally significant leadership group can 'hold the wider system'; that is, envision and sustain a long-term commitment to system change. Use of circle-format seating without tables, an ancient symbol and practice for dialogue, has been the preferred physical arrangement of the container to create an awareness in which there is energy, possibility and safety amongst a group of people. The Flame Model, developed by Bill Isaacs, is a diagnostic tool for individual and collective leadership that provides perspective on three connected levels of reality that form the core for dialogue and system change. The System Design Spiral is a holistic process tool for dialogic leadership that is applied to design and implement large-scale system change and transformation. I learned these concepts and practices principally from Peter Garrett, Bill Isaacs and Michael Jones through the 12-month Leadership for Collective Intelligence program.

My development as a dialogue practitioner has been shaped by the following engagements, among others:

- *New Terms of Engagement for a Networked World* conference, Simon Fraser University, Wosk Centre for Dialogue, Margaret Wheatley, Meha Pogachnik, 2000;
- *Dialogue and the Art of Thinking Together* workshop, Dialogos, Robert Hanig and Michael Jones, 2000;
- The *Leadership for Collective Intelligence* program, Dialogos, Peter Garrett, Bill Isaacs and Michael Jones, 2002-2003;
- Dialogue Retreat with Emergency Management Policy Division, Office of Critical Infrastructure Protection and Emergency Preparedness, Michael Jones, 2003;
- The *Authentic Leadership in Action* program, Shambhala Summer Institute, workshops led by Peter Senge, Margaret Wheatley, Michael Jones, Otto Scharmer, Arawana Hayashi and Juanita Brown, 2004;
- *Foundations for Leadership* program, Society of Organizational Learning, Peter Senge and Robert Hanig, 2005;
- *The World Needs Dialogue!* inaugural conference of the Academy of Professional Dialogue, founded by Peter Garrett and Jane Ball, 2018.

I mention these because each of us is shaped by our training and, more importantly, by those who have played an influential role in our development as practitioners. Perhaps this list gives a sense of the background and intention I bring to my work.

The dialogue work I now oversee is multifaceted and intended to achieve three fundamental goals: to enable the Agency to provide a workplace of choice where Indigenous Peoples feel welcomed, respected and supported; to ensure that the Agency carries out its integrated border management and enforcement mandate in a manner that is respectful of Indigenous Peoples' cultures and rights; and to enable the Agency to make a significant contribution to the Government's Reconciliation agenda with Indigenous Peoples, including support towards establishing renewed nation-to-nation and distinctions-based (i.e., First Nation, Métis, Inuit) relationships with the Crown.

At present, the work is progressing through a broadly defined governance system, including partnership arrangements established jointly by Indigenous and CBSA leadership and fora that are internal to the CBSA and linked with external committees responsible for overseeing the Government's Reconciliation agenda.

Partners in Dialogue

Forming and nurturing the Indigenous Advisory Circle (commonly known as 'the Circle') is crucial to our work. Our first meeting in June 2015 involved a small group of people who were previously members of the now-defunct Aboriginal Advisory Committee. It had contributed to some improvements towards Employment Equity objectives, but by 2015 it lacked leadership and had not met for years. The Indigenous employees that opened themselves to working together with me, and welcomed me into their midst as an ally, had been maintaining a mutual support network on their own that was disconnected from executive leadership and formal governance structures in the Agency. That small group was comprised of highly motivated and talented Indigenous employees who were deeply committed to making a difference. They saw an opportunity to channel their energy to make improvements, and I wanted to work with them. We quickly rebranded ourselves as the 'Circle', and today these individuals are the heart of an expanding core group that is deepening engagement with Indigenous and non-Indigenous People to develop new approaches.

When I came into the first meeting of the Circle, I spoke about accepting my role as Champion with humility, enthusiasm, some trepidation and an openness of mind and heart. I shared my intent to listen and foster dialogue to understand issues and help us think and work together in new ways to develop plans to overcome the many obstacles Indigenous Peoples faced, including lack of respect, systemic racism and challenges to recruitment, retention and career progression.

Over the past four years, the influence of the Circle at CBSA has gradually grown. I have come to see this development as a microcosm of the emerging historical opportunity for reconciliation in Canada. Renewed relationships based on mutual trust and respect are being nurtured. They are fundamental to the growth of both CBSA and Canadian society and require a transformational shift in how Government recognizes the inherent jurisdiction Indigenous Peoples have over matters that affect their socio-economic and cultural well-being. Dialogue offers the possibility of generating a new level of understanding and collaboration between Indigenous and non-Indigenous Peoples, and between First Nations and Government.

Perhaps the most intriguing and promising aspect that I have recently begun to realize more clearly about this this work is the depth of the synergy and overlap between Bohm's approach to dialogue and that of traditional Indigenous practices of dialogue. This growing sense was crystalized for me in a 2018 phone conversation with Elder Leroy Little Bear of the Darkfoot First Nation, a recipient of the Order of Canada honour in 2019, who met Bohm and engaged in dialogue with him and a number of other Indigenous leaders during the late 1980s and early 1990s. This Elder has written about being awestruck by the similarities. I felt privileged that he shared some of his experiences with me on the telephone. Perhaps I may be coming late to the party as it were, but it is still a timely insight given the practical steps we are currently taking at the CBSA. While there are also differences that warrant further careful exploration, such a blended dialogic leadership approach seems to hold real potential to renew relationships with Indigenous Peoples and move them from marginalization to accommodation to recognition to full partnership with Government such that Métis Inuit and First Nations may become co-decision-makers on important matters that directly affect their lives, including re-imagining and building the border of the future.

Progression in Dialogue

We are making progress. To elaborate further, I will highlight three key examples that provide some evidence that reinforce our belief that we are on the right path.

From the outset, I applied the 'System Design Spiral' and the 'Flame Model' to lead the change process. I began with the Indigenous Advisory Circle for the discovery phase and first-level sponsorship container. At that time, my terms of reference and scope of work as Champion of Indigenous Peoples exclusively focused inward on the Agency. We developed an annual plan of activities to educate and raise awareness and respect for Indigenous Peoples' cultures, and to improve Indigenous Peoples' representation, recruitment, retention and career development. The Chair of our Circle, an Elder and Indigenous woman employee of the CBSA, presented our plan for approval to the Executive Committee Chaired by the head of the Agency. We participated in a Government-wide initiative to enhance Indigenous Peoples' careers in the Public Service of Canada by making a significant contribution to a government-wide strategy (*Many Voices, One Mind: A Pathway to Reconciliation*). From there, we built a holistic, enterprise-level architecture across the Agency to help encourage the use of dialogue and effect the transformation we sought. Three key developments unfolded to support this.

First, my Terms of Reference were expanded in 2017 to be both inward and outward facing. This provided a foundation to create the *CBSA Indigenous Framework and Strategy,* which is principles-based and distinctions-based (Indigenous, Métis and Inuit). It comprises four domains: policy, operations, people and engagement. The CBSA Executive Committee, chaired by the head of the Agency, approved this framework in May 2018. This was a game-changer because our framework prescribes a comprehensive collaborative approach with Indigenous Peoples to transform the Agency's workplace, workforce and operations and, therefore, also the border crossing experience of Indigenous Peoples. The framework broadened the agreement for the work to be carried out and it established the next-level sponsorship container at the senior executive level of the Agency. The framework also assigned responsibility and accountability to other senior executives to deliver targeted results. This meant, for example, that the Vice President of Human Resources was required to deliver a recruitment and training strategy, and so on. Finally, the framework confirmed the source and allocation of funds needed for the actions to be taken. All of these taken together provided backing for the use of dialogue in our work.

Second, approval was provided to establish the Indigenous Affairs Secretariat. This is a small, permanent body in the Agency that serves as the hub of Indigenous matters at the CBSA and includes Regional Indigenous Liaison Officers. The Circle of volunteers has been maintained as an essential part of the architecture, but it was insufficient on its own to carry out the work. The Secretariat is responsible for supporting, coordinating and sustaining efforts to implement and evolve the *Indigenous Framework and Strategy*. The Director of the Secretariat, an Indigenous woman, has a holistic role and mandate and reports to me in support of my Champion role.

To bring to life our vision of engagement, partnership and reconciliation with Indigenous Peoples, a combination of measures were used to build capacity for dialogue-based leadership, a few of which are outlined below. I gave workshops on dialogue concepts and practices to Circle members, the Secretariat leadership and senior executives in our working group and my branch. Dialogue-based leadership training was provided to a small number of key executives and officers at the Banff Centre's Aboriginal Leadership program. We also integrated the principles and practices of dialogue based on David Bohm's work into a design-thinking initiative (ongoing) that was delivered under contract by an expert third-party with a mastery of the dialogic practice. This initiative is co-sponsored by the head of the CBSA and the Grand Chief of the Mohawk Council of Akwesasne. To date, it has enabled development of an emerging joint plan through dialogue amongst a diverse group of leaders from both government and the Mohawk community to address some long-standing border issues in the Cornwall-Akwesasne communities. These communities are located in a remarkably complex jurisdictional area, where traditional Mohawk territory, the provinces of Quebec and Ontario, New York State and the Canada-United States' border converge. In addition, the Mohawk community and its leadership, the CBSA and the location and configuration of the port of entry (i.e., a unique 'mixed corridor') have been profoundly affected by events that occurred in 2009 surrounding the arming of CBSA border service officers.

Because one of the key value-added responsibilities of the Secretariat is to apply an 'Indigenous lens' to the development and delivery of policies, plans, actions and advice, it is led and staffed primarily with Indigenous employees. Indigenous employees are complemented in the Secretariat by non-Indigenous employees possessing subject matter expertise. While the Secretariat is located at the Agency head office, it is supported by dedicated Regional Indigenous Liaison Officers in several regional offices. The Liaison Officers receive functional guidance from the Director of the Secretariat and undertake outreach activities aligned with the framework. Eventually, all regions will have Liaison Officers. Guided by the framework, we are fostering a 'community of champions' with a regional senior executive who oversees a network of regional operations executives, one from each of the Agency's existing seven regions in Canada, who serve locally, in addition to their primary operational roles, as regional champions on Indigenous matters. They receive functional guidance from the Director of the Secretariat to align their efforts with the goals of our framework.

Third, we are creating opportunities for CBSA leaders at all levels to develop dialogue skills and engage in dialogue through a series of educational and capacity-building initiatives designed to raise awareness of Indigenous Peoples' cultures. For example, in May 2018, we presented to the Executive Committee for approval our proposed CBSA Indigenous Framework and Strategy at the unique Wabano Centre for Aboriginal Health and Wellness in Ottawa. Designed by Indigenous Canadian architect Douglas Cardinal, the Centre is replete with beautiful Indigenous art and a permanent exhibition of the Truth and Reconciliation Commission. Executive Committee members were engaged in an extraordinary educational experience, including a traditional smudging ceremony conducted by Elder Annie St George and her husband Robert St George, followed by a profound and moving presentation given by a senior adviser, an Indigenous woman, in the Agency's Secretariat. The presentation elicited dialogue on the challenges and potential for the CBSA to make a significant contribution to reconciliation. Executive Committee gave resounding approval of the framework.

On another occasion, one of the Agency's Regional Indigenous Liaison Officers, an Indigenous man, provided a briefing and experiential educational opportunity for Executive Committee members on his sacred bundle, including medicines, an eagle feather and other personal items. Another event engaged Indigenous Senator Murray Sinclair, and Chair of the Truth and Reconciliation Commission, who came to the CBSA during National Indigenous Awareness Week and provided a powerful keynote address on his work followed by a question-and-answer period with a full auditorium of hundreds of CBSA employees. This event contributed to further dialogues, awareness and inquiry. For example, we hosted a national webcast across the Agency on the theme *What Reconciliation Means to Me*. This event featured a panel of four CBSA Indigenous employees, including youth and an elder, who each told their own personal and profoundly moving stories about reconciliation and offered their views on finding a path forward.

In order to build capacity and strengthen competency in dialogue and dialogic leadership skills, I give workshops on dialogue and the art of thinking and working together to different groups of CBSA employees, including members of the Indigenous Advisory Circle, Indigenous Affairs Secretariat and to other employees, managers and leadership teams. In these workshops, I introduce Bohm's work and the theory and practice of dialogue through the Four-Player System, Fields of Conversation and the Concept and Practice of Container Building and encourage the application of these methods on an ongoing basis. I have increased these offerings during the past several months to support the ongoing efforts to implement and further develop our framework and strategy. We have also begun to integrate these dialogue models and practices into the Agency's training strategy on Indigenous matters. For example, this includes the 'Kairos Blanket Exercise', an experiential Indigenous cultural awareness training process that conveys history from an Indigenous perspective. This exercise has been added as a core element of the Agency's Border Services Officer Induction Training Program.

Managing Complexity

One Indigenous colleague reflected recently that she felt 'a bit shell shocked' during the first few meetings of our Circle because of my commitment to help in concrete ways through advice, direction and the development of plans that could be implemented to improve things. My colleague noted that "no one had ever done that previously through the years". I felt welcomed as an ally from the beginning of my entry into this work, but I also sensed some wariness. At a personal level, my own wariness has dissipated as my knowledge, respect and appreciation of Indigenous Peoples has grown. More generally, I also feel that wariness has dissipated as we have come to know each other better and have made progress through years of working and sometimes sitting in dialogue circles together. As I continue to receive the gift of knowledge and learning about the history of Indigenous Peoples from their first contact with European settlers, I have come to better understand the wariness on the part of Indigenous Peoples. I accept this as being a natural, human position to hold in light of the context.

On a broader scale, some Indigenous Peoples cite examples of progress. Yet, there is realism and skepticism about the notion that relationships will be transformed, reconciliation will be achieved and a new nation-to-nation arrangement will be implemented during our lifetime. In my personal experience through the work I am doing, however, I see real commitment to collaboration, partnership and the emergence of new trust-based relationships. Clearly, the dialogue-based approach we have introduced is bringing forward a new way of working together. My belief is that dialogue is the primary factor which is fostering positive mindsets among both Indigenous and non-Indigenous Peoples and a willingness to share difficult truths and realities. I believe this provides a basis for a true, perhaps unconventional, diagnostic and open mind to perceive freshly. Some dialogue practitioners have noted that Bohm's structured approach to dialogue can generate creative thinking by helping to suspend some constraints of personal and historical conditioning. This suspension can enable individuals and a group of individuals to acquire a new perspective. I see this beginning to occur in our work. Increased trust, risk-taking, collaboration and actions are observable towards sustainable change and improvement.

In this respect, actions speak louder than words. Perhaps what I find most inspirational in my work in this area is having the privilege to meet and work with Indigenous People who have exhibited such high resilience and a relentless commitment to work and collaborate to improve things, even if those improvements are initially incremental and modest. An Indigenous colleague noted that "reconciliation is resilience in motion". I have learned that Indigenous creation stories, language and spirit are full of movement. I think this world view allows Indigenous Peoples to see and appreciate even weak signals of sustainable improvement, knowing full well that the actual speed of progress may be suboptimal and that the profound change needed may take a long time to achieve. For example, the new mandatory Indigenous cultural awareness training recently implemented for CBSA border service officer recruits may be seen as connecting to the larger story about the advancement of a new relationship between Government and Indigenous Peoples. I feel that a gradual awakening about Indigenous Peoples' reality that one may discern is unfolding across this country includes the CBSA.

Conclusions / Reflections

I would like to briefly highlight a few examples of how I believe the work described above may help to advance the field of Professional Dialogue.

First, the dialogue work under way at the CBSA is a living example that is currently both unfolding and enfolding in the spirit of Bohm's theory of the implicate order. Accordingly, one of the fundamental intentions of dialogue is to reveal the relatedness of our thought processes, and the tendency to collectively generate fragmented realities through them. In this and other respects, I see an overlap between Bohm's approach to dialogue and Indigenous Peoples' traditional practices of dialogue and ways of thinking. Elder Leroy Little Bear has noted there is a large overlap between David Bohm's dialogue approach and his peoples' approach. He noted that, before starting a dialogue, Bohm would try to have everyone clear or empty their minds as much as possible, to open up their minds. This reminded him of a Darkfoot tradition used to help a person address a concern they were stuck with and unable to resolve. A spokesperson (relative or friend) would invite people from the community to come and speak to the individual about the concern. The individual would listen throughout and not say a word and selectively take what was heard to resolve the concern. Both approaches aim to enable deep listening of many diverse views and new learning. Elder Leroy Little Bear further noted that sweat lodge ceremonies are purification ceremonies intended to clean the mind out and open it up to generate new knowledge. This objective is shared by

Bohm's approach to dialogue. In my view, there is a counter-intuitive similarity between Bohm's modern thought and Indigenous ancient wisdom, whereby the pathway of dialogue to new knowledge and learning entails not filling up the mind with more facts and information but the opposite, decluttering and emptying the mind. An angst-oriented energy and tension, created by trying to suspend judgement and allowing a 'not knowing' mindset to persist, can perhaps create a mindset of sharper awareness, one that constitutes a generative field for discovery and learning. The convergence of modern thought and ancient wisdom offers 'fertile ground' for further exploration. It may offer insights and practices for how we may create generative fields for learning that could be beneficial to advance the field of dialogue.

Second, finding the latitude to conduct dialogue and use dialogic leadership in a government context to effect large-scale systems change is fraught with uncertainty. A premium placed on results-based management and achievement of outcomes within relatively short electoral cycles can make it challenging to secure the time and space needed for dialogue. Paradoxically, this holds true even for the most intractable, complex issues that clearly do not lend themselves to quick fixes or a status quo mode of thinking. A sponsorship container at the highest levels is needed so that a senior leader has license to lead through dialogue. Such support is essential but insufficient. Strong governance arrangements that transcend traditional boundaries are also required. This is particularly true in order to work effectively with Indigenous Peoples in a nation-to-nation manner. Good governance that is principles-based is necessary to sustain collaboration and report regularly on incremental progress made through dialogue to senior leadership in both the federal government system (i.e., at the Deputy Head level, the person who is the direct report to the Minister, the elected official in Canada; as well as to the Ministerial level, such as a Cabinet Committee) and the Indigenous Peoples' governing system (i.e., at the Grand Chief and Chief level of Council, the ones who are the elected officials as well as the Elders who are the traditional, non-elected leaders). Departmental governance arrangements must be well designed to connect directly with horizontal or 'whole-of-government' governance bodies in order to strongly support courageous action in service of delivering results on Government priorities. This may entail making submissions to international bodies, such as the United Nations, pursuant to international treaty obligations that may be brought into play through special reviews.

Third, strong governance in the context of Indigenous affairs entails embracing complexity, involving multiple leadership groups and honouring arrangements within Indigenous communities. A kind of 'double jeopardy' is presented by the challenges and complexity of multiple sets of governance arrangements. For example, differing electoral cycles across the Federal Government and Indigenous Councils means that it is often difficult to manage and keep tabs on the scale and pace of change. Connections, complexity and expectations grow, sometimes exponentially – or wane – with interconnected events simultaneously influencing many players and initiatives. It is challenging to keep in step with the pace of change while also striving to influence the broader work as it unfolds. This is particularly the case with the work towards Reconciliation in Canada because it touches numerous departments and agencies that use a wide range of practices for consultation and engagement that are not necessarily dialogue-based.

Fourth, it is advisable to be deliberate and keep an expansive mindset when thinking about how to treat and understand time in the pursuit of sustainable change and resolution of concerns in partnership with Indigenous Peoples. In dialogue and collaboration circles with Indigenous Peoples, timelines are a very important consideration. In general, compressed timelines raise risks related to inadequate consultation. Time should be allotted not only for development of a shared agenda, use of flexible structure, establishment of clear objectives and principles for collaboration, setting up clear accountability, but also for inclusion of ceremony, traditional opening and closing prayers and establishing governance mechanisms together. When these measures are combined with a mindset and intention based on genuine interest and willingness to listen and engage in dialogue without 'watching the clock', such an approach is generally welcomed and constructive. Indigenous Peoples may describe such an approach as comprising a 'good mind'.

Different concepts and qualities of time are also at play (e.g., *Chronos* and *Kairos*, where the former is related to chronological time and the latter more relevant to a cyclical concept of time). To illustrate, an Indigenous hunter might say that moose hunting season begins after the first frost, rather than in accord with any particular date or month of the calendar. There may also be very different views between Indigenous Peoples and non-Indigenous Peoples about the start time and duration of meetings, including the extent of introductions or explanations of context – sometimes which can take days – before the purported agenda of the meeting may be engaged. The history of Indigenous Peoples in Canada in the geographic area we now know as North America ('Turtle Island' in many Indigenous cultures) entails varying accounts that Indigenous Peoples have resided here for up to 7,000 to 10,000 years, or 'from time immemorial'.

Canada celebrated its 150th birthday as a nation-state in 2017. While this time was one of celebration, for Indigenous Peoples of Canada it was also a period of paradox for many reasons, some referenced above. Certain observers and players, including Indigenous Peoples, refer to the 'Next 150 Years' for the development of new nation-to-nation and government-to-government relationships. The *Seven-Generation Principle* that is central to Indigenous Peoples' cultures is often cited as a measure of time required to achieve meaningful and sustainable change. In addition, change is unlikely to be consistently straightforward and without setbacks along the journey. Dialogue can be the pathway for nation-to-nation collaboration and co-decision-making to identify priorities and assign resources to make short, medium and long-term changes. As a result, dialogue will be central in establishing a mutually acceptable timeline for the set and sequence of joint initiatives that establish a path forward for Reconciliation.

Endnotes

The words *Aboriginal* and *Indigenous* are used throughout this paper to align with the chronological use of each term. In 2016, the Government of Canada began to replace *Aboriginal* with *Indigenous*. *Indigenous, Métis* and *Inuit* is the most accurate terminology to use when referring to all of the major First Nations groups in Canada. A 'distinctions-based' approach refers to a differentiated approach that comprises Indigenous, Métis and Inuit Peoples.

Special thanks to Leroy Little Bear for a powerful conversation by phone on August 16, 2018.

Heartfelt thanks to Pauline Mousseau, Loretta Landmesser, Nicole Elmy, Claudia Apel and Michael Jones for their insightful, helpful comments on an earlier version of this manuscript.

The views expressed in this paper reflect the author's and not those of the CBSA. I remain accountable for the final manuscript and any shortcomings.

Conference Session Extracts

From conversation with 20 participants considering the paper with the author

What is it that makes us people so afraid of other people who are different from ourselves? For example, when I grew up in the north of Sweden, there was no immigrants there. Ten kilometres from where I lived, there's another village, and when I was a young boy, I was told that the people living there were crazy. When I moved to Uppsala to start working within a psychiatric care at a huge psychiatric hospital, there's a community north of that county called Uppsala. And I was told that when the crows were flying over that community, they turned upside down so they didn't have to see that shit. You understand? And this problem with [the treatment of] indigenous people, we have the same problem. We have the Sami people, who have been very badly treated through the years, and still are, and we have an increasing racial problem. Really, what is it that makes us so easily be suspecting other people are trying to do something that would harm us? I link that to somewhat to this fragmentation thinking that is so common among us.

Respect for all. An attempt to treat people with respect. I worked a lot with Cambodian survivors, it's always the first word that is said. What's important for you to behave well? To respect others. For me, it's also a respect. But your question is, for me, interesting because it was so difficult. And I think difficult is to encounter the strange thing from the other, or the strange behaviour, or the strange way of living, and counter that in myself, and counter what's strange in myself.

A lot of people in our country are working with the people who are coming to the country from Syria and from other countries. And they're very involved in the work to help the people. Some of the people are really working themselves into burn-out situations to help those people coming over the borders. The question arises, then, from where do they help? From which motivation? From which point are they coming and say, "You are somebody from another culture, and I offer you my help and respect". It's not to say that there are – there's very important work to be done by the people from Austria helping the immigrants. I have guided some dialogue work with the helpers and the immigrants, and you could feel in the dialogue, in the space, that there is a wall somewhere, where the immigrating people don't want the helpers to get in.

I wanted to build on what you've said. I worked for a number of years as a parole officer, and I had many indigenous people in my case file, and many traumatized people. And there is one concept we didn't approach here. It's reciprocity. Even the most damaged people I've worked with love to give as well. And this game of giving and receiving, it took me a long time as a parole officer. I was educated in the social work thought of the time, which was that you give to people who have less. But my capacity to receive, even from damaged people, I've created more capacity to join them as human beings. And I think we never talk about reciprocity in dialogue, and somehow there's a place for that.

Postscript

The author's reflections written some months after the conference

The central role of dialogue in my collaboration with Indigenous Peoples on border management is evolving. The shift stems from the preparation I undertook to lead a dialogue on this topic at *The World Needs Dialogue!* Inaugural Conference in 2018, the dialogue that occurred there and the dialogue, thinking and work that has occurred since.

Initially, I saw Bohm's approach to dialogue as a pathway for sustainable, meaningful change. Dialogue would enable Indigenous Peoples to share difficult truths. And non-Indigenous people would be able to shed conditioned negative personal biases towards Indigenous Peoples. New perspectives and collaboration would be generated to help achieve new outcomes.

The result would be a pathway to reconciliation through a welcoming, respectful workplace for Indigenous Peoples at the CBSA and a respectful border crossing experience for Indigenous Peoples aligned with their beliefs.

There may be potential for a more profound change, a transformation of both culture and leadership, by virtue of a clearer sense of the nature of the overlap between Bohm's approach to dialogue and traditional Indigenous Peoples' practices.

A new practice of dialogue could unfold through pursuit, discovery and generation of an integrative model of modern thought and ancient wisdom.

Many traditional Indigenous practices of dialogue are sophisticated, accessible and relevant to addressing long-standing border issues. While a great deal of learning can be drawn from ancient wisdom, those who hold that wisdom see value in learning from modern thinking.

This points to the value and importance of continuing on the path of dialogue in Canada on Indigenous affairs and border services and for the contribution it might make to the domain and practices of dialogue with broad practical application.

Dialogue as a Working Model in Degerfors Municipality

Per Hilding

In 2005, Degerfors Municipality in central Sweden received financial support to develop an education programme to stimulate better staff communication, and to make its work teams aware of their responsibility for setting goals in the organisation. The programme was also aimed at promoting a good workplace climate, increased understanding of our differences and awareness about how we would succeed. We focused on a three-day training in Dialogue. All staff members in the municipality's care and nursing department, together with their managers, spent three days together without interruptions for tasks other than those included in the course. 'Be present' was a keyword, and we learned in the event how important our presence together was. Managers and staff, side-by-side, worked in groups and used feedback to gain insight into each other's differences. Our facilitators were trained by the Komanco consulting company, which at the time was owned by the Swedish Municipal Workers' Union. The facilitators worked systematically in pairs, organising the training as a process. On the first day, in addition to presentations, we carefully considered the expectations and concerns we held for these three days. We also went through value-creating practices in our approach to each other so that everyone would feel safe and in no way feel attacked or undervalued. We were all placed in a Dialogue circle without the opportunity to be 'protected' by a table. Each of us had the same ability to see and be seen by each other. The size of the groups varied, but ranged between 20-25 people. Here's an overview of our training session programme:

Day 1: We reviewed Dialogue from scratch, learning about the concepts of monologue and dialogue. We began to see the differences in our perspectives, which became evident in our initial group work. We defended our opinions with a will of steel! The groups had no real strategy for communicating with each other and the group's energy was lost in the discussions. The facilitators sat on the sidelines and noted our patterns. Afterwards, we got feedback and reflected together about our behaviour. We discovered that each of us is at the centre of the circle in some way and must develop the insight to understand what we carry within and the responsibility we have to find our role in the group.

Day 2: We started the day with a group reflection, followed by thoughts from the day before. What happened, and who am I *really* when I'm not my own opinion? We didn't solve any problems during the reflection; we were just here and now. We shared our own thoughts. On this day, the group began developing as a whole as we focused on the dynamics that our differences create. We saw what additional factors are involved in our work environment, so that we can continue developing together in the group. We looked at the system paradigm we are dealing with and the nature of our workplace operating system, in David Kantor's words: was it Open, emphasising community and flexibility; Closed, stressing order and structure; or Random, favouring spontaneity and unpredictability? We asked how we could create a reflection time in the team. We asked how feeling or action governs. How do we talk to each other in terms of meaning? We created images of what qualities we have carried with us from childhood, and what role models we have had. We examined Kantor's Heroic Modes, which he calls the *Fixer, Abandoner* and the *Protector*. Here we saw a connection to our dark sides, something new to many participants. How much do these modes control us? How have I been dark, and how did I react? Did I think that being in the 'dark mode' was unpleasant? Or was it a relief to get an explanation for certain characteristics?

Day 3: On this day we looked at how a team works with its organisation. We learned the prerequisites for success in dialogue with each other, and the key factors that are important to reaching the organisation's goals. Who sets goals, and what is required to get there? Can I influence my success or failure, and that of the group? What kinds of language do we use in our organisation? How do we talk with our senior executives or politicians? We experienced what happens when we share a common language in dialogue. We came to understand that there is a connection with being able to defend our positions, from both sides, and that we have the opportunity to correct our way of working by having many tools in our dialogue toolbox. We then took leave of each other. We left the room with energy but also knew that we would miss the group. We wrote our evaluations and our work was complete. But we learned that after a group is dissolved, we can always take another opportunity to practice at any time. There will be new people and other thoughts to listen to, to understand the context and to learn how we work in our new roles. The more we learn these things, the better we are able to continue in our joint mission.

Reflection

When we have been on a course, we know how difficult it can be to get back to the workplace and keep the knowledge alive. We may be euphoric in our energy flow, and have so much good knowledge to share. We get a cup of coffee with our colleagues and start our story; after one minute the group's interest begins to cool and the focus moves on. We find ourselves in a transient phase, where we know we are intervening in our colleagues' time. We are filled with frustration and emptiness. We have neither the forum nor the space to develop meaningful conversations. We do not have the time to teach our friends dialogue. We cannot expect that we will remain unchallenged. We can't expect anyone to listen to us if we do not have a common approach. We find that we are not able speak to our point, and we become a threat to other opinions without the option of thinking deeper together. We risk ending in crisis and possible conflict.

By contrast, we came to work the day after our Dialogue training and were noticeably touched by our common experience. We had all participated in the same course and we had heard our own voices in consensus. We had shared the course content; we sometimes did not like some things we heard from others, but we had learned to accept them and understand that we feel differently. We had a common goal and that was what we centred around. This sense of belonging and a common platform was incredible to us. We continued with the practice of dialogue, listening and understanding, as we built on the learning from the days before. We invited each other into the conversation and we talked about the concepts in a playful way, using David Kantor's labels for leadership types: "You are a Mover who wants us to get moving and get started with the job!" "You are an Opposer, so you should always question!" Everything fit within the framework of our shared knowledge. We held the feeling of togetherness and understanding of each other for a long time.

Organisation

Degerfors Municipality is a small town of about 10,000 inhabitants. One of the largest employers is the public sector, or the municipality itself. It consists of 750 employees distributed into different administrations. The municipality is divided into various parts, or so-called committees. My colleagues and I work with the Social Welfare Committee, which includes care and nursing for our elderly and disabled, and individual and family care, which manages the social network that includes special support for families, drug addiction, etc. The users of this system are the ones who receive care or nursing.

In the Social Welfare Committee the decision was made to focus on Dialogue Training for the work teams. The Committee had seen that the outcome of the education had brought such a good result that they wanted to continue. That decision led to a training of our own facilitators.

The Social Welfare Committee made the decision to continue to use dialogue systematically across the municipality. In order to save costs on consultancy fees, the committee decided that the staff of the municipality would facilitate their own personnel. They decided to appoint facilitators whose task would be dialogue work in their own organisation, first and foremost. Four of us were trained as facilitators to let dialogue live on in our organisation.

We received the training required by Komanco, which was renamed Alamanco during our engagement with them. Alamanco has been the cornerstone of our further development of dialogue. Dialogue facilitators across Sweden meet a couple of days each year in Stockholm. There we further develop the tools and work on our own development in dialogue. It is Alamanco, with its professional facilitators, that provides valuable guidance.

As facilitators we work together closely in pairs. I am a systems thinker and particularly value the practical and factual. I work well with my partner Åsa, who is less linear. She values the feelings in the group. Because a sense of grounding is important in what I do, it is essential for me to know for what purpose I am doing things. This means I am also careful to explain clearly when I teach and manage groups. Åsa, who has a more 'emotional' centring, very quickly sees how events are linked to feelings that appear among the participants. She can then make clarifications to those who are more emotional and who get lost if I am too clear in my explanations. Over the years, we have learned from each other and become dynamic. We can now work more easily with facilitators who have different personality dynamics and feel secure doing that.

Over the years we have continued to develop our dialogue work. We still train each new staff member and manager in dialogue within our department. Our basic three-day course is built on almost the same course material as it was 12 years ago. This is extremely important for us, as it gives us a common platform. We purposely use the same type of exercises, and we still work with flip charts to visualize the process. No PowerPoint.

We also have follow-ups with the work teams, as they may want to review the dialogue tools. It may also be that there is a problem in the group or even a growing conflict. Then it's often their manager who contacts us and wants a follow-up. In the follow-ups, we find out about basic problems or wishes within the work team, as well as with their manager before the conversation with the team. We never advertise in the groups that they have problems, as they often already know this themselves. We always offer guidance without touching on any situation in a way that may identify individual staff members. When we highlight the tool that most closely matches the current problem that a group may have, the problem almost always comes to the surface.

It is then often very easy to take the process to resolution, as the entire group sees dialogue as freeing, and there is usually energy to solve an ongoing conflict. At this point it is the responsibility of each one to contribute. A follow-up is often four hours long, and can be terminated earlier. Group work is part of the process, and there an incentive to investigate the problem. It shows that everyone understands their role in managing the problem, taking ownership of the situation together. Sometimes the group gets an assignment that might consist of self-reflection based on a self-review and a review of how the group is developing. Then we follow up a few months later. As we do, the focus remains on the process, and the tools of dialogue remain prominent. The group will already have talked about the different tools and understood how to use them in practice.

Dialogue as a Problem-Solving Mechanism

Dialogue has a place in personal development. Many have come closer to themselves during their gatherings. And, at the same time, some dialogues have been a direct consequence of the staff's approach to addressing problems and looking for solutions. On many levels there are examples of this.

Several levels of staff work together in different areas in care and nursing. For example, we have home services that care for users who live in their homes. They go by car and visit their care recipients' homes. They provide medicine and help with food and hygiene. The staff works exclusively in pairs and, although the overall team consists of several pairs, often the same staff teams visit the same care recipients. The users have permanently assigned care teams in addition to security alarms, so they can call if there is an urgent need.

The next level of care – and the subject of the cases we'll be exploring – is in our Care Homes for Elderly, or CHFE. Those who live at CHFE often have difficulty in managing their life in regular accommodation. At this point one then applies to live in a CHFE-home. In Degerfors we have two large CHFE facilities. Together, there are about 140 elderly in these two CHFEs combined. These CHFEs also have full staffing during the day. At night the staff levels are reduced, although access to nurses is available at all times.

All users live in their individual rooms. It's their home, and they pay rent. They have their own furniture, except a nursing bed. They receive mail and, if they want company, visitors can come at any time. For residents, there is really no difference to living in a regular apartment, except that staff are present at all times and there are common dining rooms and dayrooms.

In some departments staff are specially trained to take care of people with severe forms of dementia such as Alzheimer's. Other residents are those who have severe injuries after infarction, or severe restriction of blood to a part of the body. They may have lost muscle function and speech skills. It is stressful for the staff to take care of those users who have dementia or have had stroke, and they attach great importance to the emotional connection that has been developed between staff and users. My case study is based on the work at one of these nursing departments, where the dialogue was a direct solution to a problem.

Care Homes for Elderly
Hearing the Unspoken

At one ward after a few years, the mood started to turn dark. Staff easily came into conflict with each other and, occasionally, did not want temporary staff to visit the ward. It was difficult for anyone to understand what had happened. Without any apparent reason, a well-functioning ward had become a major concern. The same staff was intact; there had not been a new employee for a long time and no major organisational changes had been made. The CHFE's manager asked me to take part in a meeting to determine what had happened in the group. We gathered and I listened in my role as facilitator. Everyone talked loudly straight into the room, and no one seemed to care about listening to the conversation. Halfway through the meeting, it felt like everyone had something that was not being spoken, though I couldn't understand why. Everybody seemed annoyed, and some spoke quite darkly – especially two staff members whose tone was especially hard. We took a break and I spoke with their manager. We could clearly see that something was being hidden. After the break I asked the group, one by one, to describe how the work was going at the ward. Everybody would be able to tell their story without interruption. The group sat in a semi-circle – eight people facing me. The first to speak told us that everything was good and that she did not perceive any problems. She is the person who typically would talk first during the sessions. She would speak as soon as there was a gap; her role as a Mover, or initiator, in the group was clear.

The next person who spoke sat beside her and often functions as a Follower in the group. She had clear sympathies with her companion and also said that there were no problems. The rest of the group followed, and some were short in their statements. There were two people who clearly were Bystanders, or onlookers, as they only nodded without deepening the conversation. No one opposed the Mover, who repeatedly stated that there were no problems. I start asking open-ended questions. These were again answered by the same people who said that there is nothing wrong. I raised the question again, and pointed out that there is seldom a problem-free workplace. I asked, "Why are there no problems? How have you solved them?"

This was an opening for one of the participants. She pointed out that the biggest problem was that they weren't getting any substitutes on the ward. This was a problem that had been hidden during the day, but it was the main purpose of our meeting. Their manager had told me before the dialogue that it was a big problem that no temporary staff wanted to work at this ward. Why had it not been apparent to the working group? This was the first recognition. The Mover and the Follower who had taken command immediately responded that this was not correct. Then one of the silent Bystanders spoke: "There *are* some problems that prevent us from getting temporary workers. It's really strange – I've been doing double shifts several times this month for just that reason." The group became very quiet. Everyone wore a tense expression, and the silence was obvious. The second silent Bystander suddenly filled in. "I think it's because things are so divided between us." I asked another open question. "Why is that ?" The woman answered almost instantly, as if she had been waiting for my question. "It's like there are two camps, and I feel I do not belong anywhere." "What makes you feel like that?" I asked. "Because there are always some who will decide – as soon as I say something, they tell me it's not the way we're going to work here". "Can you give an example?" I asked. "Tell her about Anna", she said to the other Bystander. (Anna is not her real name.)

Apparently, in one of the rooms at the ward, lived a woman who had a severe muscle disease that made her bedridden at an early age. During the years she lived at the Home she was only able to move her head; she was completely dependent on the staff around her. She was clear in her thoughts and intelligent, well informed and verbal. I asked her to say more. "Anna is very sweet", she replied, "but she is very picky about the staff. It's not just anyone who can enter her room. She has some favourites." Another participant filled in: "Yes, it is clear that she prefers you", she said, pointing to the person who kept suggesting that there were no problems. The Mover in the group tried to divert the conversation by saying, "You can't blame a person for being popular!" Everybody laughed a bit, but it was obvious that here was something to go on.

In order not to expose one person to pressure in the group, I divided the team into smaller groups and explained one of the dialogue tools. I reviewed how we look for our roles, and that it is important for the group to take advantage of the differences in the group. The team would then talk about how they fit in their roles. All roles of the Mover, the Follower and the Bystander were represented, but no pronounced Opposer; there was no one willing to bring an opposite perspective or offer a 'course correction'. I explained to the group the advantage they would have if there were someone who would be an Opposer, and how his or her job would be to question the group about how it is working. Are they working toward the right direction? I then demonstrated a tool for feedback, and explained the usefulness of giving and receiving feedback, just to highlight these roles. I showed how to highlight by using feedback someone who may be thinking about entering the missing role, and how feedback can be used with the aim of changing a behaviour. Also, I spoke about how one must speak from the standpoint of 'I' and not hide behind the group.

I emphasised taking responsibility for a situation, moving forward and doing things in the right way, even with our opinions. The group reflected by themselves for a while, and then spent some time in small groups to discuss the roles and feedback in the group. When we then reassembled in the whole group, I asked them to share their insights. It was at this point that a new form of dialogue began, where everyone was present and no one spoke without first waiting and listening. Some asked of others, "What do you think?" or "What did you mean when you said that?" Now the group was engaged with the problem that had pervaded the group's work. During the conversation, their manager and I could see the picture emerge for the problem. Their manager was skilfully present as one in the group and participated in the dialogue, while at the same time taking a step back so as not to be perceived as governing in any way.

The Complex Problem

It turned out that one important factor was that Anna, the resident, had manipulated the staff in the only way she could in her disability: with words. She had slowly and surely involved parts of the staff in a power game where she ruled with her disease as a weapon. When she had decided a staff member would be her personal attendant, she would tie her with a strong bond. She processed this cleverly by telling the staff that there were only a few who understood her. She clearly explained how hard and unpleasant the others were. She had no confidence in all the temporary workers they sent there. She had told the temporary staff that they were not acceptable to the rest of the staff, and for their own sake they should look for another place to work. This led to a division of the staff. A few were selected and they had a very nice relationship with Anna. On the other hand, those who were not desirable were promptly treated poorly. The situation soon became so toxic that there was only one acceptable way to work, though everyone knew it was wrong. However, due to the strong hierarchy of the group the situation continued. It became apparent that it was not easy for those who were favourites to get out of the situation. This was nothing they personally enjoyed, and they themselves thought that the demands on them were unreasonable. They wanted a solution to this and welcomed the energy they received from the dialogue with their peers.

So we decided on the following actions: First, everyone in the ward would treat Anna in exactly the same way. If she said something negative about a colleague, everyone would quickly return to Anna and let her know that it was not ok to do this. Next, the staff would change every day to break Anna's dominance. They would be clear in their behaviour and they would tell each other every day what had happened in Anna's room when they were with her. Temporary workers would not go into her room without first being introduced to her in a meaningful way. In order to let Anna focus on something new, the staff introduced other routines for her health. She had access to audio books and movies from the library. It was ensured that volunteers had resources for meeting their own needs for social contacts. This happened professionally, without Anna understanding that there was a correction in her treatment. Seemingly suddenly, she enjoyed all the staff, and when she had an objection the staff completed their plan with clarity and equitable treatment. The temporary workers came to the ward with a different sense of the situation, and over time nobody refused to go to the ward.

Visual Dialogue and a New Start

During our dialogue the staff was given optional group work. They would find a task and solve it in a limited timeframe of three hours. The group consisted of 15 people. They were responsible for the way they spent their time, and we as facilitators would only be guides. The purpose was to allow the staff group to use same kind of time usually set aside for problem-solving in their daily lives – almost no time, in other words! Several things needed a solution, but hadn't taken focus; they had been set aside due to lack of time and commitment. The group raised one such issue that many had often thought about, but hadn't prioritised.

At one of our CHFE facilities there is a dining room made for 60-70 persons. During a meal the residents would sit at tables that hold eight people. They would sit on wooden chairs, and some would be in their wheelchairs. The staff never thought the mood was good during dinner. Many would set aside their food, and others were annoyed. This happened frequently as the situation became increasingly frustrating and hard words were shared. The staff chose to focus on this problem. They were tasked to solve the problem in three hours using Visual Dialogue. They organised their work in three phases:

- In the first hour, the group conducted an analysis of the current situation. What was good and what was bad about what was happening? Everyone in the group wrote down on sticky notes what they perceived as positive, and stuck them to a flip chart labelled 'Current Situation'. Then a column was made for what the group perceived as negative. In this situation, it was important that everyone in the group wrote at least one entry, positive and negative. Some wrote several formulations. After 50 minutes we stopped the work and asked the team to report the current situation analysis for us. In ten minutes, the notes were grouped on the flip chart by themes. The positive side was formed several main themes, as did the negative. After ten minutes of reporting and sorting, the group returned to work.

- In the second hour they were to create a vision of the future. One would take the positive items, bring them to the future and then add what was missing. Now all participants got to write new sticky notes with their vision of the future. Here, while focusing on improvement measures, the only restriction the group followed was to stay within a reasonable economic limit. After 50 minutes it was time to gather the notes and report on the future. Everyone's ideas were put on flip charts labelled The Future. The notes were grouped by theme, as before.
- For the third and final hour, the focus was on 'How to get there'. The question thus became, How do we deal with the future we want and take care of the negative aspects in the current situation as well as the obstacles that may be in our way? The group spent 50 minutes working with the sticky notes and the flip chart, and after wrapping up the last section the whole process was over.

The group had worked efficiently for three hours without breaks and they were full of energy. They had not solved all the questions in their way, but they had the beginnings of an action plan.

Visual Dialogue: the Results

Three days after completing the sessions, their manager called us and asked, "What have you done with my staff?" He was full of enthusiasm. The staff had come to him the day after the dialogue and asked if he had anyone free to help change the dining room. He asked if it would be expensive, but the team had answered that it would not cost much more than the time for five or six people over the course of one day. This sounded reasonable. The staff changed the entire dining room structure. They placed the tables in an unsymmetrical way, moved some of the chairs and changed the curtains. They got some old paintings and decked the room with plants. They brought in a sound system, changed tablecloths and crockery. They added some candle lights and changed the lighting.

When the dining guests arrived the next day they were met by a brand new dining room. Everyone was shown to the tables that were suitable for the needs that were important to them. Those who were in wheelchairs got more space at the table, as some chairs were taken away around them. Those who had impaired vision were seated at the window tables where the light was stronger, and with the right lights. Those who had hearing loss were placed in a corner with thicker curtains to suppress disturbing sounds. Those who weren't able to concentrate were placed where it was a bit calmer, and those who wanted to talk got good places with close contact. The whole was arranged in such a way that the dining guests did not perceive themselves being placed 'as needed', but only saw the positive aspects of being organised and cared for. The symmetrical impressions of tables that stood in lines were gone. It was warm and cosy, with clear thinking behind all the details. The group had managed to change the whole food situation for the better.

What conclusions did we draw from this work? It was clear that the Visual Dialogue had obvious timing advantages. The work was effective and singly focused on how the task was to be done. After the group relinquished the idea of solving the problem during the Current Situation analysis in the first 15 minutes, it was easy to proceed with the different parts. What was also clear was that the Bystanders found it easier to leave their thoughts on a written note. They did not need a long time to make their voice heard. In a regular dialogue the Movers seldom give space for the time needed for the Bystander's thoughts to be heard. At time-pressed meetings there is a clear advantage to working with Visual Dialogue to answer questions about what should be done and how we should accomplish our task to meet deferred future goals.

Reorganisation and Chaos

Sometimes reorganisation takes place over a period of one or two years – and it often takes less time to turn the staff's safe world into real chaos. In one of our special interventions, our team followed in the aftermath of a reorganisation that had aimed to increase cooperation across wards. In this case, the wards are located in a high-rise building. Each floor has two wards, with the wards located opposite each other. The wards may have users that need nursing care or rehabilitation and short-term care, and some wards have users with moderate or severe dementia. The context for the reorganisation was the introduction of a computerized scheduling system. It was designed so that staff would be more effective and able to cover needs in case of absences, instead of taking on temporary workers. When the work scheme was implemented, there was little time for the change. At the same time, the staff was given orders to start refurbishing the ward, and to open the doors to create more open wards.

As part of the plan, staff were to start working with personnel from other wards. This was all carried out using a very quick decision-making process, and in one month the workplace was changed. Irritation prevailed. Users became worried. Some people with dementia managed to get out of their wards and could not find the way back. While it's not the case that people with dementia are locked in, door locks are coded to make unintentional passage more difficult. This limitation is made particularly where people with dementia would find it hard to find their way back home. There is also a danger of becoming chilled if a person goes out in freezing weather in thin clothes. Restrictions are in place to protect the user from injury. Coded doors allow staff to follow up on the person's willingness to go out, and they can accompany the user or divert his or her attention to other activities. When the reorganisation was complete and doors were opened, suddenly there were no barriers to exits. Elevators were accessible as well as emergency exits and stairwells. It was the responsibility of staff to control the pattern of movement among the users. This move was controversial, and was stressful for the staff.

We began to see the risks, and that there was a need to do something. We also saw that staff cooperation was slow and disengaged. Many had corridor meetings about all that was crazy on the ward. Rumours and conflicts began to spread. Over time, the staff did receive support for the changes they suggested. Lock companies were contacted to refit code locks on several common doors and lifts. Routines to determine when doors would be open were introduced. Alarms for beds and doors were acquired. Eventually, cooperation began to flow again and conflicts were stepped down. The reorganisation that was to be a quick transition to a new way of working eventually became part of a long history. After a little over three years, all the operational problems were solved and one could work for the 'new' organisation. But sore wounds were left behind.

Why Did this Fail?

During the post-reorganisation work I analysed the situation with my colleagues. We reflected together and began to understand where things went wrong. During the organisational change, there had been no time for dialogue work. The executive organisation wanted to speed up the change process, and we passed up an important part of the dialogue. The situation brought to mind the energy principle, which says we do not renew or destroy energy – we only convert it. So it is within the natural sciences, and so it is with human behaviour. In a dialogue meeting we would have a chance to resolve our questions. If we could see an action pattern that let us take courage in our questions, then we might have the opportunity to accept a change over time. If, on the other hand, we had to stand alone with our unanswered questions we would not be able to lift our concerns. An organisation keeps its problems for a considerably longer period than expected. In our case, several issues demanded much of our energy and attention. For example, the question remained about the safety of the user, in the case of unlocked doors. Here, staff had concerns, but when we raised questions we got the answer that we should solve it later and that we should be positive about the change.

The problem was resolved, but it had been encountered during the ongoing work, which created an unnecessary energy drain with the staff. There also were many questions about the structure of the wards. The aspect that the management organisation did not take into account was that the staff, since the opening of the accommodations, had created an environment for their workplace. They had found furniture and curtains that the staff together had agreed on in colour and shape. Some had been to IKEA and bought kitchen utensils, lamps, carpets, boards and chairs. Here, the staff created a structure that was their own, which they themselves had decided. They had invested feelings in the ward they built. For the staff who worked together in this environment, this is important, but it was something which management did not take seriously, because these kinds of structures are not written on a document.

Structures are found within each of us. Together, there is an invisible structure that binds people together. If we no longer work with a colleague we have had near us for 5-6 years, that person is no longer self-evident. The worry that occurs when the structure is threatened gives negative energy, which becomes a counteracting force in the change process. Without the opportunity to talk about this in a dialogue, staff were forced to fit into a structure that might have looked similar on the surface, but it was completely different. The difference was in the structure of the system map. Other colleagues, other furniture, other users. In the eyes of the management, it was only a job that looked the same no matter where it was performed. We pointed this out, and many in management saw this, and saw it as a failure in the system. Some noted that they would have liked to have had dialogue from the beginning, but were pressed by time and the sense of commitment was different. A shortcut actually becomes the slow way of change; energy is not created and cannot be destroyed, but is converted.

Prestige Loss at School

Imagine that the organisation for which you work becomes aware of something you could do to simplify the introduction of a new way of working. As an example, we'll say that your project is to demonstrate the power of counteracting forces during a time of change. We might understand in theory the breadth of using dialogue for this, but still fail to grasp its value and instead rely on our own ideas. We may also trust that the organisation's changes will be implemented so genuinely that there will be no problem left to solve when the change is complete. Each person would share the same the perception – that he or she by themselves knows which factors are most beneficial to the process. (Of course if this were true, then all change work would be painless; nobody would want to do anything that would not be good and beneficial to an organisation.) The intention is obviously good and substantiated with an aim, in that everything would be better. Before long, however, the same problematic transition issues would occur again, as the staff would not be in phase with changes or with each other.

A few years ago we reached the school world with dialogue facilitation. At one point we received a request from a principal who was in charge of preschools for low- and middle-class students. She had been curious about dialogue as a form of development in school, and suggested that we lead a three-day dialogue training for her teachers. We took on the task with great interest, as this was another challenge for us to bring dialogue. We counted how many teachers would be involved, and when. In the end, there were two groups of about 20 in each, and we were to complete the course on school days. We worked in two facilitation pairs, using separate floors in the local school building. We removed benches and put chairs in a dialogue circle in the chosen classrooms. The teachers arrived and were divided into two work teams composed of people who knew each other. It's good to have people who know each other for the purpose of working with feedback, and especially with the Four-Player model of Move, Oppose, Follow and Bystand. In that exercise, it helps if a person has a colleague who knows them in order to find out about where one has an effective role. Everything was planned for three days with great expectations from our side.

When we met the groups on Day One, we planned to use an exercise called 'Expectations and Fears'. We asked the question, "What fear do you have about this training?" Many responded that it seemed to be a waste of their time, and that they had lots of other things to do before school starts. There was not much energy for the course. A few thought the course as a whole might be interesting, but its purpose was unclear. Some had heard that the course was good for conflict prevention, but conflicts were not common at their school, so the aim was unclear there also, and the benefit was uncertain.

The Collapse

We worked with the groups, and at the breaks we met with other facilitators to reflect and correct our course. It became clear after the morning session that one of the groups was completely out of focus. We tried to determine what was happening, but we decided to let the day go on to see if the problem persisted, or if we were able to influence the group's direction. After lunch, the situation escalated. One person came in a mood and thought it was a waste of time to sit there "at such a low level". She wanted to leave the course and saw no value in continuing. We had to stop the session and reconnect with each other and see how we might consider continuing. The whole group was rebellious, and it was clear that we had to hear from the group to see if their decision to end the course was unanimous. We could see that the other group was quieter at that moment and there was energy and a will to continue.

We put an open question to the group that was in opposition to continuing: "What is it that makes you want to quit the course?" We asked the group to reflect on that question and we gave them some time for this. When we re-entered the hall after a while, the group was calmer. We followed up the question and asked them to share their reflection with us. It came down to the fact that some people didn´t want to be questioned in their roles as educators. As teachers, this group was trained to learn, and to question a teacher's relationship to dialogue was considered a challenge: "Who would I be as a teacher if I did not have a university education to be able to manage my profession?" The dialogue, with its questions, was seen as a provocation that said that as teachers they were not taken seriously. Their image of the pedagogue being trained by facilitators of different backgrounds from theirs was clearly a challenge to some.

We took up the thread in the group and explained the purpose more clearly. The dialogue is not an end in itself, but rather it is a tool for coping with the interactions that exist in our work, as well as between the various actors that exist in our everyday lives. We used as an example the relationship in which teachers meet pupils' parents. Parents come from different backgrounds, and there are people in all stages of life. With the help of dialogue a teacher can increase understanding of why in some meetings things may go wrong. We clarified which factors contribute to increased presence in the conversation if we step aside from our roles and see ourselves in the non-prestigious conversation at the same level.

We want to work with the ability to see through the opinions we hold and understand that we as humans are not our views. When people learn to listen they get increased insight, and thus we can change our behaviour and therefore change a situation. Our course in dialogue had nothing to do with their professional roles, but was entirely a collaboration between people in training for the ability to think together. The group got the chance to gather for a while. We got a cup of coffee and, upon return, the feeling of the group was more unified. We left the question open if they wanted to continue and that was the will of the group. After the third day's end, the group was in a very good mood. We received only excellent evaluations of the course. We got flowers and we reflected on the willingness to have follow-ups, which we have done several times; they have been developmental, both for individuals and for collaboration.

A Dialogic Future in Degerfors Municipality

We have been working actively with dialogue as a system tool in the municipality since 2005. Over the years, it has survived several managers and several political changes. It has been kept alive for several reasons. As facilitators, we have remained active with dialogue and have not let it fall into oblivion. We have always had the staff with us on the journey, and they have lobbied for recognising the importance of dialogue to meet the demands of the workplace. It is a tool that works, and one with which we can feel safe. We also have many managers who have seen dialogue act as a catalyst in working to ensure the quality of communication within the work team and teamwork toward other groups.

Then it's just a feeling that you share a common platform. Everyone has the same reason for being together, and the dialogue is based on really meeting people. We sometimes get questions about how measurable the results are with dialogue. What numbers are available that might be included in a chart or table? We can't measure the obvious by any other means than it lives on because it is demanded. We have a good staff and, in the surveys that often are conducted, Degerfors users are 99% satisfied. We cannot exclude that dialogue is part of that result.

We have made a decision in the Management Board of the Social Welfare Department to train all Unit Managers, including those who have been promoted before 2018, to repeat their three-day dialogue training, as well as those managers who have not gone before. During the fall, all other staff who have been employed will also be allowed to go to the basic course. In 2019, then, all the staff will have had dialogue training and we will facilitate throughout the year, including follow-ups that we share in spring and autumn. In the spring, all staff will have at least four hours with their work teams, where we will practice important tools. The staff will then receive a reflection task until the autumn follow-up. This follow-up will be more deeply rooted in any problems or things that need to be highlighted extraordinarily. Together with each team manager we will see if there is something special that needs to be focused on, as well as a self-reflection by each of the staff that the home assignment has contributed to. Our goal is to improve communication between teams and managers as well as support the managers in their role. This is then in line with the goals set up by the Social Welfare Board for 2019.

It is my hope that this text has been able to reflect how we worked with Dialogue in our municipality for almost 13 years. Today we are three facilitators left from the original four. On the day that we may no longer exist in the organisation, I put my trust in getting a fully functioning Swedish and International academy that can be at the front edge of the future's dialogue work. We face major challenges with large cultural differences in our countries. No country is any longer isolated from the outside world, as we are all world citizens. We must be able to talk to each other based on our cultural differences and learn to understand what it means, whether in a team or as a global citizen.

We must also relate to a more individual worldview. We have all the individual needs to an increasing extent. We are no longer so collective in our worldview. We will increasingly relate to the impact of social media. This includes the spread of rumours and fragmentation, which places increasing demands on us to critically review. We must relate to the way of good conversation and create bridges with dialogue as the building block. We may seek different truths in the future but whose truth is the right one? Who are we to determine? We can only depend on ourselves and take the responsibility that each of us should take.

Conference Session Extracts

From conversation with 20 participants considering the paper with the author

Within our organisation, we're going through a huge reorganisation with so many different issues and concerns. We've got a new social director who began to introduce dialogue to us. Something as simple as our technology department and then those of us who were, I guess, on the ground working to do the supervision of those coming home from prison, we don't connect with each other because everybody's in their own little kind of silo. So we get into those spaces of – it's their work, but collectively the mission is our public safety, but everybody is pretty much working from their own standpoint and missing the piece of why we do what we do. And a lot of it is because we're very competition-based, we get into this context of, "Yeah, well you work in IT and you're supposed to take care of the treatment aspects, and that's what you do. And then here's what I do". So that's a huge issue for us.

I'll give an example of another system. We may work with a child and family service if we have younger guys or women who are on supervision for a criminal offence. We don't even share the same technology. So there's so many gaps because we don't pull our systems together because I have to get a contract for my system, which is probably better than your system. And it gets this whole thing going of these different competing ideas. We're not coming together because we don't want to share. We want to be the best. But we're not the best. We're all failing because we won't come together.

That's some of the issues that we have in working in Washington. And the climate that's happening for the United States at this point with our political system is making it worse. And everybody is scratching at these places instead of coming together to figure out how do we pull it all together to make all the systems work collectively. We say it but we refuse to do it. So that's one of the biggest issues that we're having at this point, not willing to collaborate honestly and authentically with each other.

My comment is dialogue needs structure to make its contribution. Structure needs dialogue to fulfil its mandate. And to make that very practical, I think there is a kind of energetic glass ceiling in what's achievable as a cultural take-off because of the way assistants are blame-based, they hold down the cultural flight of the organisation. I was sitting with a fairly junior person, and he told me, "The thing is, in the military, we don't like to change culture. We don't like change". And then he said, "But we do like our standard operating procedures". So what I would do is – I was interested in your comment, I like to see the map of processes that are driving results. And I like to look into the processes and the steps and identify, for example, if in a performance management system the question who's to blame, then you're going to crush the energy. Whereas the question is what can we learn? That's a different energy. And if a question is, What insight can we bring to this? then we've created opportunity for dialogue.

Postscript

The author's reflections written some months after the conference

When I first found out that I would be involved with my work internationally, I was surprised. What could there be for interest in the Dialogue that we worked with in Degerfors Municipality? When I then sat down and wrote out my paper, I got a moment's reflection in the work – that it was actually quite extensive, and for a long time. It was a feeling of greatness that grabbed me. Now other people from other parts of the world were going to take part in this. Then my feeling for Dialogue was humble.

During my Dialogue, I had to speak, straight from the heart, what conversation between people really is about when people in the small room listened to my words and asked questions. When we were together we helped to shape a new road. It was a continuation of my story. Refine your gaze forward and create a consensus, I said to myself.

It was a great experience to share. I see how, with the help of Dialogue, we can learn something new in that little time. What I did during my session was merely a much simplified and easily explained foundation in Dialogue. Speak, listen and reflect and take responsibility. I was amazed that the simplicity was so appreciated. In the simple, living is beautiful, and it is exactly how the Dialogue should be treated.

Section Five

Acorn Dialogues

Dialogue Is a Spiritual Practice

Robert M Sarly

It is sometimes said that organizing church communities is like herding cats. This is meant to be funny, but there is more than a grain of truth to it. Cats cannot be pushed into formation, but they can, in fact, be herded. All we need do is put a fish on a line. In effect, we need to find what they hunger for and hold it out there: they will come, and they will eat and be better for it. It is the same way in an effective dialogue with members of church communities who hunger to be seen, to be heard, and to be appreciated. When these nourishing virtues are offered, ordinary people will come, they will eat, and they will be better for it. Of course, we know these cats, and they are us.

Over the past 20 years, I have worked with over 60 different congregational church groups all over the United States. Church communities call me when they are in crisis, and it turns out that quite a few churches are in a crisis of one sort or another at different stages of their respective journeys. The first church dialogue I facilitated was for a small, breakaway community in Tuscaloosa, Alabama that found itself without money and at a crossroads. But let me first provide some backstory.

I was in my 50's, happily married, father of two boys, and building my career in investment banking. Then, midlife crisis came to me right on schedule, just after my 50th birthday. I was busy gathering the trappings of material success. I looked around and asked, "Is this all there is?" I could not answer myself.

I could not identify what, and who, was important to me, or to my sense of a meaningful life. I did not really know who I was; I did not actually like many people in my bubbled world, including myself. I was stuck. Possibly even lost. The opening lines to one of the many translations of Dante's *Divine Comedy* perfectly described my life: "Halfway through the road of my life I awoke in a dark wood where the true way was wholly lost." That dark wood is where I was stuck.

As a youth, I was not particularly religious. I had always been spiritually curious, but I did not feel at home in any religious tradition, and so I wandered. As a young adult, I sought out a church affiliation less for theological, or dogmatic, reasons than for finding a community of like-minded souls with whom I could share kindred experiences and perceptions of the world as I travelled through it. I was looking for a community home beyond whatever family home I might be able to make for myself. My sense of a community home was the place where I might share a meal, find a friend, or have a meaningful conversation by which

I could come to see, hear and appreciate the people around me, the world, and myself also. I sensed that I was not alone in this lost feeling, while many others had turned to the paths of money, sex, drugs and rock-n-roll for solace. But these other paths all seemed to me to offer just sugar highs that failed to last, turning into a kind of body fat that became a heavy burden to carry. I was hungry for protein.

I was especially drawn to church when our sons were small, from the notion that our family should have a values-based cultural frame in which to raise good children. However, I found that a church community is a kind of microcosm of society as a whole: its members reflect both the strengths and foibles of the broader culture, and so the communities into which I wandered were both attractive and repulsive for various reasons. They were after all populated by broken humans, in some ways just like me. Eventually we settled on a relatively open, nondogmatic group called the Unitarian Universalist Society of Wellesley Hills, in my then-home town of Wellesley, Massachusetts. We felt comfortable there.

Then after a few years, I joined my first church committee. I swore I wouldn't, but I did, and there I was. Of course, one committee is never enough, and yet even one committee is too much. The microcosm of global spirituality comes to ground under the feet of the Church Committee, where we each encounter the "otherness" of each other in a rather unpolished and unapologetic way. The first issue of discussion that blew us up, as I recall, had to do with how much money to spend on a rabbit hutch to house an actual rabbit that one church member had generously gifted to the congregation. What on earth our church community was doing in taking charge of a rabbit, any rabbit, was deeply unclear. And so it was for the remaining life of that committee.

Anyway, after some time, I had worked my way up the committee hierarchy to the esteemed position of Co-Chair of the Capital Campaign Committee. We did not need much time or effort to develop completely conflicting views of what the "people hutch" of our church home should become and how much to spend on it. A flaming row ensued, in which I was at the middle, and the congregation split into two opposing factions.

Even now, 16 years later, I can clearly recall spending the better part of a year at church at every Sunday service, without making eye contact with any of the other church leadership. It was a kind of spiritual Ice Age for me; perhaps for others also.

Then serendipity stepped in. Another congregant who noticed my distress suggested I read *The Celestine Prophecy*, and then *Ishmael* and the *Fifth Discipline*. One step led to the next and, before long, I had become familiar with David Bohm, David Whyte, Carl Jung, Lionel Corbett, James Hollis, Bill Isaacs, Chris Argyris, Glenna Gerard, David Kantor, Peter Garrett and many others who have blazed a trail of inquiry before me. The trail continues even now. Many of these trailblazers have become friends on my journey. I began to become unstuck.

In one of the episodes of *West Wing* on television some years back, the Chief of Staff character, Leo, waited up late for the return from a deposition of one of the West Wing aides. When the aide came back he asked, dumbfounded, "Leo, why are you here?"

Leo replied with this story: A man is walking along the street one day and falls into an open manhole with no apparent way out. He is not hurt, standing at the bottom of the hole, but is a little desperate about getting out. He looks up and sees his doctor walk by, and so calls out "Doctor, please help me." Hearing this, the doctor stops, takes out his prescription pad, writes a prescription, throws it down the hole, and walks on. Frustrated, the man looks up again, and sees his priest walk by, and so calls out: "Father, please help me." Hearing this, the priest pulls out his prayer book, tears out a prayer, throws it down the hole and walks on. Now anguished, the man looks up again and sees his friend walk by, and so calls out "Friend, please help me." Hearing this, the friend jumps down into the hole and is standing next to him. The man says, "What are you, crazy? Now we are both stuck down here." The friend, unfazed, replies, "Don't be silly. I've been down here before, and I know the way out."

The typical church community in my experience is often a community of would-be friends. Initially, however, they come across to each other in their nondialogic defensive posture as arms'-length Doctors and Priests. How to get these would-be friends to climb up out of themselves and jump into the hole with us has been the challenge of dialogue for me. It is also the challenge of every church community in search of, and in hopes of, finding the presence of a what I would call a Holy Spirit among us, whose task is to guide each of us home.

For example, I worked with a congregation in Salem Massachusetts, home of the Salem Witch Trials of the 17th century. This community represented an uneasy local merger of the remnant of four separate groups: a) a Christian Universalist community where God was revered, b) a humanist Unitarian community where reason was revered, and the word *God* was never uttered, c) a pagan Wiccan community where magic was practiced and embraced, and d) a gay community of loving but oppressed victims of the prejudice expressed by all the other groups. Initially finding a common language that all these subgroups were willing to use to communicate together seemed nearly impossible.

Then one day, one of the gay members confided to the whole group that his house had burned down the previous weekend, and he had nowhere to live. Figuratively, protective costumes and masks immediately began to fall away, and different people spoke out in the language we all viscerally understand, namely that of human compassion. Offers of support were made and graciously accepted, and people began to see and appreciate themselves just as people, not as members of competing groups, or worse. In this instance, their community was ready to reconceive itself as of one cloth in many colors. That openness, with some dialogic mentoring, helped build bridges between their tribal clusters and established a well of shared meaning that all could drink from, at least for a while.

In another example, in a church elsewhere in New England, the lay Director of Religious Education was engaged in an affair with the professional Minister of Lifetime Learning. When it became widely known, congregants did not know what to do. Half the congregation wanted to excommunicate both parties to the far reaches of the realm. Certainly, they wanted to fire the professional minister and expel the lay leader. Notwithstanding the fact that that church had no legal mechanism for expulsion, or excommunication, or even firing a full-time professional employee without due employment-related cause, this was no simple matter.

The other half of the congregation wanted to forgive them both, to provide counseling, and to embrace them with love and acceptance, especially if they were repentant. Various members got so steamed up about whether to tolerate or not tolerate them, they threatened to leave the church themselves, or at least cancel their financial support. Some retreated behind principle and refused even to discuss it. So they invited me in to help.

Oftentimes, I find that what the issue seems to be about is not really what it is about at all. Certainly, the standards of appropriate behavior, especially for the lay teachers of children in the church school, needed to be rehearsed and re-covenanted. But the willingness of some members to throw the whole matter of membership in this community out the window, reflected both an inattention to what brought many people together here in the first place and a fear that they were not capable of finding the repair needed to restore their beloved community. I came in as referee, my main job being to hold the container open for all to participate with safety and respect as they explored the many sides of this complex community identity issue. It was cathartic, and they did almost all the work themselves. I believe the courage they had to employ in order to discover their shared meaning together saved their congregation. They found out who they are.

Dialogue as Courageous Conversation

Let me illustrate the power of effective dialogue through a third example which was, in effect, my first dialogue facilitation in Tuscaloosa, and to which I did not even bring a background of personal understanding of what was needed. What I discovered was the interpersonal dynamics of a robust dialogue, when gently and firmly facilitated, are so strong, that the energies inherent in the membership can weave the cloth that represents the community and hold it together.

The Tuscaloosa community had recently broken away from a larger, more doctrinally conservative congregation that was geographically distant from where most of these members lived. The breakaway group could be described as generally liberal theists; they were open, welcoming, gracious and friendly. They had decided to plant a seed-congregation on a plot of land that they had purchased, to build a prayer hall, a parish hall and to hire their own full-time minister. They had raised enough funds among themselves to build the parish hall and hire a part-time minster. Then the money ran out. Hence the crisis.

They faced several strategic questions: Was this partial tactical success good enough for now? Or should they borrow (i.e., mortgage) the capital needed to complete the prayer hall? Should they recruit new members to broaden the pledge base? Should they give up, sell what they have built and rejoin the original congregation? And deeper questions loomed. Had they lost track of who they were as a spiritual group of meaning-seekers? What was important to them now? In effect, this last question is what they decided to ask themselves. They had seeded a new congregation in a new area to grow up into a mature community of beloved friends, but they seemed to have become no better than "Doctors" and "Priests" who were more comfortable just "walking on." How were they ever going to get comfortable jumping into this hole with one another, so they could help themselves back out?

A story is told by a Jungian who describes remembering himself as a child when large people brought him upstairs and put him to bed; but they did not tell him then, and have not told him since, and will not tell him ever, who he is. This conundrum may have been the actual psychological state of the Tuscaloosa breakaway congregation, who just wanted to know who they were. They had acquired some of the material trappings of an established church community: a parish hall, a part-time minister and (almost) the makings of a prayer hall, but they felt like strangers in one another's company. They had lost their sense of church. So they called me in to help.

I had met their part-time minister a year earlier at a national conference and was aware of the pioneering effort she and they had chosen to make, and of the challenges they faced in staying all on the same page as their spiritual identity evolved through congregational birth and its early adolescence. The attraction of my position as a prospective neutral facilitator to the minister and her congregation was that I was uninvolved. I knew no one in the congregation, so I was unlikely to take sides in any disputes that might arise. I had no history with their stories and, so, they could be as open with me as a child. My innocence amidst their complex issues was a virtue. However, to stay useful to all, I had to take care not to turn this innocence into ignorance. So, by way of becoming informed and still trusted, I focused my energy on shaping the container of their conversation.

Building the Container and Practicing the Unfamiliar

A courageous conversation within a community with complex interrelationships is heavily influenced by the perception of the shape of the container that holds discussion. A container that does not feel safe will stifle open, candid discussion. One that does not feel equal, reciprocal and caring will discourage the kind of overlapping identity necessary for people to establish their common ground, and for dialogic meaning to flow. I saw my principal role as facilitator as someone whose main attention was not directed towards sorting out conflicting claims to truth, held by participants, but to the stability, inclusivity and hospitality of the dialogic container itself, the conversational circle that viscerally held everyone in the room in relationship with each other. In doing so, I could occasionally ask if everyone was okay, or if people would like to take a break, or if there was any discomfort or concern that may need to be given voice or notice. I could help make people feel seen, heard, and appreciated even without addressing the subject matter being considered.

I began attending to their dialogue container several weeks before the group gathered. A few weeks prior to the scheduled three-day dialogue retreat, I asked the leadership to send me the names and email addresses of all those who had indicated they intended to attend.

Over 40 members of the full community (of 60 souls) identified themselves, and it was to those only that I e-sent an eight-question survey.

This was not rocket science; I intentionally developed the survey as a confidential exercise that was easy and nonthreatening to complete. My promise to each of the participants was to keep all responses anonymous by deleting names from replies and then compiling all responses to each question into a master form. Then I redistributed the results at the opening evening of the retreat. That way, everyone would be able to recognize their own individual position and understand where they stood within the full spectrum of the group, without personal attribution, or cause for embarrassment.

My survey questions were these: 1) How long have you been a member of this community? 2) With what other community were you affiliated beforehand? 3) What first brought you to this community? 4) What keeps you here now? 5) What do you consider to be the most serious threats to the ongoing health of this community? 6) Are you aware of any land mines or quicksand traps facing the community that are so sensitive that they cannot even be openly discussed? 7) What would you most like to see happen to this community going forward to help it thrive? and 8) What do you most expect from your facilitator at the retreat?

Gathering the Circle

We gathered on the late Friday afternoon of the designated retreat weekend, and after a brief orientation and check-in, we broke for a potluck supper on our laps, sitting in a circle of bridge chairs in their parish hall. Meeting in a circle has several virtues. First, when the chairs are carefully placed, everyone can see everyone else. Also, there is no head of table. In fact, there is no table. In the sense that a sphere can rest on any point on its surface, which in turn can support all the other points equally, so can any chair in a circle become the leader in the discussion. This in effect turns the meeting into a "leader-full" group.

After we openly reviewed the compiled survey responses, a palpable sigh of relief rolled around the circle, as we all realized that we were closer to being brothers and sisters on common ground, rather than space aliens on the devil's calling.

We reserved the long, full day of Saturday for deep learning and practice. We were in effect already a practice field, where competent performance was not yet expected. Rather we were just getting used to each other at a new and deeper level. We were just practicing. We began at 8:30 am over juice, coffee and donuts, and a little basic instruction in what I call the language and syntax of dialogue, with some basic ice-breaking exercises.

To open the session, I asked the group to do three exercises, each challenging their perception. The first asked participants to clench their hands in their laps in a specific way, then reverse, and see how they feel. Then they folded their arms over their chests as they normally would, and then reversed, and I checked in on how they felt. This is typically more challenging.

Finally, I asked them to grab a pen, and slowly outline the imaginary face of a clock on the ceiling, about a foot in diameter, going in a clockwise direction. Then, while carefully keeping their clock face horizontal, I asked them to keep their hands moving in a clockwise direction while slowly lowering their imaginary clock face down to the level of their solar plexus. Then I asked them to look down on their clock face and see which way their hands were going: clockwise or counter-clockwise? If they have done this correctly, their hands were now describing a counter-clockwise circle – seemingly opposite of the way they started – all without changing the apparent direction of their rotation. This served as a small but memorable epiphany.

In general, we can be well reminded that we are most comfortable repeating what is familiar. However, when even when only slight variations on the familiar are required, these variations produce involuntary discomfort and resistance. Also, we often understand the world from our own individual perspectives, limited though they may be. When we find that we cannot change or control the world, but we can change our perspective on it, we may be able to recognize the discovery of a hidden meaning that makes all the difference in the world, at least in our world.

The rest of the syntax of dialogue, as I presented it, comes largely from the pioneering work of Bill Isaacs at Dialogos International and MIT, in Cambridge, Massachusetts.

Basically, a courageous conversation in this model is comprised of a balance of two underlying forces: advocacy and inquiry, rather like yin and yang.

Advocacy, in turn, is comprised of the complimentary aspects of what I call "Directing" and "Opposing." Similarly, inquiry is comprised of the complementary aspects of "Listening" and "Questioning." A rich and courageous conversation will involve all four of these voices: Directing, Listening, Opposing, and Questioning.

The premise is that there are no other voices (although there may be some imaginative combination of these four) and that all four voices can and should be present for dialogue to blossom and for meaning to flow. The further presumption is that we each have access to all these voices, and when we consider entering the flow of an ongoing conversation we consciously choose which voice to use to express ourselves. Dialogically, it works best when we recognize the voice that is most missing from the collective conversation and thus most needed by the group at that moment. We enter the conversation through that voice rather than through the voice that our ego would otherwise impose on us and on the group.

There is one lesson we practiced together after lunch in Tuscaloosa on the Saturday afternoon. We found that many members of the group had highly developed "Director" voices, and especially "Opposer" voices, but not many had well-cultivated "Listening" voices, and the "Questioning" voices were particularly absent. With such a large group as we had, it did not seem appropriate to get into many of the deeper techniques for recognizing when and how to turn a pedestrian conversational dialogue into a courageous one.

However, I felt that if we had had more time, and fewer people, we would have explored additional dimensions of the flow of group meaning: the Mythic, or Heroic level of these four voices and the Shadow level of the four voices.

Several of the church elders who were present apparently felt more like "insiders" than others, and it would have been constructive to explore the roots of these feelings, perhaps through depersonalizing potential clashes of egos and unpacking a complex issue. Supplemental devices are also useful for this purpose borrowed from a variety of practitioners, such as The Left-Hand Column, (e.g., for pressing for real intent), The Ladder of Inference, (e.g., for distinguishing fact from opinion), Speaking from the first-person singular, *I* (e.g., for testing authenticity), Sacred Listening, (e.g., for slowing down the flow so that it can be assimilated and digested), and Asking Gift Questions, (e.g., for maintaining civility, respect and gracious humility amidst deep disagreement).

The beginning of dialogic practice is just that: practice. It is not perfect, or even comfortable, and space needs to be allowed for early imperfect attempts to be tried, allowed to fail, and to go unjudged. Learning how to do dialogue elegantly is a lifetime's work, one that involves courageous action and patient reflection over time. This also is part of the joy of what makes doing dialogue a spiritual practice.

It is also sometimes useful, if the members of the group are in a reflective frame of mind, to recognize each member's presence in the circle, the presence of their own awareness, as occupying one of several potential levels in one another's consciousness. Sometimes especially in an ongoing dialogic engagement over an extended period it is useful to map where each participant is in his or her learning journey, to acknowledge the different kinds of internal and external pushback that might be encountered at each stage of the conversation. In general, all dialogic voices are of equal importance, but Listening and Questioning are usually the least well developed and most influential. So, for practice purposes, reconstructive conversational mapping can be very helpful, encouraging participants to listen (sacredly) and to ask questions (preferably Gift Questions) of one another.

Finding Leadership Together

My instrumental agenda in the Tuscaloosa retreat was to discover the prospective governance group of natural leaders and centers of influence, to get the larger assembly of participants to recognize them, and to agree to a range of assigned leadership tasks and responsibilities for these few. However natural and gifted these individuals were, they were all lay members of a volunteer association who have come to accept the need to self-organize not only themselves but also the greater congregation around them. Again, my principal role in this self-discovery process was to hold the container of discussion as safe and productive and try to make sure it carried everyone in the emergent flow of meaning from the dialogue itself.

I also took my job as helping those present to begin to see themselves as a working team with mutually complimentary senses of their own capabilities and needs. In Tuscaloosa, those individuals present had never previously worked together on anything as potentially important to the common future happiness of their group, or to their own sense of individual fulfillment.

For example, in the case of the Tuscaloosa community, by the time we were wrapping up the common ground that had been uncovered and experienced by the retreat circle, the view that emerged was that the professional ministerial leadership they most needed, like

Sherlock Holmes' dog that did not bark in the night, might not be the minister whom they had hired and could only pay part-time, but someone else altogether. This process of clarification was one of general concern and consternation. There was a lot of shedding of costumes that needed to be done before this became clear and comfortable to the entire circle, and broader community.

Also, in the wrap-up for the last afternoon, one woman from the circle gave a brief testimonial in which she confessed that, although she had been a steady member of the congregational community for over nine years, this was the first time that she ever felt really seen, heard and appreciated. She had had two children and had become divorced during her years with the church, but she felt for the first time that she had come to know the congregation as friends and be known also as a friend.

She then thanked her new friends just for being there and for being who they were. When she spoke these words, there was an audible sigh of recognition as others shared her insight for themselves.

Present in the Spirit Together

The community group had achieved a flow of meaning entirely of their own, which is what the word *dialogue* means in the original Greek. When uncovered as had happened in Tuscaloosa, this was felt to have been contributed to by many in the circle but owned by no one. Contributed to by many but owned by no one!

In the flow, each participant is present with their lives, eccentricities, and baggage. Each is also aware of one another's presence. Each feels seen, heard, and appreciated in some way or another. Each also recognizes a little of his, or her, self in the presence of the other(s). When the dialogic energy flow is rich with group consciousness, individual members are sometimes aware of the additional presence of a higher being among themselves, a collective intelligence within their circle, a common emotional life-thread that feeds everyone what we each hunger for, even what one might call a Holy Spirit, or God. In effect, the group had discovered how to do church without concern for its material trappings. This was their epiphany.

Dialogue is a practice also in that it must be used continuously, or the skills that make meaning will atrophy. They must be practiced, learned and relearned with a group of people who trust each other and are able and willing to teach each other how to find their way home.

Tuscaloosa is one of many examples of taking a huge risk to reach a higher level of meaning, only to find that its flow both begins and ends beyond our own conscious control. A lot is at stake. Much depends upon our collective success. Our lives are at stake, but we are unable to succeed on our own. If only we could gather like-minded souls who will not hurt us but would bring us safely to a place where we could begin to understand who we are, and who we may become. In Tuscaloosa, the congregation was in an excellent position to establish a regular Vespers Meditation each midweek to encourage further deepening of the insights that just began to unfurl at our opening retreat. They would have also benefited from adapting their monthly Small-Group Ministry meetings to broadening their inquiry about their future as having an emerging collective awareness. Unfortunately, I lost touch with them after that retreat weekend, and so I cannot say which of many paths they chose to follow.

Yesterday's Clarity and Tomorrow's Challenges

When the goals of a group – any group, in church, or at work or even at home – are crystal clear, and the means for achieving them are similarly well-defined, command-and-control might well be the clearest way to proceed. However, in today's shrinking world, the rules of our road keep changing. It feels risky, and perhaps even foolish, to assume that yesterday's clarity will apply to tomorrow's challenges. Never mind the impact of technology and the ubiquitous Internet on traditional business practices. If we pay attention, life surprises us.

I recently read a profile of a traditional bicycle maker in India, whose business was slowly dying. He transformed his craft into a vibrant and thriving growth industry by reengaging his employees in dialogic conversation about what they were about with their bicycles, and how they could change for the better. The key breakthrough came from the staff through an internal dialogue: they realized together that if they could design the bicycle so that it could be folded in half it would much more useful to travelers, as it could be taken on the bus for the final stage of their long journeys.

We cannot mandate the courageous commitment, or the creative imagination needed to discover and unleash the Holy Spirit that lives in each of us; we just need to be ready to change despite the discomfort. Even long-standing institutions such as our churches need to face discomfort when traditional models of behavior no longer serve the evolving needs of their members. Ask the Catholic Church Fathers if this is not so amidst clerical improprieties. Ask any Protestant denomination how they are surviving amidst an increasingly secular and estranged society of wandering members. Yesterday's clarity no longer leads us through the complexities of tomorrow's challenges.

How do we even find our individual voices and then speak them out in dialogue, so that we may reengage a real, underlying common ground that is not often taught in our schools or our churches? Yet the world expects nothing less of us.

Do we know, at the threshold of an era of artificial intelligence, climate change and global refragmentation, who we are becoming? We face the challenge of awakening to a practice of more open and courageous communications among ourselves, within our own circles of friends, and among our insular tribes across the face of the earth.

Our society's midlife crisis has arrived, and we are in the midst of it. We are now invited to shine a light of compassionate understanding upon it, and act.

Will we recognize this invitation and embrace it?

Conference Session Extracts

From conversation with 20 participants considering the paper with the author

I think what we're talking about is wholeness. When we talked about holding attention, I mean, that is what dialogue does, right? We have to hold attention long enough so that we all feel that level of acceptance and acknowledgment, and we can see something that we haven't seen before. There's an emergence that happens and suddenly, whoa. We may have been in some pain or not understanding something and suddenly there's this other thing, like in your story, you saw God looking at you. It was like something happens and we have to be willing to stick with it.

But isn't that what dialogue is? That's the whole point, is that moment or that feeling. I mean otherwise, we're sitting in a circle having a conversation. But to get to that next level to have that connection or feeling, that's what we're doing, and that you have to hold attention. That's the point. That's why we're all here, I think, is to understand how each of us do that. So I mean that's what differentiates it to me.

[My comment is] connected both to your question earlier and to some of your comments and about the container. And for me spirituality is about connectedness to being touched, to kind of falling in love, not only with a person but in a more broad spectrum. And I think that the container or creating the space with dialogue, where you can be more touched, is creating a space for experience in spirituality together with other people. I also believe in how to stay in attention and to kind of put pain to work, in a way transforming the pain, rather than trying to eliminate the pain away. And then about the concepts of feeling wholeness, and oneness. I think that is an interesting distinction. For me, experiencing wholeness is kind of in time and space in this physical world. And the experiences of oneness, more of the spiritual experiences, is connecting us to something beyond the physical structures that we are a part of anyway.

I'm thinking for me sometimes dialogue, because we express it orally, sometimes it's too much in the brain. Sometimes, when I feel it really through the heart, that I understand it with the heart, that's when I feel this is the best dialogue. If I just have it intellectually in my head, I would not even accept it with the whole me, because I don't feel it. I don't touch upon my heart. I don't understand it with my heart, so it wouldn't be good enough for me.

I'm struck by the dynamic, the tension between your words of dialogue is all about the dynamic tension, and the words of oneness which sort implies no tension, because we're all merged in a oneness thing, and how both are true as we engage in an experience a dialogue. And they can't be reconciled, but they're both true, so thank you.

I would say dialogue can be a spiritual practice. I would say that dialogue can lead to a spiritual experience. It's not necessary to have dialogue to have a spiritual experience, but I think you could have fine dialogue without it being spiritual.

Postscript

The author's reflections written some months after the conference

Moving from ordinary conversation into dialogic conversation is not easy. In any one instance, much pre-investment will have already been made, mostly subconsciously, in maintaining strong defenses and immunity from attack, either intentional or unintentional. Verbal bruising from ordinary conversation is so prevalent that I preselect what will be discussed and what will not be discussed. For that which I am not prepared to discuss, no opening exists to meet. Even for those areas which seem safe to enter, full immersion, deep encounter and vulnerable exposure of weakness is presumed too dangerous to pursue, as though a yellow highway sign is placed across the way saying, "Road Closed: Do Not Pass."

To make the transition easier, I am learning, requires an invitation to enter. In a dialogic landscape, this invitation should also be two-directional, nonthreatening, in the language of trust and credible reliability, and possibly offering rewards for responding. After all, beyond the entry there be dragons, and life and limb may not be worth risking, even in the conversational imagination, just to explore the territory and be able to say, "I was there." I need to know up front, "Why bother?" I need to feel the differences in interpersonal connection and interpenetration, to be convinced.

There is no simple way to devise a universal invitation, at least to my sensibility now; however, any successful invitation would need to anticipate my fears, concerns, vulnerabilities, and hungers. "If you are cold and thirsty, won't you come in and join us for a spot of tea and good cheerful conversation?" This may allay much initial anxiety that you may be just posing as dialogic, but in fact are really judgmentally predisposed to mock and hurt me. However, other invitations may be even more gracious. One that sees me, recognizes my particular needs, and shows appreciation for my presence in the conversation may make a huge difference to my propensity to open up and participate.

My own prior dialogic work mostly described in the conference paper of last year presumed that the need to participate by prospective entrants had been pre-established and was no longer an open question. My sense now is that the initial introduction to the virtues of dialogue needs to acknowledge the distance and difficulty that most dialogic novices encounter just as a matter of needing to learn the gestalt language of dialogue, which is so very different from what they already know. Compassionate help with entry, first impressions, escalation and skill acquisition: all need to be accessible and enjoyable to be embraced with enthusiasm and commitment. Also, everyone invited needs to be seen/heard, recognized/understood, and appreciated/accepted. That is an invitation to be happy about. This is part of our ongoing responsibility to prepare for the dialogue novitiate.

Learning Dialogue in a Higher Education English Course

Mirja Hämäläinen and Eeva Kallio

With globalisation, workers today face challenges that language educators in higher education cannot ignore. As English is the globally shared language in working life, educators need to pay attention to the fact that interaction skills are one of the most called-for skills in any present-day job. Conventionally, English for working-life courses aim at providing students with such skills as telephoning, emailing, and participating in meetings and negotiations. The topic of socialising often only means learning native-like expressions for small talk. This, however, is not enough. Any consultant knows that problems at work are beyond such communication functions. In her analysis of Bohmian dialogue, Finnish philosopher Marja-Liisa Kakkuri-Knuuttila (2015) shows that David Bohm's approach to dialogue has a strong ethical emphasis. Ethics will be in more and more demand as humankind as a whole and working life in particular deal with such issues as artificial intelligence. Ethical dialogue should help in workplace conflicts too. People with academic degrees should already have the opportunity to become aware of ethical questions when using English as their lingua franca at work during their studies, and students learning English as a foreign language in higher education are easy to reach. This paper focuses on teaching English as a foreign language, though concentrating on English as a lingua franca does not exclude the native English speaker.

In this paper, we will describe a university language centre course based on Bohmian dialogue through English as a lingua franca and we suggest ways that the course can develop ethical thinking and wisdom. Wisdom in organisations is an ever-growing area of interest in organisation research and it is a big challenge to human beings in general. Can a course on ethical dialogue through English as a lingua franca develop wisdom?

Dialogue: Constructive Talk at Work – The Course

Mirja Hämäläinen, a lecturer in English at the University of Tampere, designed the *Dialogue – Constructive Talk at Work* course six years ago, having come across Bohm's 1996 book *On Dialogue* a few years earlier. Bohmian dialogue provides university students with language education in a way that raises awareness of the power of thinking together, the value of increasing understanding and equitable communication in groups (cf. Bohm 1996; Isaacs 1999; Ellinor and Gerard 1998). University language centre courses are aimed primarily at degree students, most of them Finnish. However, for the English as a lingua franca approach to make sense, the course offers four extra places for non-Finnish speakers to join each group. The maximum group size is thus 20+4.

In the first meeting of the course, students get to know each other and create values for the interaction in the group during the course. The structure of the sessions is always the same after the first session. First, in each session the instructor introduces a dialogue skill to practice. The skills offered include suspension of judgement, checking assumptions, inquiry, self-reflection, listening and voicing. Forgiveness in organisations is introduced in addition to the Bohmian topics. Students talk about the topics and do short exercises in pairs or small groups. In the latter part of each four-hour session, students work as a whole group on a theme related to working life. The instructions given to the group offer a lot of freedom, and often the students find it surprisingly difficult to accept such vague direction. The students brainstorm the topic together and, in the end, always appreciate the challenging and empowering task of defining their own job. They are instructed to work without a leader and organise the work as they wish, keeping their group values in mind, taking responsibility for the task and practising dialogue skills using English as their lingua franca. At the end of each day the group always needs to complete the dialogues as a whole group in a circle. The teacher acts as a facilitator only if needed. The main aim is to practice dialogue skills in a big group sitting in a circle without tables. What the group creates is not really important, but in all cases, the group is happy with what they got done. They proudly publish their production in their course blog with all participants' signatures.

The first groups welcomed the course as something revolutionary; in the first-ever group in spring 2013, none of the 19 students ever missed a session, and several students thanked the teacher personally for their experience. Some of them said that the course should be obligatory to all. Although students occasionally have missed a session (or a maximum of two in special cases) since that time, in most groups the attendance and commitment is very high because of the good group spirit that the arrangement and the dialogue topics seem to create.

While most of the students who have taken the course are happy with it, there are critical voices as well. Those voices are not documented as distinctly in the blog posts that students write after each session as they reflect on the dialogue topics, but they come out in the anonymous feedback collected through the university Webropol online survey system. Sometimes the teacher can witness such strong attitudes in class. Without any factual validation, it may seem that sometimes a student drops the course because it does not fit the conventional expectations for an English course. Indeed, most students start their first blog post by saying that the course is not what they expected, but that they are excited and happy that the course *is* different. And a few do find the course disturbing – they have clearly felt uncomfortable and angry because of the 'weirdness' of the class. One of the most critical pieces of feedback has been that the course is some sort of 'new-age stuff'.

Challenges

There are challenges in offering a curriculum so different from any conventional language course for work-life purposes. The general expectation is that such a course would focus on 'useful' vocabulary, perhaps some 'important' grammar, and especially the 'right' phrases to use in various work-life situations. Fluency practice is also considered important, but what that really means is not so clear. The *Dialogue* course, based on the Bohmian approach to dialogue, requires changing one's perspective. As we mentioned above, some students do not understand the value of sitting in a circle thinking and talking together in English as a lingua franca, not focussing on 'correct' or native-like language. The virtual learning environment Moodle is used in the course and it offers an extensive list of possible readings related to the course topics. Two articles are required reading for all; if a student misses one session, she or he will need to read an extra article and reflect on it in the dialogue circle to bring a contribution and compensate for their absence. The two articles for all to read have been Edgar Schein's (1993) "On Dialogue, Culture, and Organizational Learning" and Michael Stone's (2002) "Forgiveness in the Workplace". Most students appreciate the required reading and have no problems with reading an extra article if they miss a session. Very occasionally a student finds that the reading conflicts with his or her world view, and they therefore finds it unacceptable.

However, the ability to take into consideration different perspectives, to tolerate ambiguity and to compromise between many possible solutions helps develop adult thinking. These skills are part of what is required to engage in a rapidly changing working life. Integration of differences and squeezing new ideas creatively are part of this new advancement in thinking. This kind of cognitive humility is also a central component of the current construct of wisdom (Kallio, 2015; Kallio, 2018). If a student isn't able to consider multiple perspectives, he or she often becomes stuck in one-sided, absolutist thinking and is not able to consider any other viewpoint but his or her own. Those developing the new Finnish comprehensive school curriculum have taken into account emotional social and self-awareness skills linked with systems intelligence. These skills would also need to be taken into account in higher education. (Mononen, Tynjälä & Kallio, 2016.) As students on the *Dialogue* course share their reflections on the course topics both in class and in their blog posts, they become aware of their own challenges. This has been clearly stated in many blog posts with the general wording: "I have learnt so much about myself". To be able to share convincing results, the course design certainly deserves further systematic research. For now, suffice it to say that most students state that the course makes them consider aspects of communication and interaction that they have not thought of earlier. Some have reported that even their spouses are happy that they took the course!

Current adult developmental psychological theorists have identified three major levels of thinking that are directly relevant to dialogue practice. The first level is absolutism, in which a person gets stuck in his or her own viewpoint and can't take different viewpoints into account: black and white or dualistic thinking (you are either with or against me). At the next level, strong relativistic attitudes emerge; that is, when one moves past duality and begins to see multiple viewpoints, one tends to become insecure about which of the opinions is right. The person may accept diversity to the point that, in some cases, it is impossible to state that one 'closed truth' even exists. In the final stage, called integrative thinking, one understands multiplicity, and tries to integrate diversity and richness into their thought process in one way or another. This integration depends a lot on the circumstances; for example, in scholarly discussion and in teaching academic content, it is often true that the best reasoning, arguments and justifications win, but at the same time the possibility of constant construction and reconstruction of relative truth is accepted. Thus, scientific enquiry is seen as an open, creative and changeable process, even if at the moment there are reasons to accept the best current arguments, justifications and scientific data. (Kallio, 2011; Kallio, 2015; Kallio, 2018).

Relating this to dialogue in the classroom, it's easy to understand that if a student is not flexible enough – stuck in one viewpoint – and finds it impossible to accept cognitive humility or restrictions, academic free discussion can be difficult. Although in some situations absolutist thinking seems appropriate (1+1= 2), other situations are complex in a way that makes them impossible to solve straightaway, as in social situations. Human emotions are not as straightforward as pure abstraction, as so-called 'wicked problems' demonstrate. Therefore the teacher must be constantly sensitive to the ways students react. At which level of thought is the student reacting? Are students able to change their viewpoints more flexibly and listen to others carefully? How is the content of discussion integrated, or is it possible at all? Do students understand their own subjective reactions as part of the knowledge-formation process?

The questions outlined above are more than a challenge to the teacher alone. The designer of the *Dialogue* course does not claim such sensitivity and wisdom. Her approach has been from the start to admit to incompleteness, and she expresses her humility to the students when introducing the course approach: she is a learner herself. This may be one reason why so many of the students have noted the relaxed atmosphere in class. The teacher is not the authority, but rather is one member in the dialogue circle wondering about the challenges of human interaction. She does not even pretend to have perfect English skills! Although most students feel that it is easier to speak in a language not native to them when such things as correct grammar and pronunciation are not in focus, this change in the teacher's professional role is not always easy, especially for those who come from authoritarian cultures.

Multi-perspective and perspective-integrative thought is also understood to be a component of wisdom in current scientific wisdom research (Kallio, 2015). Cognitive humility is an important part of understanding one's limitations in knowledge creation. Wisdom comes also with another component in the Bohmian dialogue experiment under evaluation, as will be outlined later in this paper.

Potential

The ever-growing research on English as a lingua franca (ELF), and the current political changes in Europe have raised the question of ownership of language, as the role of the native speaker in communication is changing (cf. e.g., Seidlhofer & Widdowson, 2017). In her book *A Philosophy of Second Language Acquisition*, Marysia Johnson (2004) proposes a new, dialogic model of second-language acquisition and points out that native speakers need to be educated as well as non-native speakers. She suggests that the native speaker should offer help to make the language learner become an active participant in interaction (Johnson 2004).

In their work 'Encounters with "strangers": Towards a dialogical ethics in English language education', Alex Kostogriz and Brenton Doecke (2007) claim that English cannot be taught merely by assimilating the language learners into the native English-speaking culture. Teaching English for global work-life purposes means considering 'nativeness' and 'non-nativeness' in regards to such issues as equality and power. These kinds of questions call for an ethical framework.

Wisdom in organisations requires ethical dialogue. Kallio (2018) claims that in current wisdom theory, ethical action is of tremendous relevance to wisdom. For example, if one asks a layperson to name someone with wisdom, often they will choose a person who has *acted ethically* in difficult situations. Thus, persons who have almost sacrificed themselves, like Martin Luther King or Nelson Mandela, are often named as wise. They have transcended their own egoistic wishes in favour of the common good. Ethical thinking and action are thus an essential part of the wisdom research construct, just as they are part of Bohmian dialogue.

Reflections, Insights and Recommendations

University students need to be able to hold multiple perspectives, to integrate viewpoints, and to be ethically committed in order to participate constructively in working life in our rapidly changing society. The experiences from the *Dialogue* course show that it is possible to develop these skills as a way to wisdom through Bohmian dialogue in English as the shared language. The challenges and possibilities described above focus on the experience of the students, and new approaches to English language education are not really within the scope of this paper. The challenges that teaching Bohmian dialogue places on the teacher, however, are unique; the teacher needs not just sensitivity but also intellectual humility and a willingness to admit to being incomplete as a teacher and a human being. This may be the biggest challenge for dialogue: *equality* is not just another word to define. When the teacher functions as a facilitator in the dialogue circle, she needs courage to show her vulnerability. This is not easy, but most of the time the new role has been rewarding for the teacher. Again, research only will show whether the students are empowered by the change of power distribution in the classroom. There have been signs that the students take on more responsibility in the dialogue and even the quiet ones reflect on their contribution.

One ideal aim of the course would be, of course, for these kinds of abilities also to be developed in society at large, not just in a restricted group of university students. Dialogue, authentic listening and understanding differences could be a 'higher goal' for other communities as well. It seems that dialogic approaches are now increasingly in demand in many organisations and societies. In Finland, for example, these methods are taught for free in different organisations across the country through a generous offer of the state by means of the Erätauko-project. Deeper-level dialogic understanding seems to be a skill needed in the modern world now and in the future, rather than just more discussions.

The world needs dialogue, and education plays a key role in developing humanity in integrative thinking skills and intellectual humility. Language education is a perfect place to start paying more attention to dialogue skills and developing understanding of how people interpret and construct the world from their multiple perspectives.

References

Bohm, D. (1996). *On Dialogue* (L. Nichol, Ed.). London: Routledge.

Ellinor, L. & Gerard, G. (1998). *Dialogue: Rediscover the Transforming Power of Conversation*. New York: John Wiley & Sons, Inc.

Isaacs, W. (1999). *Dialogue and the Art of Thinking Together: A Pioneering Approach to Communicating in Business and in Life*. New York: Currency/Doubleday.

Johnson, M. (2004). *A Philosophy of Second Language Acquisition*. New Haven, CT, USA: Yale University Press. Retrieved from http://site.ebrary.com/lib/tampere/docDetail.action?docID=10169981&ppg=96

Kallio, E. (2011). Integrative thinking is the key: An evaluation of current research in the development of adult thinking. *Theory & Psychology*, 21(6), 785-801. Retrieved from http://journals.sagepub.com.helios.uta.fi/doi/pdf/10.1177/ 0959354310388344

Kallio, E. (2015). From causal thinking to wisdom and spirituality: some perspectives on a growing research field in adult (cognitive) development. *Approaching Religion*, 5 (2), 27-41. Retrieved from https://jyx.jyu.fi/handle/123456789/47759

Kallio, E. (Ed.) (2018 forthcoming). *Development of Adult Cognition. Perspectives from Psychology, Education and Human Resources*. Routledge. https://www.rout-ledge.com/Development-of-Adult-Thinking-Perspectives-from-Psychology-Education/Kallio/p/book/9781138733596/Psychology-Education/Kallio/p/book/9781138733596

Kakkuri-Knuuttila, M. (2015). Kaksi dialogimuotoa ja niiden eettinen merkitys [Two dialogue forms and their ethical significance]. *Ajatus*, 71, 203–260.

Kostogriz, A. & Doecke, B. (2007). Encounters with 'strangers': Towards dialogical ethics in English language education. *Critical Inquiry in Language Studies*, 4(1), 1–24. doi:10.1080/15427580701340626.

Mononen, L., Tynjälä, P. & Kallio, E. (2016). Systeemiajattelu – monitieteinen näkökulmakokonaisvaltaiseen ajatteluun [Systems thinking – a multidisciplinary perspective to holistic thinking]. In E. Kallio (Ed.), *Ajattelun kehitys aikuisuudessa – kohtimoninäkökulmaisuutta*.

The development of thinking in adulthood – towards multiperspectivity] (pp. 297-319). Jyväskylä: Suomen kasvatustieteellinen seura [The Finnish Educational Research Association], Vol. 17.

Seidlhofer, B., & Widdowson, H. (2017). Thoughts on independent English. *World Englishes*, 36(3), 360-362.

Schein, E. H. (1993). On dialogue, culture, and organizational learning. *Organizational Dynamics*, 22(2), 51.

Stone, M. (2002). Forgiveness in the workplace. *Industrial and Commercial Training*, 34(7), 278–28

Conference Session Extracts

From conversation with 20 participants considering the paper with the author

That's why you've got to have dialogue at school, so you build a whole new generation of human beings who are able to listen and ask questions. I work with children who are slightly mentally disabled, where degression is a coping mechanism and, beside that, some sort of psychopathology. And I do the same like you did. We also have children with fear issues, so they don't want to close their eyes. Then I ask them to look at the ground because when you're looking at each other, you get the nonverbal communication. But my experience is that when I say something, I invite you to react. So, for me, the trick is to use dialogue to get them to think. "Sometimes you have to slow down to speed up".

I've been sitting with a question around the potential of what you've opened up and so what would be possible if education was the quest for meaning rather than conveying knowledge? What if education was the quest for meaning rather than conveying knowledge?

It's like there actually are already robots teaching language. I think that language teaching has been very mechanistic. It's about the system. The conception of language has been and is still about functions and not about purpose. Is it really either/or?

I wasn't suggesting it was. If the robot teaches the skill, but the facilitator, the teacher, the human being helps create the meaning.

In leadership development and education, time is always squeezed. They're always saying, "Oh, you want three days? What can we do in one?" [laughter] So, some years ago, I started with what I call the Arthur C. Clarke principle. So Arthur C. Clarke was a science fiction writer who apparently once said, "Anything that can be taught by a robot, should be".

The first thing I do is I investigate with them where the resistance comes from. And that's a sneaky way to invite them into a dialogue, but if I can invite them to speak out their resistance, where it come from, how does it feel, and so on and so on, they're getting used – like your mindfulness.

The one thing that I've been thinking about is that dialogue, actually, it can be dangerous [laughter] in the sense that – in terms of power because it is about being equal. There's a Finnish researcher who just recently published a book on – it's only in Finnish, Dialogue in a Democracy. And when people really become aware and able to contribute it would have an impact. So this raised awareness will challenge democracies as well. And using English as lingua franca in the global world, it's a really powerful tool.

There are lots of people and you're uncertain of your English or language skills. And you start saying something. And you forget a word, and you feel so stupid. And I say, "Well, you don't have to. And this is what happens in the dialogue circle. Somebody gives it to you".

Do you know that we can train them to see this, that we can help each other? That's a totally different kind of approach from anything that has been in language education, that we support and help each other.

Postscript

The authors' reflections written some months after the conference

Writing the Acorn paper was done in haste but the process was still worthwhile. Although only one of us could join the first *The World Needs Dialogue!* conference, it was valuable to have the opportunity to present the paper with its budding ideas to the conference participants. The ideas were developed in a dialogue session in the conference. The point of recording the dialogue sessions did not seem very clear at the time; who would ever put in the time to listen to them again? It turned out to be a great idea. Going back to our session after some months was enjoyable and relevant. The dialogue gave many new perspectives to our topic as well raised several questions to look at. The three dialogues online through Zoom meetings developed the topics even further.

Of the many ideas in the conference dialogue session and in the following online dialogues, two main lines of thought continued in building understanding. These were discussed in the *Education Needs Dialogue* Practitioner Circle that was established after the online dialogues were over. We were left wondering, on one hand, what we mean by *ethics* in the context of dialogue and, on the other, by the meaning of *wisdom*. In addition, related to the topics of ethics and wisdom in a methodological way, two aspects worth mentioning here came up. The idea and urge of meaning-making as the purpose and goal of education instead of just conveying knowledge was brought up very strongly in the dialogue circle. In addition, the role of silence introduced in the circle is something to keep in mind when facilitating dialogue or teaching dialogue skills. Quieting the mind and listening are emphasized in dialogue literature, but including the concept of silence may shift the perspective a bit. There might be wisdom in the sound of silence in dialogue.

Autism Dialogue

Jonathan Drury

> *Autism is a way of being. It is pervasive; it colors every experience, every sensation, perception, thought, emotion, and encounter, every aspect of existence.*
> —Jim Sinclair, American autism-rights leader

A Brief Introduction to Autism and Neurodiversity

Autism is a lifelong developmental condition that mainly affects how people perceive their environment and how they interact with others. Autistic people experience the world differently to non-autistic people and it is often, but not always, debilitating. An autistic person may also have other conditions within the autism spectrum, learning disabilities and/or mental health issues, and may receive a different level or way of support from other autistic people.

Autistic people share certain characteristics, but being autistic affects them in uniquely different ways. Being autistic can be a fundamental aspect of identity; increasing numbers of autistic people are creating a cultural shift in this way.

Autism is a naturally occurring variation of the human genome, an umbrella term for a specific set of intersecting clusters of neurodevelopmental phenomena, most of which have a genetic or epigenetic cause. It is influenced by environmental interaction and other conditions. The traditional, pathological way of viewing autism is being challenged by a new and fundamentally different paradigm: Autism, ADHD (Attention Deficit Hyperactivity Disorder) and other conditions are not the result of disease or injury but have emerged through a combination of genetic predisposition and environmental interaction. Autisms can be viewed as neutral substrates that are neither 'good' nor 'bad' per se, and most of the related health issues are shared by everyone. In autistic people, the tendency is to group all health issues together, into what is commonly known as 'autism' or as 'autism spectrum disorder' or 'condition' (ASD/C).

Autism, then, is part of a continuum, a whole spectrum of neurodiversity and, although not yet universally accepted, this notion is increasingly supported by science and has a stable, long-standing acceptance in human society.

Here is a description of autism that I think works well:

> *Autistic individuals share a neurological type, which is qualitatively different to that of non-autistics, and which will necessarily impact, both positively and negatively, on aspects of their thinking and learning; sensory processing; social relational experiences; and communicative style, abilities and preferences. An autistic person's experience of and ability to be successful in the world, will be dependent on the closeness of compatibility, between their individual profile of skills and requirements and their physical and social environment. Levels of sensitivity to environmental factors vary between individuals, and within the same individual over time, so that the presentation of autism is ever changing. A person's neurological type, however, remains constant, and being autistic is a lifelong identity.*
>
> – Dr. Julia Leatherland

Who Am I?

In my youth I – and the other unusual people I gravitated towards – knew we were different. We fully embraced difference and celebrated it at every moment, and we didn't like most of what we saw in other people and the world they'd made. We called some people 'normals', and becoming 'normal' was the ultimate sell-out. It would mean a giving in to the ways of political problems, a dead-end job, excessive small-talk and wearing mechanistic grins on grey, troubled faces. It was the world of unhappy teachers spouting pointless information, consumerism and homogeneous populations. Most kids seemed to be heading that way and you could see they were unhappy inside, whereas I usually felt like I was on fire with the love of life, or confused by the world yet in any case stimulated by everything around me, and there was never any question of an alternative to my intense living to the full, at any price.

I got into a fair amount of trouble and, upon adulthood, started to fully realise the consequences, then the implications, of having a mind in constant overdrive; always looking for instant gratification in the next thrill or hit, or that nightly drink to make my mind quiet. A sports teacher on a school report described me as "Basically a lazy person" but I was at the top of the year in English. Early experimentation with psychedelics, then years of intense spiritual discipline, meditation, yoga and chi gong has helped me greatly. In 2014, still struggling for answers, I asked the people at the National Health Service what they thought of me and was eventually diagnosed with Asperger Syndrome (a now-outdated term under autism spectrum conditions) and ADHD.

Special Interest

Autistic people often have an enhanced special interest and I feel my main one has been the search for real presence; I ask why I am here in this body and environment and want to understand and reconcile a typically fragmented conscious experience, which has led me to a life dominated by self-enquiry. I thrive on and need order and truth, and this can and does cause problems. Recently I have been drawn towards quantum science, neuroplasticity and the non-duality tradition of Advaita Vedanta. I recently undertook a postgraduate certificate in Autism.

As part of a large cultural shift (and perhaps a response to a collective identity crisis), autism raises many serious questions relating to fundamental aspects of existence such as the nature of self, society, identity, medicine, wholeness, and unity. The word *autism* comes from the Greek *autos*, meaning 'self'. What is this 'self-ism' that has become an 'epidemic', mainly in the West?

It became clear to me soon after I got my diagnosis that Dialogue could address the fragmentation and crisis in the autism community, which I see as a magnified version of the wider problems in our communities and societies. I have always been drawn towards and intrigued by sincere communication in a safe and nurturing environment and the deep sense of unity to be found in certain company and communities. I've always had a deep sense of wanting to use Dialogue directly with the public.

You may have heard of the term *flow state* in positive psychology, but I've not previously heard of this term being used in relationship dynamics. When people communicate something very special happens; a third element occurs: the relationship. With the right intention and conditions, a *dialogue* becomes more meaningful in and of itself, and the relationship itself serves as a new perspective. I've spent all my life looking for this way of communicating with myself and others.

The word *dialogue* is made from the Greek words *dia*, meaning 'across' or 'between', and *legein*, meaning 'to speak'. In this way we can see words and meaning flowing across and between our ever-changing perceptions of our selves. I now integrate principles and skills of dialogue with coaching and vice versa in my new company, Flow.

Autism Dialogue
Background

I was introduced to Bohm Dialogue in 2010 by my Fine Art lecturer Hester Reeve. After graduating, I devised and managed a self-discovery programme for refugees and home-schooled kids, incorporating Dialogue, when I learned its true transformative power and 'found my calling'. I co-facilitated the first Dialogues at The Chisholme Institute and for staff at Hallam. In 2017 I founded Autism Dialogue in partnership with Dr. Liz Milne, director of Sheffield Autism Research Lab (ShARL) at University of Sheffield in 2017. ShARL research is aimed at gaining insight into neural and cognitive divergence "to improve public understanding of neurodiversity through research that raises awareness and breaks down barriers". We realised that autism is an ideal focus for Dialogue because of a perceived growing disparity between viewpoints about it.

In 2018 I convened, with fellow researchers, the first cross-university Autism Dialogue session in Sheffield, which produced fruitful discussions. Being a student at one institution and working with another in the city has given me a privileged position in viewing two ontological frameworks (within the respective departments of Psychology and Education) and contact with some very forward thinkers and groups as well as the whole UK autism community.

This year I am joined by Caroline Pakel, another Academy member, in co-convening the Autism Dialogue programme. I am now doing MSc Coaching and Mentoring to develop my own professional practice.

I want to develop Autism Dialogue and Coaching to see if it can improve quality of life for other autistic people and help provide a platform for them, and to bring compassion and wholeness to some of the perceived scientific and social fragmentation.

There is a good deal of energy around discussions of autism and a growing voice from autistic people, who feel unrepresented and overlooked in medical research (Pellicano et al. 2013). Often views can be polarised and expressed via electronic media, providing little scope for nuanced discussion and active listening.

Dialogue could play an important role in accelerating discussion via a common understanding and increasing professional cohesion of the whole autism arena. Dialogue could be highly beneficial in the realm of autism and has the potential to make a positive difference in the way that autism is understood by all. We are keen to carry out research into the benefits of Autism Dialogue and grow our network.

The Programme

After our initial pilot session at University of Sheffield in 2017 I ran a course of six public sessions solely for autistic adults at the Sheffield Hallam University Students' Union. These were attended by up to nine other people.

In May 2018, I started facilitating the first major programme of seven, four-hour sessions, at the Quaker Meeting House in central Sheffield. This series consists of around 20 autistic and non-autistic adults, family members, academics and professionals from around the UK. The first three sessions were for everyone to attend and the following set were exclusively for autistic people. We concluded the programme in November with a fully inclusive session once more.

[Follow-up Note: We consolidated the series with a public conference in Sheffield in December 2018 and people attended from around the country. There were presentations from previous delegates and myself and, notably, the Academy's Jane Ball and Carol Povey (Director of The Autism Centre, National Autistic Society) presented. Three parallel dialogues also took place with around 20 people in each group.]

The Practice

Autism Dialogue brings together members of the public in a way that is fundamentally different to working within existing communities or institutions, bringing special rewards and challenges.

In facilitating, I will usually begin a session with a short, guided mindfulness session to support relaxed focus and a sense of safety, and to prime a deeper awareness. I've practised this for many years and have found that mindful awareness is part of good Dialogue.

It is in our willingness to be present for ourselves and each other that the real depth and potential of Dialogue reveals itself. Immediacy presents differently in autism, partly due to sensory stimulation, so personal stories and anecdotes may help to keep the group socially oiled and relaxed.

But we also need to be wary of venturing into the realms of a support-group approach or towards problems that activism can bring. For example, general conversation might centre around autism being an ecological issue or driven by a biopsychosocial model of disability. There have been some socio-political discussions around activism and neo-liberal agendas, notions of commodification, and both disability and human rights. The systemic issues are highly complex. As participants have expressed feelings of self-acceptance and alignment, pride and gratitude for the space, these were checked by others who felt excluded by language, or felt that deeper levels of meaning were missed. Personal emotions can run high as autistic social challenges increase internally – for example, of knowing when to speak or wondering what one said was of value or not. Discussion can run deep and participants have gained important insights into such topics as cultural power shifts and even the 'permanent presence of suffering and death'. Some of us have experienced a certain raised consciousness, perhaps not too dissimilar from that which a Gestalt approach to inner work can bring.

Outside of the sessions, I receive numerous emails from participants and am mostly happy to continue a conversation with an individual outside of the group context, should a specific point need more personal exploration – although this can be counterproductive to the group. As I mentioned, I have recently begun MSc Coaching and Mentoring to complement the work and in the desire to bring the work to individuals. The focus for Autism Dialogue, however, is on the group and the potential for a peer-led community, wherein I maintain an equal position.

There needs to be greater recognition that the autism identity is a social construction with the potential to constrain and degrade. In identity terminology, individuals need to be enabled to identify with a group that is perceived as constructive and empowering rather than detrimental and limiting. (MacLeod, Lewis & Robertson, 2013)

Reporting

Many people who have attended the Autism Dialogues have reported leaving the sessions with a burden lifted or in a 'heightened state'. Other correspondence received has raised a plethora of concerns and questions, which highlights the need to establish a structured, documenting method at the outset. Whilst scientific research has yet to be undertaken, we have mounting qualitative accounts from both autistic and non-autistic attendees that indicate Dialogue can potentially lead to improving lives of autistic people and autism community cohesion.

These delegates' testimonials provide some anecdotal evidence. (Reproduced with permission):

- *I could not imagine a more autism-friendly approach to discussing autism and everything that comes with it.*
- *We were all able to agree that the categorical nature of language falsifies the more complex and shaded reality of the autism spectrum.*
- *If I had to sum it up I might call it a 'compassionate verbal collaboration'. The conversation was at times deeply personal and moving, and at others more abstract and emotionally detached, depending entirely on the speaker at the time and the way that they chose to engage with the group and topic. After leaving the dialogue session I felt an unusual calm, almost as if a burden had been lifted. The dialogue session provided a safe space to discuss autism in a personal, compassionate way, with no agenda being pushed by anyone and no targets or goals being worked towards – just a safe, civilized, and mutually respectful way to engage with the subject and each other.*
- *It's made me remember how isolating it is not to be able to be honest in the 'real'/NT world and it's helped that loneliness for a while". [NT stands for Neurotypical, a term used by the autism community to describe the predominant culture.]*
- *One thing that's really struck me is just how connected I felt (or feel) with the other participants – especially the other auties, but also the non-autistics. (It's why I hope we can find other ways to continue the conversation and stay connected in future.) What a wonderful group of people. I can't really adequately describe the combination of compassion, respect, affinity and engagement with others that I've had – it seems somewhat unique.*

In one session, which included autistic and non-autistic people, we had a formal recording and reporting exercise to support self-reflection, which raised points such as:

- *Dialogue is a type of resistance*
- *The power of personal stories is really important in social services development*
- *Cultural shifts don't have to incorporate grand vision but can begin within your own work spaces and environments*
- *Dialogue provides opportunities for the unknown to be known*
- *It can be very sad to view one's weaknesses*
- *Confusion was followed by clarity*
- *Compassion is increased and there's a desire to help it emerge*
- *How does so much get squeezed into so little time?*
- *I experienced meaning going very high then very grounded*

As mentioned, delegates presented many of their personal observations at our first conference (of which much has been published online, including audio recordings) and will be included in a forthcoming book.

External Outcomes

In Autism Dialogue, a wider aim is to support a cultural shift already taking place. Besides personal change, there is also evidence the work is influencing external bodies. A Clinical Lead Occupational Therapist from a national healthcare company announced that her team had made some immediate fundamental changes in their unit's autism service as a direct result of attending Autism Dialogue sessions and engaging directly in Dialogue with autistic people. A newly admitted autistic patient at their unit will now be formally asked what they want from the service, instead of an external team's ruling, as this person-centred approach increases. This ripple effect is seen as a positive result and we seek an increase in this type of attitudinal shift.

A Senior Commissioner from the NHS attended the 2018 conference and we stay in contact through the Sheffield Autism Partnership Board, which includes a large number of potential key stakeholders. It is often stated that that healthcare executives would benefit from attending Autism Dialogue, as many have stated they have "never even met an autistic person". I believe that major healthcare organisations could become equal partners in Autism Dialogue.

Problems We Face in Autism Dialogue

As David Bohm pointed out, society is already in a crisis of communication. An inherent problem for autism and society is an increased social misalignment and miscommunication.

Building trust or seeking social parity in this environment can be a daunting task, but many autistic people also often have great vision and, in my experience, much compassion and a deeply genuine need for collective understanding and knowledge.

A major characteristic of autism is 'black and white' thinking. Dialogue enables different perspectives to be held in the same space of enquiry and understanding. As Autism Dialogue is a generative process, we are coming up against some deep and sensitive issues, not in the least that the dominant motivating force in autistic adults appears to be a fight against many forms of authority and a predominantly disabling society ('social model'), seen to be driven by neo-liberal or 'ableist' agendas embedded within complex systems. Whilst autism is a powerful identity construct, activism is also highly charged in certain circles, and certain elements of the neurodiversity movement can be self-isolating. Twitter is one platform where a vast range of positions are defended, particularly when an example of perceived discrimination or oppression appears in the public domain, yet here there are problems, as Steve Silberman, (bestselling author of *Neurotribes*) pointed out to me recently:

> *Sadly, really, there is so much infighting in the autism community, between self-advocates and parents, between parents, clinicians and everyone else. There are so many red lines within the larger autism community including autistic people and non-autistic people, and everyone is constantly*

sniping at each other, so much so that nearly every one of my autistic friends has had to take time out from social media, because they get so attacked, sometimes by other autistic people. (Silberman, 2019)

In a position of leadership, occasionally having to use assertion and make intuitive, snap-decisions, I have inevitably been challenged, both inside and outside of the dialogue space. These challenges have strong flavours of anger and need for justice, fuelled by decades of frustration, discrimination and cruelty, in turn driven by issues at the heart of autism, for example, with controversial practices and an increasing rhetoric of clinical cures, high suicide rates and notions of eugenics.

Another issue arising in Autistic Dialogue is 'blanket advocacy', where we may find ourselves speaking for all autistic people. There is a distinct difference between the ideologies of autism and autistic individuality. As most people in the Dialogue have been able to sense and work towards a collective understanding, fractures arising here reveal a clear distinction in the way autism presents differently in each person at different moments. We have sometimes found this paradoxical aspect uncomfortable as we try constructively, in deep self-reflection, to explore our 'unique similarities' together.

An autistic individual will experience a relatively more intense social disconnection. The dialogic practice of suspension has perhaps been the most rigorous in this regard. There may be sudden tears at a moment of personal insight, followed by outpourings of care in response. There may be a misunderstanding of the Dialogue methodology and aims. This is where the safety and exploration of the dialogic space meets, not just with the question of autism per se, but also with what could be viewed as an opposing force, as together we deal with a very live and personal experience inside a highly charged microcosm of society. This public 'dialogue at the edges of meaning' is risky work and requires very careful handling. Safeguarding is being constantly reviewed and I will benefit greatly from structured supervision and Continuous Professional Development (CPD).

Another difficult issue we have explored in our mixed groups is a polarising of autistic and non-autistic people. Lack of understanding between autistic and non-autistic is a 'two-way street' and has been dubbed a 'double-empathy problem' (Milton 2012). Conversely, there is growing evidence that autistic people understand each other in specific ways unique to autistic relationships (Heasman, B., Gillespie., A 2018).

Future

Research will be undertaken to study the efficacy and effectiveness of Dialogue, likely demonstrating that it can lead directly to improved well-being for autistic people – for example, via enabling reduction in anxiety and increases in empowerment and confidence. Autism Dialogue could be at the hub of a research-based practice ecosystem derived from experientially based knowledge generation, which is lived and returned to the community.

One may say that as research into autism increases in complexity and more autistic people are becoming involved in research, good practice will forever be changing. Making use of Dialogue in conjunction with integrated practice-based research could support more realistic goals.

Professional standards, supported by this Academy, need to be in place and early partnering with healthcare organisations will support this, provided there is no perceived threat to medical progress and they can be flexible enough to listen to the autistic community who, in turn, can work with the concept of 'therapeutic intervention'. There might be opportunities internally within large healthcare organisations for dialogue as an interface between researchers and staff and service-users and their support networks.

Crucially, we must remember that autism is an innate part of a person, so it is not subject to 'cure' in any typical sense. Autism Dialogue programmes accept anyone who identifies as autistic and it isn't necessary to have an official diagnosis. This means that more autistic people could be empowered by positively identifying with their community, reducing common symptoms and thus relieving pressure from healthcare services, where waiting lists are over two years in some areas. National spending priority should be placed on applied research to help people living with neurological differences, instead of on basic genetic and biological research. Methodological challenges in research include the issue of capturing voices of those who do not speak, autistic children and those with intellectual disabilities.

We could benefit by knowledge transfer from the Open Dialogue organisation in Finland (and now in use within the NHS), which shares some of the same principles and whose work on Systems Sensitive Dialogue Intervention would be an appropriate springboard for research.

A vision for Autism Dialogue also includes an international network of trained autistic facilitators. One of the major aspects to autism is the general cultural perspective. I would like to observe autistic peer-led work in other countries, where the work intersects with and influences society, for example in education, enterprise and government.

These visions may be far-reaching; next steps include forming a network of individuals and organisations to support and lead the work ahead.

Conclusion

Autism is a phenomenon that challenges our very concepts of health, social care, culture and, for some, even existence, highlighting the urgency in getting applied research and professional standards in place as soon as possible.

An organisation or community with sound values and a strong accountability structure can adapt to – and welcomes – new challenges. Perhaps we and the other autistic-led and dialogue initiatives can together help organisations and society to be more open and see more of the positive environmental impacts autism and autistic individuals may bring. The work doesn't finish until humanity understands that the message autism brings is precisely that autism itself, whilst disabling to many, and a phenomenon wrought with complex challenges, is a huge opportunity for humanity to grow towards a more enriched and enriching world.

References

Heasman, B., Gillespie, A. (2018). Perspective-taking is two-sided: Misunderstandings between people with Asperger's syndrome and their family members. *Autism*, 22, 6 (740 – 750)

Leatherland, J., (2017). Retrieved from https://blogs.shu.ac.uk/sioe/2017/06/27/ the-autism-definition-debate-language-matters/?doing_wp_cron= 1557667947.2035329341888427734375

MacLeod, A, Lewis, A. & Robertson, C. (2013). 'Why should I be like bloody Rain Man?!' Navigating the autistic identity. *British Journal of Special Education* 40(1): 41-49

Milton, D. (2012). On the ontological status of autism: the 'double empathy problem'. *Disability & Society* Volume 27, 2012 – Issue 6

Silberman, S. (2019). Steve Silberman interview, bestselling author of Neurotribes, The Legacy of Autism. In conversation with Jonathan Drury. Retrieved from https://youtu.be/EvrR5-3_zAY

Sinclair, J., (1993) 'Don't Mourn for Us', Our Voice. *Autism Network International* 1 (3)

Pellicano, L., Dinsmore, A., & Charman, T. (2013). A Future Made Together: Shaping autism research in the UK. Institute of Education, University of London

Conference Session Extracts

From conversation with 20 participants considering the paper with the author

So I think, for me, what really interests me is the paper, and I was drawn to what could autism people actually teach us and society?

Maybe we could all really learn something of being human and vulnerable of those who really are or diagnosed or at least living themselves much more highly.

I think that's an interesting question what we can learn – and from my daughter who is also in the autism spectrum somewhere, she has this amazing sense for authenticity. One teacher she likes, the other one she hates because it's all fake and masks. [laughter]

When you're starting with a new group of all autistic people, how much set-up do you have to do before they're in dialogue or do you hold the field? I mean, like in group therapy, the therapist holds the field, but it's quite directive. So in dialogue, what makes it different is the facilitator really isn't directive. But then how do people who already are struggling with social interactions, how do they know how to participate?

But I was wondering that thing because my son is talking and talking and talking, talking, talking. And he has a problem. He's going to an auditory school, and they have these sessions together. He usually doesn't go to those because it's hard for him to sit there and listen to others. He needs to talk. [laughter] So I was wondering, could he ever function in a dialogue?

It's interesting because I've practised dialogue. It's unlike any other social interaction because the idea of the kind of image of a pool, and everybody contributes to the pool, rather than it being directly social. So it's kind of like, "Actually, you were watching while I talked to Sam". Now, that's a more usual social interaction. A dialogue is in many ways much more spacious than most other social interactions.

Yeah. Yeah. I would say that that's the nature of what we've been doing I'm sure.

Well, the space and the union of the group is more important than a one-to-one.

That reminds me of this idea of impersonal fellowship, this concept that within the dialogue space, there actually is a deep connection. It's not necessarily about me to any one of you. It's about us. And I'm even noticing that in this space, I'm noticing impersonal fellowship forming. So we haven't necessarily answered each other's questions, but we're going somewhere together.

I've been inspired in thinking about how can we use dialogue to have those working in ordinary schools to learn more about kids with autism and how to handle them. Personally, we have a terrible experience from when my son started in the regular public school. They really didn't understand anything, and they were not very open. I'm thinking dialogue groups with kids or adults together with teachers and social teachers from the schools, so they could learn a different perspective.

I really like that idea of an age range.

I am in awe of the work that you do. I know how difficult this work is in any circumstances. And to be dealing with a sensitive population, and the risks that you talked about, and the safeguarding element of containment and so on, I'm just in awe of that.

Postscript

The authors' reflections written some months after the conference

The Academy of Professional Dialogue has provided priceless mentoring and opportunities. With its support, the process of launching and developing Autism Dialogue, has allowed me to reframe personal traits into applied strengths, including hyper-empathy and monotropism (hyperfocusing). My once-disabling literal mindset and low tolerance of the limiting nature of language is now channeled through an ecology of Dialogue, environment and self. Elements of change and disruption lie inherent in the autism paradigm and, instead of suppressing it, this energy can be harnessed to enhance probing of new territory in consciousness and other fields.

By using Dialogue to explore the autistic experience, as a so-called autistic person, I have enabled a type of meta-perspective; I am a facilitator, participant, peer, learner and leader. I have witnessed others change and grow too, and whilst in the context of wider society, people may be disabled or lacking understanding, in the microcosmic society of Dialogue, the effects are enabling and empowering.

The relationship between the marginalised and those who dominate in society needs urgently addressing. It is not enough to suggest the marginalised need to make their grouping stronger or that the dominant group should acknowledge its duties to protect the rights of the marginalised. Overcoming polarised viewpoints and ideologies and the existing enmity needs a common framework. That framework is Dialogue.

In Dialogue, a true communication and language lab, the authenticity aimed for in each moment allows participants (both autistic and not), to safely relearn thinking, speaking and listening. Dialogue paves the way for improved communication and to have the best opportunity to succeed in challenging definitions of selfhood and society, Autism Dialogues should be run by, and with, autistic people and we intend to create an international network of practitioners.

By alternating groups of just autistic people with that of a mixture of autistic and non-autistic people, we explore and reconstitute some subcultural boundaries and began a more systemic enquiry.

We have realised that within the luxury of the dialogic safe container, there needs to be the added dimension of safeguarding. This is one crucial element, relevant also to other therapeutic realms, along with supervision and of course rigorous professional standards. Untethered communication with Self is the at the core of human endeavour and potential, and it is for this reason that the fusion of autism and dialogue could have far-reaching implications systemically.

Dialogue as Dynamic Energy in Living Communities

Ove Jakobsen and Vivi ML Storsletten

In our work with dialogue at the Centre for Ecological Economics and Ethics (CEEE), based at the Nord University Business School, Norway, we focus on communicative processes as a value inherent to 'living societies'. This stands in contrast to the instrumental value of dialogue in the 'smart city' concept, where conversation is often in service of designing technology and services for the future. Our goal is to develop arenas for conversation and to inspire processes that connect individuals in society and connect society to nature. In so doing, we wish to develop a collaborative economy that balances human needs with nature's 'source and sink' capacity – the effect of habitat quality on population growth or decline. To make this goal as clear as possible, we refer to the UN's 17 Sustainable Development Goals (SDGs) and the goals expressed in the Earth Charter. Both declarations make it evident that the principles of sustainability, justice, and peace are all interconnected. According to the systems view of life, all living systems interact cognitively with their environment in ways that are determined by their own internal organisation. In the human realm, "these cognitive interactions involve consciousness and culture, and in particular a sense of ethics" (Capra and Jakobsen 2017, p. 842).

Dialogue has a central role in developing living societies with a high quality of life for humans within resilient ecosystems. Therefore, it is urgent that we create an ethical framework for co-responsible actors on all levels to communicate cooperatively. Life is relationships; all forms of life are interconnected and interdependent. Humans are connected to the web of life physically through air, water and soil. As social beings, humans are connected through different forms of dialogue. Dialogues are the most important precondition for cultural development. In this perspective, dialogue can be seen as a practice necessary for developing a common understanding of norms and values that are both ethical and political.

Socrates, the ancient radical of dialogue, maintained that the purpose of dialogue is to make clear what is unclear and to discover what's right and wrong in ethics, economics and politics. He therefore valued "the experience of being corrected or becoming convinced by others more than the experience of convincing them to adopt his views" (Westoby and Dowling 2013, p. 116). Reflecting on experiences gives sense in a process of critical dialogue. By practising reflexive thinking we become aware, individually and collectively, of the complexity that characterizes human communities. How we understand the world we are living in has direct influence on our behaviour. Every society has a particular world view that regulates social and political processes to "discipline people into certain ways of ethical being, thinking and behaving that are consistent with such a view" (Westoby and Dowling 2013, p. 117).

In Western societies, where the mechanical worldview dominated since the seventeenth century, development is interpreted in terms of measurable indicators such as economic and technological growth. One of the most important characteristics of mechanical thinking is that technical solutions could be transferred independently of the cultural and natural context. Market economy, based on competition between autonomous actors, is an illustrative example of a mechanical system that is supposed to lead to growth and increased welfare wherever it is implemented and practised. The idea is that the business model is universally applicable, and therefore the technique becomes the most important instrument for social change. Today's global economy is a network of financial flows that have been designed mechanically without any ethical framework. In fact, "social inequality and social exclusion are inherent features of economic globalization, widening the gap between the rich and the poor and increasing world poverty" (Capra and Jakobsen 2017, p. 842). Hence, within a mechanical world view the models of development are universal and can be imported and exported anywhere in the world.

The problem is that the competitive market economic system has a whole lot of unintended negative consequences that are hard, if not impossible, to cure within the system. Today community development is dominated by market-oriented economics. In this state, the economy has lost contact with the natural and cultural environment. The consequences are reduced capacity for both genuine solidarity between people and caring for nature. To reduce the negative symptoms, hierarchical command lines seem necessary both for efficiency and for control. On a global level these challenges are made concrete through the UN's definition of the 17 SDGs. To reach these goals we need reflection on a deeper level about the ontological preconditions for today's economic and political systems.

Unity in diversity depends on solidarity. The idea of solidarity is central to a dialogical approach. According to Freire, solidarity involves entering into particular kinds of committed relationship with marginalized groups of people. Solidarity requires dialogic processes focused on learning about their social, political, cultural and economic realities. Community development based on 'bottom-up' social solidarity could be committed to principles and practices of mutual aid, and to the tradition of associationism (thought influenced by past experiences) developed by philosophers such as Kropotkin in the late nineteenth century. Solidarity anchored in dialogic practice goes deeper. It questions the assumptions and the causes behind the problems, instead of solely focusing on reducing negative symptoms.

If we change to an organic world view, relations become more important than objects, which means that cooperation through dialogue turns out to be the dominant principle in ethics, economy and politics. In other words, people-centred processes replace growth-centred outcomes. In an organic context, development is a metaphor implicating a qualitative change in opposition to the currently dominant ideas about growth. Dialogue becomes a central process to initiate social change. Rethinking community becomes a collective practice, a process of social change, not a project restricted for powerful leaders in economy and politics. People work cooperatively together as partners to bring about social change. Dialogue has inherent value as a 'life enhancing energy' in an 'organic context' – in contrast to dialogue as 'instrumental' value in a 'mechanical' context.

Problem Statement

To be specific, our problem here is: How, and to what degree, is it possible to inspire the change processes described by the UN's SDGs and the Earth Charter in local societies, by introducing communicative processes and dialogue on different social levels and in different social settings? We will elaborate on two different cases that concentrate on developing resilient and sustainable societies. *Case A* is about cultural development through dialogue in local communities and *Case B* is focused on developing creativity through dialogic practice in smaller groups. As a frame of reference for our reflections we will connect to two different dialogic perspectives. As a precondition we accept, in accordance with organic thinking, that "a living society is characterized by the existence of arenas where people can communicate, deliberate and decide on visions together" (Caputo, 1997).

It is important that people collectively and individually have real influence over decisions that impact their lives. In other words, dialogue is an essential ingredient in democracy. Both cases we refer to acknowledge these premises. *Case A* focuses on dialogue as an inherent value of living societies. Without communicative or dialogic relations between people, society will not flourish and creative processes will suffer. *Case B* looks at communication and dialogue as necessities for developing creative processes for using recycled materials as tools for connecting mind and body. The overall task is to eliminate, or at least reduce, the consumer-driven dominance in our Western societies.

Case A: Bodø as the 2024 European Capital of Culture

Goal 11 of the UN´s SDGs states, "Make cities and human settlements inclusive, safe, resilient and sustainable". The Earth Charter says that communities on all levels should provide everyone an opportunity to realize their full potential and enable all to achieve a secure and meaningful livelihood that is ecologically responsible. With these two declarations as a frame of reference, the Centre for Ecological Economics and Ethics has played an active role in connecting science, practice and art in diverse constellations to develop and implement 'living cities'.

CEEE will use its theoretical insight and practical experience to develop and organize projects within the framework of European Capital of Culture (ECofC). To create a viable city, flourishing cultural life is of the greatest importance – not only as a separate sector with its own activities, but also as an energising and creative driver in the process of encouraging sustainable development. Establishing dialogue-based networks that link business, education, research, artistic activities and other parts of society are necessary activities. Diversity makes societies resilient and able to resist threats from a changing environment. In a cultural setting cross-cultural dialogues, stimulating blooming relationships locally, nationally and with co-partners in Europe, contribute to developing a practically defined concept of 'living cities'. To be concrete, in the process of developing Bodø as a viable and attractive city, it is essential to establish meeting places for practising different communicative processes. In the projects focused in this article Socratic dialogue and World Café are combined in what we have called the 'Utopian Workshop'. Each of the two combined approaches brings something different to the table:

- **Socratic dialogue:** Fit for developing insight and holistic understanding based on the participants' own experience.
- **World Café:** Fit for developing common understanding and practical solutions in larger groups.

Arenas for dialogic face-to-face interaction between public 'bottom-up' processes, in combination with municipal 'top-down'-initiated processes will be encouraged. The idea is to develop Bodø as a dynamic arena for a high-quality lifestyle where science, politics, practice and culture are integrated in a sustainable ecological context. Such a balanced lifestyle is more focused on qualitative development, cooperation, trust and reciprocity – as opposed to an unbalanced and dominant focus on a societal system that promotes quantitative growth, competition, envy and self-centredness.

These common projects started in spring 2018, when Bodø Municipality and CEEE initiated a process of regular dialogue events where people representing the diversity of the population in the region meet to exchange ideas and practical experience. This activity is both a means and a goal in itself. It is a means because there is a venue for the development of a flourishing lifestyle, and it is an end in itself because dialogue helps to create and reinforce relationships that are important to develop viable and strong societies. The process is followed up through longitudinal research based on the principles of interdisciplinary science researchers working with practitioners and representatives of cultural life. Amongst other things, they will focus on integrating art to express knowledge through such venues as music, theatre, sculptural installations and paintings. We will continue the tradition of decentring and democratisation, which is characteristic of cultural policy in Nordland.

The main challenge is to connect culture with economy, society and nature through different dialogue-based activities. Our aim is to advance social life processes by connecting communities, empowering people to engage and contributing to the development of ideas on dialogue and community building. We will do this by bringing people from all walks of life together through a number of dialogue forums, each with a different focus: discussions (World Café), active listening (reflective dialogue), enlightened personal experiences (Socratic dialogues) and asking questions (Open Space). Because diversity is a prerequisite for creativity, people from foreign cultures will participate in the dialogues.

The dialogues have two different objectives: First, to develop new questions and new answers to some of the most important challenges we are facing, locally, nationally and globally; and second, and perhaps more importantly, practising dialogue as an end in itself. Dialogue vitalizes the relations between people and makes society more lively and creative. It inspires and empowers people to participate in the development of the future instead of being spectators. Arranging Utopian Workshops in primary and secondary schools is an important part of the dialogue project. The pupils represent the future. It is important to activate young people's creativity and playfulness in making utopian narratives describing Bodø and the Nordland county of the future, without taking too much notice of all the barriers typical of traditional methods.

Case B: Reuse Innovation and Dialogue

The main purpose of this second project is to develop the methods and knowledge of reuse and circulation innovation. Dialogue can contribute to the viable development of individuals, organisations and businesses as well as the local/regional community. In addition, the project will contribute to policies, plans and practices for the development of attractive and viable societies. The project's purpose can thematically be divided into four sub-objectives:

1. Provide an overview of how 'reuse innovation' impacts the understanding of the interaction between the social, ecological and economic spheres.
2. Examine how different forms of dialogue affect the development of networks of different actors at the individual, business and community levels.
3. Investigate and identify how 'recycling innovation' and dialogue can help develop new criteria for environmentally and socially responsible practices.
4. Design recommendations for political planning and community development in practice.

The Creative Recycling Centre (KGS) in Salten has worked with interdisciplinary projects within the environment, education, entrepreneurship and innovation since 2012. Creative work with recycled materials, workshops and other practical activities are central in the efforts to promote and draw attention to reuse innovation for a viable society and a sustainable future.

Through a three-year project starting in autumn 2019, KGS aims to contribute to developing awareness about recycling and sustainability (circulation economics) through practical workshops and the use of different dialogical methods. The project involves both children and adults in kindergarten and primary schools in Bodø, Saltdal and Meløy. These municipalities and communities are involved as collaborators in the effort to motivate and contribute to creativity in order to solve tomorrow's challenges.

Part of the background to the project lies in the environmental challenges we face. One example is the real danger that by 2050 there will be more plastic than fish in the sea. On the one hand, the transition to viable societal development will bring challenges; on the other, such a change in society is filled with potential for creativity, innovation and exploration of new opportunities through dialogue practice. KGS aims to be proactive in relation to this topic and will help to initiate processes leading towards sustainable societies with high quality of life based on the development of individual and collective potential. CEEE has a long experience of working on such issues and facilitating processes for developing increased understanding, knowledge and solutions through dialogue and the exchange of experience.

The foundation of the project consists of the following key topics: reusable materials, creative processes, empowerment, a sustainable-future mindset, the ability to challenge established truths, participation and co-creation, and viable societal development.

In the future it will be necessary to increase the understanding of how complex challenges can be solved through dialogue and communicative interaction. The creative potential lies in the interaction between social, ecological and economic systems. Through the project, we will investigate how practical workshops, dialogue practices and establishment of dialogue-based networks can help raise awareness about the environmental and social responsibility of individuals, businesses and organisations. Thus, the project will also result in knowledge of various implications for political planning and community development practices. Constructive coupling between science and practice is central. Goals and meaning in the project must be in accordance with the creative and reflection-rich learning processes that are already taking place in the kindergartens and primary schools.

Context of Interpretation

Working together using one's skills and knowledge for the common good is based on dialogic relations. How the context is organized has influence on dialogical practices, and those dialogical practices in turn can reshape the organisational context. More generally, dialogical processes can shift the culture, structures and traditions of a community. It is important to stimulate communicative relations between people, groups, networks, organisations, ideas and perspectives. Community development as a social practice cultivates social relationships and invokes agency. This is true not just in private and personal relationships, but also in collectively oriented public relationships. It strives to reclaim and reinhabit places as spaces of social activity or technique-oriented development.

Developing communities require dialogical relations; things cannot simply be reduced to a mechanistic process. Dialogic practices tend not to seek agreement, but rather seek *understanding*. An organic understanding of social systems brings into focus the interacting dynamics that underlie collective efforts. Humans use narrative explanations to understand peoples' behaviour in different situations, and a narrative knowledge develops when stories about events are in focus and reflected on. This leads into a process of continuous learning in thinking narratively, in seeing human lives as lived narratives (Clandinin and Connelly, 2000). A narrative approach surpasses the limitations of objective principles and activates faculties that facilitate our understanding of the world from within.

Our existence includes the three basic structures of reality: matter, life and consciousness (Polkinghorne, 1988). Narrative meaning is one of the processes in the mental realm, "a cognitive process that organizes the human experiences into temporally meaningful episodes" (Polkinghorne, 1988, p. 1). Narrative meaning draws together actions and events that affect living human beings. On the one hand, the realm of meaning is an activity, and not a static object, and is described in the form of verbs rather than substantives. Thus, identifying the realm of meaning with objects and substances will lead to philosophical confusion, as occurs in a reductionist and technical paradigm where complexities and uncertainties are reduced to measurable component parts and simplifications.

Not only individuals but also cultures maintain a range of typical narrative meanings in their myths, fairy tales and stories. Participating deeply in a culture requires knowledge about these narrative meanings in their full breadth, in addition to participating in the process of adding new contributions of cultural stocks of meaning, and deleting other meanings due to their lack of use. Community development as a social practice is not a practice of solving a puzzle or using instructions to make sense of a machine. Instead, social systems are complex dynamic processes of interacting organic parts (individuals, group and organisation) and multiple contexts (policies, plans, culture, and so forth).

While dialogic practice reaches for understanding and coherence, community development theory and practice requires something else. People need to not only connect and understand one another while also reaching for coherence; they also need to reach some mutual agreement to propel joint action. Dialogue is not only turning to the other, listening and connecting, learning and finding collective coherence and potentially shared agendas. Applied to community development it is also about practitioners eliciting a mandate from the people they are engaging with.

In the following section we will present a context of interpretation that is relevant as a frame of reference for reflecting on the two cases. As a starting point we differentiate between dialogues on the diverse levels of aggregation – namely the *micro, meso, macro* and *meta* levels.

Westoby and Dowling (2013) refer to Kelly´s (2008) methods that are appropriate to ordering and structuring community development processes, by differentiating between dialogue processes on four levels (Westoby and Dowling 2013, p. 61):

1. **Bonding (micro):** Building and nurturing purposeful interpersonal relationships through dialogue.
2. **Banding (mezzo):** Moving what might previously have been felt as a private concern into collective public action. Moving from purposeful relationships to participatory action groups. Agreeing to do something together as a group.
3. **Building (macro):** Forming and stabilising groups that can carry the work on in a sustainable way. Structuring the work. As community practitioners we are challenged to not only tackle the causes of the problems, but also to create new institutions that reflect the dreams of new ways of consuming, growing, producing commuting, working and travelling.
4. **Bridging (meta):** Linking stable groups into alliances, coalitions, co-operative arrangements, networks and federations that enable people to tackle trans-local or even global issues. People working together as communities can act both locally and globally.

We can reimagine dialogical community development as an ethical, economic and political practice for progressive and innovative social change, in which people can choose to adopt different attitudes towards each other. These would be opposed to domination, and instrumental in promoting ongoing resistance, creative transgression, dialogue and transformation. The openness towards each contributes to social innovation. Such social innovation is experienced as new ways of organising social arrangements – clearly oriented, for us as practitioners, towards progressive values of justice, equality and ecological sustainability.

Discussion

In the Utopian Workshop we close the circle by merging our ability in narrative story-telling with reasoning and visionary thinking. Dialogical processes and narratives can "promote insight, understanding and dedication, and thus inspire efforts for a better world" (Jakobsen and Storsletten 2018, p. 40).

In the first two stages (bounding and banding) we use Socratic dialogue, where the participants listen to each other's stories and reflect on similarities and differences. In addition to telling stories based on private experiences, the capability to listen to other participant's stories is of great importance. This activity contributes to connecting the individuals in communicative relations, a prerequisite for establishing collaborative networks. Socratic dialogue is best suited to groups from 10 to 30 participants.

In the third and fourth stages we use World Café as a method to describe concrete activities leading to a resilient and sustainable society based on creativity and synergic communication. People explore together, and they bring in what they know, think and feel about the questions in focus. "They work together to uncover new insights, different perspectives, and deeper questions" (Bojer et.al., 2008, p. 116).

Bonding (Micro)
Case A

To order to establish and support interpersonal relationships, it is important to invite participants to the dialogue sessions that represent the diversity in the local community in age, gender, cultural background, work experience and education. The idea is to connect people with different perspectives through identifying the experiences present in the group, in order to make the participants aware of what connects and what divides people in the existing community. The stories told open up a deeper understanding of the challenges faced by the local societies, and it makes possible solutions clearer. Change in a local society depends on preparedness to change social structures and, maybe more challenging, the participants' willingness to change themselves.

Case B

The participants will be the employees in the primary schools and kindergartens, as introductory dialogues to the creative recycling material workshops. The point is to reflect on central topics such as sustainability and recycling innovation. The stories will highlight the areas of significance for human development, primarily in the immediate daily group situations or settings in primary schools and kindergartens. It is important that the focus is held on stories and experiences about purposeful relationships.

Banding (mezzo)
Case A

At this stage the idea is to transfer private challenges into a concern for the whole community. To do this, the stories from the participants are focused and interpreted in order to find some common principles that could be used as a gateway to define practical activities. The participants bring in their own experiences, without referring to theory or authorities, and through dialogic reflection everybody contributes to find out what connects the different stories. The idea is that the dialogue should contribute to build visions of projects that build communicative relationships between the people in the community.

Case B

The dialogue processes lead to an increased common understanding of the basic principles of the project. Influence and interactions in dialogical development processes are not limited to immediate situations. They also support an understanding of how dynamic interaction processes develop in relationships between particular situations. The participants will reach a higher level of understanding about the interconnectedness of the structures and processes in schools and kindergartens. Increased understanding of the common threads that integrate the singular stories promotes collective action, in a network anchored in purposeful relationships.

Building (macro)
Case A

To follow up on the results from the Socratic dialogue, we introduce World Café to the participants. To increase the number of participants we invite participants from two or more Socratic dialogues. It is important that the World Café leads to established dynamic groups that have a focus on different smaller projects within the bigger picture. The groups should be self-selected, including people with special interests and passions for the specific projects. The idea is that change processes always start with smaller projects that are easy to make concrete and to implement in practice. An important tool for developing living self-sustained societies is to establish integrated, collaborative networks. Communicative activity is linking the various activities, and describes the stages a change process usually passes through. In addition, the World Café provides impetus and inspiration for the development of the projects.

Case B

Here it is important to connect the stories from the Socratic dialogues regarding experiences from the immediate situations, and to increase focus on how situations at a more distant level and, derived from larger environments, influence people and development. For example, this would apply at a public municipality level, where the understanding of the mandate of the schools and kindergartens may be diverse. With World Café as a method, the diversity of employees, parents, municipalities, neighbours and so on, is integrated and gives impetus to connect and formalize groups that focus on how to reach the overall goals related to sustainability, dialogue and recycling innovation. Hence, the dialogue process promotes the structure of action to emerge and materialize.

Bridging (meta)
Case A

At this stage the challenge is to connect the different working groups and projects into an integrated community project. Networks are particular patterns of connections and relationships. Networks are self-generating, and each component of the network is connected to other components. The entire network is continually creating, or recreating, itself as living systems undergo continual structural changes while preserving their web-like patterns of organisation.

The success of World Café is based on the fact that all projects are initiated by people living in the communities – in other words, voluntary, 'bottom-up' solutions. Working groups are being established to handle various challenges. For example, a group can work on projects that will increase local food production; another group finds solutions that reduce the need for fossil energy; and a third group develops projects that will provide affordable, quality housing for all. In addition to practical projects, there is also a need for development of school offerings and cultural activities buy anyone who is willing and able to participate.

Case B

In a sustainable society, relationships concern not only the connections among the people but also the relationships between the society as a whole and its environment. This means that society, culture, politics, economy and nature are interconnected, and it derives much of its character from connections to other social actors. People working together in networks in communities can also further explore the traditions, politics and social organisation of their communities. Change on the cultural and subcultural levels is then possible within their community. The building of alliances and networks develop further, and that enables people to a greater degree to act both locally and globally.

Concluding Reflections

It is usually assumed that social life consists of "a combination of our intended actions, the decisions we make and events that just happen to us" (Jakobsen 2017, p. 205). We are responsible for our actions but not for events. Actions are given meaning in terms of their context, and life is like writing a story. Initiating change processes includes creating new stories. Narrative knowledge is integrational, where different events, actions and events in human lives are drawn into thematically unified goal-directed processes; 'narrative configuration' is "the process by which happenings are drawn together and integrated into a temporally organized whole" (Polkinghorne, 1995, p. 5). The idea behind our work with Utopian Workshops, anchored in different organized dialogues, is to knit local societies together by materialising individual and collective stories. These processes have the potential to "reveal solutions to the world's most urgent challenges" (Storsletten and Jakobsen 2015, p. 348).

Since individual narratives are connected to a social context, our stories are integrated in the web of life. Developing utopian narratives is a way of communicating the kind of future we want (organically), more than a method for developing prognoses of how the future will be (mechanically).

By combining Socratic dialogue and World Café we activate peoples' individual experiences in a reflexive process and secondly activate peoples' rationality in a constructive dialogue focused on changing the society in a sustainable and life-enhancing direction. One could be forgiven for thinking that a Utopian Workshop requires a complete renovation of our individual and cultural values – but the point is rather to develop a balanced combination of ideas from the past and utopian narratives. "The primary focus is on practical possibilities and opportunities rather than campaigning against current problems" (Hopkins 2011, p. 77).

References

Bojer, M., Roehl, H., Knuth, M. and Magner, C. (2008). *Mapping Dialogue – Essential Tools for Social Change*. Chagrin Falls, Ohio: Taos Institute.

Capra, F. and Jakobsen, O. (2017): 'A conceptual framework for ecological economics based on systemic principles of life', *International Journal of Social Economics*, Vol 44 Issue 6.

Caputo, J. (1997). *Deconstruction in a Nutshell: A conversation with Jacques Derrida*. New York: Fordham University Press

Clandinin, D. J. & Connelly, F. M. (2000). *Narrative Inquiry. Experience and Story in Qualitative Research*. San Francisco: Jossey-Bass.

Hopkins, R. (2011). *The Transition Companion – Making your community more resilient in uncertain times*. White River Junction, Vermont: Chelsea Green Publications.

Jakobsen, O. (2017). *Transformative ecological economics – Process philosophy, Ideology and Utopia*. Abingdon, UK: Routledge.

Jakobsen, O. and Storsletten, V. (2018). Fridensreich Hundertwasser – *The five skins of the ecological man, in Art, Spirituality and Economics*, Bouckaert, Luk, Ims, Knut and Rona, Peter eds. Basel: Springer.

Kelly, A. (2008). *People-centred development: Development Method*, Brisbane, Australia: The Centre for Social Response.

Kropotkin, Peter (1904/2017): *Mutual Aid: A Factor in Evolution*. London, UK: Forgotten Books

Polkinghorne, D. E. (1988). *Narrative Knowing and the Human Sciences*. Albany: State University of New York Press.

Polkinghorne, D. E. (1995). "Narrative configuration in qualitative analysis". Qualitative Studies in Education, Volume 8, Issue 1, 5-23.

Storsletten, V. and Jakobsen, O. (2014). "Development of Leadership Theory in the Perspective of Kierkegaard's Philosophy", *Journal of Business Ethics* February, 2014.

Westoby, P. and Dowling, G. (2013). *Theory and Practice of Dialogical Community Development: International Perspectives*. Abingdon, UK: Routledge.

Conference Session Extracts

From conversation with 20 participants considering the paper with the authors

I really enjoyed reading what you both wrote. I think it's the most visionary and most radical of the papers that we have in the conference. I'm particularly attracted to the idea that most people think extractively, and how to get out of the situation. And what you're proposing is how people participate and contribute, and secondly, that you see dialogue as an end rather than a means.

So do you think there is a basic social economic standard from which this bottom-up change can emerge? And why do I place this question? I come from a country which is a mystery. Having absolutely everything in terms of natural resources it can, it seems not to be able to do anything with all of that. And socially it has created a certain contractive economy, yes. I mean, Argentina's the first country in the history of the known world that implodes not due to war or to natural cataclysms, just by the behaviour of its own members, right, which happened in 2001. So the whole system has become contractive and a contractive economic system that puts most people in a survival mode, where an appropriation attitude is unavoidable because you are in survival mode. So what are the standards, is my question, from which you can think of making this?

It concerns me a little bit that some of what keeps this standoff going is a dedication to salvation, saving, and so a lot of the current economic model argues in its own justification, for lifting people out of poverty, the rationale behind it. "You need us to raise the . . . " and it's very appealing, and many economists that I engage with are fine, principled people who believe that unless I can speak about what you do about a million people in the slum, in Buenos Aires, or wherever it is, if you can't speak to that with your story about ecological economy – they do this.

And then I speak with the ecologists, and they say "Look at the problems these guys are causing". And both of them in a way, they have a clear idea of what the world needs to be saved. There was something in your paper that suggested that you also have the means to save society from destruction. The dialogic process seems to be dedicated to revelation rather than salvation. And you speak in your paper about promoting understanding rather than seeking agreement.

It's really difficult to get some of the economists to agree with the ecologists. And in a way, I think that – just plays to the importance of dialogue because how do you start to get out negotiating a path through enormous complexity where solutions aren't apparent?

So I see how change very much has to start at the bottom and work its way up. But I guess I just keep thinking about how that works in communities that are already underrepresented and that don't have a voice. And I think that in those instances, it still does take a commitment from the top to be open to listening and to be open to, valuing what that segment of the community wants and what they need.

Postscript

The authors' reflections written some months after the conference

When we signed on, we did not really know what we went for, but we had a feeling that this was an important event where we, together with other dialogue practitioners, could develop ideas that we are working with in relation to research, teaching and practice. We try to combine development of methods in dialogue with practical projects focused on sustainable development of small societies in different areas in Norway. The experience-based knowledge we have developed during the participation in the Academy of Professional Dialogue inspired us to develop a course at the bachelor's-degree level where people from different organizations and companies participate in order to develop competence to facilitate dialogue based workshops in their own networks.

In the process of writing the article to present at the conference, we became more aware of the content and structure of the projects, and not least we became even more aware of the potential that lies in dialogue for social development. Inspired by being part of this international network focused on dialogue, we developed our ideas further in the direction of dialogue as part of societal evolution. We will develop the article by implementing our experience from practicing dialogues in projects focused on change towards sustainable societies.

When we were to present the article, we had to go deeper into the content and clarify for ourselves what was to be presented as the core point, and thus the article's next development phase became clearer. During the actual presentation, we received good feedback which allowed us to see other aspects of the case than we did before. When we are working with dialogues in practical contexts, our experiences from being part of *The World Needs Dialogue!* conference are highly relevant.

It was an interesting and educational experience to take part in the process from the time we announced interest until we left the conference, with many experiences and inspirations and richer in new perspectives. This is especially true regarding *dialogue*, and how we have different understandings of what the term means. The other dialogue meetings we participated in were also incredibly exciting and educational and we have benefited from the various experiences and experiences we gained in our further work on dialogue for social development.

We are looking forward to continuing and increasing our cooperation in the future in order to develop the relevance and quality of our research, teaching and practical events.

The World Needs Dialogue!
2018 Inaugural Conference Participants

David Adams *UK*	 Alan Adelman *USA*	 Lars-Åke Almqvist *Sweden*	 Claudia Apel *Germany*	 Jane Ball *UK*
 Jessica Ball *UK*	 Dionne Belk *USA*	 Trine-Line Biong *Norway*	 Chro Borhan *Norway*	 Joop Boukes *Netherlands*
 Francis Briers *UK*	 Joanna Brown *UK*	 Vicky Coates *South Africa*	 Heike de Boer *Germany*	 Eelco de Geus *Austria*
 Nancy Dixon *USA*	 Kristy Domingues *USA*	 Jonathan Drury *UK*	 Linda Ellinor *USA*	 Lena Eriksson *Sweden*

320 | Participants

Morel Fourman *UK*	Jenny Garrett *UK*	Peter Garrett *UK*	Glenna Gerard *USA*	Pierre Giorand *France*
Mirja Hämäläinen *Finland*	Geir Harald Hagberg *Norway*	Ewa Östlund Henschen *Sweden*	Beth Herman *USA*	Jim Herman *USA*
Per Hilding *Sweden*	Peter Hill *Canada*	Gerd Holmboe-Ottesen *Norway*	Bernhard Holtrop *Netherlands*	Sam House *USA*
Lorna Jackson *UK*	Ove Jakobsen *Norway*	Thomas Klug *Germany*	Thomas Köttner *Argentina*	Harriet Krantz *Sweden*
Sabine Kresa *Austria*	Eric Lynn *Germany*	Morag Mackay *Ireland*	Beth Macy *USA*	Marie-Ève Marchand *Canada*

Participants | 321

Hector Verdu Marti *Spain*	**Cara McCarthy** *UK*	**Sharon Millar** *UK*	**Daniela Merklinger** *Germany*	**Dorothy Moir** *UK*
Siv Nystedt-Claesson *Sweden*	**Maritza Nieto** *USA*	**Eddie O'Brien** *Ireland*	**Tom O'Connor** *USA*	**Conny Ohlsson** *Sweden*
Sonia Ortiz *Spain*	**Gwynyth Overland** *Norway*	**Svein Overland** *Sweden*	**Caroline Pakel** *UK*	**Cliff Penwell** *USA*
Paulette Perry *USA*	**Hugh Pidgeon** *UK*	**Mikhail Piper** *USA*	**Olga Plokhooij** *Netherlands*	**Abby Raeder** *USA*
Amanda Ridings *UK*	**Chrissi Rohn** *Germany*	**Liv Ronglan** *Norway*	**Robert Sarly** *USA*	**Mark Seneschall** *UK*

322 | Participants

Bethany Sewell
UK

Michael Stiglund
Sweden

Vivi Storsletten
Norway

Stephanie Tansey
USA

Keöne Thomas
USA

Juliane Tissen
Netherlands

Henrik B. Tschudi
Norway

Christian Valentiner
Norway

Renate van der Veen
Netherlands

Susan Williams
USA

Lightning Source UK Ltd.
Milton Keynes UK
UKHW051236290919
350496UK00008B/73/P